THE
OXFORD HISTORY
OF AUSTRALIA

THE
OXFORD HISTORY
OF AUSTRALIA

General Editor Geoffrey Bolton

THE
OXFORD HISTORY
OF AUSTRALIA

VOLUME 2

1770–1860

POSSESSIONS

JAN KOCIUMBAS

Melbourne

OXFORD UNIVERSITY PRESS

Oxford   Auckland   New York

For my family

OXFORD UNIVERSITY PRESS AUSTRALIA

Oxford   New York   Toronto
Delhi   Bombay   Calcutta   Madras   Karachi
Kuala Lumpur   Singapore   Hong Kong   Tokyo
Nairobi   Dar es Salaam   Cape Town
Melbourne   Auckland
and associated companies in Berlin   Ibadan

OXFORD is a trade mark of Oxford University Press
© Jan Kociumbas 1992
First published 1992

National Library of Australia
Cataloguing-in-Publication data:

Kociumbus, Jan.
The Oxford history of Australia. Volume 2, 1770–1860: possessions.

Bibliography.
Includes index.
ISBN 0 19 554610 5.

1. Australia—History—1788–1900. 2. Australia—
History—to 1788. I. Title. II. Title: History of
Australia. Volume 2, 1770–1860: possessions.

994.02

Designed by Guy Mirabella
Typeset by Solo Typesetting, South Australia
Printed by Impact Printing Pty Ltd Victoria
Published by Oxford University Press
253 Normanby Road, South Melbourne, Australia

CONTENTS

PUBLISHER'S NOTE

The Oxford History of Australia covers the sweep of Australian history from the first human settlement down to the 1980s. It consists of five volumes, each written by a single author with an established reputation as a productive and lively-minded historian. Each volume covers a distinct period of Australian history: Aboriginal history; white settlement, 1770–1860; colonial growth and maturation, 1860–1900; the Australian Commonwealth in peace and war, 1901–42; the modern era, from 1942 to the present. Each volume is a work of historical narrative in its own right. It draws the most recent research into a coherent and realized whole.

Aboriginal Australia is treated in its entirety, from the dramatically recast appreciation of early prehistory to present-day controversies of place, identity and belief. Colonial Australia begins with the establishment of tiny settlements at different times and with different purposes on widely separated points on the Australian coastline. From these fragments of British society sprang the competing ambitions of their members and a distinctly new civilization emerged. As the colonists spread over the continent and imposed their material culture on its resources, so the Old World notions of class, status and gender were reworked. The colonists came together at the beginning of the twentieth century and fashioned new institutions to express their goals of national self-sufficiency, yet they were tossed and buffeted by two wars and the dictates of the international economy. The final volume therefore reflects the continuity of Australia's economic and political dependence, and new patterns in the quest for social justice by women, the working class and ethnic minorities.

In tracing these themes, the Oxford History's authors have held firmly to the conviction that history needs to interpret the past as an intelligible whole. The volumes range widely in their use of source material. They are informed by specialist research and enlivened by vivid example. Above all, they are written as narrative history with a clear and dramatic thread. No common ideological orthodoxy has been imposed on the authors beyond a commitment to scholarly excellence in a form which will be read and enjoyed by many Australians.

PREFACE

My interest in early Australian history began as an undergraduate at the University of Melbourne. Philosophers and historians introduced me to the political and scientific ideas of the Enlightenment and suggested ways in which these ideas may have shaped Australia's past.

It seemed to me that, far from being isolated in a cultural and intellectual desert, the Australian colonists were particularly receptive to those great intellectual debates which, inspired by Baconian philosophy, Newtonian physics and Lockean psychology, accompanied the growth of commerce and industry in Europe and America. Colonial policies and responses were formed around the Enlightenment ideal of a world governed by 'natural' laws discoverable to human reason, and of 'natural' rights, allegedly empowering every man to pursue whatever metaphysical and commercial voyages he chose. It was as if European settlement in Australia was 'born modern' and the world which the colonists made was new and brightly lit. Knowledge itself was being seen as a form of accumulative, linear progress. Able to be written down and stored for individual perusal in books, scientific and political information was, in theory, available to every citizen and was both the means by and a measure of the extent to which certain societies had advanced, not only technologically, but also morally towards perfection. There was little place for secret and sacred knowledge, for notions of cyclical, seasonal time, and for an oral tradition of learning not as the exploration of uncharted territory, but as the re-affirmation of the known.

In writing this book, I also found inspiration in the wealth of new social history from labour, feminist and Black historians who explore 'history from below', seeking the experience of people previously under-represented in the history books and recapture 'the texture of everyday life'. It seemed to me that there were some groups of people to whom the egalitarian implications of Enlightenment theory had never been applied. I thus became concerned to examine the gap between rhetoric and reality in Enlightenment ideas. In particular, I was interested in the ways in which concepts of competitive individualism, equality, liberty and progress functioned as ideology, on the one hand expressing and advancing the social and economic position of the theorists and those people whose interests they represented; and on the other, concealing the relationships between theory and political context, turning reality upside down in order to conceal and justify the activities of these dominant groups. I wished to explore the darker side of Enlightenment theory, and in particular those debates which raged around how to codify the criminal law and make it more effective, how to stigmatize forms of political and other behaviour as deviant, how to punish the poor and put them to work, how to 'reform' the family and streamline reproduction. I wanted to know why the 'free' society being fashioned required the use of force against certain sections of the population and how the masking of these realities behind the rhetoric of freedom became so routine that even the makers and the wearers of the mask came to believe the deception.

To achieve this task, it seemed necessary to avoid writing inward-looking colonial history and more rigorously examine our relationship to changing economic and political factors not only in Europe, but also in America, Asia and the Pacific. For unless I believed that the theories were somehow self-generating, that 'discourse' had an autonomous life independent of the interests of those in possession of power and wealth, it was necessary to begin by tracing the links between the European debates and concurrent economic and political change. I wished to explain rather than merely describe the philosophical and scientific theories, defining the nature of the connections between knowledge, power and imperial expansion.

Influenced by the ideas of C. B. Macpherson's *Political Theory of*

Possessive Individualism (1962), I began to suspect that, by the last quarter of the eighteenth century, the pace of commercial expansion had so quickened that colonization could no longer be left to trial and error, or to the anarchic forces of the marketplace. Where up until this time, the annexation of overseas territory had modest, sometimes unplanned beginnings, and had taken whole centuries to achieve, from now on colonization would need to be guided by the theories first of wealthy and literate gentlemen, and later by professional experts who had the learning and the time to interpret the mass of new information becoming available from every corner of the globe, including Australia itself. The theories of late eighteenth and early nineteenth centuries were not conceived in an ideological vacuum. They were blueprints for social, political and commercial action.

This book attempts to analyse how economic, political, social and scientific theories of the period from 1770 to 1860 were used both to facilitate colonization and to normalize it. In so doing it aims to understand the lives of the men, women and children, black and white, whose labour was so crucial to those who amassed personal fortunes from the colonization of Aboriginal Australia and the Pacific.

In undertaking this task, I have incurred a special debt to Heather Radi and Geoffrey Bolton who have provided sustained and invaluable encouragement. Thanks are also due to Victoria Gollan who contributed so generously her time, critical insight, analytical skills and vast reading of international literature to the making of this book. Hilary Weatherburn provided detailed information from her outstanding knowledge of Australian primary sources. For information and advice I am also indebted to my friends and colleagues at the University of Sydney, especially Brian Fletcher and James Waldersee. Tony Cahill, Ken McNab and Barbara Caine provided assistance with British sources; Shane White with American ones. Deryck Schreuder and Soumyen Mukherjee offered comparative material on Africa, Canada and India; Richard Waterhouse made material available from his research on Australian popular culture; Ros Pesman found means from scarce History Department funds for retyping part of the manuscript; Penny Russell, Richard White and Stephen Garton provided helpful comments and friendly assistance through a series of emergencies; Peter Johnson of the Geography Department assisted with the maps. My gratitude also extends to Sandy

Mackay, Belinda Henwood and Deb Edward for assistance with research. Zenon Alexander typed the lengthy first draft of the manuscript; for typing I am indebted also to Diane O'Donovan, Jaya Thuraisingham and Suzanne Lewers. I was also assisted by the staff of the Mitchell, Dixson and National Libraries, the Macleay Museum and New South Wales State Archives. To all of these people I extend my thanks.

NOTE ON MEASUREMENTS

This book employs contemporary units of measurement. Equivalent measures and conversion to metric units are given below.

	currency	
12d (12 pence) =	1s (1 shilling)	
20s (20 shillings) =	£1 (1 pound) =	$2
21s =	1 guinea	
	weight	
	1 pound =	.453 kilograms
14 pounds =	1 stone	
8 stone =	1 hundredweight	
20 hundredweight =	1 ton =	1.02 tonnes
	length	
	1 inch =	25.4 millimetres
12 inches =	1 foot	
3 feet =	1 yard	
22 yards =	1 chain	
10 chains =	1 furlong	
8 furlongs =	1 mile =	1.61 kilometres
	area	
4840 square yards =	1 acre =	.405 hectares
640 acres =	1 square mile	
	capacity	
	1 pint =	.568 litres
8 pints =	1 gallon	
8 gallons =	1 bushel	

ABBREVIATIONS

ADB	*Australian Dictionary of Biography*
AJPH	*Australian Journal of Politics and History*
ANU	Australian National University
BPP	*British Parliamentary Papers*
BT	Bonwick Transcripts
CUP	Cambridge University Press
GG	*Government Gazette*
HRA	*Historical Records of Australia*
HRNSW	*Historical Records of New South Wales*
HS	*Historical Studies*
JRAHS	*Journal of Royal Australian Historical Society*
ML	Mitchell Library
NSW LA *V&P*	New South Wales Legislative Assembly *Votes and Proceedings*
OUP	Oxford University Press
PTHRA	*Proceedings of Tasmanian Historical Research Association*
SG	*Sydney Gazette*
SH	*Sydney Herald*
SMH	*Sydney Morning Herald*
UNSW	University of New South Wales
UQP	University of Queensland Press
VDL	Van Diemen's Land
VHM	*Victorian Historical Magazine*

LIST OF MAPS

INDIAN
OCEAN

• Darwin

N O R
T E R R

• Broome

WESTERN
AUSTRALIA

• Yalgoo

• Kalgoorlie
Coolgardie • •
• Boulder

Nullarbor Plain

• Northam • Nangeenan
Perth •
• Blackboy Hill
Rottnest Is
• Fremantle

Frankland R
Albany
King George S

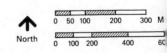

North

0 50 100   200   300 M

0 100 200   400   60

1

BLUEPRINT FOR GROWTH

Female Convict Experience   1788–1804

TUESDAY 3 MAY 1791 dawned bright and clear on Norfolk Island, a tiny pine-clad outcrop located 20 000 miles by sea from Britain at the western gateway to the vast Pacific. 'Fine weather, little wind and little surf,' wrote Lieutenant Ralph Clark in his diary:

Major Ross desired when I went out to Queensborough to take Richardson with me (which is the man that flogs the people) and give them as many lashes as I thought they deserved, when I ordered Catherine White and Mary Higgins 50 each, White could only bear 15, when she fainted away, the Doctor then wished that I would order her to be taken down, which I did, Higgins received 26, when I forgave her the remainder, as being an old woman, I ordered also Mary Teut to receive 25 lashes for the same crime as the others, she only received 22 lashes, when she fainted away, when I ordered her to be cast loose. I hope this will be a warning to the ladies out at Queensborough . . .'[1]

Catherine White, Mary Higgins and Mary Teut were three of the 550 women who, with some 1550 men, had been transported to the new British penal settlements at the New Holland colonies, authorized in 1786. Of these men and women nearly one-third were now on Norfolk Island.[2]

Though only 5 miles long and 3 in width, the island was a colonizer's dream. Unlike the sister settlement at Port Jackson, it was blessed with deep fertile soil and cascades of pure fresh water filled with eels. No indigenous people competed for these resources. Abundant limestone could be used for building. Giant pines reached nearly 70 metres in height and, as earlier British visitors had noted, offered at least 25 metres of sound timber before being impeded by a single branch; at a distance they looked like a forest of ships' masts. Around the coastline banks of wild flax grew in tropical abundance. These had similarly attracted the attention of a nation requiring canvas and rope for the large fleet of merchant vessels and warships on which the fortunes of its trading classes depended. The surrounding ocean teemed with 'very fine fish'; towards the north of the island a mountain-top seethed with birds which came in from the sea in thousands to breed. These were so tame that they could be caught with the hands or effortlessly knocked senseless with a stick.[3]

A mere three years before there had been no sound but the cries of the parrots, doves and sea birds, the sigh of the wind in the pines and the constant beating of the sea. Late in February 1788 Lieutenant Philip Gidley King had arrived from Port Jackson with twenty-three prospective settlers. Searching for an anchorage around the rocky and dangerous coast, by 6 March they had found a passage through a reef to a beach they called Sydney Bay. Though access was difficult, they had put ashore the people, tents, tools and provisions, hoisted a flag and declared themselves to be in formal possession. By March 1790 Major Robert Ross, commanding officer of the marines, had arrived with two companies of soldiers and 215 settlers, mostly convicts. In August, there had arrived another 200 convicts and the population had grown to more than 700, making the settlement nearly half as populous as Port Jackson. A second settlement, Queensborough, was established in the valley. Convict men were felling the mighty trees. Pigs, goats, and dogs had been introduced. Grubs and rats were proliferating on the settlers' corn. Hundreds of 'Mount Pitt' birds were slaughtered daily.

The flogging of the three women was not part of the formal plan for colonizing this outpost of the British mercantile empire. This ambitious and novel experiment in social engineering, authorized by Lord Sydney five years before, aimed at creating a community in which men and women classified by the British criminal law as delinquent might be transformed into useful colonizing material.[4] Cruelty, however, especially when directed by males towards women of an inferior socio-economic class, was part of the plan's unwritten agenda and reflected current

assumptions about male and female sex roles, property and procreation, sexuality and family life.

Certainly Lieutenant Ralph Clark did not consider himself as a
sadist. He was a particularly upright and sensitive young man,
who conformed to the romantic sensibility and evangelical self-
discipline, strongly—but not incompatibly—influencing young
people of his class at the time. On the convict transport *Friendship*
in 1787 he had been careful to avoid the deplorable lapses of
fellow officers Captain Meredith and Mr Faddy, and ship's
surgeon Dr Arndell, who frequently kept him awake by drinking
and singing well into the night, even on the Lord's day. In
contrast Lieutenant Clark spent his leisure time reading fashionable tragic plays, saying his prayers, keeping a daily diary of his
conduct, and writing home to his beloved wife and child.
Married just three years, he had only left his wife and two-year-
old son in the hope of financial reward and promotion. 'God out
of his great goodness give her health and that of our dear Sweet
Boy,' he wrote in May 1787, a week after sailing, 'if I had either
his mother or him I would eat him up with love and kisses'. At
the end of June his thoughts still dwelt on his angelic wife and
happy home. His only happiness now, he declared, was in kissing
Betsy's picture and the little piece of young Ralph's hair which
he had brought away with him. These treasures, he confided to
the diary, he would not part with—not even for a captain's
commission. In August when the Fleet lay at Rio, while Mr
Faddy and others sought riotous entertainment Lieutenant Clark
spent his time in collecting butterflies to send to his family. In
November at the Cape, with the Fleet due to leave this last port
of call for the faraway Pacific, Clark was devastated when a ship
came in from England but carried no letter from Betsy.

At the scene of the flogging on Norfolk Island Lieutenant
Clark would have denied there was anything uncharacteristic or
reprehensible about his behaviour. Indeed, his contempt for the
convict women had been present even before he left England and
included a prurient interest in their sexuality which existed
comfortably beside the romantic posturing he reserved for his
wife. Most of the civil and military authorities shared his views.
Convicts were rascals, and women convicts were dishonest in the
double sense of the word. Not merely would they lie, cheat or
steal, they were also probably unchaste and as such a dangerous
temptation to innocent married men.

Thus the most despised of the twenty-one female convicts in Clark's charge on board the *Friendship* were those who were involved when members of the crew broke through a bulkhead 'and had connection with them' before the Fleet had sailed from off the Isle of Wight. Clark was outraged when, three days out from Portsmouth, the seamen refused to work unless given an extra ration of beef per day. They only wanted it to give to 'the damned whores the convict women of whome the[y] are so fond', since having intercourse with them. Off Tenerife he had the same four women put in irons for 'fighting'. A fortnight later the seamen once again broke through the bulkhead and four women were caught 'in the mens place'. Within two days one of the four, Elizabeth Dudgeon, had been flogged for impertinence to Captain Meredith. 'The Corporal did not play with her but laid it home which I was very glad to see.' Elizabeth was twenty-three-years old, had no trade, and had been tried for and convicted of the theft of nine guineas. Like most of the convict women, she had been recruited from the burgeoning ranks of the urban poor.

On other ships the treatment of the women acquired a special cruelty derived not only from the military authority of the officials but also from their assumptions about male superiority and its right both to exploit and punish sexuality in working-class women. According to Dr Smyth, surgeon on the *Lady Penrhyn*, by December 1787 the officers on that ship abandoned ordering the women to be flogged with 'a Cat of nine tails on the naked breech' because, as Smyth put it, there were 'certain seasons when such a mode of punishment cd. not be inflicted with that attention to decency wh. everyone whose province it was to punish them, wished to adhere to'. In any case, thumb screws were more effective. Cutting off their hair and shaving their heads was also discovered to work particularly well, though while undergoing these punishments the women were so abusive that it was necessary to gag them.[5]

The reason men like Smyth and Clark were able to treat the convict women less as human beings than purely sexual objects in need of savage discipline was also due to the fact that the women offended developing notions of what ideal female behaviour should comprise. In the new, respectable, middle-class society which was emerging it was coming to be accepted that female sexuality should be expressed only within formal marriage, and should be centred on reproduction rather than sensuality. Yet on the convict ships the women had little choice but to accept the sexual advances of male 'protectors' who hopefully would fend off the advances and insults of the ship's officers and crew and provide some comforts and privileges to make the long voyage less intolerable.[6]

Nor did the fact that these sexual relationships often culminated in motherhood induce respect or restore the women's humanity. Since liaisons were often formed during the long periods of incarceration on board while the ships were filled and made ready for sail, it was not unusual for childbirth to occur during the voyage. Surgeon Smyth recorded four births and one miscarriage during the nine months' voyage to Botany Bay. For destitute women, motherhood too was seen in sexual terms, especially if it occurred outside marriage. On the convict ships, evidence of pregnancy, far from being seen as requiring special concessions and care, became an overt statement about a woman's prior sexual activities, thus increasing both the scrutiny and the moral censure of the male officials.

Moreover, it was difficult for the convict women to avoid having their pregnancies come under the eye of the ship's surgeons. In contrast, childbirth ashore, unless complications developed, was customarily managed by women whose knowledge was more than equal to existing medical procedures. The presence of a medical man who had been in touch with the sick or the dead only increased the chances of puerperal fever. Even the wives (still few in number) of civil and military officials making the voyage to the Pacific settlements did not always seek the intervention of the surgeon when a child was born *en route*. Mrs Eliza Marsden, wife of the second chaplain, coming out on the store-ship *William* in 1793–94 was delivered of her first child 'a fine girl' with no other assistance, her husband wrote, but such as he could give.[7]

On the *Friendship* on 3 August 1787, Sarah McCormick, one of the four women who had been involved in the bulkhead affair, was taken ill of an unspecified complaint. The matter was drawn to the attention of Dr Arndell who pronounced her unlikely to live. According to his diagnosis, she was quite 'eating up with the P[ox]', a circumstance which prompted Clark to dwell again in his diary on how the women had gone to the seamen, adding vindictively, 'I hope She has given them some thing to remember her'. By 5 August Dr Arndell found occasion to bleed Sarah no less than eight times, while on the 24th the unfortunate doctor was obliged to stay sober while Captain Meredith and Mr Faddy got wonderfully drunk celebrating 'little Ralphie's' birthday, for the doctor did not expect Sarah to live till morning. In spite of Arndell's predictions (and his treatment) Sarah survived. On 3 October she and Elizabeth Pully, another of the celebrated four, informed the innocent doctor that they were with child. It was three months since the infamous bulkhead incident. Clark hoped that the Governor of the new colony, Captain Arthur Phillip, would make the fathers marry the two women and stay for ever at Botany Bay.

Scant interest was paid by the authorities to the fate of the new-born, nor to the other children (thirteen in all) of the few women who persuaded the authorities to allow their youngest child to accompany them to the colony. Most such pleas were rejected. The need to found a new colony in the Pacific arose at a time when few labouring men and women of Britain were yet so desperate or so hungry that they would voluntarily leave their communities to look for work abroad. The plan for convict colonization was premised on the knowledge that a system of forced migration would be essential. Moreover, the deliberate fracturing of convicts' family and kinship networks in Britain could be rationalized by the belief that it was necessary to break the organized criminal and political connections in which, it was said, convicts were always implicated.[8]

The First Fleet also carried forty women and fourteen children coming out with the 160 marines. Whereas officers were not permitted to bring their wives, the rank and file of the armed services were recruited, like the convicts, from the labouring population of Britain and as such were seen as suitable colonizing resource, always provided they could be persuaded to stay on as settlers. Indeed, it was assumed that in the event of an invasion by a rival trading power or of a rebellion by the convict labourers, these men, having undergone militaristic discipline, would spring to the colony's defence. Some children died at sea but about thirty-six are thought to have disembarked at Sydney Cove. These were joined by about twenty-two from the Second Fleet and perhaps a dozen from the Third Fleet in 1791. By 1801 about a hundred children would have accompanied the 6000 convicts who were transported to New South Wales; a small percentage of those convicts were themselves aged from eleven to fourteen.[9]

Caring for the infants and children on the voyage added to the vulnerability of the women. In later years it became routine to provide ten sets of 'child bed linen' for every hundred female convicts on board, but the number of 'swaithes, pilches, blankets and napkins' provided by the officials was scant and mothers of the new-born needed to make their own arrangements for the extra materials they and their infants required. On the *Lady Penrhyn* it was noted that they were plundering the sailors of wearing apparel and cutting it up for mysterious purposes of their own. On the *Friendship* one of the women to whom Arndell gave his clothes to wash had the audacity apparently to lose no less than seven pairs of stockings overboard. 'D . . . . d B . . . . . . s', thundered Clark, and threatened that if they were to lose any of his attire given them to wash he could cut them to pieces. On the *Lady Penrhyn* Smyth preferred to wash his own trousers by towing them astern, but had no redress when one day they were unceremoniously eaten by a shark.[10]

Despite the officers' callous disregard for the needs of the women and children, it was largely because of their ability to produce children and thus build the population of the new settlements that the women had been sent. In the world from which this little Fleet had been launched, demographic issues were coming to be seen as of enormous significance. Indeed, political and economic theorists were locked in debate about how best to reorganize gender relations and the family so as to achieve efficient population growth, expertly geared to sustaining wanted rates of commercial expansion both at home and overseas.

This was the case especially in Britain where the economy and society were already being shaken by industrialization. Here, in contrast with the European nation-states, the feudal authority of monarch and church had been broken in the mid-seventeenth century by the English Revolution. Then, under a political settlement reached in 1688, power had been firmly grasped by a ruling group comprised of great landed magnates, wealthy traders and the upper echelons of army, church and law. Now in control of parliament and therefore of trade, finance, the judiciary and the armed forces, these people identified their wealth with that of the nation. Between 1702 and 1783 they engaged in no less than four major wars against their chief rival, France, by which time they had succeeded in changing the pattern of European trade.

British ships now dominated the New World and a wide spectrum of nobility, officials, navigators and adventurers, gentry and clergy had a stake in the concept of aggressive empire-building as a business proposition.[11]

These imperial policies demanded unprecedented numbers of unskilled and semi-trained men. A relatively peripheral campaign like that against the French in the Caribbean in January 1762 involved eighteen battleships and a hundred support-vessels carrying 12 000 soldiers. Many men died in campaigns such as these, either from scurvy, the ravages of tropical disease, or from being shot, speared with splinters of Spanish mahogany or English oak, or crushed under recoiling guns. In addition, colonization required a growing population to provide labourers, police and settlers, especially given the death rates of native peoples.[12]

The problem of sustaining demographic resources was the more crucial because of the growth of manufacturing. Though most factories were still very small operations, producing machine parts, small metal goods, pottery and especially textiles, they were increasing in number throughout the eighteenth century as capital created from overseas trade became available for reinvestment at home. Moreover recent technological innovations such as James Watt's steam engine (1769), Arkwright's water frame (1769) and Hargreave's spinning 'jenny' (1770) were rapidly being applied to production. This growth of manufacturing was in turn stimulating further overseas expansion in a cyclical process which increased the pressure on human resources.

Like the merchants and landholders the new factory owners had a special interest in demographic growth, for instead of making their money essentially from buying cheap and selling dear, in their factories profits depended on keeping wages as low as possible. This required an oversupply of potential labourers which, though it strained the system of parish relief for paupers, enabled employers to pay the lowest possible wage. Industrialization would be premised on the ideal of a nuclear family unit dependent on the earnings of a single male breadwinner with a wife who could devote herself to child-bearing. As well as pushing women into reproduction, this arrangement meant that the man would now be forced by these growing responsibilities to accept whatever work and pay was available. Moreover, this concept of a nuclear family ensured that women, along with children and the aged, formed an additional pool of reserve labour which could be called upon by employers during times of peak production. Meanwhile, even the work which was traditionally available to women, such as domestic service, laundry work, millinery and dressmaking should ideally be temporary and always lowly paid.

Fortunately for British industry, to some extent its special labour needs were initially met more or less spontaneously by the destruction of subsistence agriculture and the dispossession of the British peasant from the land. This large-scale relocation of labour resources and shattering of the family economy entailed misery and starvation for many people and might have been expected to result in a demographic disaster. In fact, however, it coincided with a population explosion. England's population in 1750 was about six and a half million but, partly due to increased resistance to some forms of infectious disease, by 1801 when the first official census was taken, there would be nine million people, many of them crowded into the unplanned and ill-drained streets of the growing ports and factory towns.[13]

The new industrialists were also fortunate in that initially their labour requirements and those of the ruling coalition were closely entwined. Thus cotton from the plantations overseas was now being processed by families usefully removed from the land by the enclosing landlords. Even villagers who still clung to their cottages could be set to work to produce textiles and other goods under contract to manufacturers. All were conveniently enmeshed in a web of cash transactions, buying up locally made manufactured products and imported tropical ones like tea, sugar and tobacco, as well of course, as the food they no longer produced themselves.[14]

Despite this initial compatibility of labour interests and common concern for demographic growth, very few of the trading and aristocratic families were manufacturers themselves. Certainly some benefited from the multiplier effects of industrialization on mining, urban growth and the construction of canals and turnpike roads, but the new industrial producers were more often former master craftsmen or yeomen farmers who had just sufficient property to raise the funds needed to begin production. By the end of the eighteenth century they were becoming concerned that some of the policies pursued by the ruling alliance were no longer meeting their special labour needs.[15]

This divergence of interests became apparent in features of the criminal justice system which had been developed over the past century as an instrument of labour control. Acts of Parliament had steadily tightened the definition of larceny and housebreaking. Activities like wood-gathering, deer-stalking and fishing were redefined as criminal poaching, wood-theft, and trespass. The aim was to facilitate dispossession from the land and force the former peasants to understand that in a cash economy they might use, eat and possess only those commodities for which they could pay. Resistance was heavily punished with liberal use of the death penalty. Whereas in 1688 there had been about fifty capital offences, 187 more were added to the statute books between 1660 and 1819. Some fifty were created by the notorious Black Act of 1723, which either criminalized or made more severe the penalties for activities like breaking fish ponds, killing cattle, cutting trees, firing houses, barns and haystacks, sending anonymous letters demanding money or goods, or forcibly rescuing from custody anyone accused of these offences.[16]

However, as some spokesmen for the industrialists were pointing out, an economic system which required a surplus labour pool could not afford to deal so drastically with its human resources. Certainly, from the 1760s judges had chosen to commute many of the sentences, but they had instead developed the practice of exiling offenders into forced labour abroad. By 1765 perhaps as few as 50 per cent of those who were sentenced were actually executed. This meant that some 1200 people were hanged annually, while the number transported rose to almost 1000. By the 1770s transportation had become a major part of the English criminal law, not only bolstering the labour force overseas but creating an extra source of profit for private contracters and shipowners, who removed the convicts to the plantations of Virginia or Maryland.[17]

In 1775 when the American War of Independence brought an end to this arrangement, the diverging interests of the new industrialists and the ruling coalition reached a crisis. Transportation might intimidate workers but it also took too many of them away, putting them to work in the interests of an old-fashioned colonial system for which the industrialists had little use. Yet the British authorities had not relinquished their desire to continue colonization and they maintained the steady flow of convicts, stockpiling them on some of the numerous ships, too old ever to sail, which now littered the Thames and harbours around the south coast. A classic mercantilist expedient which reflected the ruling alliance's stake in shipping, trade and war, the prisoners spent their nights on board these former emblems of British sea power while by day they carried out maritime work about the harbours and ports. The politicians and their advisers debated plans for new colonies in Africa and the Pacific where, it was thought, convict workers might usefully be employed. In the interim, the hulks rapidly became overcrowded, and, to the alarm of citizens in the surrounding towns, were said to be a source of contagious gaol fever and potential rebellion.[18]

Faced with this crisis, and convinced of the centrality of population growth to imperial expansion, the British authorities needed a blueprint for combining demographic and economic growth. To find it they looked to the numerous theorists who were seeking to analyse the relationship between land, population, sexuality and national wealth. Already in England John Locke, an early spokesman for the social contract and the rights of man, and apologist for the political and economic principles on which the settlement of 1688 had been based, had carefully defined land as a commodity, rationalizing both its enclosure at home and its annexation abroad as in accordance with Natural Law. Theorizing the nature and potential of the human mind, Locke was also concerned with the control of women, assuming that they were 'naturally' subordinate and therefore should 'consent' to be governed by men. By the 1760s, Lockean postulates had been further developed by theorists like J. J. Rousseau and it was apparent that the 'rights of man' meant precisely that, new forms of freedom for selected white adult males. In order for the new 'liberal' society to be held together, labour found and profits made, other sections of the population would have to be brought under new, more efficient means of control. By the 1780s, new theorists such as Adam Smith and Jeremy Bentham, were providing a comprehensive analysis linking ideals of contract and property to the control of marriage, sexuality, reproduction and 'crime'.

Bentham in particular was concerned to theorize both current penal policies and demographic issues, attempting to adjust both to the needs of the industrialists. From 1788 he lobbied for the replacement of transportation with more scientific and profitable forms of punishment. By 1802 he had designed a special disciplinary institution which, he claimed, would both intimidate the poor and exploit their labour at home. Known as a 'Panopticon', this would be different not only from the workhouses and hulks but also from the disorderly 'houses of correction' or 'Bridewells' which, dating from the Elizabethan period, were the other main means of disciplining the unemployed poor. Modelled rather on the factory, in the Panopticon or penitentiary the inmates would be set to operate ingenious machinery which would be punitive and onerous, but which would also efficiently produce goods. All of the profits would go to Bentham but he in return would guarantee that the inmates would have been so thoroughly educated by the process that they could be safely and economically returned to the factory. It was a classic industrialists' alternative to the hulk.[19]

Bentham's awareness of the escalating costs of maintaining the 'surplus' poor also led him to argue, in contradiction to many writers, that the economy might be better served by encouraging couples to plan and space their children. Other theorists believed the solution to finding a blueprint for ideal demographic growth lay in sparing the lives of children already born. In Britain infanticide had been made a serious criminal matter in 1624 and, though the practice of executing mothers for this offence was declining and the law would be repealed in 1803, in that year abortion would be defined as a capital crime. Meanwhile reformers were turning their philanthropic efforts towards consigning destitute children to foundling homes and hospitals; others believed that the factory itself was an appropriate institution for feeding and disciplining the children of the 'surplus' poor while at the same time deriving some profit from them. Among these reformers and theorists was a sprinkling of well-to-do women, for whom literary pursuits and charitable work (especially involving children and other women) were some of the very few public roles they were permitted to perform beyond their primary role as dependent bearers and rearers of children in their own homes.[20]

These debates about how to reconstruct the family and streamline reproduction would accelerate from 1798 when Thomas Malthus, an Anglican clergyman and political economist, enunciated an impressive and apparently scientific law of population. Bringing together and popularizing arguments previously put by writers like Daniel Defoe, Sir James Steuart and Joseph Townsend, Malthus argued that population was limited only by the lack of material resources needed to feed and clothe the lower orders. To explain precisely how this 'check' to population operated, Malthus argued that whereas the wise and prudent classes checked their reproductive capacity by exercising 'moral restraint', the foolish and improvident, like mere plants and animals, produced more children than they could possibly support. 'Misery and Vice' would be their inevitable lot in this 'struggle for existence' until their numbers were cut by starvation and disease, and the whole process would begin again.

Underlying these controversies was the central issue of whether profits could best be maximized by increasing or containing population growth. On the one hand, industrialization required a reserve pool of labourers and consumers; on the other, the poverty caused by their intermittent unemployment appeared to some as a drain on the public purse. Yet if workers did limit their numbers, the employers would lose their needed pool of what the theorists called 'surplus population'.

Whether they approved of limiting or maximizing women's reproductive capacity, the real service of these debates was not in demography but rather in ideology. Thus Malthus's work, which had been initiated by alarm at the new Speenhamland system of 'child endowment' for paupers and the increase in parish rates which it had caused, contributed to the prevailing castigation of the poor which implicitly rationalized the shattering of their family life. Just as important, anticipating the time when the industrialists too would require overseas expansion, Malthus's theories allayed the traditional fear that colonization was a drain on population, normalizing imperialism as a search for living space which should be allocated to those societies whose material production and population growth were greatest. Malthus assumed that human reproductive capacity and 'ardent' sexual passions were infinite and that therefore all societies had always reproduced at full capacity. Even the 'apathetic' American Indians would bear large families, he declared, if they settled in some fertile spot or otherwise adopted 'civilized' ways. He therefore concealed the fact that rapid population growth was only specific and necessary to capitalist society where profits depended on an over-supply of workers.[21]

These debates about population had grave consequences for women. Irrespective of their political persuasion or immediate sources of wealth, all of these theorists shared a belief that population growth, and thus women who sustained it, could be manipulated in the interests of manufacturers and merchants. All assumed that women's bodies existed merely to reproduce.

This concept of women as reproductive units affected all women, rich or poor, black or white, for though it was chiefly more workers which were needed, not more leaders, the theorists applied the ideology to women generally, thus masking the fact that it benefited only the holders of economic wealth. However, having fewer means to escape or alleviate the consequences, it was working-class and black women who bore the full force of this essential requirement for rapid economic growth. Though in some circles the increasing emphasis on their demographic importance was welcomed as elevating their status as mothers, for labouring women it meant being regarded less as human beings than as human capital, mere statistical items whose sexuality was an exploitable resource. Thus for the women in New South Wales this new definition of women in terms of their reproductivity was not only one of the reasons they had been sent to the colony but was also one of the reasons why they were being treated with such contempt.[22]

European intellectuals were also advancing a new view of male sexuality and this too was reflected both in the formal plans for penal colonization and in the actual experience of the women of New South Wales. This ideal was centred around an aggressive, procreative sexuality now coming to be seen as normal rather than sinful and therefore desirable in every male. As Malthus put it, arguing that colonization was an inevitable consequence of population pressure, the men of a colonizing country were necessarily barbarous, energetic adventurers, delighting in war and overturning the peaceful inhabitants of the countries upon whom they rushed, who could not long withstand the energy of men acting under such powerful motives of exertion. The prodigious waste of human life involved was of no consequence, for the mighty power of procreation (especially evident, according to Malthus, in British colonies) would soon replenish it.

Some medical writers were arguing that good health in males depended on regular sexual emissions; others were stigmatizing male homosexuality as wasteful and non-reproductive and creating fear of the physiological consequences of 'unnatural' sexual practices between males. Scrutiny of the growing numbers of men isolated from family and community and incarcerated in houses of correction, hulks and barracks helped draw attention to these issues. The Navy sharpened its punishments for sodomy among sailors, especially during the Napoleonic wars. Prejudice against homosexuality was also engendered in the general public. A poem published in London in December 1786, soon after the decision to found the penal colony, had no compunction in including 'gay powder'd coxcombs and proud dressy fops' among the thieves, villains, strumpets and whoremasters who should, it was suggested, be exiled immediately to Botany Bay.[23]

Some theorists, believing casual heterosexual relations were an antidote to male homosexuality, went so far as to argue that perhaps female prostitution should be tolerated, even encouraged. After all, such heterosexual liaisons might produce children anyway. Besides, the aggression needed in the colonizing male was best achieved by teaching him that it was part of his role as the more chauvinistic sex to seek out sexual liaisons with women wherever possible. This was a natural male right, part of the new 'liberty' which all men, it was said, might now enjoy. If they chose, they could even purchase a liaison with the cash they earned from their new but admittedly uncertain work as stablemen, street-sweepers, waterside workers, builders' assistants, carters, street-sellers, beggars and cadgers. The female sex was a piece of property to be fought over, possessed, and disposed of exactly like the land and the other marketable commodities. Indeed, in the case of the prostitute, the female sex actually became a commodity, part of the network of cash transactions which the casual poor had to be taught to use, preserve and respect.

Given the scale of urbanization, the forced mobility of men and the desperate poverty of mothers and girls, there was no shortage of candidates obliged to test these theories. Prostitution offered an expanding field of economic survival for destitute women, for clients offered themselves at every level of society and on an unprecedented scale. At one end of the spectrum was the growing number of men cut off from marriage and family life by poverty or by service in the armed forces. At the other end of the spectrum were the roués and buffs who had long had no doubt that the pursuit of sexual gratification was an appropriate pastime for men and who were taking advantage of the social dislocation and the economic vulnerability of the female poor to promote a consuming interest in illicit sexual activity. Reflecting the size of this upper-market clientele, writers such as John

Cleland, Daniel Defoe and Samuel Richardson were making the increasing sexual accessibility of the female poor a major theme in that new literary form, the novel. There was also a flourishing trade in pornographic literature, with journals like *The Rambler* and the *Bonton Magazine* finding that explicit discussion of subjects like flagellation found a ready market among the literate classes.

This anarchical doctrine of the 'liberation' of the male libido was at odds with the need to establish paternity and guarantee laws for the inheritance of property. It was to solve this problem that increasing emphasis was being placed on the very different, asexual ideal for women: that of the virtuous wife and mother. That is, a rigid theoretical distinction had to be made between those women whose sexuality was to be used purely for reproduction and those who were to be used to stimulate aggression in the male. In practice, of course, these roles would be blurred. Numerous women would prostitute themselves in marriage and experience male sexual aggression whether they were married or not, and numerous 'prostitutes' would marry and bear children.[24]

These preoccupations with the stimulation and control of male sexuality, no less than reproduction, influenced the official plans for the penal settlements. According to Lord Sydney, the presence of the convict women was essential in order to prevent those 'gross irregularities and disorders' which, he said, would necessarily arise otherwise. Ideally these women should serve the needs only of the convict men who, after arrival, were to be permitted access to their company. To serve the marines, a ship would be sent to collect women from New Caledonia and the Friendly Islands, thought from explorers' reports to be especially sexually alluring.

In these plans, attention was also paid to the reproductive function of the convict women as wives to the convict men. On the expiration of their sentence, or upon being pardoned for good behaviour, convict men were to be entitled to a plot of land and, should they be persuaded to take a wife, the amount of land granted would increase from 30 to 50 acres. Another 10 acres would be given for every child. The assumption was that by being provided with land plus a woman to discipline and call their own, they would at once be prevented from lapsing into those vices which were known to prevail where men were herded together, and be encouraged to turn into model if miniature capitalists. The marines, too, after three years' term of duty, were to be eligible for a grant of land which would increase in size with marriage. This had been promised as early as 1786 in order to encourage enlistment, and regulations to this effect followed in August 1789. Single non-commissioned officers were to receive 130 acres and privates 80 acres, plus 10 acres for a wife and 10 for each child born when the grant was issued. No provisions were made for granting land to officers, it being assumed that farming was incompatible with their duties and that no one of this class would consider forgoing society to settle in such a remote part of the globe.[25]

Nor were arrangements made for granting land to the women. British property laws assumed that on becoming married a woman forfeited property to her husband. However, this also reflected the assumption that the women convicts, forcibly taken from their homes and communities in Britain, were to be made part of the property of the colonizing male. Similarly, although arrangements were made for some of the families of well-behaved male convicts to accompany or follow them to the new colony, parallel privileges for women convicts were not part of the blueprint. Their family life had to be absolutely destroyed in order to reduce them to the sexual and reproductive objects which the system required.

Though the distribution of land grants to male expirees was carefully planned, precisely how the women were to be allocated in this singular piece of social engineering was by no means clear. It puzzled the Governor, Arthur Phillip, as early as 1787. He was in no doubt that the proposed consignment of Island women was intended only for the marines. To serve the convict men, he hoped the 'natives' might be persuaded to allow access to some of their women, but otherwise he would have to depend on the convict women to arouse the desired sexual and property values in the male offender. Musing gloomily over this problem before the Fleet sailed, he assumed the women convicts would be singularly unsuited to these important tasks. Certainly they should at all costs be prevented from sexual contact with the military garrison, for he did not wish convicts 'to lay the foundations of an empire'. He therefore proposed classifying the women according to the received idea of female utility. The most virtuous were to be protected during the voyage and on arrival, made available for marriage. The more 'abandoned' were to be used for approved 'visits' by the convict men, though only at

certain hours and under certain restrictions. Given these enlightened plans for turning the male offender into an aggressively
masculine holder of property, Phillip planned to show little
mercy for sodomites. Any man found guilty of this offence
would, along with murderers, suffer secondary transportation to
New Zealand, where Phillip hoped the Maoris would obligingly
eat him.[26]

In view of these constructions of male and female sexuality, it
was hardly surprising that the female convicts were the objects of
such officially sanctioned and highly visible brutality. Even a free
woman coming out as the wife of a convict did not escape the
abuse entailed by this assessment in purely sexual terms. For
instance, Mrs McNamara, one of some seventeen wives of
convicts permitted to sail with the First Fleet, was put into leg
irons by Lieutenant Clark 'for being impertinent to the convict
cook'.

As on the ships, on the shore the approved exploitation and
punishment of the women's sexuality was allowed to run its course.
The scene early in February at Port Jackson when the women in
the First Fleet disembarked was noted by most of the authorities
who kept a record. According to Surgeon Smyth, 'the Men
Convicts got to them very soon after they landed & it is beyond
my abilities to give a just discription of the scene of Debauchery
and Riot that ensued during the night'. Clark's reaction was more
judgemental:

what a seen of Whordome is going on there in the woman's camp—no
sooner has one man gone in with a woman but a nother goes in with
her—I hope the Almighty will keep me free from them as he has heather
to done but I need not be affraid as I promised you my Tender Betsy I
will keep my word with you . . .

It was left to the urbane Captain Tench, one of the most highly
educated of the official party with a 'wide reading in contemporary English literature' to put the official view. While on
board, the convict men had been kept 'rigorously apart' from the
opposite sex,

but, when landed, their separation became impracticable, and would
have been, perhaps, wrong. Licentiousness was the unavoidable consequence . . . What was to be attempted? To prevent their intercourse
was impossible; and to palliate its evils only remained. Marriage was
recommended, and such advantages held out to those who aimed at

reformation, as have greatly contributed to the tranquillity of the settlement.[27]

Meanwhile, what the officers saw as 'anarchy and confusion' reigned in the women's camp. Sailors attempting to keep up relationships made on the ships or hoping to form new ones were attacked by the male convicts even as they approached the women's tents, the convicts attempting to force them back on board their ships. 'Palliatives' handed out included a sentence of 200 lashes to a marine, Thomas Bramwell (or Bramage), for striking one of the convict women. She was Elizabeth Needham from the *Lady Penrhyn* who had according to Smyth, 'connections' with Bramwell during the voyage. Since disembarkation, the two had quarrelled, and Thomas had struck her because in Clark's words, 'She would not goe up in the woods with him to X . . .'.

Overall, the official view that it was impractical to protect the women prevailed. This was reflected in the failure to provide adequate shelters for the women and children; in some cases there was no protection against the weather, let alone against unwelcome advances from the men. The women and children in the party removed from Port Jackson to Norfolk Island in March 1790 had to sleep out in the bush after landing, as they could not walk across from Sydney Bay to the town before dark. Another group who arrived in August 1790 had the same experience, and a man who stole some of their possessions while they were asleep received only five lashes as punishment.[28]

The officials' blueprint for the exploitation of female bodies did not extend to young girls who, reflecting Lockean ideals on child-raising, theoretically were not to be turned into sexual commodities until ready for reproduction. Thus in September 1789 Henry Wright, a marine, was sentenced to death for raping eight-year-old Elizabeth Chapman. However, his sentence was commuted to life transportation to Norfolk Island because, according to the Judge-Advocate, David Collins, though this was a heinous offence, it was not one which required immediate example. Fortunately the chastity of the female part of the settlement, he declared, was not so rigid that other men might be driven to 'so desperate an act'. Despite this Henry Wright continued to use little girls. On 18 July 1791 on Norfolk Island Lieutenant Clark noted in his diary that Henry had been forced 'to run the ga[u]ntlet through all the men and women here, for attempting to deflour . . . Elizabeth Gregory, a girl of about ten years of age'.[29]

Neither was pack rape of the women officially condoned; in such cases a protective paternalism obscured the ruthlessness of the system. In the first such trial, held in May 1795, six men were acquitted of raping Mary Hartley at the new settlements along the Hawkesbury River, although two were found guilty of assault. In November eight men were charged with raping Marianne Wilkinson; three were found guilty and received heavy sentences. Even so, it was admitted by Collins that 'these unmanly attacks of several men on a single woman' had frequently happened, and some were not reported.[30]

The hardships suffered by the women during the early years of the colonial experiment were not all part of the written and unwritten official agenda. Some arose from a series of misfortunes which for a short time seemed likely to destroy the little settlements and their European inhabitants.

The voyage of the First Fleet had been accomplished exactly to schedule and without losing a single ship. By July 1788 a formal flag-raising ceremony held at Port Jackson claimed the eastern half of the continent as far as the 135th degree of longitude for Britain. Governor Phillip had made a detailed plan for a town at Sydney Cove, with generous streets 200 feet wide, allotments with frontages of 60 feet, large freestone buildings and even a library; he planned to call the new town Albion. On the western arm of Sydney Cove an observatory was almost complete, through which Lieutenant Dawes planned to observe an approaching comet. Captain Hunter of the *Sirius* had charted the shores of Sydney Harbour and expertly sounded its depths. Other officers had made detailed drawings of fish, sharks, possums, dingoes, emus, and parrots, and dried and stuffed whole specimens for consignment back to England. Captain Shea had shot two kangaroos and Lieutenant Clark was planning to kill another and have it stuffed and sent back to Betsy.

However nearly all the streams evaporated rapidly in dry weather and no stream capable of turning a mill had been found. Saws blunted and broke on the hard unfamiliar timber, which shrank and warped as it dried. Rushes brought from a nearby cove proved a highly inflammable roofing material, as did fronds of cabbage-tree palm. The only clay suitable for making bricks was located a mile inland, and the brick kiln constructed there collapsed repeatedly in heavy rain. No chalk or limestone was found, and lime for laying the bricks had to be produced from burning shells. Even more serious, the first sowing of crops failed, for some of the seed had been overheated during the passage from the Cape and much was destroyed by weevils. Of the crops which grew, some withered in the dry soil, others were eaten by field mice. In July 1788 only about 12 acres of land were under cultivation. Of the livestock which survived the voyage, much had since perished. By September few of the government-owned sheep survived. Of the sheep brought out by the officers with a view to later sale to the convict establishment, only those raised like pets and put to graze on the short grass near their owners' tents were still alive. Pigs and poultry proved more resilient, but periodically escaped to relish or rampage through the precious garden plants brought from Rio and the Cape. Five rabbits survived, but all of the government's cattle, comprising two bulls and four cows had departed in search of greener pasture and were presumed lost.

From the moment of disembarkation, food supplies were in question. By July Phillip realized that supplies of provisions would have to be sent from England for at least four or five years. Medical supplies were dangerously low, forcing Surgeon White away from his studies of the local flora and fauna to experiment with red eucalyptus gum to treat dysentery, and yellow gum for lung infections. Leather was needed for mending shoes, and thread to repair clothing was in short supply. Even on the better-watered and more fertile Norfolk Island there was cause for alarm. Autumn winds seared the gardens, and in addition to the rats, unwelcome grubs had proved resistant even to King's ingenious repellent using a mixture of two plentiful materials, ashes and urine.[31] In October 1788 Governor Phillip dispatched the *Sirius*, one of the only two remaining ships in the colony, to the Cape to purchase fresh supplies but she did not return until the following May. Then in December 1789 the storeship *Guardian*, loaded with supplies from England, struck an iceberg twelve days out from the Cape. Horses, cattle, sheep, and goats were among the vital supplies jettisoned in order to save the ship which limped back to Table Bay.

It had been to relieve the famine at Port Jackson that in January 1790 it was decided to transport Major Ross, a large detachment of marines, and more than 200 of the convicts to Norfolk Island. In March, having just unloaded her human cargo, the *Sirius* was wrecked in Sydney Bay and most of her provisions were lost. With only the *Supply* left to communicate with the outside world and provisions for perhaps seven months on half-rations, this was a disaster to daunt the most determined of empire-builders. Some of the officers declared that perhaps the experiment had been far too ambitious and the little settlements were too isolated to survive, much less ever to become a hub of naval or commercial activity in the Pacific.[32]

In fact the leanness of the ration was relieved by June 1790 with the arrival from England of the *Lady Juliana* and the store-ship *Justinian*. Periodic food shortages, however, continued to occur across the ensuring decade and even the Marsden family on their farm at Parramatta had occasionally to sit down to 'balm tea' or 'wheat coffee', sometimes without sugar.

Though all suffered privations during the hungry years, the hardships fell chiefly on the convict women with children. As early as September 1788 when the women's ration was two-thirds that of the men and the children's was one-third, Phillip admitted that the children's allowance especially was far too small. In May 1790 one woman died after eating a mixture she had concocted of 'flour and greens'. A man's ration at the time was two-and-a-half pounds of flour, two pounds of rice and two pounds of pork per week. The women were also desperately short of clothing. By April 1792 when the hardships and privations were occasioning cases of insanity, officials noted that many of the victims were female. They were puzzled for an explanation since the women were 'not harassed with hard labour' like the men.[33]

During the early months at Port Jackson the women were kept, according to Tench, 'in a state of total idleness' except for a few who were kept at work making pegs for tiles and picking up shells for lime. On Norfolk Island during the first decade employ-ment for the women included piling up the roots of trees where the men had grubbed them out for burning. Later they carried the potato harvest from the fields to the storehouse. Some were designated to mind the hogs and could be severely punished for losing any, or letting them get into the corn. It was not till the late 1790s with the development of colonial trade and of local industries, together with the growth of the free population, that some women were able to subvert the reproductive aims of the system and play an economic role in the capitalist society being created. At the end of December 1799 the total population of the mainland settlements had reached 5100 of whom half were living in Sydney, 1466 at Parramatta and Toongabbie, and the remainder on farms along the Hawkesbury. In that year, of fourteen licensed liquor vendors, two were women. They included Elizabeth Needham who, having survived Bramwell's beating, had become one of the very few women in that first decade to have succeeded in acquiring land of her own. In addition to her liquor licence, she held 40 acres of land in the Bulanaming district, granted on 15 September 1796.[34]

Elizabeth Needham's case was exceptional. Out of a total of nearly 1000 grants made by 1799 only twenty-two went to women. It was not till 1803 or 1804 that even those women with business skills could find openings in Sydney. Nor had many women found employment in the government institutions for the sick and insane, though two or three were midwives. The majority of women continued to find that, as on the ships, they were forced to seek a male 'protector' as soon as possible. Those most at a disadvantage in this procedure were the ones with the greatest need—the women with young children to care for. Lacking protection, accommodation, clothing, sufficient food and access to paid work, some women resorted to theft. As early as February 1788 one woman was flogged at the cart's tail for stealing from another convict woman. In November 1789 Ann Davis was found guilty of breaking into the house of a convict man, Robert Sidaway, and stealing several articles of clothing. She became the first woman executed in the new colony.[35]

In these circumstances it was inevitable that most women saw marriage or cohabitation as the only possible solution to their difficulties. In his address to the convicts on 7 February 1788 Phillip had strongly recommended marriage, promising every assistance to convicts who chose to wed. Three days later a number of couples took his advice. According to Clark some of the men had wives and families in England, and others, according to Collins, were motivated only by the Governor's promise of being rewarded with certain comforts and privileges denied to the single male. Most couples who married at this time were likely to have been acquainted previously, as were Susannah Holmes and Henry Kable. Both came out on the *Friendship*

Susannah having borne Kable's child when she embarked. Many couples were deterred from marriage by the fact that only an Anglican clergyman was permitted to officiate at marriage services. This would remain a major problem for Catholics, male and female, till amended in 1834.[36]

Some women who were young, pretty, and preferably un-encumbered with a child, found 'protectors' among the officials. Thus Ann Yeates, who arrived on the *Lady Penrhyn* in 1788, formed a liaison with the stern Judge-Advocate Collins, producing a daughter in November 1790 and a son in April 1794. Elizabeth Burleigh lived with and had many children by Dr Arndell in addition to her son John, who arrived with her in 1788. Esther Abrahams, who arrived on the *Prince of Wales*, lived with Lieu-tenant George Johnston and eventually married him, though not till 1814. A less long-lived relationship was Ann Innett's interlude with Lieutenant King on Norfolk Island. Sent back to England by Phillip in March 1790 to report on the difficulties faced by the settlement, when King returned to the island in November 1791 he was accompanied by a new wife, Anna Coombe, who six weeks later presented him with a son. Anna temporarily 'adopted' Ann's two sons, whom King imaginatively named Norfolk and Sydney, while Ann was left eventually to marry an ex-convict, albeit a wealthy one. Margaret Dawson from the *Lady Penrhyn* became de facto wife of William Balmain, formerly Assistant Surgeon on the *Alexander*, while even Lieutenant Clark eventually became a 'protector'. He chose twenty-year-old Mary Branham. Mary was already pregnant on that Tuesday morning on Norfolk Island when Clark supervised the floggings of the three women, and in three months their daughter Alicia would be born.[37]

Convict women needed to find a long-term 'protector' even among men who held them in contempt because their chances of return were slight. Whereas time-expired men could work their way back on a ship, for most of the women this was not a viable option. A sprinkling of expirees did manage to secure a passage back, the first being Dorothy Handland. A 'dealer' by trade, she had been sentenced for perjury in 1786 and was said by Surgeon Smyth to be eighty-two years old when she embarked on the *Lady Penrhyn* in 1787, but such cases were unusual. As Governor Bligh recalled twenty years later, unless she had realized some money or some stock, a woman's only chance of return was to prostitute herself to the master or mate of a passing vessel.[38]

Even fewer options were available to women under sentence. In contrast with male convicts, female absconders had little chance of surviving outside the settlement, as Ann Smith discovered. Arriving on the *Lady Penrhyn* in 1788 she 'eloped from the Camp' within a week of landing, as according to Smyth, 'she had often said she would do'. Other than a small piece of her petticoat, no trace of her was ever found.

In general, the few women who escaped and survived could do so only by joining a party organized and controlled by men. In March 1791 Mary Bryant escaped with her husband and two children in a tiny cutter which took them on a two-year voyage along the Queensland coast and across the Arafura Sea to Timor. In November 1794 Mary Morgan fled the colony by joining convicts John Randall and his wife on the *Resolution* with the master's compliance. There were also the sixty-six women on the *Lady Shore* which was seized in a mutiny off Rio in August 1797 by a party of Irish and French deserters who had been pardoned on condition they join the New South Wales Corps. Though they successfully steered the ship to the Rio Grande, there they were made prisoners of war while the female convicts were sent into the service of the Spanish colonists.[39]

Most women were likely to find the 'protection' offered by their male partner unsatisfactory. The first convicts' houses at Port Jackson were primitive, with lattices of twigs in place of windows, and walls of mud. On Norfolk Island, by 1796 not more than ten settlers had been able to erect better dwellings than log huts, which were neither warm nor durable. Those built by the settlers on the Hawkesbury and Georges Rivers were usually 'wretched hovels' of bark, initially consisting of two rooms with later additions at the back and sides called 'skillings'. Kitchens were basic in the extreme, and women and children were constantly exposed to the risk of death from burning and scalding. In August 1795 Jane Forbes, the wife of a settler at Prospect Hill, fell into the fire while preparing their breakfast 'and received such injury that she shortly after expired'.[40]

Some convict husbands followed the example set by the officials and used corporal punishment to discipline their wives. Ann Jenkins arrived on the *Mary Ann* in July 1791 and in September married George Sharpless who, in a fit of jealousy, gave her 'such a dreadful beating, that her life was for some time in danger'. Judge-Advocate Collins was unsympathetic.

Sharpless, he remarked, could only have been pretending to be jealous for Ann was, in his opinion, the 'perfect antidote to desire'.

From August 1789 convicts could be assigned into private service, and many convict women found themselves compelled to perform unpaid domestic services for approved settlers. Though some were assigned to the few wives of officials then in the colony, most went to the civil and military officers where their labours were likely to include sexual services. 'The cattle that were brought in the *Hunter* and which were sold by auction at this time, were not greater objects of contest than were these females', commented Collins following the arrival of ninety-four women convicts on the *Britannia* from England in July 1798. By the time of the Bligh regime (1806–08) it had become customary for men who wanted servants to go on board newly arrived transports and select them from among the new arrivals. Bligh admitted that the female convict had no choice in the matter unless she could name another person who would apply for her. According to Bligh it was impossible to prevent what he called this 'prostitution', nor was there any necessity for any regulations repressing it: 'men who were settlers wanted female servants, and pitched upon particular women for whom they applied, who perhaps cohabited together; these things could not be prevented . . .'[41]

Under this system the attitudes of the male authorities towards the female convicts hardened further. One of their severest critics during this first decade, Governor Hunter (1795–1800), complained that they were 'at the bottom of every infamous transaction committed in the colony' and he authorized magistrates to order women who disobeyed orders or neglected duties, to suffer 'such exemplary punishment, either corporal or otherwise, as the nature of their crime may merit'. Hunter believed that corporal punishment of the women convicts had in recent years declined, and that this was the reason why they had 'grown disorderly beyond all suffering'.

By the time of Hunter's retirement in 1800 however, officials were questioning existing policies on the women. It was noted that cohabitation was more common than marriage and as Bligh later put it, a 'habit of getting children and quitting the country was increasing'. This habit, needless to say, extended to the officials. Having ignored the pleas of his wife for an early return, David Collins departed in 1796, making little provision, if any, for two children then aged six and three, born of his liaison with Ann Yeates. Ralph Clark had sailed back to Betsy at the first opportunity, but he too left his mistress and their child in Sydney when he departed with the marines in December 1791. Encapsulating the expansionist and pro-natalist preoccupations of this age, perhaps it was fitting that both Clark and Betsy were among its victims. Within three years both were dead, he probably in action against the French at Haiti, she after giving birth to a dead child. Little Ralph, then aged nine, also died in 1794 serving on the same ship as Clark.[42]

Back in New South Wales, it was largely the Crown which supported the deserted women and their numerous children, for as an experiment in reproduction the colonial system had worked too well. By December 1799 the number of children in the colony had grown from the mere thirty-six who had disembarked in 1788 to 862. From an insignificant minority of 3.2 per cent of the total population they now comprised 16.9 per cent. By the end of the 1790s there were as many children as women. Both groups were heavily outnumbered by the men, who numbered 3385 or 66.3 per cent of the total population. This was thought to be completely at odds with any other demographic structure anywhere at the time.[43]

This phenomenal increase in the colony's children was partly a reflection of the fact that most of the women who had arrived since 1788 were of child-bearing age.[44] Moreover, children survived because of the absence of the main infectious diseases which elsewhere decimated the young. As yet measles, whooping cough, scarlet fever, and diphtheria were absent, and colonial children escaped the gastroenteric diseases which were thriving in the over-crowded poorly drained urban centres in Britain. Also, because there were so few children coming out on the convict ships, infectious diseases were less readily propagated. Sick children either died or recovered before the end of the journey. Thus, although some of these ships could make a very fast passage—like the *Mary Ann* which took only 143 days in 1791—there was little chance of these diseases being transmitted to children already in the colony.

In contrast, children on vessels returning from the colony suffered heavy mortality. The *Gorgon*, carrying the marine corps and their wives and children back to England in 1791–92, lost ten children after leaving the Cape. Among the dead was Charlotte, the daughter of Mary Bryant, who along with the other survivors of the escape had been captured in Timor by a British officer and transferred to this vessel at the Cape.[45]

Because so many men declined to support the colonial mothers and children as part of their permanent property, there was increasing concern in official circles about the cost of the existing policy to the Crown. Of the 862 children in New South Wales in 1799, no less than 828 were 'on the Store'. Of these, one-third were the children of people who were not or had not been convicts, for as Hunter pointed out in 1797, it was not only the offspring of convict men but those of the military who were 'destitute'. The authorities accordingly sought statistical data on family patterns and from 1800 onwards began to collect information about the number of marriages celebrated. In doing so however they ignored stable de facto relationships. Following a muster in 1807 Samuel Marsden estimated that nearly 60 per cent of the colony's children were 'illegitimate'. A survey made by King (who succeeded Hunter as Governor from September 1800 to May 1806) placed the proportion nearly as high. These figures were also accepted by Governor Bligh who pointed out that there were then only 395 married women in the colony of New South Wales and some 1035 'concubines'.[46]

No one was in any doubt that the increasing number of children was an economic asset to the colony, provided the youngsters were not off-loaded by their fathers onto the government store. By 1797 even Hunter was prepared to reverse his strictures on the convict women when he considered their function from a reproductive point of view. 'If we estimate their merits by the charming children with which they have fill'd the colony, they well deserve our care.'[47] This growing interest in the reproductive contribution and moral welfare of the convict women did not entail an improvement in their status. Instead there was a tendency to make a distinction between their alleged 'depravity' and the 'innocence' of their colonial-born offspring. Somehow the women were still at fault, and increasingly the solution was seen to be in bringing both them and their daughters under greater control of the nascent colonial state.

This reflected further developments in overseas theory and practice concerning control over reproduction and the protection of property. Especially following the publication of Rousseau's *Émile* (1762), it became apparent that not only women but also children would have to be brought under discipline. The followers of Locke and Rousseau were arguing the human mind was a *tabula rasa* and all learning derived from experience. Therefore children were not mere little adults, but empty vessels who should be isolated from the adult world and their minds filled with approved values and skills. Only thus could they be trusted, when grown, to understand and obey the new rules about property, labour and sex roles. Ideally this training process should involve not only formal schooling but a highly structured, supervised home life. Like the prisoners in the Panopticon, the child was to be under constant vigilance, night and day. Allegedly devoted to the protection of 'innocence', this formula actually focused attention on early manifestations of sexuality and advised punishments and preventatives likely to achieve the aggressive sexual behaviour wanted in the male and the fecundity wanted in the female. Particularly debated was the role of corporal punishment, which in Britain was extensively used in the schools for the sons of the rich despite the fact that it was thought to arouse rather than repress sexuality. Some of the dialogue on this topic was itself pornographic while also contributing to the prevailing association of flagellation with pleasure rather than pain.[48]

Highly compatible with growing evangelical influence, this concept of the innocence of childhood was central to the development of an ideology of 'rescue' which rationalized the practice of rounding up the destitute young and incarcerating them in miniature workhouses or factories designed specially to house the young. This practice saved children from starvation and so helped to keep worker numbers high. It also ensured that children, separated from parents said to be 'hardened' in their habits and unfit to have the care of the malleable young, were schooled into their future roles as obedient semi-skilled workers and mothers.

In the convict settlements these sentiments were early endorsed by the clergymen. As Reverend Richard Johnson put it, there was an urgent need not only for day schools but also for an 'orphan school' to rescue children from immoral and delinquent mothers. Already separated from their husbands and kin, it seemed that the most destitute of the convict women were now also to be separated from their children. Lacking, as yet, a leisured class of ladies or gentlemen to establish charitable schools and orphanages on the British model, it was recognized that these facilities would at first have to be provided by the State.

The first experiment of this kind was made by Lieutenant King as early as February 1788. Along with other officials such as David Collins, King had been favourably impressed with a Spanish workhouse for 'the daughters of the labouring poor' visited while idling about Santa Cruz on the voyage out. On Norfolk Island in 1796, perhaps moved by concern for his own illegitimate offspring, he had established an institution for 'such orphan female children as have lost or been deserted by their parents' who were 'of such an age as to require a strict hand and eye over them'.[49] In Sydney in 1801 King opened a similar institution for some thirty 'orphan' girls. His wife and Mrs Paterson attended daily to see that the girls were 'properly managed', and Mrs King acted as 'matrimonial agent', seeking out for the older girls approved husbands who were believed to have the means to support them. By 1802 forty-nine inmates were being taught reading, religion, needlework, spinning, 'and some few writing' prior to marriage or apprenticeship into the service of approved settlers.[50]

King's experiment in educating and disciplining females to their reproductive role was not merely confined to girls. Alarmed by the age imbalance of the population, he began to seek a way to avoid the excesses of the unsystematic free market in women which had developed. He implemented a Benthamite programme of reform for the women who would be set to manufacture needed products. On Norfolk Island it had always been hoped to establish a 'manufactory' to produce linen and canvas from the wild flax growing there. By 1791 the first samples were produced by male and female convicts, and in 1793 plans were made to kidnap two Maoris and bring them to the island to teach flax dressing.

On the mainland Hunter had similarly employed a few of the convict women from Ireland in 'spinning linen out of the white flax of the country', which was cultivated along the Hawkesbury. By 1801 an attempt had also been made to begin a woollen 'manufactory' to produce clothing which was still in short supply and which might be issued from the government store. By March 1802 every woman who could spin had been employed since October 1800, together with 'convalescents and invalids . . . unfit for any other labour'.[51] As in the British workhouses the aim was not merely to employ the women but to control and, if necessary, punish them. In August 1804 King announced that the upper floor of the new gaol at Parramatta had been made available as 'a secure place of assignment for delinquents and a house of industry'. Nine looms were now at work by which 100 yards of cloth could be produced weekly, manufacturing linen, sailcloth and hemp.

King believed the two small rooms could function as an 'asylum' where the pregnant and nursing mothers and other unassignable women could be put to work, together with a place of discipline where those whose services in assignment were 'unsatisfactory' could be sent. However, shortly before the conclusion of his regime in August 1806 he was noting problems. On the one hand 'incorrigible females' had to be sent to the coal works at Newcastle in order to prevent overcrowding in the manufactory. On the other, women saw the new institution less as a workhouse than as a shelter where, for the first time since the colony had been founded, they could be independent of sexual exploitation by the men. They were now in a position at least partly to subvert the pro-natalist plans of the authorities.

Thus, although women were supposed only to go to the manufactory before being selected as housekeepers and servants, already Governor King had doubts about the efficacy of any plan which proposed 'to lock all the females up who are not married until they are so fortunate as to obtain husbands'.[52] Such a plan would conflict with the concern to maximize reproduction and correct the demographic imbalance of the colony. As succeeding governors would discover, there was no easy solution to this problem until the massive human removals required by this phase of industrialization and colonization were largely complete. Meanwhile, there remained the related problem of disciplining the male convicts and especially of persuading them, at the conclusion of their sentences of hard labour, to settle down and win a living for their wives and children on their tiny plots of colonial land.

2

THIRTY ACRES
Male Convict Experience   1788–1804

Reached Ruse's farm, and begged to look at his grant, . . . A lot of thirty acres, to be called Experiment Farm, . . . Ruse now lives in a comfortable brick house, built for him by the governor. He has eleven acres and a half in cultivation, and several more which have been cleared by convicts in their leisure hours, on condition of receiving the first year's crop.[1]

TWO YEARS AFTER the first landing at Botany Bay the colonial authorities had, according to plan, allocated land to male emancipists and expirees in the little settlements at Norfolk Island and New South Wales. After completing their term of hard labour, ex-convict men were encouraged to stay in the settlements and cultivate their 30 acres of land—or more if they were prepared to marry and have children. Tools, provisions, grain, cattle, sheep and hogs were also to be provided. The land was a gift, free of all taxes and quit-rents for ten years provided that the ex-convict agreed to live on and improve it, while also reserving for the Crown all timber fit for 'naval purposes'.[2]

These plans were a novel solution to the problem of how to establish colonies located on sites thousands of miles from the home country. This was especially difficult in places like New South Wales where the local population had no interest in private property and commerce or trade and therefore no technology, law or labour system based on them. Moreover, how was a native population, which initially outnumbered the invaders, to be persuaded to perform these tasks? The classic and time-honoured solution to this problem had been to import slaves. By the 1780s British investors were purchasing some 38 000 slaves annually. Two-thirds of the world's slave trade was transported in British ships.[3] But slavery was currently coming under attack by evangelical reformers, who had inherited from their Puritan forebears a great faith in personal liberty and the rights of the individual. Often members of Dissenting families, the industrial lobby, too, was opposed to slavery. Like Continental theorists, Rousseau and Montesquieu, these people were quick to apply egalitarian rhetoric to labour, for they had discovered that for manufacturers, it was not economical to rely on a captive work-force which, along with its family, had to be fed, clothed and housed daily. Profits could only be maximized by employing free, mobile labourers who could be paid a cash wage adjusted, not according to their needs or those of their families, but according to how long they spent on the job actually operating the machine.

In Britain, a campaign to abolish the trade and liberate the slaves rapidly developed into a national crusade. In 1787 a British philanthropic organization was permitted to establish Sierra Leone on the west coast of Africa as a colony where liberated slaves might be resettled as free citizens. Here they would be taught to participate in 'legitimate trade', that is, to purchase from, and produce goods wanted by, manufacturers in Britain. An Act making it unlawful for British subjects to participate in the slave trade was passed in 1807 and Sierra Leone became a Crown Colony in 1808.[4]

New South Wales was the only other colony to be founded by Britain during a temporary twenty-five year period of re-evaluation of colonization which set in after the loss of the American colonies and which reflected the increasing polarization of merchant and industrial capital. During this period, not only were the critics of the ruling alliance attacking the slave trade, they were also attacking the administration and the privileges of the East India Company, a traditional source of wealth from overseas expansion enjoyed by the entrenched élite. Chartered in 1600, this now rather tarnished jewel in the British mercantilist crown had secured key bases on the Indian archipelago. These functioned as repositories for armed vessels to be used against the Dutch and the French, and as sources of local goods such as cotton, indigo, silk and sugar, which could then be traded for spices along the Malabar coast. Similarly, opium from India was traded with China to obtain tea. In addition, the Company had been granted a monopoly of the carrying trade in all raw materials harvested in a huge area stretching from 51 degrees East to 180 degrees West.

The foundation of the new colony right in forbidden seas showed that the termination of the Company's exclusive privileges was only a matter of time. Indeed, New South Wales, like Sierra Leone, anticipated the future interest of the industrial lobby in colonization. Already, newly independent American competitors were challenging the Company's claim to the resources of the Indian and Pacific Oceans, and as early as 1773 a Regulating Act marked the beginnings of attempts to bring the Company's affairs under the scrutiny of parliament. In 1784 Pitt's India Act had implemented a system whereby the Company's Charter would come under review every two decades.[5]

Not only the East India Company but the whole commercial system of which it was a part was coming under attack. In his influential *Wealth of Nations*, published in 1776, Adam Smith had produced a critique of the traditional rationale which across the seventeenth and eighteenth centuries had provided historical explanation and moral justification for European policies on trade, colonization and war. This rationale was known as Mercantilism. Smith had no quarrel with its starting point, which was that it was not possible to have a society which merely produced sufficient food and other goods to satisfy its own immediate needs. Every society, the theorists agreed, must be like European ones, producing a surplus which could be made available for commercial exchange. Believing in the legal concept of private property, the theorists assumed that every surplus commodity must have an owner. Indeed, how could any surplus ever be sold unless it was exclusively the private property of an individual or group? Theorists also agreed that the wealth derived from the production of surplus goods for a market did not belong to the labourers who produced it but to the person who owned the means of production. However, mercantilist theory had gone on to postulate that not only individual traders but whole nations were locked into competition for control of the world's surplus which, they believed, was limited and fixed. It followed that a nation could only increase its share by forming trading monopolies to exclude other nations or individuals, or by plundering the wealth of rivals. This could involve the seizure of goods *en route* to markets, or even better, the actual 'treasure' or bullion which, along with population, was the measure of a nation's wealth.

In such an economic system, the possession of colonies was absolutely vital. Some, like the Spanish acquisitions in America, might be direct sources of gold and silver. Others might contain products which could be sold to other nations and thus, by helping maintain a favourable balance of trade, avoid inroads into the nation's treasure chest. Even if they produced none of these things, colonies were still needed as strategic bases to cut off the trade of rivals and protect one's own. They might also reduce dependence on foreign sources of needed goods, or more important, supply 'naval stores'.

By the mid-eighteenth century, many of the forests of the main colonizing countries had long ago been reduced to heathland, partly by the pressure of providing timber for domestic purposes and fuel for iron production, but especially from the need for timber to replace ships constantly being lost in trade or war. The Spanish, for instance, needed no less than 3000 trees, each with a yield of 600 feet of board, to build even one medium-sized battleship, and their slaves were attacking the mahogany forests of Cuba for this purpose. In addition, they needed forty pine trees from Mexico to construct the yards and the three masts required for one of these ships. In a less happy position were the British who were relying on the goodwill and icy harbours of the Baltic countries to supplement supplies of native oak.

Mercantilist colonies were valued not only for their productivity but also as markets for European goods. It was considered the acme of perfection if all of these goods could be carried in the nation's own ships, as Britain's mid-seventeenth century Navigation Laws prescribed. The carrying trade was a source of wealth and its seamen constituted a useful reserve of skilled manpower in the very likely event of war.

According to Smith, however, the idea of a fixed total of international trade for which nations had to struggle was fallacious, for the wealth of nations and of individuals lay not with acquiring captive colonies, but getting rid of the old mercantilist monopolies together with the duties, embargoes and navigation laws by which they were protected by the State. Making use of the prevailing rhetoric of liberty, Smith argued that these monopolies were now anachronistic encumbrances which fettered the free workings of the market, stifled enterprise and restricted a limitless potential for productivity. Moreover the individual trader, he argued, selfishly striving for the greatest possible personal gain, automatically employed his capital in the manner most advantageous to himself and society, for by running a personal risk he was better able to judge the value of markets and investments than any statesman or legislator. Smith therefore advised the gradual relaxation of the present metropolitan monopoly of colonial trade, adding that colonies should at the same time assume responsibility for their own defence and administration.[6]

Founded during this transitional period between mercantilism and industrialization, the new convict colony was a compromise between these two different concepts of empire. On the surface it appeared to be a classic old-fashioned mercantilist settlement, clinging to the peripheries of a continent located half-way between the Spanish settlements of South America and the Dutch ones at the Cape. For though a large slice of the Australian continent had been claimed for Britain, mercantilist colonization by no means assumed that it was necessary to waste time, money and human resources on settling the interior of territorial possessions. Perhaps useful plants and minerals would be found there, perhaps the indigenous people would be persuaded to buy or sell goods, but in the meantime, it was the strategic coastal base and its defence which were vital, not what lay behind the coastal fringe. Thus, labour would be focused on not merely producing flax and procuring timber from New Zealand to refit the fleets in India but also, hopefully, cultivating tropical products which presently had to be purchased from European rivals. The convict men could also build the roads, bridges, wharves and warehouses needed for shipping out these products and importing British manufactured goods. This infrastructure would be even larger should the colony develop into a base for a southern whale fishery, seen as especially important now that ambitious and newly independent American competitors were moving into the North and South Pacific. Thus would the convict colony help create a network of commercial exchange stretching from the Pacific and Indian Ocean to China and beyond.[7]

In the choice of state-employed convicts instead of slaves to provide the initial labour force, and in the vision of them as future petty land-holders, the new settlements were a modern departure from mercantilist practice. Joined by any marines who could be persuaded to stay, these people and their farms would provide a useful buffer zone between the new colonial base and the possibly hostile natives. It was they who would bear the brunt of Aboriginal resistance while laying the basis for future capitalistic enterprises. In the meantime, these men were to be farmers, not traders, and to conciliate the interests of that declining monolith, the East India Company, token regulations were passed forbidding colonists to encroach on its monopoly. The failure of the authorities to provide a currency for the colony by which the farmers could sell any surplus they produced suggested that it was expected that initially they would not do more than clear the land, feed themselves and ward off Aboriginal attack. All larger transactions would be based on bills of exchange and promissory notes under the control of London financiers.

As early as 1789 Governor Phillip was ready to begin this experiment in convict land settlement. James Ruse, a convict who had been sentenced in Cornwall for seven years in 1782 for breaking and entering, and who had previous experience in farming, asked for a land grant. Since food was in short supply, the Governor was especially anxious to see how quickly an ex-convict, albeit one with knowledge of farming, could support himself in the new country as a settler. In November 1789 Ruse began this experiment on just 2 acres of land lent to him at Parramatta. In September 1790 he further conformed to official wishes by marrying convict Elizabeth Perry. By February 1791, in just over one year, he delighted officialdom by being able to take both himself and his new wife off the rations issued by the government store. Though the feat would prove both unusual and temporary, in April 1791 he became the first emancipist to receive title to 30 acres of land.[8]

According to the officials, at first relatively few convict men felt inclined to volunteer for this stint of pioneering labour. By November 1791 there were only forty-four ex-convicts settled on land grants at Parramatta and Prospect Hill, and nine on Norfolk Island. By 1803, however, a total of 464 male ex-convicts had been persuaded to cultivate farms. This represented 25 per cent of the total number of emancipists in New South Wales, a very high ratio of farmers to labourers by contemporary British standards.[9]

Soldiers and seamen proved initially to be the most willing

settlers. On Norfolk Island there were thirty marines and nine seamen settled by November 1791. Just over a year later there were eight marines settled at the Field of Mars near Port Jackson, with 81 acres under cultivation. In January 1794 Henry Hacking, quartermaster from the *Sirius*, was among the twenty-two settlers who, probably at the suggestion of Ruse, received land grants along the fertile flood-plain of the Hawkesbury River near the present town of Windsor. Settlers in this area were destined to become of central importance, both in creating a source of food for the colony and in dispossessing the Aborigines from its peripheries.[10]

Given these plans for the male offender, it followed that male convict experience was likely to be completely different from that of the women. Where it was the women's role to provide sexual services and produce the next generation of labourers, the men were to be taught, as an early advocate of the colony, James Matra, wrote, to 'work or starve'.[11] Yet right across the early years of the settlements, the ability of the men to work, either as landless labourers or on their own farms, was severely limited by the fact that, reflecting the greater numbers being crowded into the male transports, many arrived permanently weakened by sickness and disease.

Officially the new colonizing experiment was not supposed to reproduce the overcrowding and disregard for human health which characterized the slave trade. But the Reverend Richard Johnson left a graphic description of conditions of the men on board the Second Fleet vessel, the *Surprize*, where the death rate was one in seven:

Went down amongst the convicts, where I beheld a sight truly shocking to the feelings of humanity, a great number of them laying, some half and others nearly quite naked, without either bed or bedding, unable to turn or help themselves. Spoke to them as I passed along, but the smell was so offensive that I could scarcely bear it. . . . Some of these unhappy people died after the ships came into the harbour, before they could be taken on shore—part of these had been thrown into the harbour, and their dead bodies cast upon the shore, and were seen laying naked upon the rocks. . . . Upon their being brought up to the clean air some fainted, some died upon the deck, and others in the boat before they reached the shore. When come on shore many were not able to walk, to stand, or to stir themselves in the least, hence some were led by others. Some creeped upon their hands and knees, and some were carried upon the back of others.[12]

As Phillip noted of the men on the Third Fleet, which arrived between August and October 1791 with a death rate of approximately one in ten, many were so debilitated that it would be a long time before they regained their strength and could begin the work of providing food and shelter for the settlement. Indeed, some were beyond recovery.

The proportion of the male convict population ill, infirm or permanently weakened by sickness, continued to be swelled by the landing of the sick. The *Atlas*, carrying 151 male convicts and twenty-eight female ones from Cork, lost sixty-three of the males (though only two of the females) by the time of arrival in July 1802. Fever and dysentery had broken out after the male convicts had been crowded together to make room for the master's cargo of goods which he was bringing out for sale in New South Wales.[13]

Other than dysentery and inflammation of the eyes, the convict labourers and farmers were vulnerable to a range of accidents incidental to their work. A considerable number were hurt or killed when felling trees. At Norfolk Island in 1791 James Elliot had his hip broken when clearing of the site for the town of Phillipsburg; another man suffered a similar fate while cutting down a tree wanted at the sawpit. A third, Henry Palmer, died of brain injuries after a tree which Clark ordered him to cut fell on him, while a convict boy, Charles McFarlain, suffered a fractured skull when an axe slipped from his hand and rebounded off the wood. On the mainland, convict Simon Burn lost an eye while employed in splitting palings for the government.[14]

Even at this early stage it was discovered that men worked better for a wage than under punishment. Therefore, though the hours set for male convict labour varied over the period, they always included time off for the men to work on their own account. In January 1794 according to Collins, for sawing one hundred feet of timber in their own time for private individuals, a pair of sawyers demanded seven shillings. By 1797 this was the standard rate for this task. In that year when there were over 700 men working for private settlers, a man could earn £1-5s per acre for burning off open ground, and £1-4s for breaking up new ground. In November 1795 one group of labourers working at reaping formed a 'combination' to raise their pay. However, though wages were nominally high, men were often paid in the form of over-priced goods rather than cash.[15]

While under sentence, male convicts who impressed the authorities could be placed in positions of trust, such as that of storekeeper or overseer. If they were then considered to have exercised due honesty and diligence, they were excellently placed for emancipation and a land grant. George Barrington, emancipated in November 1792, was one who was rewarded in this way. Sentenced for seven years in September 1790 for stealing a gold watch, he had been made principal watchman at Toongabbie before receiving a conditional pardon and 30 acres near Parramatta.

Expirees who declined a land grant could get work in a wide variety of occupations. Those skilled in a trade were always in demand in fields such as carpentry, tailoring, bricklaying, shoemaking, and the cloth and hat trade; the unskilled found work in potteries, smithies, tanneries, breweries, shipping, and the seal fishery. Expirees and the pardoned could also join the New South Wales Corps, a special military unit raised in Britain in May 1789 to replace the marines. In October 1793 twenty-three men were pardoned for this express purpose, seven of whom had been transported for life.[16]

By 1802 Governor King had introduced a new scheme to encourage the convict 'to gain his livelihood by honest means'. Whereas under Governor Hunter a 'ticket-of-leave' meant a certificate given to expirees, under King this name was given to certificates enabling selected convicts to work full-time on their own behalf, provided they did not demand 'extortionate pay' for their labour or transgress any of the orders and rules of the colony. If they did so, they would be recalled to government labour and face such other punishments as the case was thought to merit. While open to women as well as men, this system was of greater value to those for whom paid work was available.[17]

In addition to tickets-of-leave there were special opportunities by which men could and did earn pardons. Fourteen out of the twenty-one men who survived after the *Guardian*'s collision with an iceberg in December 1789 were rewarded with pardons after they were sent on to the colony with the Second Fleet. Instructions were given that they were also to be supplied with tools and implements appropriate to their needs. Similarly, John Ascott, a carpenter serving a seven-year sentence, was pardoned for his part in attempting to save the livestock and food on the *Sirius* after it was wrecked on Norfolk Island in March 1790.

Male convicts who were trained in a trade crucial to the survival of the struggling settlement during the hungry years, were especially likely to win a pardon. One such was James Bloodsworth. A builder by trade, he had been sentenced in 1785 to a seven-year term and had arrived in 1788. He immediately attracted attention as 'a most useful member of the settlement' and was appointed master-bricklayer at Sydney Cove where he helped design and erect many early buildings, including the first Government House and the storehouse at King's Wharf. After being pardoned in 1790 he was promoted to superintendent of bricklayers. He was also successful in farming a 50-acre grant at Petersham, increasing the holding to 245 acres before his death in 1804. Another who received an unconditional pardon in November 1792 for his 'diligence, unremitting good conduct, and strict integrity in his employment for several years as the public baker of the settlement' was Robert Sidaway. A watch-case maker serving a life sentence, Sidaway had become the colony's first baker. Following his pardon Sidaway went on to build the colony's first theatre. Between 16 January and 23 July 1796 Sidaway and the manager, convict John Sparrow, produced five popular plays: *The Revenge, The Hostel, The Fair Penitent or Fatal Curiosity, The Busy Body* and *The Poor Soldier*. The cast included one woman, Mrs Davis, but the other five performers were all male.[18]

In the early 1790s male convicts with a knowledge of the mechanics of mills operable by manpower were in a potentially fortunate position. Flour was in very short supply; iron handmills sent with the First Fleet had proved useless, and no windmills had yet been constructed. Two master millers sent out by the British authorities had proved unequal to the task. In February 1794 a male convict died after eating two pounds of unground wheat. Thus, when convict James Wilkinson offered to construct a 'walking mill' at Parramatta, he had no difficulty in attracting the attention of Major Francis Grose, commander of the New South Wales Corps and administrator of the colony for two years following the departure of Phillip in December 1792. Inspired by this convict challenge to the official millers' expertise, Wilkinson's fellow prisoners volunteered to perform the heavy part of the work, cutting and bringing in the timber needed to construct the principal wheel. At the same time ex-convict John Baughan (or Bingham), a cabinet-maker by trade, offered to construct a mill more quickly and it was completed in March 1794, one month ahead of Wilkinson's. Two years later an Irish convict was paid £25 for the construction of another mill on the western side of Sydney Cove. Meanwhile, in addition to these large operations, in 1793 a convict blacksmith was paid £2-2s per week to produce handmills.[19]

In spite of these successes in teaching the convict men to 'work or starve', the penal settlement almost immediately produced both the need and the opportunities for some men to resort to theft. Purloining of food and clothing from the officers' tents and from each other was becoming common by June 1788, while the reduction of the rations from November 1789 caused a great increase in offences against private property. Theft from the settlement's struggling gardens proved difficult to control, but did not occur in areas and at times when vegetables were plentiful. Very young convicts, long deprived of adequate food, had special problems in resisting temptation. Such a one was John Bennett, a seventeen-year-old convict coming out on the *Friendship* in 1787. When given permission to come up on deck at night 'to make water', Bennett took the opportunity to slip into the boat where other convicts had hidden their provisions. Eating until he could not stir, Bennett then fell asleep among the leftovers till 2 a.m. when he was suddenly awakened by the sound of having his legs clasped into irons. It was predicted by Lieutenant Clark that Bennett would be on the gallows within six months, a prophecy which came true. Flogged for theft within three weeks of landing, on 2 May he was hanged for having stolen three-and-a-quarter pounds of biscuits, four pounds of sugar, together with a piece of canvas (used for carrying the stolen provisions). He was one of the first people executed in the new penal settlement.[20]

Another whose ravenous appetite caused him trouble was 'Black Caesar', one of nearly a thousand Africans who would be transported to the Australian colonies. Most had been slaves in the Caribbean or North America; others had been brought to Britain as children where 'a little black boy' trained as a footman or waiter was seen as an elegant addition to the retinue of a wealthy family. By the 1770s there were thousands of these people in Britain eking out a miserable existence, most as servants and some by entertaining or begging about the streets. Their numbers were increased following the war with America, when demobilized African sailors joined their fellows on the streets, where many of them died in the bitter winter of 1786–87. Caesar had been tried for theft in England and had arrived on the *Alexander* in 1788 to serve a life sentence. According to Collins, 'his frame was muscular and well constructed for hard labour' but he could in any one day devour the full ration for two days, and to satisfy his appetite 'he was compelled to steal from others, and all his thefts were directed to that purpose'. Despite absconding twice in 1789, each time liberally equipped with provisions, Caesar was initially treated leniently by the authorities, probably because of his reputation for enormous physical strength and its utility to a settlement relying on manpower. In March 1790 he was pardoned by Phillip and sent to Norfolk Island.[21]

Though the men enjoyed commercial opportunities denied to the women, their official punishments were brutal in the extreme. On the transports, where numerous schemes were laid by the male convicts to seize the ships, much greater use was made of fetters than in the case of female convicts. Savage punishments were handed out to those who planned or attempted mutiny. On the *Albemarle* on 9 April 1791, two convicts allowed on deck early in the morning rushed the guards, disarmed them, and the leader was about to attack the helmsman with a cutlass when he was shot by one of the officers. He and one other were immediately hanged from a yard-arm. This, according to the officer, 'had the desired effect upon the other convicts who then confessed they had intended to sail the ship to America'. On the *Britannia* in 1797, six male convicts died after being punished with 300 lashes each following a suspected plot to take the ship. Others who suffered the same punishment but survived, only did so by drinking their own urine.

In the settlement punishments were similar. On Norfolk Island in 1790 fifty to one hundred lashes were routinely ordered for work-related offences. Flogging, however, was never intended to interfere too long with a man's capacity to work. Two carpenters ordered fifty lashes each for neglecting work at Charlotte Fields on Norfolk Island in December 1790 were expected to return to work next day, and when they did not were put on half rations. In cases of extraordinarily harsh sentences, the punishment was administered by instalments to allow the convict time to recover. At Port Jackson in August 1795 James Barry, found guilty of attempting to break into a settler's house at the Ponds with intent to steal, was sentenced to 1000 lashes but received only the first 270 of them in the first session. Some variations were made for extreme youth. On Norfolk Island in April 1788 Lieutenant King punished Charles MacLennan, a fourteen-year-old boy, with three dozen lashes for stealing rum out of the surgeon's tent. This was similar to the punishments handed out to adult males by King at that time. On the other hand, in October 1791 another convict boy on Norfolk Island was sentenced to thirteen lashes only for theft, and the punishment was inflicted 'on the backside'. As for women, slightly less pain and a great deal more humiliation was seen as appropriate for the young.[22]

As in England, executions were performed in public. There, the authorities, suspicious of the disorder around the scaffold as relatives battled with the surgeons for access to the corpse, had recently decided to authorize dissection following hanging in a certain number of the death sentences. Similarly, in New South Wales the surgeons were routinely provided with a supply of corpses for experimental purposes. It was also considered appropriate to hang some bodies in chains in prominent public places where it was hoped they would terrorize the population and exhibit the power of the law. As in England, last-minute reprieves at the gallows were also considered exemplary. Sixteen-year-old Samuel Wright, sentenced to death for stealing clothing, was given this salutary lesson in August 1793. Reprieved at the very moment he was about to ascend the ladder, according to Collins, he fell on his knees in an agony of gratitude and joy, and the watching prisoners were suitably impressed.[23]

In the light of these experiences, it was hardly surprising that numerous male expirees left permanently and returned to Britain. By 1820 some 10 per cent of all expirees had done so. Convicts under sentence also dreamed of returning home. For many the idea of escape was a constant and sustaining ideal; by 1820 the number of absconders is estimated to have equalled the number of convicts returning to Britain, that is, some 10 per cent of the total transported. They were, of course, principally male.

On 26 September 1790 five male convicts seized a punt at Parramatta and absconded down the river to Sydney. Here they acquired a more worthy boat with a mast and a sail, and set off down the harbour for Tahiti. With them they took one week's provisions each, clothes and bedding, three iron pots and some other items. A boat was sent to search for them and they were supposed to have perished in the frail craft, until in August 1795 four of them were found alive at Port Stephens where they had been cared for by Aboriginal people.

Far more common were the attempts to escape on vessels leaving the harbour. In February 1793 the master of the *Bellona* consented to having the ship smoked before its departure for Canton, in order to force out stowaways. Four men under sentence duly appeared on deck. In October 1795 no less than fifty men managed to secrete themselves on board the *Endeavour* leaving for India, a rash attempt which culminated in compulsory disembarkation at Norfolk Island.[24]

Daunting problems faced those convicts who chose hard labour and wedded bliss on small parcels of farming land of their own. For despite the encouragement of material aid provided by the governors, these farmers needed additional access to capital, some farming knowledge, and a considerable measure of luck to wring a living from their parcel of land. As on the government farms at Port Jackson and Norfolk Island where 'ye rats' and 'ye grubs' constantly frustrated the horticultural endeavours of the newcomers, so the ex-convicts' crops suffered. Most could not afford to feed and clothe assigned convicts, while the high cost of free labour was even more prohibitive, limiting the amount of land which a single emancipist could clear and cultivate. As with the government farms, periodic droughts took their toll of harvests, while during the hot summers fire was another threat. In December 1792 James Castles, an expiree settler at Prospect Hill and a farmer by trade, had his hut accidentally burned down, 'with all his comforts', and three bushels of wheat that he had just reaped.

For those settled along the Georges and Hawkesbury Rivers, there was the additional problem of floods. A flood on the Hawkesbury in May 1799 took the settlers and the government by surprise, in spite of the fact that local Aborigines had warned some of them that it was coming.

The river swell'd to more than fifty feet perpendicular height above its common level, and the torrent was so powerful it carried all before it. Many of the people were taken from the ridges of their houses by a few boats they had amongst them just in time to save their lives. . . . Many hogs, other live stock, poultry, with much of the produce of the last unfortunate harvest, and the domestic effects of the people, were carried away before the torrent. Fortunately, we lost but one man.

Earlier but less serious flooding had occurred in January and August 1795. In March 1800 further flooding occurred, this time also on the Georges River, where a number of marines had been settled since April 1797.[25]

The emancipist farmers were further disadvantaged in the commercial relations which developed over the decade. Among the problems with which they had to contend was the competition from the many officials who had turned to farming and trade. Civil officials who had moved into farming included Dr Arndell, Surveyor Thomas Alt and the Reverend Samuel Marsden, all of whom had formal grants of at least 100 acres by 1794. In addition, a decision to allow land grants to military officers had been announced in January 1793. Elsewhere in British colonies military officers had to resign their commissions in order to qualify for land grants, but as early as May 1788 officers of the Marine Corps, who had purchased livestock at the Cape for sale later to the government, had requested they be granted land to farm. Moreover, some of those living with convict women wanted, they said, to leave the land to these women and their families after they returned to England. In 1793 the amount of land to which officers were now entitled was not specified, the only stipulation being that it should be located in regions 'as would be suitable for a *bona fide* settler should it ever come into the hands of such a person'—which presumably meant fertile land not on the frontier. Governor Phillip and the officers of the marines had already left the colony when this dispatch arrived, but in fact Major Grose had already given one grant to a fellow officer of the New South Wales Corps and immediately issued seven more. Favouring the area most safe from Aboriginal attack, that between Sydney and Parramatta and around the harbour, Grose and his successor, fellow officer Captain William Paterson, (in charge from December 1794 until September 1795), continued to make formal and informal grants to officers. By 1796 officers owned 31.5 per cent of all land under cultivation, plus all of the horses, cattle and most of the sheep in the colony other than the livestock owned by the government. By 1800 thirty-four officer-farmers had accumulated over 14 000 acres and 4000 sheep while the number of convicts allocated into their service had dramatically increased.[26]

The small settlers petitioned the governors for assistance, pointing out that not only could they not afford to feed and clothe convict labourers, but they were less likely to be allocated such labour in the first place. They also complained of unfair practices when selling their produce to the Government Store, an institution which began as an army commissariat but which rapidly became the chief market for colonial produce. Here, the wheat and stock of the officers was given preference and the small settler waited longer to be paid.

In addition, the officers had come to control the importing and retailing of essential goods. This they had done by buying up the cargoes of passing vessels whose masters would accept their paymaster's bills as a form of currency which was equivalent to sterling when cashed in Britain. At the same time, the absence of any alternative source of currency or credit effectively prevented competition. In October 1792, led by their commander, Grose, the officers formed a syndicate to charter the *Britannia* for a speculative voyage to the Cape and regular importation of speculative cargoes followed, selling in the colony at profits as high as 150 per cent or more. Over the next decade there were few officers not involved in at least some of this trade, the chief participants being Paterson, Johnston, Foveaux, Hill, Rowley, Laycock and Macarthur. By 1800 the arrival of professional merchants and itinerant sea captains acting for merchant houses in England and India brought an end to the officers' monopoly, but by this time they had moved strongly into farming where, by selling their surplus grain and livestock to the government store, they had discovered a second means of gaining access to sterling. The government paid for its purchases with Store receipts which, when sufficient had been collected, could be converted into treasury bills. These, like paymasters' bills, could be used to purchase imports. It followed that for large dealers like the officer-farmers, the government market for local grain and meat was virtually a source of foreign exchange. This was the reason that so many of them had turned to farming from 1795.

The high prices charged by the officers for commodities such as spirits, tobacco, sugar, tea, soaps and clothing forced up the price of free labour and the cost of maintaining assigned servants, whom they could pay in kind. Attempting to raise capital to meet these difficulties, many of the emancipist farmers fell into debt or lost their farms, in many cases to their chief competitors. By 1800, of fifty-four ex-convicts who had been settled on the Hawkesbury five years before, only eight remained.

Settlers on Norfolk Island faced a similar plight. By 1798 they were complaining of the huge profits being reaped by the Sydney traders at their expense. 'They certainly labor under very great inconveniences', Hunter admitted to the authorities in Britain. It was true that the Sydney merchants generally exacted profits of some 500 per cent, 'so that the labor of twelve months will go but very little way in the purchase of those trifling comforts which, until they arrived here, they may have been all their lives accustomed to receive'.[27] Most of the soldiers and seamen who had settled on the land were similarly affected. Arndell and Marsden, appointed to conduct a survey of the settlers in March 1798, found only three of the eight marines remaining on their farms at the Field of Mars. Convicts under sentence could not sue or be sued for debt, but emancipists could. Many were imprisoned as debtors in the old goal at Sydney, later described by Bligh as 'a miserable place'.

As the land granted to the emancipists and marines began to be acquired by the officer-traders, so a custom developed of castigating the small-holders as unworthy and inefficient. Arndell and Marsden, like many of the officials, believed that though the emancipist farmers had suffered from certain financial disadvantages, most had been ruined because they were 'idle, vicious, given to drinking, gaming, and other such disorders as led to poverty and ruin'. This censorious pair declared that the drunkenness among the settlers had been caused by too much government assistance, which served only to encourage idleness and dissipation. As most of the governors were aware, however, heavy drinking was a custom which had developed from the want of currency. In its absence, rum among other products, was used as a form of barter. A by-product of the booming sugar trade, rum was an excellent substitute for currency for it was light to carry and infinitely divisible. In the early days of the settlement any rum brought into the settlement by seaman from passing ships was seen as a threat to order, and was proscribed. By 1793, however, as more officers moved into trade and farming, it began to be argued that the convict labourers preferred to be paid with spirits, and even that 'liquor given to them in this way operated as a benefit and comfort to them' provided it was issued at the rate of half a pint a day. These changes in the distribution of rum as currency and in the extent of officer farming occurred during the 'Interregnum' period, when the colony was administered by

Paterson and Grose. From this time, consumption of spirits became a major hazard to the economic survival and health of farmers and labourers. Not only did rum retail at six shillings a bottle by the end of that year but, according to Collins, the 'passion for liquor' had become so predominant among the convicts that 'it operated like a mania'. Nevertheless, in general the male convicts and emancipists may not have consumed more spirits than labouring and seafaring men at that time elsewhere. However, the effects on them were compounded because many men were already weakened by starvation and disease.[28]

Would-be farmers were further deterred by the very real fear of Aboriginal attack. Convict and ex-convict men at work in the bush early became the main target for Aboriginal spears, as the Eora and Dharuk people—onto whose land the convicts had so unceremoniously been discharged—set out first to control, and then to repel the invaders. The relations of the convict men with the Eora were at first friendly, the Aboriginal people coming down to help them haul in the seines which were early set to catch fish on the harbour. Even six months after the landing of the British, relations between some convicts and some Aborigines remained amicable, one family living on a bay adjoining Sydney Cove being 'visited by large parties of the convicts of both sexes on those days in which they were not wanted for labour'. Here the Aboriginal people received such presents as the convicts could afford to take them, 'but none of them would venture back with their visitors'. By February 1788 it was becoming apparent to the Eora that the newcomers were not temporary sojourners in their land, and that none of them had any respect for Aboriginal land management which for thousands of years had ensured food resources were not depleted. Over at Botany Bay a boat crew from one of the British transports did not hesitate to shoot at local people after a misunderstanding over the exchange of tools and weapons. At Sydney Cove the British were wilfully attacking the limited food supplies, some for the sport, some out of curiosity to examine the strange new fauna so foreign to British eyes, and some for a change of diet after the privations of the voyage. In April, John Macintyre, a convict specially designated to shoot animals and birds for the Governor's table, shot an emu, 7 feet 2 inches (220 cm) high. The flesh was found to be 'very well flavoured' and the skin was sent home for the perusal of Lord Sydney and wealthy amateur scientist, Joseph Banks, who was one of the main planners of and advisers to the new colony. Cockatoos, parrots and even crows were being sampled, and in some cases pronounced 'better than salt beef', with snakes and lizards being tasted by the more adventurous among the invaders. The seines set in the harbour sometimes netted at once sufficient fish to feed 200, but these catches were not necessarily shared with the people who were extending their hospitality to the newcomers and who were facing starvation by the first winter. Nor were the Aborigines entitled to sample the strange, often slow-moving livestock which the strangers had brought with them. The uncouth invaders set their emaciated minions to attack the vegetation with axes, tear up the land with shovels and hoes, laying the soil bare, moving rocks, and overturning sacred sites. 'Happening to be at Camp Cove at a time when these people were much pressed with hunger,' Collins later recalled, 'we found in a miserable hut a poor wretched half-starved native and two children.' The man 'was nearly reduced to a skeleton', though the children were in a better condition.

Nor did the invaders confine their depredations to Sydney Cove and Botany Bay. By February 1790 one hundred of these convict labourers were at Parramatta, clearing the land there of the fauna and the fruits which were so vital to Aboriginal survival. 'With the assistance of one man and half-a-dozen greyhounds which I keep,' Elizabeth Macarthur, wife of the officer-trader, boasted at Parramatta in August 1794, 'my table is constantly supplied with wild duck and kangaroos; averaging one week with another, these dogs do not kill less than three hundred pounds weight.'[29]

Though not responsible for the invasion and the unwilling participants, it was inevitable that the convict men should be seen by the Aboriginal people as the principal offenders in violating tribal law and easy targets for judicial punishment or guerilla action. By April 1788 at Sydney, one convict sent to cut rushes for thatching returned to the settlement wounded by a spear; another who went out to collect 'vegetables' in the bush was bruised and beaten. In October 1788 following further attacks, convicts seeking vegetables to supplement their rations were ordered to go with armed parties of marines who were also joining the search for bush foods. Sources near Sydney being depleted, parties were now venturing as far as Botany Bay. In one such group, a convict man, Cooper-Hanley, became separated from the armed marines and was later found dead.

Governor Phillip had been instructed not to countenance retaliatory attacks on the Aboriginal people, for little was as yet known as to their numbers, technology and social organization. Until this information was available, officials could not be sure whether these people had anything to trade, nor whether they were more of a military threat inland than immediately around the harbour. It was also crucial to find out whether they had a social hierarchy, religion or a system of law which could be adapted to the needs of the British. Perhaps leaders or kings would be found who could be persuaded, as had been the case in some parts of Africa and India, to force their people to cooperate with the invaders.

Diplomacy was also needed because the Europeans were outnumbered and equipped with cumbersome and unreliable weapons. Eighteenth-century firearms were inaccurate except at very close range and could not easily be loaded without breaking cover. Moreover, the time taken to load them through the barrel gave the Aborigines some chance in combat, both with soldiers and settlers. In wet weather the loose gunpowder might not ignite, or could burn very slowly, 'hanging fire'. Even if it burned briskly, any target was still given brief warning by 'the flash in the pan'. Aborigines around Sydney were well aware of these facts. In September 1790 the Governor himself was speared during a parley at Manly Cove, and the unreliability of the colonizers' weapons thus impressively demonstrated. One warrior picked up a spear from the beach with his toes, fitted it to his woomera or throwing stick, and launched it with such accuracy and power that it ran clean through Phillip's shoulder before any of the surrounding marines fired a shot. The wound, however, did not dispatch him, for Aboriginal weapons were far less murderous in their design and fatal in their effects. Only temporarily and occasionally would Aborigines have the upper hand in what was, from the outset, an unfair fight.

In his determination to keep the peace at least until more was known about Aboriginal society and law, Phillip took no action after the spearing. He also punished ruthlessly a group of convict bricklayers who, in March 1789, organized themselves into a punitive expedition and armed with stakes set off towards Botany Bay to avenge the death of one of their gang who had ventured into the bush in search of sarsaparilla leaves (prized by the convicts as a liquorice-tasting substitute for tea). Near Botany Bay they found a group of Aborigines, but in larger numbers than they expected. In the ensuing affray the convicts were soundly defeated, leaving one of their number dead in the field and another, a boy, severely wounded. Six other convicts were injured. All the adults received sentences of 150 lashes for attempting to take the law into their own hands.[30]

The spearing of the convicts around Sydney and Botany Bay continued until the tribes in these areas were decimated by an epidemic of an imported disease—whether smallpox or another is still debated vigorously—which attacked them from April 1789 on. Smallpox had already contributed to the extermination of the indigenous populations of the New World, and in North America it had recently been deliberately introduced to facilitate European invasion. In Britain inoculation had been practised since early in the eighteenth century and the surgeons were well acquainted with the latest information on how the disease was spread and how it could be prevented. At Port Jackson the surgeons had brought with them 'variolous material in bottles', presumably as a precaution against the outbreak of the disease. Yet no attempt was made to use this material to vaccinate the Aboriginal people, even those well known to and in touch with the Europeans. The effects of the 'mysterious' outbreak were convenient in the extreme, for it attacked only the Aboriginal population. When the *Sirius* arrived on 6 May from the Cape with the stock of provisions so badly needed by the Europeans, Lieutenant Bradley noted that 'we did not see a canoe or a Native the whole way coming up the Harbour and were told that scarce any had been seen lately except laying dead' upon its shores. Bodies had been found all around the settlement, some with children lying dead close to them, and some in the act of making the utmost exertion to crawl from their caves to runs of fresh water.[31]

Meanwhile, the Governor had embarked on a new strategy to find out more about these people who were initially so dangerous to the survival of the struggling colony. All the officers, and most especially Judge Advocate Collins, were noting in their journals every detail of social and material culture which seemed to them to be significant, but they remained baffled as to how this strangely egalitarian society was governed, and their researches

were of little use to Phillip. Tench was blind both to the
Aborigines' humanity and to their technology, in spite of their
assistance to him in exploring the hinterland behind Port Jackson.
King was fascinated mostly by their nudity, and during an early
parley at Botany Bay, having offered one of the women a handkerchief, was delighted when she tolerantly suffered him to apply
it 'where Eve did ye fig leaf'. George Worgan, surgeon of the
Sirius, was prompted to use his handkerchief as a gift to woo a
group of women who were busy fishing near South Head but was
outraged when they treated it with the utmost indifference,
throwing it into the 'dirtiest Corner' of their canoe and going on
with their work. Most reported cruel treatment of Aboriginal
women at the hands of Aboriginal men, implying that this was a
customary tradition and that their own attitudes towards women
were somehow more civilized and tender. This spared them from
acknowledging their own promiscuity and violence towards the
convict women, as well as the exploitation and rape of Aboriginal
women by whites which was under way by 1791.[32]

In December 1788 Phillip arranged for the seizure of an
Aboriginal man whom he hoped would be persuaded to live at
Government House and in due course disclose useful information
about the society from which he had been taken. However,
Arabanoo, the man captured, showed no inclination to collab-
orate with the British and was singularly unimpressed by what he
observed of *their* social organization. Indeed, so barbarous was
their behaviour to their own kind, that when he saw the officers
preparing for a sumptuous feast at Government House, he fully
expected that they were cannibals and that it was their intention
to eat him. In May 1789 Arabanoo succumbed to smallpox after
trying to care for some of his dying countrymen. Undeterred by
this setback, the following November the Governor arranged for
the seizure of two more Aboriginal men, Bennelong and Coleby,
and incarcerated them at Government House. Coleby soon after-
ward escaped, notwithstanding an iron fetter which had been
rivetted to his ankle. By June 1790 Bennelong, too, had managed
to get away, but following the spearing of the Governor, chose to
return. Perhaps he did so in the belief that the Aborigines, by
inflicting this ritual punishment on the person of the governor
himself, had won and he, Bennelong, could now begin to oversee
the incorporation of the newcomers into Aboriginal civilization.
At length Bennelong discovered that his people were not in

control but he nevertheless stayed on, for by 1791 there was little left to go back to. Starvation and disease had taken their toll; traditional religious life and kinship arrangements could no longer be sustained. In December 1792 Bennelong left for England with the departing Governor and another Aboriginal man. There, viruses rampant in the cold climate undermined the health of both and only Bennelong survived to return with Hunter in September 1795. Coleby, too, kept in touch with the British and in 1816 was actually promised a 30-acre grant. Bennelong died in 1813, broken by alcohol; the fate of Coleby is unknown.[33]

Following the failure of these attempts to capture Aboriginal adults and use them as sources of information or as 'chiefs' who might have some influence over their own people, the authorities in New South Wales reverted to other methods. Influenced by the current philanthropic concept of 'rescuing' pauper children and training them to be a pliable labour force, the colony's officials shifted their focus from kidnapping Aboriginal men to kidnapping Aboriginal children. As a result of the scale of the destruction of Aboriginal society there was no shortage of children to 'adopt'. After the smallpox epidemic, Reverend Richard Johnson took Abaroo, a girl of about fourteen orphaned by the disease, and Surgeon John White acquired Nanbaree, an Aboriginal boy. In 1796 Marsden 'adopted' a four-year-old whom he called 'Samuel Christian' (or 'Tristan') and an infant, 'Harry'. Botanist George Caley, who arrived in 1800, took Moowat'tin or 'Daniel', a boy who was said to have been reared from 'infancy' by emancipist settler Richard Partridge at Parramatta.

At first these experiments seemed successful. The Johnsons reported that Abaroo very quickly learned to speak English and to wait at the table, while Tristan was prevented from learning to speak his parents' language altogether. By the time he was six years old he too had been transformed into an excellent waiter. But all these 'successes' in turning Aboriginal children into dutiful labourers proved short-lived. Abaroo ran away after only fourteen months' training and returned to her people. Tristan was taken with the Marsden family when they departed for England in 1807 but managed to escape from the family at Rio after being punished by 'his master' for drinking. In 1814 he was recognized in Rio by Captain John Piper, an officer-trader, and brought back to the colony, only to die in the Sydney Infirmary soon after. Moowat'tin's life was also destined to be short. Having proved himself invaluable as a guide and interpreter to Caley, accompanying him on numerous field trips and a voyage to Van Diemen's Land, Moowat'tin sailed for England with the botanist in 1808. In 1811 he returned to the colony to work as a labourer for, as he said, he could not live in the bush now. In 1816 he was convicted of raping the fifteen-year-old daughter of a Parramatta settler and executed.[34]

As non-Aboriginal numbers were strengthened and it became apparent that Aboriginal people would resist enslavement and had nothing the invader wanted but their land, the official attempts to maintain diplomatic relations with them were abandoned. As early as December 1790 Governor Phillip had launched the first of the hundreds of official punitive expeditions which would follow for the next 140 years. The occasion was the spearing of John Macintyre, his 'game keeper', by an Aboriginal resistance leader named Pemulwuy. In a savage response, the Governor ordered a party of military to shoot any six Aborigines and bring back their heads in bags, as well as to take two alive for hanging. Encumbered by their knapsacks, arms and uniforms, this party returned to the settlement after three days in the bush, exhausted and without heads or captives. This was hardly surprising, for the Aboriginal people had been forewarned of the expedition by White's little orphan, Nanbaree. A second party was equally unsuccessful, sinking up to their necks in what Tench called the 'rotten, spungy bog' around Botany Bay and having to extricate each other with the ropes intended to tie up the captives.[35]

Though Aboriginal resistance would continue at Port Jackson, by February 1790 the main scene of conflict was shifting to the Parramatta region. Here, in the buffer zone, the emancipist farmers on their tiny blocks were expected to clear the land of Aboriginal resistance, as much as of rocks, stumps and trees. There was never any possibility of amicable relations between Aborigines and convicts who became farmers, for they were forced into competition with each other for the land. Further, unlike the convicts at Port Jackson, the expirees were armed. At first they satisfied themselves with firing over the heads of the resident Aborigines to put them to flight, and like the officials, setting such children as were left behind to work about their homes. By September 1794, however, following the murder of a settler and his servant on the Hawkesbury, they organized their own punitive expedition and killed seven or eight Aborigines 'on the spot'.

By the following year the Hawkesbury settlement was in a state of open war. There were then some 400 settlers in the region, their farms stretching 30 miles along both sides of the river. Most of them were male convicts, emancipists, and expirees. The Aborigines, starving, were systematically descending on the farms to carry away the corn. The war would continue till 1805.[36] Though the government would have preferred to allow the ex-convicts to settle the Aboriginal problem, in May 1795 the threat on the Hawkesbury to food supplies in Sydney was such that Paterson was prepared to send in the troops. He authorized an official punitive expedition of two officers and sixty privates from the New South Wales Corps. The soldiers marched out from Parramatta with instructions to destroy as many Aborigines as they could meet and hang the bodies from gibbets to be erected at prominent places. Some seven or eight Aborigines were killed in this operation and prisoners were taken.

For the government however it was more economical to force the ex-convicts to do their own killing; but convicts and ex-convicts might use their guns to resist the authorities rather than the Aborigines. As the Judge Advocate, Richard Atkins, wrote in 1805, in any other country the settlers could be safely left to deal with the natives, but in this colony such as 'experiment might be subject . . . to great inconveniences'.[37] Atkins's fears were well-founded. The Hawkesbury area was the scene not only of warfare with the Aborigines but of much convict resistance as well as a major convict rebellion in 1804. Particularly feared was any potential alliance between runaway convicts and Aborigines. Such a relationship could have proved very dangerous to the authorities, especially during the dry summers at the turn of the century, when it was feared that either of these troublesome groups of people might set fire to the ripening or harvested crops. Troops were stationed along farms on the Georges River in 1802 to prevent Aborigines from firing the wheat and arson was suspected but unproved at Toongabbie in January 1797. Convict escapees were often treated kindly by Aborigines, especially in areas where as yet the full force of the invasion had not been felt and the Europeans had not broken too many Aboriginal laws.[38]

Especially threatening to the authorities was the alliance formed between emancipist John Wilson and Aborigines during the Hawkesbury River war. Described by Collins as 'a wild idle young man', Wilson had arrived on the *Alexander* in 1788 and was serving a seven-year sentence imposed in October 1785 for stealing nine yards of cotton cloth. Soon after his sentence expired Wilson chose to live with the Aboriginal people near the Hawkesbury, learning part of their language. He underwent ritual scarifying of the chest and shoulders and was given a tribal name. Although his knowledge of bushcraft, learned from his Aboriginal friends, was sometimes exploited by the authorities for the purposes of exploration, Wilson chose mostly to live with the Aboriginal people. From August 1795 he was joined in this life by another ex-convict, William Knight. By February of the following year it was widely believed that these two were assisting the river people in their hostilities and had shown them how useless a musket was when it had been fired. Proclaimed an outlaw in May 1797 Wilson continued to dwell periodically with the Aboriginal people until executed by them after attempting to take a young woman against her will.

Convict and ex-convict outlaws working in the area at the time included Black Caesar, who by July 1794 had returned from Norfolk Island and taken to his former practice of living in the bush and plundering farms for supplies. Having been speared by Aborigines in February 1790, possibly during an attempt to join forces with them, in December 1795 Caesar attempted to in-gratiate himself with the authorities by declaring that he had killed Pemulwuy who had been conducting a determined cam-paign of resistance since spearing Phillip's gamekeeper. By now, however, the threat of alliance between escaped convicts and Aborigines was such that Caesar was neither believed nor trusted. Following an offer of a reward of five gallons of spirits for his capture, Caesar was shot by a Hawkesbury emancipist farmer in February 1796.[39]

By the late 1790s at least seven or eight other convict runaways were operating in the bush. By November 1801 two of them, William Knight and Thomas Thrush, were believed to have allied themselves with Pemulwuy. In raids ranging from Sydney to Parramatta, Pemulwuy's desperate feats included an attack on a convict at the Brickfields in 1795, the spearing of a marine settler at Georges River in May 1799, and an attack on an armed punitive expedition within the town of Parramatta in March 1797. On this occasion a party of local settlers and soldiers had armed themselves and had gone to hunt and harass Aborigines who were plundering the farms for food and clothing. After being at this task a night and a day, they returned fatigued to Parramatta. Within half an hour Pemulwuy, with a group of his supporters, followed them into town. As Collins wrote, Pemulwuy 'in a great rage, threatened to spear the first man that dared to approach him', and threw a spear at one of the soldiers.

The conflict was now begun; a musket was immediately levelled at the principal, which severely wounded him. Many spears were then thrown, and one man was hit in the arm; upon which the superior effect of our fire arms was immediately shown them, and five were instantly killed.

Though shot in the head and other parts of the body Pemulwuy survived. Described as 'extremely ill' he was taken to hospital but soon contrived an escape, despite the encumbrance of 'an iron about his leg'. When joined by Knight and Thrush in 1801 he was working in the area around Parramatta and Toongabbie, and was said to have incited other Aborigines there to plunder the settlers, murder four white men, and cruelly use some of the convict women. In March 1802 a reward was offered for William Knight, Thomas Thrush and one other, and as a token of how seriously the 'diabolical and outrageous' association with the natives was viewed, this included not five, but twenty gallons of spirits plus two suits of slops. Pemulwuy had already been declared wanted 'dead or alive' the previous November, but in view of the great agility of his band, he was not easy to catch. Accordingly the government turned to a technique which would be routinely used by the Europeans across the continent. This was to make use of tribal divisions within the Aboriginal people, a strategy which was doubly useful. It at once prevented unity between Aboriginal groups and secured the skilled services of Aboriginal guides who could be used either to track other Aborigines or wanted convicts and emancipists. In the case of either convicts or Aborigines, the result was to divide and rule.

Pemulwuy was an early victim of this technique. Some of Pemulwuy's former companions claimed that they were sorry to have been incited by him to attack the settlers. King and senior officials therefore decided to give orders for every person to do the utmost to put a stop to Pemulwuy and at the same time to inform the Aborigines that when he had been given up to the authorities they should be readmitted to official friendship. By

June 1802 Pemulwuy was dead, shot by two settlers, and his head presented to King, allegedly at the request of the Aborigines in his band who wished to be allowed to return to Parramatta in peace.[40]

The same strategy was used against other Aboriginal leaders in this area, including Mosquito or 'Bush Muschetta' and Tedbury, son of Pemulwuy. It was only through the co-operation of other Aborigines that Mosquito was captured in mid-1805; Tedbury survived at least until 1810, attacking farms, stealing sheep and bushranging along the Parramatta Road. His eventual fate is unknown.[41]

Similar divisive tactics were used by the authorities to control the Irish, that other potentially disruptive group who, throughout the period of scarcity and famine could possibly, if united, have brought the settlement to its knees. Arriving since October 1791, they included a number of educated political prisoners. Some had been involved in the Defender Movement; others, like 'General' Joseph Holt and Michael Dwyer, had seen military action when open war broke out in Ireland in 1798. In New South Wales, in September 1800, King estimated that, exclusive of the Defenders transported in 1794, at least 235 'seditious people' had been sent out following the Irish Rebellion plus many other Irish transported for felonies. There was also Maurice Margarot, one of six Scottish Jacobins who arrived from October 1795 onwards and who, though appearing to act as a spy for King, was thought likely to be in touch with the Irish radicals and other educated convicts. For the authorities, these fears were exacerbated by rumours that French ships were about to arrive and liberate the convicts. According to Collins, rumours of a French presence in April 1798 inspired one refractory fellow, while working in a gang at Toongabbie, to thrown down his hoe and give three cheers for liberty. Collins considered him rightfully flogged.[42]

In August 1798 following an attempt by Governor Hunter to compel the convicts to keep the Sabbath by attending the colony's only church, an Anglican one, this building was set alight, and being covered with thatch it was completely burned down within an hour. In 1799 similar mysterious conflagrations consumed the first of the new, strong log prisons at Sydney and Parramatta. In 1800 the fear of the authorities climaxed with the discovery of an actual plot. A group of Irish convicts planned to take Parramatta, then at daylight move on to Sydney, capture the barracks there, secure the shipping in the cove, and depart for Ireland on a government ship, the *Buffalo*. The makers of this plan estimated they had some 300 supporters and believed many of the settlers would possibly join them. They also had a supply of pikes, similar to those used in Ireland. Made by an elderly hut-keeper at Parramatta, these devices were designed to permit a person on foot, first to unseat an armed horseman and then to run him through. Following the discovery of the plot, suspects were interrogated to find out where the pikes were hidden. One of the accused said they were on the 30-acre farm of emancipist Joseph Pearce. Others declared they were sunk in the lower part of the harbour. Twenty-year-old Paddy Galvin was rash enough to say he knew where the pikes were and subsequently fell into the hands of Samuel Marsden and Richard Atkins, who had him flogged to solicit more information. But Galvin was 'just in the same mood when he was taken to the hospital as when he was tied up'. 'They are an unaccountable set of beings', grumbled Marsden, 'I am sure he will die before he will reveal anything of the business'. Notwithstanding these impediments to the course of justice, two committees of enquiry arranged for twenty-four ringleaders to be publicly flogged, five of them with sentences of 1000 lashes. Together with others believed to be implicated in the plot, they were then exiled 'to a distant and remote part of the Territory by a speedy Conveyance', their number including one of the convict priests, Father James Harold. In addition to these measures, the authorities attempted to increase the armed force of the colony, inviting a number of 'the most respectable in-habitants' to join volunteer associations of fifty men each. Known as the Sydney and Parramatta Loyal Associated Corps, each was commanded by a military captain and other officers, supplied with arms and ammunition, and given some formal army training by a sergeant in the New South Wales Corps.[43]

The *Buffalo*, on which the convict hopes had been based, sailed for England on 21 October, but neither this nor the torture of the suspects prevented further resistance. In 1800 on Norfolk Island, to which the exiled rebels had been sent, a plan involving an uprising by one hundred convicts was discovered and ruthlessly put down, two of its leaders being hanged without trial. On the mainland in 1801 another uprising was suspected and pikes found, but this time King decided that sadly, the authorities had not been able to elicit enough evidence to hang anyone.[44]

Notwithstanding these precautions, the local Irish males refused to be metamorphosed into industrious colonists. On the evening of 4 March 1804 some 200 convicts at Castle Hill, a government farm founded in 1801, overpowered the officials and seized arms and ammunition. The leaders, Philip Cunningham and William Johnston, then organized the convicts into four sections which were to scour the agricultural settlements adjacent to Parramatta to collect further arms and recruits, then reconvene outside Parramatta. This time the plans were much more ambitious and carefully laid. Colleagues inside the town were to set fire to the farm of John Macarthur, and during the diversion this would create the rebels would take the whole settlement. It is possible that they planned, as in 1800, then to escape down the river to Sydney and so to the open sea. But two of the four bands failed to arrive at the planned rendezvous outside Parramatta, and though they had collected at least twenty-six muskets, plus swords and pistols, reaping hooks, and pitchforks, and were some 250 to 300 strong, they had not secured sufficient supporters to attack the town. Also their confederates in Parramatta failed to light the diversionary fires, and even worse, by dawn Governor King arrived in person on horseback, closely followed by Major George Johnston and fifty-six men of the New South Wales Corps who had left from Sydney on foot at about one in the morning.

Though the major part of the Corps remained in Sydney to prevent any rising by convicts there and to forestall any escape from Parramatta to the sea, the rebels abandoned the plan to take the town. Unlike Pemulwuy they declined to pit themselves against superior firepower and set off instead for the Hawkesbury, perhaps hoping to secure more arms and recruits. By mid-morning the rebels were overtaken on the road 10 miles west of Toongabbie by Major Johnston. At least nine of the rebels were killed and many wounded in the first round of firing which lasted fifteen minutes. Many more died in the pursuit which followed, for Major Johnston had some difficulty in controlling the zeal of his men. Parties of settlers were among those who continued to pursue and capture the convicts till the following Friday, and stray rebels were still being captured at the end of the month. On Johnston's orders Cunningham was hanged immediately without trial at the Hawkesbury, on the staircase of a public store. Ten rebels were selected and tried for armed rebellion, of whom all were found guilty. Eight were hanged; three at Parramatta, three at Castle Hill, and the last two at Sydney. Meanwhile a further nine men were awarded sentences of 200 to 500 lashes each, and at least thirty more were selected for dispatch to the Coal River, a penal station north of Port Jackson.[45]

The Castle Hill Rebellion was the largest and most organized manifestation of male resistance in this period, and as such it was outside the more general pattern of sustained but largely small-scale and often individualistic responses. Further, it was unusual because it was not betrayed, though during the rebellion convicts at Parramatta sent an address of loyalty to the government, while the convicts in the Loyalist Associations joined the soldiers in putting down the rebellion.

The authorities' generally unstated aim was to divide and rule, and this was assured of success in a community where a system of rewards encouraged betrayal. Whenever soldier and settler, convict and Aborigine, were divided between and against themselves, in spite of the fears of the authorities, any form of group political action could not succeed.

Indeed, notwithstanding the initial threat of famine and the profiteering of the officers, the chances of success of the experiment in convict colonization had been reasonably favourable ever since the First Fleet departed from England. The venture had been solidly based on previous experience of colonization and war, together with the latest demographic and economic theories. Where previously it had taken centuries for colonizers to secure a foothold in a new land, in New South Wales it had taken just over a decade, and having reached the stage where the colony was a viable economic and strategic base, the British would now turn to scientific theory for advice on how to begin to exploit the interior. After all, it was only through navigational science that their presence in the Pacific had been made possible and they were already discovering that the scientific knowledge to be gained in the colonies was essential for production at home and further expansion abroad.

3

HUNTERS AND COLLECTORS
Science and the South Pacific

EARLY IN APRIL 1802 two ships stalked each other in a bay near the Coorong on the southern coastline of New Holland. One of them was the *Investigator*, a sloop of 334 tons under the command of Lieutenant Matthew Flinders. A twenty-eight-year-old naval officer, Flinders had been commissioned by the Admiralty to lead a scientific expedition which, it was hoped, would eventually lead to the discovery of profitable raw materials and safer sea routes for trading vessels.

'We have now possessed the country of New South Wales for more than ten years', Joseph Banks had written peevishly in May 1798, urging such an expedition. Yet so far not one article had been produced of use to the mother country. Mercantilist colonization had not required the settlement of continents, but it did require the exploration of them and especially, as Banks put it, knowledge of whether there were 'vast rivers, capable of being navigated into the heart of the interior'. Had not Mr Mungo Park just discovered precisely such a navigable river, conveniently running eastwards across Africa? It was impossible to believe that such a large body of land as New Holland would not contain a similar waterway, giving access to people with goods to trade or to other sources of raw materials. It was for this purpose that Flinders had been sent to investigate the coastline of the entire continent.[1]

The French were asking similar questions. Perhaps concealed

behind a deep strait or bay as yet unclaimed by Britain, there existed a river mouth which would give easy access to the interior and its people. It was no coincidence that the other ship working along the Coorong was a French corvette, *Le Géographe*, under the command of Nicholas Baudin who held a similar commission from Napoleon's revolutionary government.

Despite this underlying commercial purpose, both these expeditions were conspicuously scientific. On the *Investigator* even some of the guns had been removed to make room for the astronomical instruments, encyclopaedias and learned personnel, while the French vessel fairly bristled with botanists, mineralogists and artists specially commissioned for the voyage.

Though the European search for knowledge of people and places far from their own foggy shores had long been impelled by commercial considerations, it was navigational science and industrial technology which had made colonization possible. By the time British and French vessels 'discovered' the Pacific in the second half of the eighteenth century, scientific investigation of the area, together with its flora, fauna, minerals and especially its people, was vital to the construction of biological, geological and anthropological theory on which further commercial and industrial expansion depended. Indeed, the European economy had never relied more intensely on scientific knowledge. As the navigators were acutely aware, they themselves had now to be scientists, expert in mathematics, astronomy and hydrography, for there was nothing quite as valuable as publishing an accurate map to secure a nation's claim to territory by right of prior discovery—though tin plates, carved trees and raised flags were still also used for this purpose. By the late eighteenth century all the main colonizing powers had produced at least one legal theorist who—from Grotius and Locke to Pufendorf, Wolff and Vattel—argued that trading nations had a moral right to take newly-found land and that it was by such emblems that the division of the spoils among themselves was ideally to be regulated.

Thus Baudin's instructions included a clause directing him to spy out whether or not the British had established a settlement in Van Diemen's Land, the east coast of which had first been mapped by the French. Already, with a sister ship he had charted the western coast of the continent northwards from Cape Leeuwin, paying special attention to the area around Shark Bay which had been claimed for France by St Allouarn in 1772. Baudin was also instructed to examine the north coast of Australia which, as non-annexed territory, was said to be available to first European comers. Flinders' expedition, on the other hand, was partly funded by the British East India Company which he had previously served and which hoped that his new, accurate charts and geological and botanical information could be turned to immediate commercial advantage.[2]

Late eighteenth-century technology demanded specialist knowledge of global human and material resources. Particularly needed, for example, were sources of minerals, metals and fuels, oil to lubricate the new machines and dyes to improve the textile industry. There was also pressure to search out new foodstuffs to feed the growing urban populations which industrialization required. Plants were sought which might contain medicinal qualities or new fibres and adhesives, and animals which might be used to improve or replace known species useful to humankind. Moreover, mechanization meant faster production which was beginning to increase the demand for known raw materials such as sugar and cotton, as well as enlarging the need for overseas markets for manufactured goods.

The key to achieving these goals was seen to lie in natural science, where methodology was based upon building up an encyclopaedic fund of knowledge, so that no page in the Baconian 'Book of Nature' remained unturned. Ideally, the properties of every rock anywhere on earth were to be known, and of every living species, so that all might be ordered into a coherent classificatory system and the task of determining their long-term and short-term utility could begin. Given these preoccupations, the shores of the Australian continent were seen not merely as a source of immediate wealth but as a vital repository of scientific data, a virtual laboratory containing undreamed-of specimens, the collection of which was rapidly becoming an end in itself.

Accordingly, despite their shared scientific interests, neither Flinders nor Baudin was particularly pleased to see the other. Although it was essential to the accumulation of scientific knowledge that scientists stay in touch with others working in the same field, there was no disguising the fact that as servants of the wealthy classes, they were locked into competition with each other. In science, as in colonization and trade, both national profits and personal fame depended on getting there first. The navigators, and also the naturalists they had on board, were intent on building their own empires.[3]

Though Baudin and Flinders achieved the navigational feats they had been sent to perform, both were destined to be cheated during their lifetimes of the honours attainable from such exploits. Baudin failed to return to France, dying *en route* at Mauritius in September 1803. Flinders, too, was unlucky. Already, in 1791 George Vancouver on his way via the Cape to a mapping assignment in the North Pacific, had charted the coast from Cape Leeuwin to the Recherche Archipelago. Then in 1797 George Bass, a naval surgeon who had arrived with Governor Hunter on the *Reliance*, had ventured in a whale boat down the coast from Port Jackson, to slip between the islands south of Port Hicks and sail as far as Westernport. Impressed by the great swell and the direction of the tides, Bass suggested that, far from being attached to the continent as previously supposed, Van Diemen's Land might be the largest of a group of islands lying off the continent's southern coast. The following year he accompanied Flinders on a voyage commissioned by Hunter to verify this. Flinders was in command of this expedition and, circumnavigating Van Diemen's Land, had discovered a promising new river mouth at Port Dalrymple on its north coast. However, the honour of having proved the existence of the Strait—and of carving some 700 miles off the journey from the Cape—remained with Bass.

Five years later, Flinders' achievements on the *Investigator* were similarly ill-fated. Assisted in his on-shore enquiries by the Sydney Aborigine, Bungaree, he would go on to circumnavigate the continent and collect information for the most accurate map of its entire outline to date. Then while returning to Britain in 1803 he would be shipwrecked off the Queensland coast and later imprisoned for almost seven years on Mauritius by the French, for after the brief Peace of Amiens the authorities there were under no obligation to regard this expert naval officer as a simple scholar of purely peaceful persuasions. This delay enabled members of the French expedition to publish their researches first, François Péron from 1807 onwards and Louis-Claude Freycinet in 1811. Even worse, they designated the entire south coast westward from Wilson's Promontory 'Terre Napoleon' and to its principal features assigned French names. To add injury to insult, Flinders's cat Trim, his companion on the *Investigator*, fellow survivor of the shipwreck and scientific expert, as Flinders put it, on lunar observations and the anatomy of shipboard rats, vanished during the long internment and was presumed eaten by a hungry slave.

Despite these personal losses, Flinders' map, eventually published the day before his death in 1814, marked a turning-point in cartography and navigational science. Except for a small section of the north-east coast, the whole outline of the southern continent which for so many centuries had baffled and intrigued geographers, traders, and monarchs of Europe, had at last been filled in, and from now on the continent would be known by the name Flinders called it on his map, Terra Australis or Australia. Minds would by then be turning to a new question—what lay within those last huge continents which, to Europeans, seemed to be waiting for the beneficent palm of the missionary and the merchant?[4]

European investigation of the New World had been increasingly dependent on science since the initially hit-and-miss affairs of the fifteenth century. As the journeys necessary to reach the sources of treasure, trade, and benighted savages became longer, sophisticated developments in industrial and human technologies were required. Changes had to be made to the design of ships, and new kinds developed which could carry the cannons and the men required to defend the trading vessels and the territories being acquired across the Atlantic and Indian Oceans. Skills had to be developed in the charting of coastlines and the calculation of distances, and methods evolved for maintaining the health and discipline of soldiers and crew. Thus the questions that were being asked of science were shaped by the demands of expanding European capitalism.

The charting of the coastline of New Holland had a crucial place in this process, for the continent occupied a key area in the south-west Pacific which had long been of interest to European traders. As early as the twelfth century, cartographers and geographers had believed that the known land masses of the northern hemisphere must have an antipodean equivalent to keep the world balanced and evenly spinning. Designated Terra Australis Incognita, in the European commercial imagination this unknown land gradually assumed fabled proportions and was thought to be rich in spices, minerals and treasure beyond compare. By the beginning of the sixteenth century, this imagined continent was of special interest to the Portuguese, whose caravels had pioneered European commercial expansion to the East Indies via the Cape and who were then prowling the ocean south of the Moluccas. In 1516 they colonized Timor and by the 1520s their traders had attempted to chart the coastline of a larger land mass further to the south. Though Portuguese knowledge of this land was apparently kept secret, maps of the area produced by French cartographers at Dieppe during the 1540s and 1550s are thought to be based on prior Portuguese discoveries. These charts showed a large promontory called 'Java La Grande' which, joined at its base to a sprawling polar land mass designated 'Terre australe', stretched promisingly northwards across temperate regions and almost as far as the East Indies. However, on these maps, instead of scenes of gold mines or productive commerce, naked savages were depicted as occupying the interior, together with exotic wildlife ranging from elephants, camels and unicorns to crocodiles and flightless birds. No attempts were made by the Portuguese to colonize 'Java La Grande'.[5]

Also interested in the suspected continent were the Spanish. By 1565, following the path which Magellan had forged around the Horn, they had plundered the wealth of the Aztec and Inca people and established a colony in the Philippines. Their galleons were riding the north-east trade winds out of Acapulco to Manila and returning home, laden with eastern goods, on the westerlies which blew across the Pacific from May to September. These exploits were taking the Spanish across some of the emptiest tracts of the North Pacific, and their imaginations were fired by the notion of a Great South Land. Inspired by a Peruvian myth that part of the Incas' gold had been secured from islands west of America, they believed the southern continent to be a possible source of the Christian fable, King Solomon's mines. Beginning in 1567 they launched no less than three exploratory expeditions westwards to search for it. First came Mendana, who reached a group of islands which he duly named the Solomons, even though he found no gold there. In 1595 he sailed again, this time in the company of de Quiros and with the intention of establishing a colony as a base for further exploration. Falling upon the Marquesas, this party killed some 200 people before abandoning the project and departing for Manila. In 1605 de

Quiros made a final attempt to find the fabled land, sailing with Torres and planning, should Terra Australis again elude him, to explore New Guinea instead. This time de Quiros descended upon Vanuatu where he again attempted to establish a colony but departed within a month for Mexico while Torres, who had become separated from him, returned to Manila via the strait which now bears his name.[6]

Following these disappointments, the Spanish virtually abandoned exploration of the south-west Pacific and the task of defining the mysterious southern land more precisely passed to Holland, an emerging trading state. Following the establishment of their own East India Company (or VOC) in 1602, Dutch traders, protected by military force, began to challenge Portuguese monopoly of this area. Keen to explore new commercial possibilities, as early as 1606 the VOC commissioned William Jansz to explore the area south of the Moluccas. Sailing in the *Duyfken*, Jansz charted the east coast of the Gulf of Carpentaria which was later named after a VOC official. However, though confirming that a large land lay to the immediate south, Jansz found the local people to be extremely hostile and found no material resources to inspire additional exploration or settlement.

Indeed, further Dutch investigation of the area was stimulated largely by the need to prevent damage to ships and cargoes for, far from proving to be a source of wealth, the southern continent proved at first to be a costly impediment. This was particularly so from 1611 when their vessels began to attempt to reduce the arduous twelve months' voyage from Holland via the East African coast, by taking advantage of the 'roaring 'forties' which blew eastwards from the Cape. Navigators were expected to be able to judge the exact moment when they had sailed far enough to the east and then make a steep left-hand turn to sail north for the Sunda Straits and Java. This was by no means easy to do, owing to the difficulty of calculating one's precise position at sea. Whereas mariners had long been able to calculate latitude by taking the altitude of the sun above the horizon at noon, longitude was a problem. It could only be arrived at by 'dead reckoning', that is, by measuring the daily run of the ships, no easy task, especially in stormy weather. Not surprisingly, many Dutch ships miscalculated the distance they had travelled from the Cape, and sailed too far eastwards before making the turn for the Sunda

Straits. Many then found their way northwards blocked by sections of coastline which appeared to be part of the same troublesome southern land.

Consequently, the early reconnaissance of this continent's coast by the Dutch was as much a product of accident as design. For instance, it was after an unplanned encounter with an island off the West Australian coast that, in 1616, Dirck Hartog nailed a plate to a tree (found eighty-one years later by his compatriot, Willem de Vlamingh). Similarly, in 1627 another Dutch trader had occasion to draw in some of the Great Australian Bight, naming this part of the continent Pieter Nuyts Land, after a Dutch official. Meanwhile, in 1623 the VOC commissioned Jan Carstens and Dirck Melisz of the *Pera* and *Arnhem* to make another official investigation of the northern area. Like Jansz, they were sent to look for treasure, in this case gold along the south coast of New Guinea, and again like him, they found their plans intercepted by another appendage of that exasperating southern continent, the Cape York Peninsula. Least favourably impressed of all the Dutch traders and navigators was François Pelsaert, wrecked on the Abrolhos Reef in 1629. Forced to row to Djakarta in a long-boat to obtain help, he abandoned two mutineers on the desolate shore, believing that this would serve both as a punishment and, should they ever be picked up, a source of additional information about the resources, if any, of this apparently barren land.[7]

By the 1640s the Dutch had safeguarded their route eastwards by establishing settlements at the Cape, Mauritius, Madagascar and India and had conquered much of the South-East Asian archipelago. Their VOC was now ready to commission its most ambitious, official exploratory voyage aiming both to chart the difficult and dangerous coastline to the south and hopefully find a route past it which might give access to the Spanish settlements in South America and allow that trade to be interrupted and plundered. For this task they appointed Abel Tasman, who carried with him a mixture of goods ranging from European cloth and blankets to Chinese sandalwood which would be traded for a sample of the resources of the Great South Land. Tasman also carried instructions to keep an accurate daily journal describing every detail of the inhabitants and the resources encountered, for by now such scientific information was becoming essential in order to streamline future expansion and maximize profits.

Sailing on two journeys in 1642 and 1644, Tasman made a sweep of the seas to the south of the Dutch trading empire, charting sections of both known and unknown coastline. The first land sighted was the southern coastline of today's Tasmania where, at North Bay on 3 December 1642, a sailor was made to swim ashore and plant a flag. This new possession was named after Anthony Van Diemen, governor of the Company. Tasman also charted part of the west coast of New Zealand, as well as parts of Tonga, Fiji and northern New Guinea. Thus, Tasman appeared to have circumnavigated what was thought to be a very large land mass indeed. This still-baffling continent the Dutch called New Holland. The fabulous Terra Australis was assumed to lie further to the east or west of it, perhaps deep in southern seas.

Tasman's failure to find new sources of treasure and trade disappointed the VOC. As Van Diemen wrote, Tasman had found nothing 'profitable', only apparently 'poor, naked beach-runners' without any interest in trade. Eighty years passed before the Dutch launched Jacob Roggeveen on another search for the Great South Land. Leaving the Netherlands in 1721, he followed a route around the Horn pioneered in 1615 by private Dutch adventurers, Schouten and Le Maire, but discovered little more noteworthy than the bleak, treeless Easter Island with its inscrutable stone statues in human form. The Dutch then withdrew support from Pacific exploratory ventures, just as the Spanish had done after Mendana, de Quiros and Torres failed to find King Solomon's gold.[8]

Meanwhile, by the second half of the seventeenth century British and French imperial expansion was overtaking the Dutch. Both were moving from the position of mere pirates attacking the treasure ships of Holland and Spain towards becoming major trading nations with colonies of their own.[9]

In England, as the extent of financial and human resources being risked in adventures overseas increased, gentlemen of leisure and learning organized themselves into societies dedicated to finding scientific solutions to such problems as how to calculate longitude and how to preserve the health of men during long periods at sea. Of these, the Royal Society, founded in 1660, was the most important. Ostensibly devoted to promoting the accumulation of useful knowledge about the forces which turned the world and affected the distribution of its raw materials and population, its connections with commerce were obscured by an overt posture of scientific objectivity. Methods were to be distinctly empirical, based on the study of Nature itself rather than theoretical speculation and revelationary ideas. By the time William Dampier published his *New Voyage Around the World* in 1697, Isaac Newton was about to become the President of the Royal Society, and this organization was producing precise instructions to seafarers and travellers on how to assemble accurate data on coastlines, ports and weather patterns. Traces of this method were already present in Dampier's work, which was dedicated to the President of the Royal Society. Ex-pirate and plunderer of the Caribbean, Dampier was interested in the possibility of using New Holland as a base for English ships seeking access, like the Dutch, to the resources and markets of Spain's American colonies. He made two voyages to New Holland in 1688 and 1699, and published two accounts giving the new detailed quasi-scientific descriptions of the land and its people which the gentlemen readers of such accounts now required.[10]

To facilitate astronomical methods of calculating longitude, the audacious French had the temerity to establish a Royal Observatory in 1671 at Paris. The British, however had been quick to counter this move by establishing a similar institution at Greenwich in 1675. By 1738 the British scientists and navigators had the satisfaction of seeing on their own charts the prime meridian between the North and South Poles in exactly the position where it ought to be, namely, slicing cleanly through Greenwich. London was to become the centre of the globe with all positions marked to the east and west accordingly.

The publication in 1728 of *Newton's System of the World* meant that now the observation of heavenly bodies could be mathematically described and their future positions predicted. By the 1760s it was thought that herein was a solution to the problem of finding longitude — simply by comparing local time, measured by the position of the sun in the heavens, with Greenwich time, which could also be calculated by mariners measuring the position of the moon relative to the sun. In 1766 the Astronomer Royal, Nevil Maskelyne, published the first *Nautical Almanac*, a book of tables intended to simplify the calculations involved by setting out a calendar of lunar positions over time.

The moon, however, was not always visible. Obviously it was preferable to carry an accurate timepiece, but clocks with pendulums could not be relied on to function on a heaving ship. In 1764 John Harrison designed the first suitable chronometer for keeping accurate time at sea, and thus it was that the clock, already very much the tool by which the work-time of the labouring masses was to be measured at home, became symbolic of and vital to the development of technology to facilitate overseas commerce and trade.[11]

Over the same period, experiments had been made in solving that other problem which hounded the success of the early sea voyages—scurvy. In 1747 naval surgeon James Lind had found that orange and lemon juice were effective in the treatment of the disease, and put forward a detailed regimen for maintenance of health during long sea voyages. This centred on special attention to diet plus plans to impose cold bathing, skin friction, and forms of group exercise on the soldiers and crew. Ships were to be kept scrupulously clean with special emphasis on ventilation and fumigation. Compulsory attention to these details could usefully function also as new methods of disciplining the crew. Lind's *Treatise on Scurvy* was published in 1753. Together with Maskelyne's lunar tables and Harrison's ships' clocks, the technology was now assembled which would make possible the voyages of James Cook. These in turn would greatly broaden the scope for British imperial strategies in the South Pacific, while also introducing new standards of accurate mapping which commerce now required.[12]

By the 1760s British and French curiosity about the Pacific had never been more intense. Their charts were now peppered with tantalizing scraps of coastline and 'wandering islands', reported by mariners who had been pushed by unusual winds and currents outside the relatively narrow corridors to which most shipping was confined. Interest in the area quickened following the Seven Years' War as the British moved to consolidate their new possessions in India and North America, and safeguard access to trade with China and Japan. In 1764 John Byron was sent to take possession of the Falkland Islands in the South Atlantic, then search for a passage through the American continent in the vicinity of Drake's New Albion (California). This would bypass Spanish possessions and give access to the Pacific, thus securing a share in the lucrative North American fur trade currently being developed by Russian, Spanish and French investors. Ideally, iron and textiles would be exchanged at bases on the North American coast for sea otter and other pelts which in turn would be marketed in Canton for tea.

Byron's circumnavigation of the globe in twenty-two months was the forerunner of numerous new, state-run, geopolitical voyages under naval command which would reveal the Pacific and its people to Western eyes. During his homeward route via the East Indies to the Cape, Byron noted the absence of a great swell from the south-west, and vast flocks of birds flying south, suggesting the imminent presence of the long-sought Terra Australis. Within two months of his return a new expedition was dispatched along a more southerly track. Under the command of Samuel Wallis, this unveiled not the Great South Land but Tahiti—a seafarer's Garden of Eden, strategically located half-way across the dangerous ocean desert of the South Pacific. Destined to become of central importance to future voyages, Wallis lost no time in declaring this abundant isle a British possession.

Long interested in finding bases in the southern Indian Ocean and already challenging British ambitions in the Pacific, the French, too, were active. In 1739 Lozier de Bouvet was excited by the discovery of a coastline in the South Atlantic which he believed was part of Terra Australis and which he named Cape Circumcision. French exploration in the area began in earnest in 1766 when Louis XV sent two lavishly equipped ships under Louis de Bougainville. Sailing east to Tahiti via the Cape and returning by the same route, Bougainville dashed some hopes by establishing that wherever Terra Australia was, it could not be between Espiritu Santo and New Holland. On his return journey he explored as far as the Coral Sea and possibly the Great Barrier Reef before turning north for Java, ending forever speculation that the continent was to be found in this location.[13]

As in the modern space race, so important now was science as a tool of imperial expansion that, ironically, it could be used as a cover for commercial and strategic espionage. This became evident in plans to dispatch a new British expedition to the South Seas in 1768. It was then fifty-two years since Edmond Halley had published a paper explaining that a transit of Venus was a useful means of calculating the distance of the sun from the earth provided that the transit was timed at points widely separated, especially in a north-south direction. In 1761 the Royal Society had dispatched Mason and Dixson to the southern states of

America to observe a transit, but their plans were foiled when they were set upon by a French frigate soon after leaving Portsmouth. Determined not to lose the next opportunity (and the last till the year 1874), the Royal Society had succeeded in extracting £4000 from George III to finance an expedition to the other side of the globe. Symbolizing the new role of science as both 'a weapon and a cover', the point chosen was Tahiti. A 368-ton barque, the *Earl of Pembroke*, was purchased by the Admiralty for the voyage and with her she carried 'Secret Instructions'. On completion of the transit she was to sail on a systematic search for the Great South Land, chart it and claim it for the uses of British commerce. To lead this venture the Royal Society suggested Alexander Dalrymple, a Scottish hydrographer and employee of the East India Company. From 1759 Dalrymple had made numerous voyages of trade in the East Indies, negotiated a trade treaty with the Sultan of Sulu and had been elected deputy governor of Manila which the British captured as a trading base in 1762. He was also interested in Torres's testimony of a passage to the Pacific south of New Guinea and was a passionate believer in the existence and commercial viability of the Great South Land. To his bitter disappointment, the Admiralty refused to give command of a Royal Navy ship to a civilian and suggested instead a Lieutenant James Cook. This officer was seen as an ideal choice because he had experienced action against the French during the Seven Years' War off the North American coast. He was also known to be 'a good mathematician', though largely self-taught, and had conducted surveys of the St Lawrence River and the Newfoundland coast.[14]

Though departing in August 1768, just too soon to have the advantage of Harrison's clock, Cook's expedition took on the appearance of a purely scientific mission of no immediate advantage to shipping, strategy or trade. With him he carried the latest lunar tables, telescopes, quadrants and sextants, while his vessel was given a new name more suited to an age of heroic scientific enquiry — *Endeavour*. The voyage also seemed largely scientific in purpose because it included an unprecedented number of experts in natural science. Indeed his decks were cluttered, as those of Flinders and Baudin would be, with the paraphernalia of a swarm of intellectuals from every branch of this particular tree of knowledge. There was Daniel Carl Solander, a student of famous Swedish botanist, Carl von Linné, better known as Linnaeus, and

Herman Spöring, a former professor of medicine in Finland. Also on board were natural history artists, Alexander Buchan, who was to specialize in painting the scenery and the people encountered, and Sydney Parkinson, who was to make accurate drawings of animals and plants.

In charge of this party of luminaries on the *Endeavour* was none other than Joseph Banks himself. Then an ambitious and indefatigable young man possessed of independent means, Banks had already made a collection of rocks, plants and animals from Newfoundland and Labrador, on the strength of which he had been elected a Fellow of the Royal Society in 1766. Enjoying also some influence with the Earl of Sandwich, in 1768 he had little difficulty in persuading the authorities to allow him and his staff to join the expedition then leaving for the South Seas. For the convenience of his distinguished and very cosmopolitan party, Banks added four servants, two dogs, a large library, numerous contrivances for catching and preserving insects, nets and hooks for snaring marine life, quires of paper for preserving botanical specimens, boxes and cages for transporting living ones, and a special telescope through which the curious might pass the time examining the bottom of the sea.

Scrutineers rather than buccaneers, these naturalists and artists have often been seen as the embodiment of pure scientific enquiry, turning away from careers dependent on colonization and war to devote themselves to the eclectic world of science and art. Given the central importance of collection and classification of species to solving the problems raised by industrialization, however intent these people were in exploring theoretical territories of their own, they were, like the navigators, agents of commercial expansion. It was expected that the artists on these voyages would spend their time drawing coastal profiles and other phenomena of obvious use to strategy and trade, as well as subjects such as Patagonian penguins and the New Holland flying fox, whose relationship to commerce was equally important, albeit more long-term and obscure.

Despite some tension between the personal ambitions of the navigator and those of the naturalist, Cook's first voyage to the South Seas was an unqualified success for both. Arriving at Tahiti on 12 April 1769, within a month his crew they constructed a small fort on Matavai Bay from which they might intimidate the local people and take the observations. By 3 June everything was ready; Green, Cook, and Solander observed the transit despite the heat of the day, which they also measured, and which they said reached 119°F (48°C). While the physical scientists were thus occupied, Banks and most of the crew were studying the Tahitians whom they found much more engaging. Given Wallis's cruel bombardment of the area prior to his five weeks' stay in 1767, the Tahitians proved ready to accommodate the visitors, providing fresh food and sexual encounters in return for metal goods. It was an arrangement which Banks especially found attractive. Like Bougainville, who had been there the year before, he described the Tahitians, in mock heroic style, as godlike Greeks, their men like Hercules, Ajax, and Epicurus. Their women were elegant, their attire natural and beautiful, their bodies were as if copied from Renaissance art.[15]

Cook, too, found time to observe the people, and though he was less inclined to philosophical speculation he displayed a similar curiosity about every facet of their technology, economy and their sexual life. He also mused at length upon the presence of venereal disease which, he assumed, had been introduced by the French and which, at the time of his departure, infected half his men. Nevertheless he made no attempt to prevent their intercourse with the people, even permitting them to bring women on board the ship at night. At sea, however, he was a disciplinarian who attended scrupulously to the regimen for health laid down by Lind, and considered that further experiments with methods of preventing and treating scurvy were part of the scientific purpose of the voyage. A quantity of sauerkraut had been supplied by the Admiralty, and Cook insisted that its prophylactic qualities were tested to the full. So triumphant was he at the end of the first voyage in not losing a single man from scurvy that 19 000 pounds of sauerkraut and 5000 pounds of salted cabbage were put aboard for the next voyage, plus malt and 30 gallons of a new remedy known as 'mermalade of carrots'. Each man was compelled to eat one pound of sauerkraut twice a week, oftener if thought necessary. Cook's remedies were so successful that he later gave a paper on them to the Royal Society and published it in 1776. Some of his crew however were less impressed: 'it was No Uncommon thing when Swallowing Over these Mess[es] to Curse him heartyly & wish for god's Sake that he Might be Obledged to Eat such Damned Stuff Mixed with his Broth as Long as he Lived'.[16]

Cook's other passion was to correct the inaccuracies and avoid the errors made by less mathematically gifted seamen equipped with less sophisticated instruments. After leaving Tahiti in August 1769, using his lunar tables Cook systematically sailed due south to latitude 40 degrees to search without success for Terra Australis, and then west to check that the coastline of Tasman's New Zealand was not part of it. By March 1770 the task was done and Cook was free to decide a homeward route. In the event of the absence of any Great South Land, the only remaining mysterious coastline awaiting the navigational skills of the scientist was the eastern margin of New Holland. Cook decided to steer west for this coastline, chart its northward course, and then look for the passage through to the East Indies via the rumoured Torres Strait.

On 17 April 1770 this move was rewarded. Lieutenant Hicks on board the *Endeavour* sighted land, and the ship swung in to chart what proved to be the eastern coastline of New Holland. Two days later a landing was made at Sting-ray Harbour (later named Botany Bay) where, having fired at the local people, the party remained undisturbed for over a week. Three more landings were made along this coastline including, from 11 June, an unplanned seven-week sojourn at the Endeavour River after the ship was holed by coral on the Great Barrier Reef. Having repaired the ship Cook continued to sail as close to the coast as possible, and by so doing could confidently confirm Torres's report. 'New Holland and New Guinea are two Separate Lands or Islands,' he congratulated himself on 23 August, 'which until this day hath been a doubtful point with Geographers'. Now satisfied that there were no more discoveries to be made in the area, for the Dutch had charted everything to the west, on the previous day he had gone ashore to an island off the northern tip of Cape York Peninsula and officially taken possession of the entire eastern coast that he had surveyed. Raising a flag, he claimed the coastline from 38 degrees south to 'Possession Island' in the name of George III.[17]

Cook's second and third voyages were equally important to commerce and colonization. With the use of the new chronometers for the long second journey in the *Resolution* (13 July 1772–30 July 1775), he was able to scour the southern Indian and Pacific Oceans in a search for the Great South Land so thorough and so prolonged that journeys of this kind would later become proverbially associated with his name. Having descended so far south that the ship was threatened by pack-ice, and becoming increasingly sceptical of the existence of the missing continent, Cook nevertheless did not think the Pacific area 'sufficiently explored'. After a leisurely cruise through Tahiti and the Society Islands, where his men were again permitted free intercourse with the local people, Cook 'fell in with a large country' which he named New Caledonia. He also discovered a much smaller and uninhabited land which would soon become part of Britain's first colonization venture in the Pacific. Of this he took possession and named it Norfolk Island.[18]

Suspecting that the British presence in the Pacific was not purely 'scientific' and they might be planning to establish a base at Tahiti, the Spanish followed suit with three expeditions to the Pacific in 1770, 1772 and 1774, while from France came Jean-François de Surville in 1769 and Marion Dufresne in 1771.[19] Cook was no sooner back in Britain than in February 1776 he had offered his services to the Admiralty for a third British expedition, its principal aims being to check French reports of a new island south of Mauritius and continue the quest for the needed North-West Passage. Travelling via Van Diemen's Land and New Zealand, in January 1778 Cook chanced upon the islands now known as Hawaii, superbly located in relation to the North Pacific. After a northern summer spent in Arctic waters Cook returned to this second Tahiti to chart its islands and refresh his crew. Here on 14 February 1779 his career was brought to an abrupt end. By now a Fellow of the Royal Society and something of a celebrity, he had become impatient with Islanders who challenged both his property values and his power by expecting to control access to shipboard commodities in exchange for the use of women and food. In Tonga he had ordered floggings for 'theft' and when that failed, he ordered ears chopped and had men's arms slashed with a knife. At Moorea when a goat was taken, he staged a punitive expedition, burning houses and smashing canoes. At Kealakekua Bay when he shot a man during a beachside confrontation over a missing cutter he and four of his party were surrounded and killed. In all some thirty Hawaiians died during this attempt to discipline the invaders.[20]

Where Cook's scrutiny of the Pacific had failed to present investors either with a Great South Land or a North-West Passage, Banks had enjoyed a field day. Although Cook refused to sacrifice 'a day's fair wind to the accommodation of the Naturalists', Banks had seized every opportunity to collect botanical and other information. At Tahiti, he also collected Tupia, a priest who volunteered to accompany the party to England as a human specimen of the voyage's ethnographic discoveries. When Cook called at Botany Bay on 21 April 1770 Banks and his staff descended like locusts on the new species of plants found growing there, collecting seeds and taking cuttings which they dried on sails spread in the sun, for they soon used up all 200 quires of paper which they had brought for this purpose. Like the officers later at Port Jackson, they also shot 'Loryquets and Cockatoos' and set their dogs to catch the mysterious quadrupeds they encountered. During the longer stay at the Endeavour River they made several sallies inland where, however, research was impaired by the stings of 'indefatigable insects'. These seemed as persistent in taking specimens from the Englishmen as the men of science were in collecting entyomological samples from the new land.

Unlike Tupia, none of the local inhabitants of this New Holland coastline showed any interest in joining the living specimens on the ship. At the Endeavour River, Sydney Parkinson attempted to compile a short vocabulary of their language, but when Banks refused to share a catch of turtles with them the Aboriginal people made a circle of fire to windward of the interlopers and their goods upon the shore. Spreading rapidly in the dry grass, the flames almost destroyed Banks's tent before he hauled it down and dragged it to safety. As at Botany Bay, the naturalists and navigators did not depart without having found occasion to shoot at the inhabitants, leaving at least one person wounded at each of the two places where landing was prolonged.[21]

Banks's plans to accompany the second expedition were aborted after he declared the *Resolution*'s cabins to be too small for the large party he had planned to take. His reputation, however, was already made. In 1771 both he and Solander were presented to George III, and received honorary degrees from Oxford University. Linnaeus was delighted with the collection of specimens, and by 1776 Banks had moved into the large London house which became his museum. By 1778 he was President of the Royal Society and ultimately he became also a member of the Engineers Society, the Board of Longitude, the Coin Committee and the Committee of Trade, and the Privy Council. Banks's success reflected the fact that the specimens brought home by the naturalists on all of the voyages created sensational interest in Britain. Though the navigators shared in the acclaim, it was the more exotic and unexpected discoveries of the naturalists which gained the lion's share of the attention. When the *Endeavour* returned to England, not only Cook's manuscripts but those of Banks, Solander, and others were given to a celebrated writer, Dr John Hawkesworth, to be edited into *An Account of the Voyages Undertaken by His Present Majesty for Making Discoveries in the Southern Hemisphere* (London 1773). The official account of the third voyage (1784) included over sixty drawings by draftsman John Webber of exotic places, flora and fauna, and copious extracts from it were published in journals and newspapers of the 1780s. This new scientific information about the South Seas and its people was also romanticized through its influence on poetry, theatre and the picturesque tradition in art, so that it was elevated into cultural ideology while its underlying commercial significance was further obscured.[22]

In fact, however, these collections and accounts systematized more than a century of scientific effort to increase the store of knowledge available to merchants and manufacturers. The British were now in a position where the information necessary to colonize the Pacific was available to be applied. Thus it was that they turned to Banks whose practical experience and scientific contacts made him the ideal adviser to the British state. His collections and observations provided the basis on which plans to establish a colony in the Pacific could be formulated, its site determined and its prospects assessed. Indeed, until his death in 1820, he remained at the centre of a web of networks connecting British colonization and science, networks which reached out to include numerous civil, religious and military officials involved in the administration of early New South Wales.

Even before the foundation of the colony, which he strongly recommended, Banks was promoting schemes for the commercial exploitation of the newly-found products of the Pacific. He was influential in organizing an experiment in the transportation and acclimatization of the fabled breadfruit trees of Otaheiti. If these could be cultivated in the West Indian colonies they could be used to replace food supplies which were no longer available after the loss of the American colonies and needed to feed the slaves. In 1787 the Royal Society for the Promotion of Arts and Commerce had offered a gold medal for the first person who could successfully transport the trees alive. Banks recommended William Bligh, master of the *Resolution* on Cook's fatal third voyage, to undertake this new and challenging experiment in navigation and natural science. Bligh sailed on the *Bounty* in November 1787, calling in August 1788 at Van Diemen's Land, the east coast of which was now a key stopping place where French and British expeditions took on wood and water and made ethnological observations *en route* to the Pacific. Sailing on to Tahiti, by December he had collected over a thousand breadfruit plants and was ready to depart for the West Indies with the plants successfully transplanted into pots, boxes and tubs on board.

Bligh's botanical experiment with the breadfruit was cut short by mutiny on 30 April 1789, for while he had been focusing on the precious plants some of his officers and the crew had been experimenting with the other delights for which the islands were now famous. This, in Bligh's view, was the reason for the 'revolution' on board his ship. While the mutineers, led by Fletcher Christian and guided by a valuable Kendall timepiece, sailed the *Bounty* back to the paradise of Tahiti, Bligh and eighteen of his followers, including the young midshipman, Matthew Flinders, found themselves at sea in a 23-foot open boat and engaged in an unplanned test of their navigational skills. Equipped with only four cutlasses, some bread and water, a quadrant and a compass, these expert measurers nevertheless steered for the north coast of New Holland and thence via Torres Strait to Timor, where they completed their remarkable 3600-mile journey on 1 June.

Despite the ignominy of having lost his ship, Bligh's career was far from blighted for it was acknowledged that he had contributed to cartographic knowledge of the continent. Sailing closer to the shoreline than Cook had been able to do, he produced a detailed map of a section of the north Queensland coast. For the authorities a less welcome result of his voyage was that, becoming well-known, it inspired escape attempts from Botany Bay, as convicts like William and Mary Bryant successfully emulated the journey of the unlucky captain.[23]

Meanwhile, the British settlements in New South Wales were proving a catalyst for further scientific enquiry, and the collection of information about the Pacific and its products was being pushed on apace. Banks corresponded with the early governors, giving precise directions for the gathering of specimens, many of which, like the New Holland platypus and the Port Jackson shark, were new to natural science. As Hunter noted in his *Historical Journal of the Transactions at Port Jackson and Norfolk Island*, published in 1793, it was no uncommon thing to see 'a skait's head and shoulders to the hind of a shark, or a shark's head to the body of a large mullet, and sometimes to the flat body of a string-ray'. In 1798 Banks dispatched George Caley to work full time on the collection of specimens from the colony while, during his exploratory work with Flinders, George Bass collected material which he later published, ranging from the anatomy of the wombat to the feeding habits of the black swan. By 1802 when Flinders and Baudin met at Encounter Bay, information gleaned from the Pacific on new forms of animal and vegetable life had overturned established theories and was demanding new methods of classifying and theorizing every species of life on earth.[24]

These developments, especially in biological science, had serious consequences for the people who were being dispossessed from the land both in overseas colonies and at home. Given the pace of economic expansion and the extent of political turbulence, especially in Britain and France, it was becoming increasingly important to understand whether human nature and numbers were related to environmental or biological factors. Though as yet no reliable system had been developed by which human reproductive capacity could be compared or people's physical strength as labourers, a whole new science of ethnology was being created, having as its unstated basis the need to control the working population both in the colonies and at home. In Europe it was thought that some of this information could be obtained by studying captive human specimens incarcerated in asylums, hospitals and the like. Theorists could also turn to information available in the Old Testament and in the history of the ancient Greeks. However, with the growing acceptance of the *tabula rasa* theory, the study of 'primitive' people living in a 'state of nature' remote from European social institutions and law was increasingly seen as absolutely essential. A huge literature on the American Indians had already been amassed for this purpose.

It was predictable that, when developed, this new science of human nature would not be culturally neutral but would serve an ideological as well as economic purpose. From the seventeenth century on European writers had argued that the people of Africa and the Americas, currently being enslaved, were bestial and stupid, mere beasts of burden who could with impunity be treated as such. In his *Leviathan* (1651) Thomas Hobbes argued that people's bodies were mere commodities, and used assumptions about European superiority to justify authoritarian rule and economic exploitation. It was theories such as these which informed Dampier's denigration of the New Holland Aborigines in 1688—though he had also been especially irritated by their disinclination to reveal their source of water supply and to recognize their lowly status by shouldering the 6-gallon casks of water he wanted carried to his ship. The first Englishman to set foot on Australian soil, Dampier was also the first to shoot one of its inhabitants.[25]

Published in 1735 and laying the basis for scientific racial theory, Linnaeus's *System of Nature* reflected and developed these prejudices. Employing a concept which dated from antiquity, Linnaeus classified people into races according to the colour of their skin, dividing them into four main physical and psychological types. Those with the darkest skins were labelled *Homo Afer* and, described with an employer's eye, were said to be lazy, careless and cunning. In smug legitimation of their own economic system and denigration of the people they sought to control at home and overseas, philosophers ranging from Turgot to Adam Smith hit upon the theory that all societies 'progressed' through definable stages of hunting, pastoralism and agriculture until they reached a commercial phase which, needless to say, was considered the most advanced. This concept conveniently modified the Great Chain of Being, a notion dating from antiquity and postulating a fixed hierarchy of species stretching upwards from vegetables and animals via man and kings and so to God. The new 'progress' model was not only more fluid, secular and ostensibly egalitarian but also more compatible with developing evolutionary theory. Moreover, it suggested that all 'nomadic' people, whether vagabonds at home or those who did not engage in agricultural and commercial pursuits overseas, could be conveniently classified as an inferior type.[26]

While providing a useful advance over skin colour for the construction of theories about the classification and control of human resources, this theory was still based on mere philosophical speculation and was difficult to translate into quantifiable fact. Even worse, it was temporarily thrown into confusion by enthusiastic descriptions, brought back by Bougainville and

Banks, of Tahitian people existing, so it was said, in a happy state of primitive simplicity. Commerson, Bougainville's botanist, wrote an essay identifying the Tahitians with the idealized society described by Rousseau in his *Discourses on Inequality* (1755) and Diderot, writing his own *Supplément* to de Bougainville's account of his voyage (1776), actually went so far as to suggest that 'primitive' people enjoyed some advantages over civilized ones.

Wallis, too, returned with an idealized picture of Tahitian life but the concept of the noble savage was especially popular with the French. This was partly because they were in the process of seeking alliances with non-European people in India and North America to use against British claims in these areas. It was also because the celebration of Tahitian life was so compatible with the ideas of Rousseau. The son of a Swiss watchmaker, Rousseau was much more aware than some of his fellow philosophers of the danger of extending liberty, equality and fraternity to all men. He was thus particularly concerned to explore Romantic theory and to pursue its backward-looking, quasi-feudal implications rather than its egalitarian, utopian ones. To followers of Rousseau, for 'childish' savages, as for the child, the economic opportunities which were to be made available to some sections of the population under the new liberal regime would have to be indefinitely postponed. Moreover, the concept of the noble savage was clearly a temporary phenomenon. It could only be entertained while the Islanders consented to be trading partners who obeyed the European rules of property, sexuality and exchange. For the noble savage was essentially a trading savage, a notion underlying Lord Sydney's assumption that Islander women would co-operate in the peopling of New South Wales. It was an image which corresponded to late mercantilist colonization theory, for soon the expanding industrial economy of Europe would require both the labour of newly discovered native people and their land. Then, the coercive implications of the savage as a child with no property, in need of education and conversion, would be fully developed and applied.[27]

Indeed, no sooner had the occupation and colonization of the Pacific begun than the concept of 'nobility' was found to be inadequate. In some cases, the same theorists who were commending the natives of the Pacific for their 'noble' willingness to trade were also gathering the more quantitative 'scientific' information which the new, quicker colonization of whole continents was going to require. Thus, when at the Horn, Joseph Banks was concerned to correct the myth-making of unscientific observers like John Byron by measuring the height of the so-called Patagonian giants. Similarly at the Endeavour River, he had no compunction in spitting on his finger and rubbing it on a man's skin to determine the precise shade.

In Britain, Cook's death was made the catalyst for a change in enthusiasm for the noble savage. At the same time, reports reaching missionary ears of unholy domestic customs and religious rites practised in the Pacific did nothing to convince those in Christian circles of the original innocence of the noble savage. Already Cowper's *Task* (1783) used the new information about primitive peoples to argue that natural man was a rude and brutish creature who only very slowly could be made to acquire civilized habits, while Thomas Haweis, founder of the London Missionary Society, conceived the idea of a mission to the South Seas after reading Cook's voyages.[28]

In France, in 1783 Julien Crozet argued that far from being simple children of nature, primitive people were brutish and treacherous (*Nouveau Voyage à la mer du sud* 1783). Crozet had sailed with Marion Dufresne in 1771 in what had proved an ill-fated venture. The plan was to pick up spice plants from the Moluccas for acclimatization in Mauritius and *en route*, return to his homeland a Polynesian, Aotourou, who had been persuaded by de Bougainville to visit France. Unfortunately Aotourou had contracted smallpox at Mauritius and subsequently died, but Dufresne unperturbed, attempted to make contact with more specimens of the noble savage in the course of a call on the east coast of Van Diemen's Land early in 1772. He had conceived the novel idea of sending naked Frenchmen ashore bearing gifts to establish amicable relations whenever unclothed inhabitants were encountered. Unimpressed by the Frenchmen's novel contribution to anthropological theory or perhaps, by their bodies, the Van Diemen's Land Aborigines had responded with a shower of stones and spears. Dufresne was wounded in the shoulder and in the ensuing skirmish at least one Aboriginal man was killed. As with Banks, so important was the new ethnological science for Marion that he measured the body and washed the skin. Three months later in New Zealand, where Dufresne had called to take on a cargo of timber, the Maori people showed a similar unwillingness to further either his ethnographic or commercial enquires and brought the Frenchman's enquiries to a permanent end. In retaliation Crozet massacred some 250 people. He also took possession of these timber and flax-rich islands, which Dufresne had already named 'France Australe'.[29]

Though the French had clearly capitalized on his experience, Dufresne's demise was another blow to the concept of the noble savage. Within two decades there was a third martyr to the cause of navigational and ethnographic science in southern seas. He was Jean-François Galaup, Comte de La Pérouse. Sent by Pacific enthusiast Louis XVI on an ambitious scientific expedition in August 1785, La Pérouse was to examine carefully 'the genius, character, manners, customs, bodily constitution, language, government, and number of inhabitants' of all lands visited, as well as their 'garments, arms, ornaments, utensils, tools, musical instruments'. He was also to visit Nootka Sound, search for the North-West Passage, and scrutinize the coasts of Kamchatka and Japan. La Pérouse had an angry altercation with natives at Samoa where twelve of his party were killed. Arriving at Botany Bay on 24 January 1788 his two ships, though innocently named *La Boussole* and *L'Astrolabe* (the *Compass* and the *Quadrant*), caused consternation to the British officers who had arrived only a few days previously to create their laboratory for turning convicts into colonists. Relations between the commanders however, proved amicable, but the embittered La Pérouse soon fell out with the Aboriginal people and found occasion to shoot at them. When by 10 March his researches at Botany Bay were over and he dropped over the rim of the Pacific, never to be heard of again, it was conjectured that other 'ferocious' savages had disposed of him.[30]

Thus even though some writers and artists continued to develop the concept of the noble savage, others were arguing that far from leading a life of innocent joy in harmony with their environment, in areas where that environment was less favourable than Tahiti native peoples had failed to develop from, or regressed to, a degraded, preternatural state. Within this new theoretical framework, the already despised Africans came in for savage criticism in books like Edward Long's *History of Jamaica* (1774), and the Patagonians and Aborigines became special objects of scorn. James Bennet Monboddo's *Of the Origin and Progress of Language* (1773–6) used voyagers' accounts from as far back as Dampier to argue that natives like the Fuegians and Tasmanians, who lived in cold climates, were primitives and as such had a biological affinity with apes. In Germany in 1781 J. F. Blumenbach's *On the Natural History of Mankind* put forward a new classificatory system to replace the old Linnaean one with allegedly quantifiable fact. He divided the human species into five main races, declaring that a combination of colour, hair, skull and facial characteristics was the key to classification and control. His 'caucasian' type was, of course, said to be superior, while people with different skin colour and skulls were said to have degenerated from this ideal.

Meanwhile, the French were using expeditions launched to search for La Pérouse as an opportunity to conduct further navigational and ethnological enquiries in the Pacific. Bruny D'Entrecasteaux's party carried out detailed charting of the east coast of Van Diemen's Land and investigation of its inhabitants in April 1792. Appointed during the early years of the Revolution in France, the naturalist for this expedition, Jacques-Julien Labillardière, has often been seen as more egalitarian and sympathetic towards Aborigines than other European observers of the time. However, Labillardière merely believed that, rather than having regressed, the Tasmanians had the potential for 'progress' towards a superior 'agricultural' stage of development. Moreover, he shared with the British officials in New South Wales the assumption that because the women contributed towards food gathering, they were brutally treated and the men therefore were especially savage.[31]

By 1800 the growing need of industry and industrialists to find ethnographic knowledge to facilitate their economic policies was especially evident in the findings of the Baudin expedition. Organized when the Revolution was losing all popular support and becoming reactionary, Baudin's naturalist François Péron, and his colleagues had been selected by a newly formed and equally élitist version of the Royal Society—the Institut National, members of which included France's answer to Joseph Banks, comparative anatomist Georges Cuvier, plus the newly installed First Consul of France, Napoleon Bonaparte. The expedition had been provided with naturalists and mineralogists and had new 'scientific' instructions for the study of 'primitive' people in their natural environment. These guidelines had been prepared by Joseph-Marie Dégérando at the request of a 'Society for the Observers of Man' which had been founded in Paris in November

1799. In addition to Cuvier, its members included biologist Jean-Baptiste Lamarck and physician Philippe Pinel. Dégérando was still prepared to argue that his so-called 'savages' were merely in a state of arrested development and could be made to progress if brought under the influence of philanthropy, guided by science. He declared that, when taught how to trade, savages would learn new 'needs' and 'desires' which would soon take them on to the higher stages of commerce; but already Cuvier's theories were denying even this fate for colonized people. Like Blumenbach, he was developing a research technique designed to prove that certain people were inherently inferior and even with the most well-intentioned and scientific philanthropy in the world could never be made equal to Europeans. To establish his findings Cuvier needed a supply of skulls and whole skeletons, and he gave detailed cannibalistic instructions to voyagers on how to prepare these. Each skeleton was to be

boiled in caustic potash for several hours to remove the flesh, after which the bones were to be put in a bag, labelled and sent back to Europe where they might be reassembled. It would also be desirable to bring back some skulls with the flesh still intact. One had only to soak them in a solution of corrosive sublimate, set them out to dry and they would become hard as wood, their facial forms preserved without attracting insects.

It was true that the sailors might oppose this work as barbarous, but men of science had no such qualms. 'I have put it in spirits and forward it by the Speedy', King wrote to Banks in June 1802, cheerfully dispatching Pemulwuy's skull. After all, this was an age of enlightenment and the progress of knowledge must not be impeded.

François Péron had been taught by Cuvier and was a friend of Dégérando. Presumably he found the native skeletons by no means easy to prepare, for he brought back only one (from Mozambique). However, he used a new invention, a dynamometer, by which he thought he could test accurately the physical strength of the 'natural man'. Predictably, his results showed that physical prowess of European men far surpassed that of any other groups investigated, including Tasmanian and mainland Aborigines, and Malaysian people of Timor. Péron was also responsible for providing numerous verbal pictures denigrating the physical appearance of Aboriginal women. Like other men of his class, he showed a voyeuristic interest in Aboriginal sexuality and even alleged that he had found objective scientific evidence that Aboriginal men were less virile than Europeans, thus explaining their supposedly retarded population growth. [32]

In 1803 Malthus used evidence from New Holland to enlarge on his theory that in human societies it was 'the struggle for existence', the competition for food and other resources, which limited population growth. Needless to say, the Aborigines were cited to make the point in a chapter entitled 'The Checks to Population at the Lowest Stage of Human Society'. In 1809 Lamarck in his *Philosophie Zoologique* declared that the experiences in the lifetime of an animal species could be biologically inherited by its offspring. This theory, which would inform social and biological science until at least the end of the nineteenth century, was derived from information obtained by Baudin and Péron.

In 1826 Dumont D'Urville, commander of another scientific expedition, would describe Flinders's fellow-voyager, Bungaree, in particularly derogatory terms. 'These are stupid brutes of the first degree. They have lived for forty years alongside European civilization, and they have remained as stupid and savage as ever; brandy is the only thing they have understood.' [33]

These views added fuel to the new rationalizations for the conquest of non-European peoples which the ever-growing scientific community had provided and which the liberal industrializing classes now required in its efforts to speed up production and trade. The brief flirtation with allowing colonized people a degree of equality was over. Like the working classes of Europe, indigenous people were to become the object of liberal sociological theories, allegedly grounded in objective scientific fact. The opinions of these theorists flew around the globe at remarkable speed. As early as 1795, for example, philanthropic families in New York were discussing comparative anatomy and 'physiognomy' and even the results of the philanthropic experiments in educating Aboriginal children in New South Wales. [34] In due course, this body of scientific theory would be imported back to the colonies where some of it had originated, and be used by missionaries and land-takers alike to excuse and facilitate the next stage of colonization there. Faster than anyone had expected, the little settlements in New South Wales were already functioning as launching pads for the commercial exploitation of the resources of the Pacific.

4

FREE TRADE

New South Wales and Van Diemen's Land to 1821

IN FEBRUARY 1804 former Judge Advocate David Collins wrote to Governor King from the headquarters camp of a newly established settlement at Sullivan's Cove in Van Diemen's Land:

I found Port Phillip wholly unfit for the settlement, and the idea of fixing one at Port Dalrymple I abandoned . . . because I conceived the local situation of the River Derwent more adapted for commercial purposes. Its position at the southern extremity of Van Diemen's Land gives it an advantage over every harbour yet discovered in these straits, and I entertain a hope that when it is generally known that an establishment is formed, so directly presenting itself as a port of shelter to ships from Europe, America, or India, either for whaling or other speculation, it will be greatly resorted to.[1]

Collins was not wrong. Soon to be known as Hobart, this little camp was destined to become a second major Pacific base securing for British and Sydney traders a lion's share of the commodities to be harvested from the surrounding seas.

By 1800 the commercial function of the British settlements in the Pacific was undergoing further development. On Norfolk Island flax had not been exploited and it had been found that New Zealand timber was much better for shipbuilding. Moreover, as the wreck of the *Sirius* had so grimly proved, the want of a safe anchorage meant that Norfolk Island would never be suitable as a base for shipping. In contrast, Matthew Flinders had shown that the whole of Van Diemen's Land abounded with superb harbours

91

and those around the Derwent River were, he reported, 'capable of receiving all of the British navy'. In addition, he reported, its coastline and offshore islands were alive with seals, whose fur could be utilized as a southern component of the fur trade with Canton or, it was discovered by 1804, sold in England where it was made into a waterproof felt material comparable to beaver. Also, the animals could be boiled down to extract oil, an item of extreme importance in this period before large-scale production of petroleum and vegetable oils.[2] Then, as Collins pointed out, there were the whales. As well as being used as a lubricant, for lighting lamps and in textile production, whale oil was used for candle- and soap-making. Also, the bone, especially from the baby whales, made umbrella frames and corsetry. Long regarded as an essential industry which usefully trained men for the sea, British interest in Pacific whaling had been growing with the decline of the old Greenland fisheries. It was further quickened in 1788–89 when whale merchant Samuel Enderby sent the *Emilia*, manned with experienced Nantucket men, around the Horn and on to a successful venture. Five out of six of the Third Fleet vessels were British whalers and interest in the area was further aroused from 1796 when war with Spain closed the whaling grounds off South America to British ships. By 1802 Enderby was able to inform Banks that one of his vessels had just returned from Port Jackson with 170 tons of sperm oil worth £13 000.

Much to the chagrin of the British, the lucrative sealing, whaling and trading potential of the area south of Port Jackson was, as Governor King wrote in November 1803, starting to be 'encroached upon and Annoyed by the Americans'. As everyone was very much aware, when the British lost the thirteen American colonies they acquired a formidable commercial rival committed to the principles of free trade. By 1804 American vessels were plying the Pacific north and south of Hawaii, and having penetrated the fur trade were buying nearly one quarter as much tea as the East India Company. As early as November 1792 the first American vessel, *en route* to China from the Cape, had called at Port Jackson with goods for sale and within a year numerous American whaling and sealing ships were operating in the area. By May 1804 these audacious and skilled seamen were actually erecting dwellings on the islands around Bass Strait and even building a ship from the remains of the *Sydney Cove*, a trading vessel sent from India with a speculative cargo for Port Jackson

in 1797 and the first of many more ships which would be wrecked
in the treacherous waters east of the Great Australian Bight. By
1811, some fifty-seven American vessels would have visited
Sydney.[3] As if this threat to the strategic and commercial possibilities of the area was not enough, there was also the presence of
the French. As early as May 1802 King was convinced that the
principal object of the Baudin expedition was nothing to do with
collecting botanical specimens or measuring the strength of
Aboriginal men. Rather, the French were looking for a place to
make a settlement similar to the one at Port Jackson, probably on
the northern coast of Bass Strait. They might even be planning to
lay claim to the whole of Van Diemen's Land.

The anxiety of the authorities in New South Wales increased
in June 1802 when Le Géographe and its companion ship Le
Naturaliste called at Port Jackson to take on supplies and to get
medical help for the large proportion of their crew suffering
from scurvy. By December when Baudin left the harbour for an
unspecified destination, rumours were rife around Sydney that he
was about to make a settlement. King responded by sending the
armed schooner Cumberland in pursuit, and a flag was raised,
albeit upside down, on King Island in Bass Strait, right in front of
the French.[4] The British authorities, too, were alarmed. Not
content with mere emblems of possession, in December 1802 they
decided a second colony in the area should be founded without
delay. For its location they chose the extensive harbour at Port
Phillip. Located half-way along Bass Strait on the southern
coastline of the continent, this looked on paper to be an ideal
strategic and commercial site.

In this period of prolonged warfare with France, surplus
manpower available for colonization was extremely limited.
Plans for providing labour and defence in this new settlement
were a scaled-down version of those evolved to establish New
South Wales. One detachment of marines was provided for its
defence, and the settlement was to comprise chiefly male convicts
whose good behaviour was to be encouraged by sending after
them, at the public expense, their wives and families 'as indentured
Servants'. David Collins, now back in Britain and in straitened
circumstances, was appointed Lieutenant-Governor, and the
Reverend Robert Knopwood, an impoverished spendthrift chaplain from the West Indian service, was put in charge of spiritual
matters. In addition to the civil and military personnel, a

government mineralogist, A. W. H. Humphrey, was also appointed. Some 455 persons from this little convoy landed near Sorrento on 9 October 1803.[5]

This first settlement at Port Phillip proved temporary. The soil was found to be 'nothing but a complete bed of sand, and the timber was of so miserable a kind that it was impossible to get a straight piece twelve feet long'. Even worse, the bay was difficult to leave, ships being compelled to wait until they had 'the Top of the Tide' and 'a leading Wind', so the bay would never be of use either as a naval base or for whaling. Deciding to abandon the site, Collins was given permission to move the settlement south to Van Diemen's Land. On 30 January 1804 the little party made their difficult exit from Port Phillip Bay, leaving behind and alive at least one convict absconder. He was William Buckley, who would be found living with the Aboriginal people when the British returned to settle these shores in 1835.[6]

In choosing to make the Derwent the new site for his settlement, Collins was not alone. Already Governor King, in his anxiety to secure these southern waters for British trade, had dispatched another colonization party independently from New South Wales and this was now successfully established at the mouth of that capacious river. Access to the Derwent was unimpeded by the islands and currents which bedevilled Bass Strait and, located midway between the Indian Ocean and the Pacific, it looked likely to become the Cape Town of these southern seas. Under the command of Lietuenant John Bowen, King's miniature version of the First Fleet had sailed from Sydney in August 1803 and was even more reduced than that of Collins. Though both comprised just two vessels, Bowen's ships carried only forty-nine people. They included Jacob Mountgarrett, a surgeon who, like Bowen himself, had only arrived in New South Wales the previous March. There was also one sergeant and seven soldiers of the New South Wales Corps, accompanied by three women and a child. Twenty-one male convict labourers were sent to prepare the ground for the first sowing of grain and, to serve them, three female convicts were provided. Nine cows, one bull, twenty-five ewes and two rams also disembarked from the little vessels, together with some other livestock privately owned by the three free settlers in the party. Even so, reinforced by some forty-two extra male convicts sent in October 1803, this little colony was well established when augmented on 15 February 1804 by the arrival of the group from Port Phillip. Somewhat reluctantly, Bowen was obliged to hand over control to Collins, who immediately decided the site of the existing settlement at Risdon Cove was unsuitable and moved it across the river to a place he named Hobart Town.[7]

Meanwhile, plans were also going ahead to plant a settlement to guard the mouth of the Tamar River at Port Dalrymple. As early as June 1803 the British authorities had decided to transfer there many of their settlers and convicts from Norfolk Island. In the event, most of the settlers from Norfolk Island would be relocated on the Derwent, but on 5 November 1804 an expedition led by Captain Paterson arrived to assess the suitability of the northern site. With him were Mrs Paterson, seventy-four male convicts and two convicts' wives, plus sixty-four members of the New South Wales Corps with their twenty women and fourteen children. In 1807 the principal establishment was moved up the Tamar River as far as its junction with two freshwater rivers named the North and South Esk. The site of this settlement was named Launceston.[8]

By 1810 the authorities were speaking with enthusiasm of the open fertile country that lay between the settlements in the north and south of Van Diemen's Land. According to Surveyor-General John Oxley, the country between Launceston and the River Derwent was blessed with an abundance of deep rich loam along navigable rivers where farm buildings could be constructed out of reach of floods. In 'Many Places the settler would have 100 Acres fit for Cultivation in the same or even less period that it would require to Clear 20 Acres at the principal Agricultural Settlement in New South Wales'.[9] Lieutenant Edward Lord agreed. An officer in the marines who had joined the expedition under David Collins, Lord declared that the new country was spared the formidable mountain range which virtually enclosed Sydney and the Hawkesbury, and the first loaded dray had been driven from Hobart to Launceston without felling a single tree. By 1810 the population of the island had grown to 1321, which was 11 per cent of the total white population now settled in New Holland.[10]

Exploration parties venturing up the high reaches of the Derwent and the Huon Rivers found a beautiful new kind of timber, of fine pale yellow colour. Very light to carry and wonderfully resistant to damage and decay caused by insects, its

measured up to seven feet in diameter, and even more
enient, often already lay fallen on the ground. Clay suitable
for making bricks was abundant, and at Hobart a rushing stream
flowing down from snow-capped Mount Wellington was early
seen to be capable of turning a mill of virtually any dimension.

Even so, as at Port Jackson, in the early years only a limited
number of fit and able-bodied people was available to put
Western technology to the uses of the settlement. In Hobart
during July 1804 the labourers were attacked by scurvy. By
November 1804 eleven convict workmen had died since August,
nine of them from scurvy, among them skilled artificers such as a
sawyer and a brickmaker. A further twenty-one were ill with
the disease. Also, seed sent from England failed to germinate,
livestock perished and dozens of ducks and chickens fell victim to
two new kinds of predatory carnivors. Described as larger and
more deadly than the ones at Port Jackson, and as having bushier
tails, these sported either white spots or black stripes about the
back and became known as the Tasmanian Devil and Tiger
respectively.[11] Nevertheless, these settlements were never in real
danger of collapse for the British authorities were now able to
draw on the experience gained in establishing New South Wales.
More was also known about the southern climate and its animal
and vegetable products, thanks to the navigators and naturalists.
Collins, for instance, during the first winter took to sending
convicts to hunt kangaroos and issued the catch as fresh meat
supplied as rations from the government store. Fish being scarce,
especially in winter, the kangaroos were also hunted by convicts
and settlers on their own account. Convict James Grove declared
that the meat was 'equal in quality to most foreign—not English—
roast beef'; emus, too, were hunted and eaten. Whales were
abundant, and a few were taken, scraps from them being used to
feed the pigs in spite of the fact that, according to Collins, this
diet made their flesh taste like lamp-oil. Up to 1808, kangaroo
remained a major source of fresh meat for Europeans in both the
northern and southern settlements, varying in proportion to the
amount of salt-meat available.[12]

The British authorities were now also aware that the impact of
this pressure placed by the white settlers on the local food
resources would mean war with the Aboriginal inhabitants,
largely repeating the pattern set at Port Jackson, Parramatta and
the Hawkesbury. The authorities had been informed by Bass and

Flinders in 1798 that the local people were 'inferior' to those of the mainland and, as such, even more indifferent to notions of trade. Thus it was unlikely that the officials would be able to make use of internecine struggles such as were developing in Hawaii and Tahiti where dominant families, enriched by trade, were now conveniently fighting each other for supremacy. It was also reasonably certain that the Aboriginal people were not sufficiently numerous to expel the invaders. Consequently, the official instructions to ascertain the number of Aborigines and the likelihood of deriving some advantage from accommodating them, which had been issued to Phillip, were noticeably absent from Collins's instructions. Where Phillip waited almost three years before staging the first official punitive expedition, in the new settlements reprisals began almost immediately.

The catalyst for this first demonstration of the might of the invaders was almost exactly the same. In May 1804 when the Moomairremener people, hunting kangaroos at Risdon, saw fit to relieve a white gamekeeper of his catch, as at Port Jackson when Pemulwuy speared Macintyre, the gamekeeper's master opted for an instant show of force. Lieutenant Moore, in charge of the settlement while Bowen was exploring the Huon area, decided that a large group of Aborigines approaching the camp, though it included women and children, was harbouring malevolent designs; a notion prompted because at the same time, reports were being received that another party of Aborigines was attacking Mr and Mrs Birt at their farm. Moore sent two soldiers to the farm where two Aborigines were shot; while at the camp Surgeon Mountgarrett suggested 'dispersing' the Aborigines there by firing at them with the cannon. After this was done, the survivors were pursued by convicts and soldiers. At least three Aborigines were killed in this affray, and Dr Mountgarrett showed a truly scientific interest in the corpses, offering to dissect one and send the skeleton of the other to colleagues at Port Jackson.

At Port Dalrymple, Colonel Paterson was equally prepared to dispense with the careful diplomacy which had been necessary at Port Jackson in the early years. Having ordered the punitive raid against the Hawkesbury River Aborigines in 1795 he had no qualms about the overt use of violence and force, so when within two days of landing he was confronted by some eighty Aborigines who came into the camp expecting to be recompensed by the trespassers with a variety of gifts, one Aborigine was killed and another wounded. As on the mainland, the Aborigines responded to this treatment by harassing the settlement but there was no way in which they alone could remove the invaders. When Alexander Riley and Private Richard Bent were investigating the possibility of overlanding the surviving cattle up the river to reach the future site of Launceston, they were stopped by about fifty Aborigines, pursued, ambushed and both were speared. However, despite an uncomfortable 15-mile walk back to their boat, the wounded two survived.[13]

As in New South Wales, it was not the intention of the authorities that free settlers of the financial status of Alexander Riley should be inconvenienced by Aboriginal resistance. The son of a London bookseller, Riley's two sisters had married officers of the New South Wales Corps and preceded him to New South Wales where he arrived in June 1804, expecting to make a fortune from trade. Within three months he had been made a magistrate at Port Dalrymple and by 1805 had been appointed by Paterson to run the local commissariat store.[14]

When Van Diemen's Land was founded, officers were forbidden by the authorities to trade, to avoid the disasters which officer trading had caused to emancipist farming. A plan introduced in New South Wales in 1797 and finalized in 1802, to retail consumer goods through the Commissariat Store at reasonable prices, was introduced at the outset in Van Diemen's Land. It followed that the officers never enjoyed quite the same opportunities to charge exorbitant prices as had prevailed in New South Wales until 1800 when the arrival of resident merchants from Madras and London marked the end of their monopoly. The absence of drought and floods, as well as the experience gained by the farmers from Norfolk Island, also provided advantage for small farmers, which had been absent in the older colony. Nevertheless, Van Diemen's Land rapidly became, as Bligh stated in 1809, 'Sydney in miniature'. In February 1805 some of the officers successfully applied to Collins for an advance of special 'commissary notes' equivalent to sterling with which to buy stock and other articles from the captain of the *Lady Barlow*. Others found kangaroo products a lucrative source of business, bringing more profitable returns from the Commissariat than agriculture. Also the officers were permitted to acquire land for farming, the first grants being made to them by January 1806.

Thus, in due course, the officers' control over the government

market through the Commissariat Store and therefore their access
to foreign exchange was similar to that in the older colony. By
1813 even the New Norfolk farmers were becoming heavily
burdened by debt. Unable to secure a high price for their grain or
to lower production costs, many slipped into subsistence farming
and, though still in possession of their land, were wretchedly
clothed and housed. Meanwhile, by 1812 the colony was exporting grain to Sydney and meat from 1815, a practice which, along
with their sales of potatoes and kangaroo skins to New South
Wales, further increased the officers-farmers' access to sterling.[15]
Indeed, in Van Diemen's Land, there were so many opportunities
for blatant favouritism in selling goods to the government market
that former Norfolk Island commissary, William Broughton,
writing to Macquarie in October 1816, declared that such was the
state of the settlement that if, like Sodom and Gomorrah, its fate
depended on finding six honest men, it would be 'swallowed up
in all its iniquity'.

In fact, of course, the line between what constituted acceptable
business practice and what was seen as dishonest was by no means
clear. Broughton was complaining that the secretary of Governor
Davey had the audacity to borrow some grain from the Government Store on the pretence that he needed it for seed, then
exchange it for a cargo of spirits which was available from a
visiting ship. 'This, Sir, is what is called here, *Financiering*', wrote
the aggrieved commissary. Broughton had arrived in 1788 as
servant to Surgeon White. Lacking both capital and powerful
patrons in England, he was one of the few civil officials who
failed to make money from trade.[16]

As in New South Wales, the southern settlements soon proved
to be a veritable speculator's paradise. This was the more so since
in both colonies after 1800 finance raised initially from importing
and from farming could be reinvested in a variety of profitable
maritime activities which, in turn, provided an export staple and
thus leverage for the importation of further goods. Notwithstanding the monopoly of the East India Company, local trading
networks rapidly developed which reached out from both colonies
to enlarge the markets being developed by British and American
investors, westwards to India and the Cape, and across the
Pacific from the coast of Chile to China itself. Of these maritime
industries, one of the most profitable was, as the authorities had
predicted, sealing. One of the first to exploit this market was

Charles Bishop, an American who had established a boiling-works on Cape Barren Island in 1798, and who later partnered Bass in various maritime ventures. By 1800 Robert Campbell was another who had moved into the industry. By 1806 there were some eight private vessels registered in the colony for sealing.

This savage, destructive activity attracted colonial merchants because it was an export industry which improved their access to foreign exchange and because it did not require expensive, sophisticated equipment. The seals, having exchanged their natural habitat to breed on land, were easy prey. Nor did the trade require a highly paid, skilled workforce. A single vessel left groups of hired ex-convict labourers with minimal provisions on the islands of Bass Strait, returning at the merchant's pleasure to pick up the men plus the oil and skins from the animals they had clubbed to death. The men were expected to provide their own shelter on the often treeless and exposed shores by constructing tents out of seal skins. This caused no loss to the merchant, for he himself contracted to pay his labourers on a system of lays, that is, as a fixed percentage of the total yield. As a further saving to the employer, this was not paid till the men were returned to Sydney and then, as often as not, the men had no choice but to sell the skins back to the employer at whatever price he chose to pay. Generally minimal rations were supplied, for the gangs were expected to supplement their diet with fresh muttonbirds, Cape Barren geese, and kangaroos caught by their dogs. Sometimes groups were left marooned on their island prisons long after all of these sources of food were exhausted. Others lost their dinghies after landing on the rocky outcrops where the seals congregated to rear their young. Chance rescues of starving gangs by passing vessels were a feature of the industry from its inception. Other forgotten men set sail in small boats, often of their own construction, to arrive starving at the already hungry settlements in Van Diemen's Land.

As in Chile and Peru, the slaughter of the seals was ruthless and indiscriminate. By 1803 King was concerned that some measure of control was necessary to protect the industry. He was also concerned about the economic exploitation of the men, though only because of the problem which this was causing by increasing the number of women and children left 'on the store'. His regulations regarding pay and labour conditions proved impossible to police, while indiscriminate killing of the seals also continued, the depletion of seal numbers being conveniently attributed to the American gangs.[17]

Much of the early profitability of sealing was also due to the fact that, from its inception, the industry relied on the unpaid services of a large number of Aboriginal women. All around the coast of Van Diemen's Land and along Bass Strait the women were immediately at risk, not only from starvation and disease, but from exploitation by sealing gangs. The women were in great demand partly for sexual purposes and partly because of their bushcraft and the special expertise they developed in hunting seals and making boats. Especially in the early days of the trade, as in Tahiti, some of these women went to the white men with the consent of their family, in this case as part of reciprocal arrangements for the exchange of food. However, in contrast with the fur trade in North America, because the trade in seal skins developed so swiftly, the period in which Aboriginal people were able to control or derive any advantage from it was extremely brief. Also, because the skins were obtained along the coastline, the Europeans had no need to depend on expert 'middle-men' to organize produce from the interior and thus no call to maintain diplomatic relations for any length of time. Because no French settlement had eventuated, opportunities to play rival groups of European traders against each other did not develop.

Thus, the sealing trade became notorious for its abduction of Aboriginal women and girls; others, facing starvation, had no choice but to work for the white men. In 1815 William Stewart, a Sydney trader who had arrived from Calcutta in 1801, informed the Colonial Secretary that small-scale sealing enterprises of some six or seven men using whale-boats were taking Aboriginal women by force. He alleged that they were practising cruel punishments upon any women who failed to catch sufficient seals or attempted to get back to their people. Some were half-hanged, others cut about the head with clubs or flogged with 'Cats made of Kangaroo-sinews'.

In writing about sealing, recent historians, concerned to include the experience of indigenous people in national history, have been drawn to arguments which bestow 'agency' upon the Aboriginal people. Far from being passive victims of Western aggression, the women especially are seen as 'adapting' to the trauma of the sealing invasion and even becoming 'the social guardians and economic exponents of a new society'. No matter how much one might wish to see the Aboriginal people as active makers of their own history and to acknowledge the tenacity with which they defended their land, coped with disease and attempted to lessen the effects of invasion by incorporating aspects of European culture into their own, the fact remains that they could not make their history as they chose. Like other oppressed people, they had no power to determine the choices available to them. Nor did the act of choosing or adapting redress the destruction of traditional community and the economic exploitation which was the source of their suffering.[18]

In 1831 the Arthur regime investigated the number of escaped convicts and ship's deserters living on the islands of Bass Strait and attempted to 'rescue' the women, liberating them from what was seen as 'slavery' and incarcerating them in a mission. No such interference in the industry occurred during the first decades. The early governors were not concerned about whether or not the Aboriginal women were slaves, nor about miscegenation.

Whaling, too, had a devastating impact on coastal people. While deep-sea ventures in search of the sperm whale required more capital than most colonists could as yet raise, all around the coastal bays of Van Diemen's Land shore-based parties in small boats began to hunt the black whalebone or bay whale which came into the shallow waters to breed. In 1818 an English ship caught thirty whales in the Derwent and by the 1820s traders could congratulate themselves that though the seals were almost extinct, and the islands which had sustained the labourers were now overrun with dogs, whaling remained a viable option. By the 1830s bay whaling stations ringed Van Diemen's Land and New Zealand and littered over 3000 miles of coastline from southern New South Wales to Swan River. This was in spite of the fact that local investment in whaling was discouraged by 1809, when any oil harvested by colonial ships had to pay a heavy duty if exported to Britain. Further protection for British whalers was provided from July 1813 when oil bound for Calcutta was taxed if supplied via Hobart or Sydney. However, profits for local investors in the industry improved dramatically from the late 1820s when the duty on whale and seal oil was cut. Deep-sea whaling also flourished at this time, being less affected than bay-whaling by the extermination of the species. Having begun off California, Chile and New Zealand, during the 1820s new whaling fields were discovered in equatorial waters. The industry continued to bring numerous ships into Australian ports until the late 1840s.

Whaling was dangerous and poorly paid work, especially on the ocean-going vessels. Whales in Australian waters could weigh as much as twenty-five elephants, almost as much as the smaller ships, and they could smash the long rowing boats in which the men pursued them. Whalemen also risked losing fingers sliced off by icy ropes or being dragged under murderously cold water when being towed at speed by a huge harpooned animal in its death throes. In return they could expect to be paid with one-sixtieth to one-eightieth of the total commodities produced at the end of a voyage. As in sealing, this method of payment was found advantageous by employers as it induced the men to try to improve the catch and take greater risks.[19]

Vessels also radiated from the eastern Australian ports in search firstly of food and later of luxury commodities like pearl shell and bêche-de-mer (or trepang, an edible sea-slug), for sale in Canton. In Tahiti, aware that the local supply of foods like coconuts, breadfruit and pork were quickly exhausted, to offset future shortages Cook, Bligh, Vancouver and the Spanish had all distributed European seeds and livestock. The Spanish pigs, in particular, had flourished and by 1793, the first of numerous cargoes of pork was collected to augment food supplies in New South Wales. Commercial exploitation of this market began in 1801 when King sent the Porpoise to obtain further supplies. Private trading quickly followed, Garnham Blaxcell and John Macarthur being among those who found a steady market for pork at the government store. It is estimated that over the next twenty-five years some three million pounds of salt pork were supplied to New South Wales, the Islanders being paid with a variety of tools, clothing, arms and ammunition.

What the pork trade was to Tahiti, so sandalwood was to become for Hawaii and much of the South Pacific. Strongly in demand in Canton where it was prized as incense for burning on ceremonial occasions, the trees from which this wood was cut grew up to 2 feet in circumference upon high, inaccessible slopes. Beginning at Fiji (1804–10), followed by the Marquesas (1815–16), Hawaii (1815–28) and finally New Caledonia and Vanuatu (1840s and 1850s), it was soon found that the Pacific people, especially if their traditional economy had already been destroyed by the demands of passing trading and whaling vessels, could be persuaded to cut and supply the timber in exchange for axes, scissors, nails, metal fish hooks and sometimes muskets, powder and shot. As in Tahiti, dependence on these goods locked the people into the developing Pacific trading networks. If persuasion failed then force was used, and in many cases the industry came to rely on bloodshed and brutality equal to sealing at its worst. The sandalwood trade was also extremely wasteful, for the most highly perfumed and therefore most profitable wood was nearest to the roots, so that the trees were literally cut out of the ground and whole stands were rapidly destroyed. This meant that the traders would move on to another area, but in the interim the industry gave rise to the same kind of political upheaval and devastating internecine war as had occurred in Tahiti.[20]

In the Australian colonies, the task of imposing order on developments fell upon the hapless governors. Caught in the transition between mercantilist and industrial capitalism, they found themselves in the impossible position of trying to prop up a form of convict colonization which was quickly becoming anachronistic. With American and French competition in the burgeoning Pacific trade, attempts to protect either the East India Company's monopoly or the system of ex-convict agriculture which had been designed to shield it were now out of touch with economic realities and were therefore, according to the traders, morally and politically indefensible. From Hunter to Macquarie in New South Wales, and from Collins to Sorell in Van Diemen's Land, every administrator became involved in angry confrontations with merchants and traders who declared that the governors were the short-sighted, old-fashioned servants of a despotic state, intent on intervening in a world of business about which they knew nothing and cared less.

At their most extreme, these disputes culminated in the *coup d'état* when, in January 1808, the unfortunate Governor Bligh, having recovered from his débâcle on the *Bounty*, now himself unable to steer the colony through a much more difficult sea of troubles and was once more unceremoniously relieved of his command by a rebellious crew. Arriving in the colony in the wake of disastrous floods in 1806, Bligh had seen agriculture as a priority over commerce and had been even more determined than Hunter and King to stamp out the trade in rum which was ruining so many of the small farmers. Choosing to support the interests of these 'plain sensible farming men of moderate expectation', he soon fell out with the colony's rapacious and powerful 'aristocracy' of traders. On 26 January, the twentieth anniversary of white settlement, the choleric John Macarthur persuaded his fellow officers that it was necessary to arrest the Governor in order to put an end to a brutal 'tyranny'. A move which had recent precedents in other British colonies, the arrest was also expertly timed to advance the traders' maritime activities, since the ship *Elizabeth* was setting off for China from Port Jackson loaded with sandalwood, while the brig *Harrington*, under a joint agreement between the captain, Macarthur, Blaxcell, and Surgeon Thomas Jamison, slipped in with an illegal cargo of goods from China. This sold for £20 000, well over half of which was clear profit.[21]

Hobart's equivalent to John Macarthur and Major Johnston was Lieutenant Edward Lord. Receiving his first land grant in January 1806, by October of that year Lord was the largest stockholder in the colony. No supporter of Bligh, in April 1808 Lord visited Lieutenant-Colonel Foveaux, who had taken over in Sydney, and obtained from him an appointment as a magistrate and an additional grant of 500 acres which he took up near New Norfolk. When David Collins died suddenly on 24 March 1810 Lord had his own chance to become Governor of the colony. He applied to the Secretary of State in Britain to be Collins's successor, meanwhile taking charge of affairs and, it is said, burning all the papers at Government House immediately after Collins's death. Though these plans were thwarted by Macquarie, Lord did succeed in being granted a huge 3000 acres of land through the influence in Britain of his brother, a member of parliament. By 1813 he owned his own brig, was a major importer of foreign goods, and was on good terms with the new governor, Thomas Davey. By 1820 he was said to be the richest man in Van Diemen's Land, the owner of three ships, warehouses at both the major ports, 6000 cattle, 7000 sheep and 35 000 acres of land.[22]

Fellow merchant and shipowner, John Ingle, was another with whom it was wisest to be friends. A member of David Collins's initial contingent to Port Phillip, in October 1805 Ingle became a leading merchant by virtue of his friendship with Lord and obliging relatives in England, who were on hand to despatch the cargoes of merchandise he then sold in the colony. He is also said to have benefited handsomely from the extravagant arrangements

made by Lord for David Collins's funeral procession on which
the government incurred commissariat spending of over £500. By
1813 he declared that he was the owner of goods worth more
than £23 000.

Perhaps most characteristic of the kind of adventurers with
whom the governors had to contend was Rowland Loane. He
arrived at the Derwent in 1809 on his own ship *Union* with a
cargo of goods worth £20 000. On his passage up the river he was
intercepted by the deposed Governor Bligh, who after more than
a year of negotiations with the military officers regarding his
departure, had finally been prised out of Sydney on the *Porpoise*.
At the end of March 1809 the ex-Governor was anchored on the
Derwent, hoping to win the support of Lieutenant-Governor
Collins for his cause, and meanwhile investigating every boat
which came up or down the river 'on the Public Service'. Much
to the irritation of Collins, who saw this as a slight upon his
authority and status, all such boats were ordered 'to come within
Hail of his Ship, upon pain of being fired at if they did not
comply'. Unperturbed by these developments, Loane seized the
opportunity of going on board and clinching a quick deal with
Bligh, upon which the disgruntled ex-Governor found himself
the owner of three-and-a-half tons of rice, eight casks of meat,
three hundredweight of sugar, and 200 gallons of spirits. After
settling this transaction, Loane went on to Hobart where he sold
his ship and went into business as a general merchant and
speculator in land. Meanwhile Bligh was destined to put his
purchases to use since Collins did not co-operate in his cause and
he therefore remained on the Derwent until the arrival of
Macquarie in January 1810.[23]

Despite this particular piece of colonial 'financiering', like the
other governors Bligh was by no means opposed to private
enterprise. What all wished to discountenance were the extremes
of profit-taking which the absence of currency and the location
of the colonies on developing Pacific trade routes had made
possible. Ruthless, *laissez-faire* business practices, devoted to the
short-term profits of local speculators, might serve to secure for
British manufacturers sources of raw materials, but they also
jeopardized the experiment in convict colonization and the
interests of the British ruling class.

The governors were especially vulnerable to accusations of
tyranny because, in order to administer the initial experiment,

they had been awarded virtually absolute power. Though answerable to the British government, the governors of New South Wales could appoint justices of the peace, pardon convicts, remit punishments, regulate trade, grant land and proclaim marital law. They also enjoyed wide powers over the legal system. The Court of Criminal Jurisdiction was composed of the Judge Advocate and six military or naval officers appointed by the governor, while the Civil Court was composed of the Judge Advocate and two other appointees. In Van Diemen's Land, the powers of the lieutenant-governor were more circumscribed for he was subordinate to the governor of the older colony; no courts of law had been created there and all prisoners had to be sent to Sydney for trial. Even so, the arbitrary powers of the lieutenant-governors were strongly resented by the free settlers, who rightly saw that all these arrangements were foreign to the political system in England and its colonies of settlement.[24]

It was also true that, in attempting to strike a balance between the old demands of the East India Company and the rapidly developing system of Pacific free trade, some of the governors' decisions seemed both arbitrary and unfair. In January 1805 King had permitted an illegal cargo of oil to be dispatched to London on the *Lady Barlow*. This was the property of Robert Campbell, an agent for a Calcutta business house, who had arrived in the colony in 1800. In contrast, the following May, King decided to refuse permission for an American vessel, *Criterion*, to land a cargo from Canton. Similarly, in September 1806 Bligh disallowed Edward Lord and his colleagues to dispatch a ship to China via Fiji, but next February permitted Campbell's brig *Perseverance* to sail to Canton.

However, from discouraging the enterprise of men like Ingle and Loane, Riley or even the officer-traders themselves, the governors saw their role as that of supporting commerce and trade, not only by authorizing land grants and providing a market for foodstuffs but also by the construction of the roads, hospitals, schools and other necessary public buildings on which further economic expansion would be based. The British state aimed to facilitate, not to oppress, colonial enterprise. Thus it was that Hunter had welcomed the discovery of coal in 1797, and King had pushed further exploration for this product around the Hunter and Georges Rivers by 1802, sending samples for the perusal of Joseph Banks. The Admiralty encouraged notions of exporting timber, iron, flax, indigo, and bark for tanning leather. Lord Hobart had ensured the appointment of mineralogist Humphrey and Castlereagh instructed Bligh to experiment with growing coffee. As a House of Commons committee, reporting on the transportation system in 1812 pointed out, the aim was to improve the colony's natural and commercial advantages for without so doing 'the exertions and industry of the convicts' could not be advantageously called into action during their servitude, and 'but little inducement would be held out to them to become settlers after their emancipation'.

Some of the governors themselves took part in the profit-making from colonial trade. Governor Davey was granted 3000 acres of land at Coal River (Newcastle) and acquired 5000 more by grant when he was replaced by Sorell in 1817. Governor Bligh began office in New South Wales with 1345 acres of land around Sydney, gallantly granted him by Governor King, in return for which Bligh granted Mrs King 790 acres at Werrington which she graciously named 'Thanks'.[25]

Free settlers who were beginning to be attracted to the colonies by the possibilities of trade were given every encouragement. Garnham Blaxcell, who arrived in 1802 as acting purser on the *Buffalo*, was appointed by King to several influential positions, such as deputy commissary from which he gained a foothold in successful trading ventures. Similarly, the ambitious Blaxland brothers, friends of Joseph Banks, though they thought themselves entitled to much more assistance than they received and became the avowed enemies of both Bligh and Macquarie, were in fact provided with a free passage for themselves, their wives, children and servants. Arriving in New South Wales in 1806 they were also presented with stores, livestock and equipment, plus huge land grants and numerous convict labourers. Thomas Birch, medical officer on a whaler which arrived in Hobart in 1808, who invested in whaling, town land and the importation of spirits, met no opposition when he constructed a 60-ton schooner and a 120-ton brig, in spite of the theoretical prohibition on the building of local craft. By 1816 Birch was said to own Hobart's finest house which he leased, on occasion, both to Governors Macquarie and Sorell.

Designed to protect the East India Company's monopoly and deter the escape of convicts, the rule against boat building had been in force since 1788 and had been restated by Hunter as recently as 1797. However, ship construction was to become one of the most lucrative local industries, with some 120 vessels being registered in New South Wales by 1821, the majority of them locally built. Indeed, by the time Birch began his operations, the governors had tacitly recognized that the importance of the Hawkesbury grain trade, of coal and cedar from the Hunter and especially of the need to develop the local sealing industry, far outweighed any proscription of the Company on the construction of ships.[26]

Just as the governors did not intervene in the traders' ruthless treatment of the Aboriginal people, or their exploitation of their labourers and of natural resources, so also in their relationships with their business partners the traders were given a free hand. In the days before the growth of banks, limited liability companies and other institutions of finance capital, the scope for defrauding one's partner was immense. The practices and the principles of Alexander Berry, for instance, were not unusual. A surgeon in the service of East India Company vessels since 1802, Berry was one of those who used the space allotted to officers on the Company ships to bring out goods for sale on their own behalf. By 1806 this had netted him sufficient capital to charter a ship and purchase a speculative cargo of goods from the Cape for sale in India. Like so many of the traders, Berry needed a partner to make this venture a viable proposition and he found one in a former student and friend from the Edinburgh Medical School, Francis Shortt. Learning at the Cape of the market for provisions in the British penal colonies, the partners altered their plans, purchased a Spanish prize-ship which they renamed the *City of Edinburgh* and filled her with a cargo of supplies including 22 000 gallons of wines and spirits to be sold in Van Diemen's Land and New South Wales. Leaving Shortt at the Cape, Berry sailed with the goods, disposing of many of them at Port Dalrymple, despite the fact that in 1807 Governor Bligh, concerned about the threat of Van Diemen's Land trade to both Sydney and London mercantile interests, had closed all its ports to shipping. Arriving at Port Jackson in January 1808 just two weeks before Bligh's deposition, Berry curried favour with the military junta and soon disposed of the remainder of the rum and the other goods, many of which were obligingly sold for him by Simeon Lord, a local trader, who in this way realized some £15 000 on Berry's behalf.

Berry had agreed with Shortt to return to the Cape with a

cargo of sawn timber plus the remaining profits, but instead seized an opportunity offering to contract with the government for the removal of the Norfolk Island settlers to Van Diemen's Land, for which Colonel Johnston, who had replaced the Governor, thoughtfully offered payment in the form of dressed colonial timber. This operation took four months to complete, by which time Foveaux had been appointed Acting-Governor in New South Wales. He alleged no timber was available to honour the contract. While awaiting the outcome of legal action Berry entered into a new partnership with Simeon Lord to obtain a speculative cargo of sandalwood, pork, and timber from the Pacific.

Meanwhile, at the Cape Shortt had received no payments from Berry and was being harassed by their creditors. He dispatched an agent to Sydney to obtain from Lord the profits due to him from the sale of the initial cargo, and to intercept the bills of exchange which Berry had drawn on Simeon Lord's London agent in Sydney. Shortt's agent arrived at Port Jackson too late to claim the bills before they were dispatched to London aboard the *Boyd* and, in the end, it was Berry who intercepted the bills. His *City of Edinburgh*, loading timber in New Zealand, heard that the *Boyd*, in pursuit of a similar cargo, had been attacked by a party of Maoris. Among the passengers were the first wife of the fastidious commissary, William Broughton, who had been returning to London and little Betsy Broughton, aged five, who was one of only four survivors. Sailing to the scene of this débâcle, in one stroke, the lucky speculator Berry rescued the daughter of a key figure in the colony's financial transactions, forestalled the attempts of his erstwhile partner Shortt to get his hands on the bills, and collected a valuable cargo of sandalwood, pork, and New Zealand softwood spars. He completed his coup by sailing around the Pacific for another two years, thus avoiding his partner, and picking up some extra profit from trade down the South American coast.

Eventually Berry lost the *City of Edinburgh*, her cargo and the bills in a storm off the Azores in 1813, but the ship and the cargo had been heavily insured and in Cadiz Berry found another partner. This was London agent Edward Wollstonecraft, who agreed to handle the insurance claims and contribute to new trading ventures. By 1819 the new partners would be in Sydney ready to seek fresh fields of fortune and adventure. The unlucky

Francis Shortt pursued Berry for payment of the debt till the end
of his life which, fortunately for Berry, was not an unduly long
one for he died at Port Jackson in 1827. Berry was permitted to
seek his fortune abroad while powerful friends in the colony,
Reverend Samuel Marsden and E. S. Hall, defeated the claims of
his old partner in court in 1813. It was more than a decade before
Berry was ordered to pay a mere £6000 to close the original
partnership.[27]

Lawyers did well as traders flourished, for colonial businessmen
were extremely litigious. Moreover, members of the legal profession participated in trading activities and adopted the attend-
ant moral values which were permeating society in the colonies
and Europe. 'I am sure you will be pleased to hear that my profits
upon a small quantity [of spirit] I bought at Rio, and some wine I
bought at the Cape, will pay for the furnishing of my house', Ellis
Bent, the new Deputy Judge Advocate wrote to his brother soon
after arrival in Sydney in 1810. 'For 57 gallons of brandy, which
cost me £17/2/-, I have £142/10/- and, for a pipe of Cape wine
which cost me £20, I can get £120 whenever I like'. Bent also
trafficked in private promissory notes, then still commonly used
instead of coined money and which were convertible at a sub-
stantial discount into the sterling of a treasury bill. He also
insisted that all payments by his clients were made in sterling.
Comfortably installed in the new house which Macquarie had
built specially for him, and with over 2000 acres of land also
provided by the Governor, Bent expected to be making £1000 a
year from stock-breeding alone by the end of 1813.[28]

Governors' attempts to regularize the colonies' monetary
system formed another area of potential collision with the immediate material interests of the traders. As early as March 1810
Macquarie asked the British authorities for permission to establish
a bank, as a solution to the shortage of credit and cash. For many
of the colonists, transactions continued to be paid by barter.
Wages were still often paid in rum and tobacco. The abundance
of personal promissory notes was also a problem. Known as
'currency' because they were peculiarly local in origin, some fell
apart from constant handling; others were forgeries; and not all
were of equal value, for some people at all stations of life made a
habit of writing such notes and then declaring themselves bankrupt. Yet while there was a shortage of exports relative to
imports and British expenditure in the colonies, sterling would

remain at a premium and opportunities would abound for traders to capitalize on the varying value of 'currency'.

Macquarie's first request for a bank having been refused, he was promised instead a shipment from India of £10 000 worth of Spanish silver dollars with which to replace the system of barter and promissory notes. Planning to increase the effectiveness of this measure, Macquarie multiplied the dollars' value by stamping out of the centre of each one a 'dump' which was equal to about one-quarter of the original coin. Issued from January 1814, the new coins were nevertheless insufficient to replace all payments in the colony except those made by store receipts and official commissariat notes. The situation was not helped by the refusal of Bent to ban recognition of the promissory notes in the courts. Nor was the problem improved by an agreement undertaken in 1813 by a 'commercial society' of leading traders, to accept no promissory notes except those issued by themselves at an agreed exchange of 50 per cent premium on sterling. While some traders made short-term profits on promissory notes, future commercial expansion would be better served by creating a bank which would help regularize the monetary system and provide easier credit facilities, while also providing respectable gains for its shareholders. Late in 1816, therefore, Macquarie called a meeting of the magistrates and principal merchants in Sydney, and Alexander Riley, J. T. Campbell and Drs D'Arcy Wentworth and William Redfern were among those who agreed on the utility of forming a trading bank, which opened the following year. In Van Diemen's Land a similar bank was formed in 1823 with Edward Lord and former officer of the New South Wales Corps, Anthony Fenn Kemp, prominent among the seventy-three shareholders, most of whom were Hobart merchants and storekeepers.[29]

During this early period, even a few emancipists were able to enter this world of contracts and courts, wheeling and dealing. However, they only did so by fully absorbing the rampant individualism of the commercial world and in particular, by absolutely betraying allegiances to each other. The few among them who were able to avoid spending the rest of their lives in wage labour or toiling on their 30-acre plot mostly began by retailing goods on behalf of the officer-traders who, wishing to conceal both their association with the lowly status of trade and their personal connection with the extortionate prices they were charging, declined to be seen behind the counter of a shop. Thus, assigned convicts, soldiers, and in some cases women, were given a chance to profit in a small way from the trading networks which were developing. Simeon Lord, serving a seven-year sentence for stealing cloth when he arrived in 1791, was one who had moved into the ranks of the affluent in this way. Assigned to Captain Rowley, Lord retailed spirits and general merchandise purchased by the officer-traders. By September 1798 he bought a warehouse and other buildings in Sydney, and by 1800 had launched himself into a long career as a trader whose activities ranged from sealing and sandalwood to pastoralism.

Also prominent among the few emancipists who gained entrance to the world of the merchant capitalists was Henry Kable. Sentenced for fourteen years for burglary in 1783, Kable had followed the conventional means by which convict men improved their lot, being appointed first as an overseer and then as a constable, before being dismissed in 1802 for illegally buying pigs from a visiting ship. By 1800 he had accumulated sufficient capital, probably by working as a middleman between the officers and the Sydney consumers, to enter what became a major field for the ex-convict merchants, the sealing industry. Joining forces with emancipist boat-builder James Underwood, Kable moved from exporting seal skins to a wide range of speculations, including sandalwood and whale products, in partnership with Simeon Lord. Meanwhile he bought up the land grants of fellow ex-convicts, in some cases before the land was even occupied. By 1811 he owned a store and a brewery at Windsor.[30]

A sprinkling of women also moved into entrepreneurial roles, acquiring shops and especially inns of their own. A list of liquor-houses issued in Sydney in 1815 showed that thirteen out of a total of sixty-seven were in the names of women, at least four of whom had been convicts and one had a ticket-of-leave. Most of these women acquired their assets through the death of a trader-husband or de facto husband. One such was Mary Reibey. Sentenced for horse-stealing in 1790, in 1794 she married Thomas Reibey, an employee of the East India Company's vessel *Royal Admiral* in which she had been transported. He acquired land on the Hawkesbury and began a business transporting grain to Sydney. From this he raised sufficient capital to use his former association with the East India Company and began a small importing business at a trading establishment in Sydney, which he named Entally House, after a district in Calcutta. By 1805 he joined a partnership which enabled him to enter the sealing trade. Two years later he and his partner had bought the schooner *Mercury* to facilitate trade with the Pacific Islands. In 1811 his death and that of his partner left Mary Reibey in charge of the business, which she continued to manage successfully till her death in 1855.[31]

Some emancipists also prospered by developing the colony's nascent secondary industries, of which flour-milling was perhaps the most important before 1821. The most modern mill was run by a steam-engine imported by a free settler, John Dickson, who had arrived with it in 1813, but it was emancipist Samuel Terry who was one of the largest suppliers of flour to that most risk-free of markets, the government. Convicted of theft in 1800, by the time Terry's sentence expired in 1807 he had distinguished himself by serving in the Parramatta Loyal Association, had been self-employed as a stone-mason at Parramatta and had set up a shop there which he ran with the help of convict Mary Shipley, with whom he lived from 1801. By 1810 Terry had a son by Rosetta Madden, a widow of some means who had arrived free on the *Hillsborough* in 1799, probably with a convict husband. Mrs Madden was one of those women in the colony who acquired a business upon the death of a spouse. Terry went on to prosper through the inn which he acquired upon marrying her in 1810, and also through farms on the Nepean River and in the Illawarra, as well as from dealing in city allotments after Macquarie began to excise small grants in built-up areas. By 1820 he had 1450 cattle, 3800 sheep and 19 000 acres of land, which comprised almost exactly one-half of the amount of land then held by former convicts. Like the officer-traders, Terry was extremely litigious. By 1821 he had brought at least twenty-eight actions in the Supreme Court and was known to be assiduous in collecting his debts. Like the officers, too, he had acquired a considerable portion of his wealth through the liquor trade, though as a retailer his dealings there were more conspicuous than theirs. Thus it was he who became a special target for accusations, not only for extracting extortionate profits, but also for encouraging small settlers to become intoxicated at his inn and sign away their possessions as security for debts.[32]

The governors of this period had no objections if some emancipists were moving into these entrepreneurial roles. Indeed, they actively encouraged it. Just as they did not as yet censure the sexual liaisons of colonial gentlemen, so too they were aware that the small number of emancipists moving into business could only enlarge the much needed colonial employer class. For instance, D'Arcy Wentworth, a medical practitioner who had been advised to transport himself to Botany Bay in the course of being prosecuted for highway robbery in 1787, was permitted a successful career as a government medical officer. Though falling out with Bligh, who court-martialled him for putting convalescent patients to work for his private advantage, in 1810 Wentworth was appointed a magistrate and, in partnership with Garnham Blaxcell and Alexander Riley, successfully tendered for the construction of a new and capacious hospital to replace the old one at Dawes Point, the agreed price including a three-year monopoly on the importation of rum. Wentworth was further favoured by Macquarie in being appointed principal surgeon of the hospital and being permitted to pursue his commercial activities virtually full-time while the day-to-day affairs of the new institution, completed in 1817, were run by another emancipist surgeon, William Redfern. Indeed, it was Macquarie in particular who followed the spirit of the old formula of promoting industrious ex-convicts to positions of power, a policy which won him the special ire of the increasingly jealous 'exclusive' class.

Despite the common aim of governors and merchants to develop the colonial economy, each group was committed to a different method of achieving this aim. There could never be peace between them. Perhaps there would have been more than one 'rum rebellion' but for the fact that, except in the case of the unlucky Bligh, the traders did not have full influence over the army. As it was, their disputes with the governor more often merely culminated in a furious and petty correspondence with his superiors. When Macquarie declined to grant John Macarthur more land or to pay his price for pure-bred sheep, Macarthur used family connections in London to destroy the Governor's reputation and precipitate his recall. In 1818, ex-military officer and Van Diemen's Land trader Anthony Fenn Kemp attacked Sorell's personal life, pretending to take great exception to the fact that the Governor chose to be seen publicly with Mrs Kent, an officer's wife with whom he was living at Government House. In fact, Sorell's liaison with Mrs Kent dated from his term as Deputy Adjutant-General of the British forces at the Cape from 1807–11, and she had accompanied him to Van Diemen's Land when he took up his appointment as Lieutenant Governor in April 1817. In 1824 Sorell, too, was removed from office.[33]

For their part, the governors responded by using the very considerable powers they enjoyed, dismissing traders from the magistracy, denying them convict servants or, in some cases, imprisoning them for misdemeanours. This was not because they disapproved of profit-taking, but because they believed that the traders must play by the rules. To ruin too many emancipist farmers and to traffic too blatantly in their land was to upset prematurely the blueprint for convict colonization before the land had been cleared and brought under cultivation. By refusing too often to pay debts, the traders were challenging the law without which commerce would be turned into chaos. By regularly evading government duties they were challenging the whole basis of mercantilist capitalism. The traders, however, were in an unusually strong position to pursue economic self-interest and make their own rules because of the growing political strength of the industrial lobby in Britain and its attacks on the old mercantilist economic system. Men like Macarthur, for example, though obliged to concoct devious schemes to evade the East India Company's charter and trade in their own ships between Fiji, Canton and Calcutta, were well aware that though the removal of the Navigation Laws was not on the immediate political agenda, the demise of the East India Company was only a matter of time, a point which was proved in 1813 when its charter was not renewed.

Moreover, mercantilist economic theory was being further discredited. Claiming to have advanced on Adam Smith and the Physiocrats, new advocates of free trade such as S. de Sismondi, James Mill and David Ricardo gained public attention between 1800 and 1820. Where Smith's method was now seen as insufficiently scientific and his economic principles as too static, these new political economists claimed to be advancing towards certain knowledge of progressive and evolving laws which controlled the means by which wealth arose, was distributed or destroyed. Collectively, their arguments provided the traders (and subsequently some historians) with a classic rationale for attacking any intervention by governors in the economic sphere as misguided and uneconomic, a muddle-headed attempt to keep the colonies as dismal 'prisons' instead of permitting the flowering of free trade and the wealth and liberty which this was said to engender. As if this was not enough, the rhetoric of individual liberty was being developed by Jeremy Bentham in his writings on colonization, economics and constitutional law. Long opposed to convict transportation and mercantilist colonization, Bentham's pamphlet *A Plea for the Constitution of New South Wales*, published in 1802, had argued that there was a legal loophole in the documents establishing the governors' authority to make laws, and consequently their autocratic power was not only morally repugnant but unconstitutional. Applying the positivist method and pleasure-pain psychology of his Panopticon ideal to political organization, by 1810 he had formulated his influential *Catechism of Parliamentary Reform* and by 1820, together with Mill, had become the principal theorist of Philosophical Radicalism, a new branch of traditional English liberalism closely geared to the needs of the industrial middle class.

Given these developments, it was small wonder that the colonial traders were prepared to stage miniature declarations of independence of their own. For though, like the British mercantilists, they owed their economic status to buying cheap and selling dear, they borrowed their political tactics and their justifying rhetoric from developing liberalism. Benthamite ideals provided them with both a political and economic rationale, not only in 1808 but in 1814 when Ellis and Jeffrey Hart Bent, having declined to appear in court with three emancipist lawyers, George Crossley, Edward Eager and George Chartres, challenged the right of the Governor even to enquire into their case. Any such action on the part of an autocratic governor, they declared, was inconsistent with the special dignity and independence of the British judicial system. To deal with the problem, the Secretary of State was obliged to remove the Bents from office and replace them with John Wylde as Judge Advocate and Barron Field as Judge of the Supreme Court.[34]

Indeed, by 1814, allegations that the governors' powers were equivalent to those of a Nero or a Caligula were entering a new phase. This was the case especially in New South Wales where, between 1812 and 1815, an economic depression resulted in a shake-out in the ranks of the traders. Caused partly by a local glut of goods from India plus the onset of drought, the depression effectively removed some of the traders from the scene. Garnham Blaxcell and Alexander Riley were among those who left the colony, while John Macarthur, back in England from 1809 to 1817 awaiting court martial for his part in the deposition of Bligh, also suffered a series of reversals which marked the end of his mercantile experiments. The abolition of the Government Store in 1814 was intended to widen the market for a new generation of professional merchants who began arriving from 1815. In Van Diemen's Land, though merchants were spared the rigours of the depression by virtue of their exports of grain to New South Wales during the drought, these years were also a turning-point, with new merchants like Joshua Fergusson, George Gatehouse and Thomas Kent arriving from around 1816.[35]

For survivors of the depression and many of the new arrivals, the conflict with the governors was beginning to change. Although in New South Wales Macquarie's implacable opponents successfully secured his recall in 1821, factions among the colonial élite would move towards actually allying themselves with the governors and against a new colonial liberal group comprised largely of wealthy emancipists. 'If the colonists were not restricted from this fishery', thundered William Wentworth, native-born son of the emancipist surgeon, writing of the whaling industry in 1819,

it would soon become an immense source of wealth to them . . . But it is in vain that nature has been thus lavish in her bounties to them; in vain do their seas and harbours invite them to embark in these inexhaustible channels of wealth and enterprize . . . What a miserly system of legislation is it which thus locks up from its own subjects a fund of riches, that might administer to the wants, and contribute to the happiness of thousands!'[36]

Wentworth need not have worried. By 1819 the struggle between mercantilists and industrialists in Britain was also entering a new phase. Though the old ruling class of aristocrats and traders was still firmly entrenched, industrialists were growing in number and wealth. Even better, their spokesmen—the liberal theorists—were beginning to drop their former hostility to colonies and to perceive a new and enlarged function for them as repositories for British capital investment and markets for manufactured goods, in a new kind of empire which would be based on free trade. Indeed, all of the cruelties, the massacres, the starvation and ecological disasters unleashed by the Western demand for tropical food stuffs, corsetry and sealskin hats, were about to be eclipsed by a new invasion of speculative traders. The catalyst for this was the development of a new market—that of the recently industrialized woollen industry in Britain and its demand for fine merino wool.

5

INVASION OF A CONTINENT

Exploration, Survey, and Pastoral Capitalism
1813–1832

IN 1829 THE *Caroline*, a copper-bottomed, full-rigged ship of 340 tons, pitched and tossed her way down the South American coast past Rio. On board, recently relieved of their precious fleece but rugged in British flannel against the cold, were 150 merino sheep. This little ark and her helpless cargo were bound for Swan River, a new British colony on the south-west coast of the land the Dutch had called New Holland. The vessel had been chartered for the voyage by a Sussex yeoman farmer, Thomas Henty, and on board going out as emigrants were three of his sons, together with thirty-three servants and their families. They included a carpenter, shepherds, and stockmen who had signed on to serve for five years in return for a free passage and £20 a year with board. Neither they nor their employees planned on ever going back.[1] Though the Hentys hoped to profit from farming and trading speculations in the new colony, at the centre of their plans were the merino sheep. By 1815 increasing competition from the United States had begun to threaten the great and steady wealth which, since 1770, British planters and manufacturers had won from their monopoly of the cotton industry. Casting about for a supplementary source of profit, the British industrialists sought to improve the long-established woollen manufactory. By now they had successfully developed not only the technology to mechanize the industry but also new overseas pastures on which to grow quality fine wool. To feed their hungry machines and find markets for their capital and their manufactured goods they would seek control of nothing less than whole continental interiors and their people, not just access to coastal hinterlands and informal mastery of the waterways of the world.

As in India and Canada, so in Australia the needs of the industrialists entailed the acquisition of unprecedented amounts of territory and new methods of colonization. The colony on which the Hentys' hopes were fixed was quite different from that founded in Van Diemen's Land twenty-five years before. Swan River was established by British entrepreneurs who saw the colony as a field of investment for gentlemen of means, who would be willing to risk their capital and their own persons by settling overseas. For this purpose they would be granted a great deal more land than the meagre 30 acres permitted to ex-convict settlers in the eastern colonies. Also, since they disliked the concept of a captive labour force, there were to be no convict 'slaves' at Swan River. Instead, the new gentlemen immigrants would import 'free' labourers, bound by legal contract to serve them for a fixed number of years. The ideal was to reproduce nineteenth-century British rural society in microcosm, transplanting squires and parsons, their wives, children and servants in order to produce wool and further develop British commercial dominance in the Antipodes.

Prominent among the investors in this new concept of colonization was Thomas Peel. The nephew of the man who had founded the British cotton manufactory and cousin of the Cabinet Minister, in 1828 Peel had joined a syndicate of financiers negotiating with the Colonial Office to found the colony as a business proposition. They proposed to transport 10 000 emigrants, their stock and supplies, to the Swan River within four years, placing them each on blocks of 200 acres, if the Colonial Office would grant the Company four million acres of land.[2] Though these discussions lapsed, by now the authorities at the Colonial Office were moving towards the idea of a new colony occupying not merely the Swan River area but the entire western third of the continent. Such an acquisition would function both as a southern extension of the empire in India plus, in effect, lay claim to the whole of Australia.

The first steps were taken in 1824 when a warship under the command of Captain James Bremer was dispatched to establish settlements at Apsley Strait and Port Essington, midway across the northern coastline of the continent. The founding of these outposts had been initially advised by Captain P. P. King (son of the former governor), who had charted the coast from 1818 to 1822 and who saw the region as a second Singapore. The East India Company and other British merchants had also been interested, wishing to protect their trade routes to China and forestall Dutch claims to the area. However, the commercial viability of this northern coast, which European visitors had for so long found inhospitable, remained uncertain. The first British trading ships which ventured into the area were captured by pirates. Fresh water and harbour facilities were deficient at sites located close to the routes of the Indonesian fishermen, who were expected to provide trepang for exchange with Canton. In August 1826 a military detachment was sent from Sydney to found another base at nearby Melville Island, where trepang had been found in the straits.

As had happened so often before, French ambition stimulated the annexation of the continent's remaining third. Where no British officer had ever surveyed the southern coast between Cape Leeuwin and Shark Bay, no less than four French scientific missions, beginning with Freycinet in 1817, had explored Australian waters—Duperrey in 1822, Hyacinthe de Bougainville in 1824 and Dumont D'Urville in 1826. Fears were growing that these visits masked a more sinister interest in the fertile southwest portion of the continent to which the French had already theoretically laid claim. Indeed, it was true that by this time economic and political change in France was creating a pool of convicts who were considered a potential overseas labour force. In 1819 a Report on Transportation actually recommended founding a French version of Botany Bay on the south-west coast. Although French interest later shifted to the less provocative location of New Zealand, in November 1826 Governor Darling dispatched military parties to prepare for settlements at Westernport and King Georges Sound. Darling had arrived in New South Wales in November 1825 following a four-year term of office by Governor Sir Thomas Brisbane. His settlements at King Georges Sound proved to be the basis of permanent colonization in that area. This was followed early in 1827 by a survey of the area around Swan River with a view to assessing its strategic and commercial possibilities.[3]

In charge of this Swan River expedition was Captain James Stirling, a naval officer who had a special interest in the project. In 1823 he had married Ellen Mangles, whose father was a director of the East India Company and owner of extensive interests in the East Indies. Stirling hoped the temperate Swan River region would become the hub of trading patterns in the area, exporting oil, seal skins, and trepang to China, and horses and grain to India and Mauritius (now, happily, also a British possession). Returning to Port Jackson in March 1827, starry-eyed at the prospect of profits, he reported wide grassy plains, rich loam and abundant water. He urged an immediate settlement and asked to be made its commandant.[4] The new Secretary of State for the Colonies, Sir George Murray, was a close friend of the Stirling and Mangles families. In due course it was decided that the settlement would be a crown colony governed by Stirling but largely developed by outside capital. Large grants of land were to be made to independent settlers in proportion to the number of labourers and the amount of stock and equipment they brought with them.

Peel was granted priority of choice of 250 000 acres with a further 250 000 after he landed 400 settlers. He, in turn, formed an association which undertook to grant 200 acres to every person who brought out one male and one female emigrant. Individuals who paid their own passage were to receive 100 acres each. The association also undertook to select artisans and labourers for Swan River who were to be paid three to five shillings a day and could qualify for a 50-acre grant if prepared to be indentured to the association for five years. The first ship sent by the association, the *Gilmore* with 179 emigrants, arrived in December 1829, too late to qualify for land grants. Peel proved a hopeless organizer and many of 'his' immigrants went hungry.

Meanwhile, Charles Fremantle was hastily despatched from the Cape to take possession of the entire western side of the continent. Arriving in May 1829 Fremantle found the river more difficult of access than Stirling had suggested, but duly landed, raised the flag and was comfortably in possession when the official party arrived from Britain in June. It included Stirling and his wife on the *Parmelia*, escorted by the *Sulphur* with a garrison from the 63rd Regiment, their wives and children, artificers and their families, and private settlers. By the time the Hentys's *Caroline* negotiated the difficult port in October 1829 the shores were littered with the goods and the livestock already unloaded from other ships.[5]

In contrast with the period when the eastern colonies were founded, there was now no shortage of well-to-do gentlemen willing to settle permanently overseas. The Henty family was a classic example. The father, Thomas, had inherited 281 acres of rich land in Sussex and from the end of the eighteenth century he had been one of those efficient yeoman farmers, enclosing the land, taking a keen interest in modern capitalistic farming methods and in the improvement of stock breeds. Like others, Henty was facing depressed conditions in the post-war years and a lack of openings for his numerous children. Farmers of this kind lacked the means to follow the example of the British industrial magnates who were buying up rural estates to achieve a pseudo-aristocratic life on the land and a seat in parliament. They could, however, aspire to a similar status if prepared to emigrate to the Australian colonies.

A second group that inclined towards this ideal were the numerous army and naval officers placed on half-pay at the conclusion of the wars. For them, there was little prospect of advancement in the armed forces, for the British, having now defeated the colonial ambitions of their main commercial rivals and having been the first to industrialize, were in a position where they could turn away from investment in wars with Europeans and devote themselves to single-minded territorial expansion around the globe. As early as 1816 the war office was experimenting with the idea of a settlement for veterans in Canada. Regulations for the granting of land in the Australian colonies, issued in 1826, offered veterans capital to invest in colonial land in return for their commissions.

John Septimus Roe epitomized the kind of ex-naval officer attracted to the idea of a leisured, genteel life on colonial land. Born in 1797 he had been still only a midshipman when unfortunately peace descended in 1815 and he was obliged to find less promising employment surveying coastlines surrounding the Indian Ocean. In due course this won him appointment as the Surveyor-General at Swan River and he had arrived with his new wife, Matilda, on the *Parmelia*. Many other settlers were veterans of the land war against Napoleon, such as John Molloy, who with his wife Georgiana, sixteen servants, tools and stock settled at Cape Leeuwin in 1830.[6]

For most of this new breed of gentlemen settlers, aspirations to status and wealth in the new colony were centred less on farming and trade than on wool production. In Britain, interest in this industry had been growing across the eighteenth century in an effort to reduce reliance on imports from the traditional supplier, Spain. Already, in 1789 that indefatigable collector, Joseph Banks, had been able to acquire for the King a few specimens of the Spanish ram and by 1801, a small flock grazed on the grass at Windsor. During the Napoleonic wars further interest was engendered by manufacturers fearing a continental blockade. By 1804 it had become customary to auction a few of the Royal flock to British breeders. Among the purchasers was Thomas Henty and by 1821 he was supplying merinos to settlers in New South Wales.

In the Australian colonies, as early as 1801 some traders were becoming interested in sheep-breeding, not only for mutton to sell to the government store but as a source of wool exports to improve access to foreign exchange. Prominent sheep-holders among the military officers at that time included Captain Joseph Foveaux, paymaster William Cox, commissary John Palmer, and quartermaster Thomas Laycock. By 1801 Reverend Samuel Marsden had also invested in sheep, including some Spanish merinos which had been purchased by chance at the Cape in 1797 by a naval officer sent there by Hunter for supplies. Other purchasers of these Spanish sheep included Captain Kent, Captain Thomas Rowley, commissary James Williamson, and John Macarthur who, by the 1820s, would be claiming to be the founder of the wool industry.

Macarthur had been no more knowledgeable about sheep than his fellow speculators, but he had been luckier. In November 1801 he had been transported back to England by King for court-martial following a duel with Paterson, his commanding officer. Happening to take with him some samples of wool from his flocks at Elizabeth Farm, Macarthur arrived at the very moment when the war with France had not only raised fears for continental supplies but had caused British farmers to concentrate on corn and meat production. Impressed by the high prices being paid in England for wool, Macarthur rapidly developed a vision of New South Wales as the prime supplier of this commodity and of himself as an expert on the improvement of colonial fleeces. This was in spite of the fact that during his absence, his estates and his experiments with sheep-breeding were managed by his wife, Elizabeth. (This was again the case during his prolonged banishment from the colony following the Rum Rebellion, from 1809 to 1817.[7]) By October 1805 Macarthur was back in New South Wales pronouncing that a flock could double itself in less than two and a half years, and that within two decades some five million colonial sheep could be counted upon to produce twice as much wool as England now purchased from Spain. With him Macarthur brought his nephew Hannibal, and permission to resign from the army, with an order for 5000 acres of the best pasture land, plus a further 5000 acres if tangible results were forthcoming. A number of Spanish rams from the Royal flock accompanied him, as did Walter Davidson, nephew of Sir Walter Farquhar, an influential British physician whom Macarthur had fortuitously acquired as patron while in England. Davidson, too, carried permission for a large grant of 2000 acres of colonial land.

Though the full impact of the pastoral invasion did not begin till after 1815, sheep numbers in New South Wales rose steadily, almost trebling between 1803 and 1808. At first many owners preferred to continue raising sheep and cattle for the meat market rather than for the export of wool. However, it was news of Macarthur's plans and the encouragement of Banks which had prompted the arrival of Gregory Blaxland with a number of Spanish sheep in 1805. By this time Samuel Marsden had more than 1000 sheep, and when he visited England in 1807 he took with him samples of wool from his flocks which he had made into a suit. George III was impressed, and Marsden, too, returned with a gift of merinos from the Windsor stud. Missionary Rowland Hassall was another promoter of the wool staple, borrowing a Spanish ram from Marsden and acquiring 1300 acres of land by 1808. Even so, it was not till the exhaustion of the other fields of mercantile speculation that greater attention was given to exports of wool. Sheep numbers in New South Wales rose from 32 000 in 1810 to 74 000 in 1814, and exports of wool to England increased from a mere 4000 lbs shipped by Marsden in 1812, to 35 000 lbs by 1813. By 1821 New South Wales and Van Diemen's Land sent nearly 200 000 lbs of wool to England, and the pastoral invasion of the continent was under way.

In Van Diemen's Land the development of sheep production increased most rapidly. This colony did not suffer the drought and economic depression which struck New South Wales in

1812—15 and, because of the ready availability of fine grazing land, by 1819 the number of sheep was almost double that in the older colony. They were, however, still being raised largely for meat. In 1820 Macquarie arranged for the sale of 300 Macarthur rams to the island's prominent breeders with a view to improving wool production.[8]

Although settlement was still confined to the coastal fringe of the continent it was already realized by settlers and government that the nascent pastoral industry was going to require vast quantities of land. Profitability depended on utilizing native grasses on relatively treeless well-drained plains which did not have to be 'improved' and where flocks and herds could be grazed pending their sale to newcomers to the industry. These grasslands, created by thousands of years of controlled burning by Aboriginal people, were rapidly destroyed by the voracious, hard-footed European beasts. Every native animal had trodden with a padded foot, and had eaten the grass cleanly with its two sets of teeth. It was soon found that a single sheep required 3 acres of native pasture, and that native grasses germinated poorly and deteriorated rapidly when heavily grazed. To pastoralists, it seemed logical to solve this problem by constantly moving their expanding flocks and herds further inland.

Not only did pastoralism require much larger holdings of land than agriculture, but it was also incompatible with small-scale farming. Owners of large flocks and herds preferred land in remote areas where they would be spared the expense of fences to prevent their stock trampling on the unenclosed crops of small holders. In Van Diemen's Land, by 1820 there was a system of grazing licenses to facilitate this, with owners of large flocks being given permission to place their livestock on large areas of land unoccupied by Europeans and with ample spaces of land between them to prevent the flocks of different proprietors from merging. In many cases the custom developed of simply moving stock out on to well-watered, unoccupied land—a practice which later became known as 'squatting'.[9]

This unprecedented demand for land put pressure on the state to provide exploration and survey, especially in New South Wales where access to suitable pastoral land was impeded by steep, coastal ranges and dense rainforest which effectively prevented knowledge of what lay beyond. The result was that up till 1815, while the flocks had spread rapidly across the midlands of

Van Diemen's Land, pastoral capitalism in New South Wales was largely confined to a fan-shaped area to the west of Port Jackson, known as the Cumberland Plain. Meanwhile a succession of government officials, scientific experts and would-be pastoralists hurled themselves against the rugged escarpments which defined its northern and western limits. In May 1813 the mountains were successfully traversed by a party of three pastoralists who were fortunate to strike one of the few possible routes. In the absence of consultation with the Dharuk people—who knew and used a pathway via the Burragorang Valley—a passage across the mountains could only be found by following Aboriginal paths which kept to the tops of the ridges and never descended into the precipitous valleys.[10]

William Charles Wentworth was one of the triumphant trio. He was then twenty-three years old and already owner of 1750 acres granted on the Nepean River. Another in the party was William Lawson, who had arrived as an officer in the New South Wales Corps in 1800, and was owner of a 370-acre farm at Concord and a 500-acre grant at Prospect. The third member of the group was Gregory Blaxland, by then owner of a 4280-acre grant at Evan, 500 acres at Cooke, and sufficient livestock to be sorely in need of new pasture by 1813. All three received 1000-acre grants in the new country for their achievement.

The crossing of the Great Dividing Range immediately to the west of Sydney marked a turning-point in land exploration and the invasion of the continent. The three pastoralists returned with descriptions of excellent pastoral land, and by November 1813 Macquarie dispatched the Assistant Surveyor, George Evans, aided by an Aboriginal guide, to make a scientific report.[11]

As with ocean exploration, now in the invasion of continents, science and the state were needed to support and protect the interests of investors, but where mercantilist capitalism had harnessed navigational science and navies to its needs, in this new phase of expansion it would be largely military engineers who built the roads and bridges and provided the surveys needed to facilitate the invasion of the heartlands. In New South Wales, April 1814 found Macquarie, the first of the governors to be recruited from the army, already planning to have convicts construct a cart road from Emu Plains to the new country. The 101-mile road was completed in January 1815, a gang of thirty convicts having quarried through the sandstone escarpments to construct precipitous passes and build more than a dozen bridges. The men were supervised by William Cox, a former Lieutenant in the New South Wales Corps. Cox was rewarded for the convicts' efforts with a grant of 2000 acres near Bathurst, which he called Hereford. By 1820 he also owned Clarendon, a large estate at Windsor, and his flocks were said to be among the best in the colony.

In April 1815 Macquarie and his wife travelled over the new road in a carriage, walking down the steep descent from Mt York to the plains on the other side. Early in May they were on a westward flowing river, known to Wiradjuri people as Wambool but now renamed the Macquarie. Here the Governor planned to erect a town 'for the convenience and accommodation of such settlers as may be indulged with grants of land in this new discovered county'. He named the new town Bathurst after the Secretary of State for the colonies. By 1818 a massive movement of settlers, convict labourers, flocks, herds, horses, dogs — and infectious disease — were pushing outwards from the Cumberland Plain in what would prove one of the largest and most rapid land seizures in history. [12]

Science and the state were also important in determining whether the Aboriginal people inhabiting the interior were more numerous and more formidable than those on the coast. Equally important was the continuing search for any large, navigable river which might provide a cheap means of shipping out exports, without becoming, like the Mississippi and the St Lawrence, the means by which a rival commercial power might gain a foothold in the interior. Throughout the 1820s state-funded exploration came to focus on solving what became known as the mystery of the rivers. This new land-based attack on the old problem of locating river highways began immediately the Blue Mountains had been crossed. Within one week of the viceregal ceremony at Bathurst, Macquarie again dispatched Evans, this time with a party of four men and two pack-horses, to travel overland southwest of Bathurst and see if the Macquarie River turned in that direction. Evans found that it did not, but came upon a second considerable river flowing to the north-west. This was named the Lachlan, and Evans had reached it at a point about eight miles downstream from the site of present-day Cowra. He followed it almost as far as the present site of Forbes. 'A very little rain would make the River Navigable for Boats', he decided, for the

banks were wider than South Creek at Windsor and the soil
equally rich.[13]

In March 1817 the first of numerous overland versions of the
large-scale, government-funded, marine expeditions was dispatched to investigate the inland rivers. Led by the Surveyor-
General, John Oxley, with Evans as second in command, this
party included Charles Fraser, colonial botanist, William Parr,
mineralogist, and eight servants and assistants. They carried
provisions estimated to last for five months and expected to
travel, as far as practicable, via the rivers whose courses it was so
vital to chart. Floating down the Lachlan in light boats, Oxley
hoped to arrive somewhere between Spencer's Gulf and Cape
Otway, still thought a likely site for a river mouth. Like the
scientific expeditions sent to survey the Pacific, the party was to
note the soil, the woods, the animal and natural productions, the
climate, and return with an accurate description of the number
and social organization of the natives. The country over which
they passed was to be 'regularly chained and laid down upon a
chart'. A detailed daily journal was to be kept, the temperature
measured by 'Fahrenheit's Thermometer' two to three times a
day. Useful specimens of plants and minerals were to be collected,
and even a vocabulary of the Aboriginal language was to be
compiled. With them they carried 'a small theodolite by Ramsden',
'Kater's pocket compass', 'an excellent sextant, pocket chronometer and artificial horizon', and 'mountain barometers' to
measure altitude. The use of these scientific instruments reflected
the growing need in Europe for accurate mathematical surveys of
the land, partly to facilitate military operations and partly
because, with the growth of enclosure, it had become essential to
define land precisely as parcels of private property. In 1791 the
English Board of Ordnance had been founded to begin a survey
of the entire British Isles based on new trigonometrical methods
and directed by military personnel.[14]

However, as explorers in Australia especially were to discover,
the penetration of continental interiors presented problems for
which neither lessons learnt at sea or even recent experience in
large-scale land war offered preparation. Early in July 1817
Oxley's mission was abandoned. Far from being navigable, the
Lachlan River was found to fracture into myriads of tiny water-
courses hidden in a forest of reeds, while an attempt to trek
overland southwards towards Spencer's Gulf encountered only

waterless, grassless plains. Fortunately, striking a new course to the north, the party came upon a section of the Macquarie, still flowing westwards through rich pasture lands. Oxley followed it back to the Bathurst Plains, and by 29 August they were enjoying the hospitality of Mr Cox on the margins of this settlement.

Inspired by Oxley's description of the magnitude of the Macquarie, by May 1818 plans were made for a second expedition. Again led by Oxley, this was instructed to set off down the river following its course past a fertile valley, now named after the Duke of Wellington. Though accompanied by Evans, Fraser, and an entourage of scientific equipment, this second party again failed to solve the mystery of where these western-flowing rivers went, for like the Lachlan, the river seemed to culminate in 'an ocean of reeds'. Abandoning it altogether, Oxley and Evans struck out across country to the north-west, only to discover another puzzling western-flowing river. Even more exasperating, far from idly petering out in reeds and rushes, this river was in flood. Crossing it with difficulty, the explorers nevertheless named it after Viscount Castlereagh, an influential British politician. Now heading eastwards for the coast, they ascended the range which the Aboriginal people called the Warrumbungles and came across a sight equal to the Bathurst Plains from Mt York: 'The view which was on all sides presented to our delighted eyes was of the most varied and exhilarating kind. Hills, dales and plains of the richest description lay before us . . .' Oxley's enthusiasm was partly due to his relief at having extricated himself and his party from an intimate encounter with the black-soil plains near Barradine during a wet season. He named the new sheepwalks the Liverpool Plains, after the Prime Minister, and viewed them with a pastoralist's eye. An intimate friend of John Macarthur, by 1815 Oxley was the owner of 1000 acres of valuable country near Camden and received further grants at Minto and Appin in 1817.[15]

Though the Liverpool Plains were of importance to pastoralism, Oxley was no James Cook. He catalogued the Riverina area as 'desolate plains', unlikely ever again to be visited by 'civilized man' and gave apparently scientific verification to the idea that the western rivers, instead of being navigable Mississippi highroads to a fertile interior, culminated in a vast inland sea. This belief became the catalyst for further state-funded exploration, for it stimulated speculation in scientific circles that this supposed shallow lake might overflow via a still unknown coastal river system into the surrounding seas. Some believed that the Brisbane River might connect the imagined lake to the Pacific. Others dispensed altogether with the theory of an inland sea to argue that a great, north-west river existed which, meandering cheerfully across the site of today's Northern Territory, picked its way through the Kimberleys before entering the sea somewhere near Broome. Some thought it more likely that the Macquarie marshes communicated with the Alligator River, discovered by P. P. King adjacent to Melville and Bathurst Islands. One supporter of this view pointed out that the descent of such a river to sea-level over such a distance would be similar to that of the Nile between Cairo and Rosetta. In support of this vision, creatures resembling alligators were reported to have been sighted in the Macquarie River.[16]

It followed that future state-funded and quasi-military expeditions to conquer the inland of this mysterious continent would continue to be encumbered with boats. This was the more so after Allan Cunningham, a protégé of Joseph Banks, took up the theory of the great north-western river. One of a bevy of botanical collectors posted about the globe to collect specimens and acclimatize plants for the Royal Gardens at Kew, Cunningham had been a member of Oxley's first expedition and, in spite of the privations of that journey, had managed to return with 450 botanical specimens as well as considerable exploratory experience. In March 1823 he had undertaken a venture of his own, aiming to find a route from the Mudgee district to Oxley's Liverpool Plains. With some difficulty and much luck, he was successful. Located between the present-day sites of Coolah and Bundella, Cunningham named his passage Pandora's Pass. Inspired by this success, in April 1827 he departed on another land expedition, this time to investigate the rumour that the Brisbane River might be connected to a great inland sea. Again he was successful in finding excellent pastoral country, which he named the Darling Downs. Cunningham also proved conclusively that the river was not 'an overflow channel from inland marshes'. Accordingly, he came to be one of the most ardent supporters of the idea of an Australian Mississippi, even after new light was cast on the mystery by Charles Sturt in 1828–29.[17]

A young military officer and protégé of Darling, Sturt departed from Wellington Valley in December 1828 in charge of another official assault upon the mysterious rivers. It being the third year of a drought, the party successfully penetrated westward beyond the marshes which had defeated Oxley and stumbled upon another major river, this time flowing to the south. Sturt dutifully named this after Governor Darling and the following year was placed in charge of a second attack on these contrary, antipodean rivers. Aiming to avoid the frustrations of the Lachlan and Macquarie systems altogether, and to approach the Darling from a more southerly point, Sturt's party set out southwards from Sydney in November 1829 only to find themselves in a battle with the Murrumbidgee. Equally reluctant to share its secrets with the invaders, this river confronted their whale-boat first with rapids, fallen timber and a shallow, shingly bed and later, as its current quickened, with over-arching branches which ripped off the boat's protective awning and sank the accompanying skiff. Eventually hurled without ceremony into the waters of a much larger river which they named the Murray, Sturt's party was carried past a junction which they correctly assumed was the Darling and southwards towards Bass Strait. Here to their supreme disappointment, they established that the river system entered the sea surreptitiously and uselessly at the back of a sandbar guarding that old threshold of exploratory endeavour, Encounter Bay. For all but diehards like Cunningham, it was now accepted that the task of annexing the interior would have to be achieved without the aid of the western-flowing rivers, and Sturt's party faced the long and arduous task of rowing back up the recalcitrant rivers, arriving at last in Sydney on 25 May 1830.[18]

While these large state-funded and scientific expeditions were wrestling with the rivers, numerous other exploratory activities were being undertaken privately by pastoralists. As the crossing of the Blue Mountains had demonstrated, in comparison with ocean exploration, costs were not prohibitive, especially to people already enriched by pastoral pursuits or trade and with a vested interest in the result. Advanced scientific skills were necessary, less for the discovery of new land than for apportioning it later to investors. The possibility of successful, privately-funded expeditions was also increased by the fact that land explorers could make full use of the unpaid services of Aboriginal people who had expert knowledge of how to travel over the land and survive its challenges. Aboriginal guides provided vital information about food, water and shelter, and knew how to seek out local people who would provide knowledge about pathways, passes and the whereabouts of rivers. In addition, there were now available numerous ex-convict and native-born men who had followed the example of John Wilson in first learning skills from the Aborigines and ultimately exploiting their bushcraft and usurping their expertise. Most explorers, not to mention stockmen and police, either sought Aboriginal assistance or used people who had acquired some of these skills. In 1819 Hawkesbury settler and constable, John Howe, assisted by Miles, an Aboriginal guide, found a route from Windsor via the Colo River to the rich pastoral land along the upper reaches and tributaries of the Hunter River. For his part in the 'discovery' of the route, Benjamin Singleton, who had found part of the track in 1818, was, like Howe, rewarded with land grants in the Hunter River area known at St Patrick's Plains.

Then there was Hamilton Hume. Native-born son of an early, 30-acre settler, Hume had made his first journey of exploration as far as Berrima in 1812, aided by an Aboriginal boy. In 1818, in a party which included ex-convict James Meehan, Hume reached southwards to the Goulburn Plains and by 1822 had also carried out exploration in the Yass, Braidwood and Illawarra districts as far south as the Clyde. Two years later, in partnership with pastoralist William Hovell, Hume undertook a much more ambitious private expedition, travelling south-west from Sydney overland to Corio Bay, opposite Westernport. Though they discovered that snow-covered mountains occupied part of the south-east corner of the continent and found excellent pastoral land on their western slopes, Hume and his partner did not avoid the trials which, it seemed, were necessary to induce the continent to part with its secrets. Among the ranges inland from Bass Strait they fell upon thick undergrowth and knife-like grass which cut into skin and clothes. Here one of their convict servants took what Hovell called 'an unfortunate tumble' which 'not only took away part of his trousers but the front flaps of his shirt also, thereby leaving him in that state that had there been any doubts of his manhood before, these doubts were now removed'. This ragged party arrived back in Sydney on 18 January 1825, the two leaders competing with each other to be the first with the news of fresh pastoral land. Both were rewarded with grants of 1200 acres.

Also advancing the overland invasion to the pastures south of

Sydney was ex-naval surgeon and pastoralist, Charles Throsby.
Having accompanied Meehan and Hume in 1818, by 1820 Throsby
had been as far south as Breadalbane and the following year had
crossed the Molonglo and inspected the Limestone Plains. Throsby
was assisted in these pursuits by his ex-convict servant, Joseph
Wild, who in May 1823, together with at least one Aboriginal
guide, was sent to assist an official expedition investigating this
area. Led by Captain Mark Currie and engineer, John Ovens, this
party crossed the Limestone Plains and ventured up the Murrumbidgee as far as the Bredbo River where they came upon the open
grasslands called Maneroo or Monaro.[19]

In the eastern colonies, mere exploration of the inland was not
sufficient to change the country into a giant sheepwalk overnight. Whereas at the Swan River it was assumed that large
parcels of land would be required for each pastoralist, until 1825
the convict colonies were, in theory, still committed to the 30-
acre grant. This was too small for pastoral capitalism. Also now
that there was an abundance of immigrants with capital it made
no sense to grant land to emancipists and ex-convicts who,
ideally, should now become labourers in the service of pastoralists,
not independent farmers or even worse, pastoralists, with land of
their own. Like the privileged monopolies, the original land laws
of the convict colonies were now coming to be seen by sheepmen
and traders as an outmoded remnant of the old commercial
system and in urgent need of reform.

The case for altering the land laws was supported by John
Thomas Bigge, Chief Justice and Judge of the Vice-Admiralty
Court at Trinidad, who was selected to conduct a searching
enquiry into the function of the convict colonies in January 1819.
Bigge and his secretary, Thomas Hobbes Scott, arrived in New
South Wales in September of that year, partly to report on
convict discipline but also to enquire into every aspect of the
judicial, civil, and ecclesiastical establishment, revenue, and
trade. In the course of his enquiries, Commissioner Bigge became
the confidant of John Macarthur, and an ingenious scheme was
evolved by which the land regulations would be changed so as to
exclude ex-convicts and small holders permanently from the
burgeoning pastoral industry. As Macarthur informed the Commissioner, the aim should be to place 'a body of really respectable
Settlers' upon the land, with grants of 10 000 acres as well as
extensive adjoining reserves. This 'new aristocracy' would supply

Great Britain with wool using convict labour which would be almost totally privatized. They would also employ any paupers that Britain might care to send forth. Macarthur also suggested that these gentlemen settlers be given magisterial powers by which labour discipline would be enforced.[20]

New land regulations ushering in changes based on this concept were announced by the Secretary of State, Earl Bathurst, in January 1825. Land was to be distributed either by full grants or purchase, with the latter considered the most desirable. Portions were to be offered in large blocks of 1920 acres, and a single person could purchase up to five of these parcels, paying by quarterly instalments if preferred, though there was a 10 per cent discount for cash. To the further advantage of men of capital, the purchase price and the discount were refundable after ten years, provided that over that period the purchaser had maintained a reasonable number of convict labourers, the quantity being calculated in proportion to the amount paid for the land. Blocks which had been on the market for six months could be given away in portions of up to 2560 acres, and only to applicants who possessed capital equivalent to one-half of the grant. In issuing this new land policy, the British authorities also spelt out further means for assisting pastoral capitalism and controlling access to its profits. A general survey, to be conducted prior to the annexation of land, was to subdivide the two eastern colonies into counties, parishes and hundreds, and land was to be allocated for public roads and quays, villages and towns. No less than one-seventh of the land in each county was to be reserved for the support of Anglican churches and schools. Labourers could also be grateful for the small sections of public land which were to be set aside for their 'health and recreation'. No mention was made of the Aboriginal people; it continued to be assumed that they had no prior claim upon the land.[21]

The 1825 regulations marked the end of land grants to eman-cipists and immigrants without capital and foreshadowed schemes, like that of Stirling and Peel in Western Australia, to promote private investment in large holdings. As later developed in the theories of the systematic colonizers, the principle was that these holdings would be worked by a landless labour force imported from Britain and financed essentially by the colony. In 1831 the ending of free grants altogether and the insistence that all land be sold at a minimum price of five shillings an acre was a further step in this direction. By 1828 only 14 per cent of the emancipist population held land in New South Wales.[22]

Implicit to Bigge's brief was the need to decide whether the rising class of land-owning entrepreneurs like Wentworth, Macarthur and Oxley were sufficiently numerous for the large role played by the state in establishing colonial production to be phased out without detracting from the changing needs of British industry. It was also necessary to decide whether or not they were ready for the creation of more liberal judicial and legal institutions modelled on those in England and long recommended by the theorists of the new commercial system such as Bentham. During the 1820s the struggle of British industrialists for wealth and power was still in the transitory phase so it was hardly surprising that, in adjusting colonial land and political policies to those changes, Bigge and the British State opted for a compromise. They decided that although the colonial capitalist class was not yet numerous and powerful enough to take full control, major new official positions enlarging the local state should be created. These included the office of Colonial Secretary, created in 1821, and of Colonial Treasurer, created in 1823. Also in 1823, a small Legislative Council of between five and seven persons was established in New South Wales to advise the governor. The same Act which created the Council also authorized the position of Attorney-General, a major step towards the establishment of an independent legal system in the colonies. Separate Supreme Courts were established for New South Wales and Van Diemen's Land, each with a Chief Justice replacing the office of Judge Advocate. In June 1825 an Order-in-Council separated Van Diemen's Land from New South Wales and gave it a nominated Legislative Council with the same authority as that of the older colony.

These measures did not satisfy local land-owners, especially wealthy emancipists like Dr William Redfern and Edward Eager, and sons of emancipists like William Wentworth, who were treated as inferiors by wealthy families who had arrived free. Believing that they were now being discriminated against by the new official class, they carried the old attack on the governor's authoritarian powers throughout the 1820s, making stirring statements about the 'tyranny' of Whitehall whenever official policy threatened their status or economic position. In 1824 Wentworth and Robert Wardell established a newspaper, *The Australian*, in opposition to the semi-official *Sydney Gazette*, and used it to promote liberal and lofty ideals, and in particular to declare war on Governor Darling. In 1826 they took advantage of the death of a soldier, Joseph Sudds, while under punishment authorized by Darling, to dispatch a petition to Britain demanding the 'rights of Englishmen', trial by jury and 'taxation by representation'. They also demanded a legislature elected on a franchise wide enough to outweigh the influence of 'certain private families'.[23]

Despite these political differences, the British authorities were aware that the material interests of the wealthy emancipists and the free emigrant pastoralists were identical. Indeed, to the British, origins counted far less than wealth as a qualification for holding huge acres of land for development according to the needs of British industry. Certainly, both groups participated in the rush to acquire pastoral land which followed the ending of the 30-acre grant; men of capital scrambled to obtain a free grant if entitled to one, or purchase pre-emptively if they could afford to, or to graze stock informally on good unoccupied land further out. Many pastoralists combined all of these options, that of grazing stock on distant land especially, for in New South Wales the surveyors made slow progress in the huge task of mapping and subdividing the colony. An initial survey completed in May 1829 listed nineteen counties, and in October Oxley declared this land open to settlement. In the meantime, land was granted and purchased before survey and, under a leasing arrangement introduced in October 1828, land-owners could lease runs immediately adjacent to their holdings for only two shillings and sixpence a year for 100 acres.

Despite this convenience 'squatting' now became an essential part of pastoral capitalism, as Peter Cunningham explained. Formerly a surgeon on a convict ship and now a large land-holder in the Hunter Valley, in 1827 Cunningham published a book for intending emigrants. Here he advised the newcomer to go out into new country with a knowledgeable 'bushman' and an Aboriginal guide and look for land which had 'a good grazing *back-run* behind it', but which was otherwise surrounded by land so indifferent that no other settler would be likely to live nearby. He advised the prospective pastoralist to pay no attention to settlers describing the land as poor, for this was the standard ploy to prevent selection of the back-runs. It followed that there was never any chance that settlement would be confined to the nineteen counties or 'limits of location' as they were known.[24]

Especially during the drought which set in from 1826, herds, flocks and convict servants were pushed out from the Cumberland Plain over Pandora's Pass to the Liverpool Plains and further north to the highlands (called New England by the invaders), westwards towards Mudgee, and south-west towards Yass and Monaro. In 1825 Robert Campbell, already the owner of 1500 acres at Bathurst, was granted 4000 acres at Limestone Plains on the present site of Canberra. In 1827 he was permitted to purchase another 5000 acres across the Molonglo River, and had stock on a run much further to the south which he called Delegate. By 1832 there were at least eighteen outstations on Monaro stocked with 50 000 cattle and sheep, many of the investors of this region being the owners of land in the area from Moss Vale to the Limestone Plains. Other land-takers in the south-west were new arrivals, in many cases veterans of the Peninsular War. These included Francis Rossi who was offered the position of Superintendent of Police in New South Wales in 1824 and was granted 2560 acres near Goulburn where he settled in 1834. Captain Terence Murray arrived as a serving officer in the 48th Regiment in 1817, left for Madras in 1824, but two years later retired on half-pay and returned to take up a grant of 2560 acres selected at Lake George in 1829. For the convenience of these invaders, convicts were set to build a road from Parramatta to the Goulburn Plains in 1819. By 1826 it had reached Cowpastures, and by August 1830 some 150 miles had been completed, including the difficult section over the Razorback Pass.

Settlement further to the south was temporarily checked by the Snowy Mountains, but the invasion continued to the south-west on the other side of the Great Dividing Range. Here, occupation of the land along the lower Murrumbidgee quickly followed the expeditions of Hume and Hovell and of Sturt. Prominent among those who moved stock south-westward were the Macarthurs, who by 1832 had outstations in the Tumut district and at Gundagai. By this date stations along the river had reached as far as Wagga.[25]

North-west of the Cumberland Plain, the grant or purchase of extensive areas of land along the upper Hunter during the 1820s acted as a springboard for the development of outstations beyond Pandora's Pass. By 1831 there were some twenty-three squatters on the Peel River near the present site of Tamworth, with others as far north-west as the Breeza Plain. In the absence of navigable rivers, the expensive task of road-building had begun in this area. By 1827 the first section was completed on a road which eliminated the circuitous Colo valley route by crossing the Hawkesbury River at Wiseman's Ferry and then taking the settlers northwards through Wollombi to Singleton.

Invaders descending onto the Liverpool Plains included numerous land-holders from the Hawkesbury and Hunter Valleys and a gigantic organization of British investors, called the Australian Agricultural Company. Incorporated by royal charter in 1824 and raising capital in England of £1 million from 10 000 shares valued at £10 each, this large speculative venture obtained permission from the Colonial Office to select one million acres on a location of its own choice. To determine the site, a colonial committee of advice was formed. When other local land-takers failed to display interest, this came to comprise three members of the Macarthur family. In addition to James, fourth son of the rapacious speculator, there was James's cousin, Hannibal, and brother-in-law Dr James Bowman. A surgeon on the convict ship *Lord Eldon*, Bowman had arrived in 1817. In 1823 he succeeded (where Oxley had failed) in wedding Elizabeth Macarthur, whose dowry included 2000 merino sheep. In 1824 he completed this triumph by acquiring through grant and purchase Ravensworth, a 12 000-acre estate superbly situated between Singleton and Muswellbrook.

The selection of a site for the Company's huge holdings was plagued with difficulties. Oxley's recommendations included the Liverpool Plains or the head of the Hastings River, but meanwhile the Company's first agent, Robert Dawson, arrived in December 1825 with 720 French and Saxon sheep. On the advice of the local committee, Dawson visited another area suggested by Oxley near Port Stephens and, impressed by the harbour there, he recommended this site. The committee agreed, but within two years it was found that the place was far too swampy, rugged and heavily timbered for sheep. Many of the flock had died for the inexperienced Dawson had been persuaded to purchase old and diseased specimens from the Macarthur family, often at high prices. When in 1827 Dawson declined 'to make the Company Grant a dumping ground for all the old sheep in the colony', the local committee made him the scapegoat for the ill-chosen site and suspended him. Hastily dispatching James to London to counteract Dawson's view of the issue, the Macarthurs duly emerged from this fiasco unscathed.

The huge grants allowed to the Australian Agricultural Company made it unpopular with local land-takers. Nevertheless, many of them owed much to the market it created for their livestock. Some Hunter Valley pastoralists whose grants were like Bowman's, strategically located close to the main stock routes to the north-west, found that initially they had no need to acquire outstations. This was because of the sustained demand for their surplus livestock from pastoralists passing through to take up land further out.[26]

In Van Diemen's Land, the invasion of the pastoral capitalists had been equally rapid. As at Swan River, there were limited amounts of suitable land and this was rapidly taken up by the first arrivals. They included not only the retired army and naval officers and sons of English, Irish and Scottish farmers, but also a wave of settlers from New South Wales, with the result that 4000 free settlers arrived between 1817 and 1824. By 1830 the European population reached 23 500, of whom some 6000 were free settlers. There were then a million sheep in the island, again briefly surpassing the number in New South Wales. In 1823 no less than 439 260 acres were granted, the largest amount ever to be alienated in a single year.

By the time of the arrival of Governor Arthur in May 1824, a large part of the eastern half of the island was known and occupied. From 1824 on assaults were made on the mid-northern and north-western sections, headed by appointees of the huge Van Diemen's Land Company. Created in London with the approval of the Colonial Office, shareholders in this venture were granted 250 000 acres in the north-west of the island in 1825, but between 1826 and 1828 exploration of the vast area set aside for the Company found little pasture suitable for sheep.

The choice of the Company land had been the responsibility of Edward Curr, who had arrived in Hobart in 1820 on a business venture and was granted 1500 acres of land at Cross March. Returning to England in 1823, he published *An Account of the Colony of Van Diemen's Land* principally designed for the use of emigrants, and was consulted by the Colonial Office on the plans to form the Company. Curr became one of its directors and returned in 1826 to locate the boundaries of the Company's land in the north-west. To his alarm, Curr found only heavy timber and wild country and urged the directors to press for a grant elsewhere. This they declined to do with the result that the venture was never enormously profitable. In 1831–34 the cold, disease, and the attacks of the Tasmanian carnivorous animals destroyed the precious flock of Saxon sheep, and by 1833 Curr was recommending abandonment of sheep-rearing and the adoption of a scheme of tenant farming to provide the Company with profits from rent and a market for its remaining stock.

The fate of the Van Diemen's Land Company underlined the shortage of pastoral land in the colony. Between 1827 and 1835 the Survey Department sent expeditions into the south-west corner of the island. J. H. Wedge, George Frankland, J. E. Calder and John Charles Clarke explored the upper Derwent and its tributaries, discovering the sources of the Huon and the Derwent and reaching as far as Lake Pedder and the upper Gordon River. Pastoralist William Sharland, a member of the Survey Department, had travelled as far west as Frenchman's Cap by 1835 but no more sheepwalks were to be found—a disappointment which by that year would be causing Van Diemonian pastoralists to turn their attention to the land across Bass Strait in their search for land for their expanding flocks and herds.[27]

The state-facilitated land invasion not only provided exploratory parties and convenient land regulations but also put down Aboriginal opposition. Loaded drays and lonely hut-keepers and shepherds were easy targets for Aboriginal spears, as were the sheep themselves. Indeed, sheep provided a useful alternative to some of the traditional food supplies the settlers' presence was destroying, and whole flocks were removed by Aboriginal people to carefully hidden yards where they constituted both a future food supply as well as a means of hitting back at the invaders and arresting their destruction of the grasslands. Sheep could be disposed of simply by breaking their legs or stampeding them over a steep cliff. Though Aboriginal people found little use for the cumbersome firearms of the invaders, they readily acquired their hunting dogs, their cutting tools, and adapted their iron and glass to make Aboriginal weapons more deadly, capable of dispatching not only European men but also their horses and cattle.[28] Since the pastoralists were now confident of their military superiority and were equipped with a captive cheap labour force, they showed little interest in sparing Aboriginal lives and new heights of official and unofficial violence were reached. In April 1816 when Dharuk resistance along the Hawkesbury, Grose, and Nepean Rivers was forcing some settlers to abandon their farms, Macquarie responded by sending three detachments of troops to cleanse these areas which he declared were 'infested' with Aborigines. They had instructions to drive the Aboriginal people off the land, to take some prisoners and to 'Inflict exemplary and Severe Punishments'. This meant shooting any who attempted to escape and hanging their bodies from trees in conspicuous places. Sent out on 10 April, these three parties combed the riverlands west of Sydney for twenty-three days. Captain Wallis's group, surprising one native camp by night near William Broughton's farm at Appin, took five prisoners and killed fourteen Aborigines, some of whom fell to their death when forced over precipices in the area. The violence in the Appin region had been initiated by the settlers who, in some cases, had already conducted their own exemplary punishments. One Aboriginal woman had her scalp cut off and left to dangle across her forehead as an example of white ways, while her infant had been thrown into the fire and burned alive.[29]

With the crossing of the Blue Mountains and the taking up of huge parcels of land west of the Dividing Range, new experiments in punishment and dispersal were tried. In June 1824, following the death of seven stock-keepers near Bathurst, Governor Brisbane requested permission to raise a troop of colonial cavalry, declaring that existing infantry and police had no chance of success in that region. Actions described by Brisbane as 'sanguinary Retaliation' by whites in the area were also proving an embarrassment. On 14 August 1824 Brisbane, advised by Attorney-General Saxe Bannister, decided upon a new procedure which would legalize killing by settlers as well as troops. He declared the whole of the country west of Mt York under martial law. This proved extremely effective. The detachment of troops under Major Morisset at Bathurst was increased to seventy-five men divided into small parties headed by magistrates, themselves land-takers in the region. By December 1824 Governor Brisbane was able to report that this 'system of keeping these unfortunate people in a constant state of alarm soon bought them to a sense of Duty' and martial law was revoked on the 31st of the month.[30]

From April 1788, convict men working on the fringes of the settlement or gathering 'sweet tea' to supplement their diet became the target for reprisals by the Eora people attempting to control the invasion. The use of the woomera increased the velocity and accuracy of the spear but Aboriginal weapons were not designed for large-scale warfare.

Convicts and marines struggle to retrieve supplies and livestock following the wreck of the Sirius at Sydney Bay, Norfolk Island, in March 1790. The loss of the Sirius was a disaster, leaving the settlements perilously short of food and clothing and with only one ship left to send to the Cape or Batavia for relief.

The British at Port Jackson were more surely in possession when painted by the artists of the Malaspina expedition to the Pacific in March–April 1793. Government House, located at the crest of the hill, commands attention. The wide road leading up to it follows the line of the present-day Bridge Street, passing the houses of Judge-Advocate, Chaplain, Surveyor and other officials.

Fernando Brambila's 'View' of the settlement at Parramatta at Rose Hill shows the colony's heavy reliance on convict manpower, not only for farming but transport. Arriving at Port Jackson on 11 March 1793, Malaspina's expedition had already visited the Philippines, Norfolk Island and New Zealand. On 12 April it departed for the Friendly Islands (Tonga) which it claimed for Spain.

By 1826 when the Wonnarua people had to be 'dispersed' from the Hunter to make way for the British flocks and herds, Governor Darling had at his disposal the 'colonial cavalry' envisaged by his predecessor. The new mounted police was established in September 1825, with two officers, two sergeants and twenty privates, all recruited from the British army then serving in the colony. The horses were old and unfit but equipment and personnel were not. By June 1826 sixty sets of cavalry equipment had been despatched to New South Wales and forty to Van Diemen's Land, where Aboriginal people, taking advantage of the especially rugged terrain which surrounded the sheeplands, were waging a guerilla war and attacking settlers, shepherds and stock. In the Hunter Valley, by the end of 1826 combined resistance by the Wonnarua and Wiradjuri people had been broken by the military, aided by local land-owners. Principal among these was Robert Scott and his brother Helenus who, arriving from India in 1821, had been granted a total of 4000 acres of land near Singleton. As on the Hawkesbury in 1805, such cruel and indiscriminate slaughter raised the issue of who was allowed to flout the law by openly killing Aboriginal people. Ignoring private punitive expeditions by land-takers like Scott, the Darling administration felt constrained to stage a formal enquiry into the particularly brutal murder of at least three captives by military parties under the command of Nathaniel Lowe, a lieutenant in the 40th regiment. One man had been tied to a tree, shot at until he fell and then left to strangle; another had been tied up behind the new gaol at Wallis Plains and used for target practice until his head was blown to pieces.[31] However, Lieutenant Lowe and his men were in no way endangered by these enquiries. The first was held at Glendon, the Scotts' station, and the magistrates in charge of the hearing were Captain Allman, commander of the troops stationed at Newcastle, E.C. Close and Robert Scott himself, none of whom had any interest in discrediting the new mounted police. The second was a full trial, with Lieutenant Lowe in the dock, but the Hunter Valley magistrates refused to co-operate with acting Attorney-General W.H. Moore, the trial was delayed until May 1827 and Lowe was defended with spirit by leading barristers Dr Wardell and William Wentworth. The outcome came to depend on the credibility of three key witnesses, all ex-convicts. Contradictions were found in their evidence, and other witnesses called for the defence declared the three were not to be trusted even under oath. Lowe was acquitted amid cheers from his many friends in the court.[32]

At Swan River, despite a proclamation issued soon after its foundation that the Aboriginal people were British citizens, under the protection of British law, the numerous war veterans among the settlers proved especially merciless in dealing with resistance. Governor Stirling himself organized and participated in one particularly murderous reprisal at the new town of Pinjarra in October 1834, where Aboriginal men, women and children were cut down by deadly cross-fire. One member of this killer party, Waterloo veteran Captain Richard Meares, later had a mural painted of this 'battle' on the dining-room wall of his house at Guildford, opposite another one depicting a scene at Waterloo.[33]

In spite of the views of land-takers like Meares, Lawson, Wentworth or Cox, who either overtly or implicitly advocated the slaughtering of Aboriginal families,[34] not all those devoted to the new concept of the colonies as a place where people were replaced by sheep believed that this should imply a policy of extermination. Many industrial capitalists in Britain, aware of the need to expand markets for their goods, were especially interested in the preservation of native peoples. Just as they favoured the idea of gathering up the British poor, the orphaned and the outcast into asylums and refuges in order to guarantee a surplus labour supply and prepare it for the factory, so in the colonies they fancied the formula of collecting indigenous peoples into missions and reserves. Here, protected from the assaults of the land-takers and clothed in blankets made in Britain, they would be re-educated to emerge eventually as dutiful workers and consumers.

Though not yet sufficiently influential to shape the planning of the early convict colonies, groups of Evangelical reformers concerned about worker education and prison discipline had dispatched Richard Johnson and then Samuel Marsden to mend convict morals and promote marriage and reproduction in New South Wales. From the 1790s, hearing of the alleged idolatrous practices and idle habits said to prevail among native people, Evangelical, Wesleyan and inter-denominational organizations were formed to launch the first of numerous missionaries into Africa, India and the Pacific.[35]

Not that the missionaries, either at home or abroad, necessarily perceived their philanthropic efforts as serving any political function, nor did they necessarily derive any personal wealth from the advancement of colonization and industry. Most saw themselves as participating in that fervent religious crusade which, aiming to save the lives and souls of the unchristian masses, was now sweeping Britain. Whether or not these ardent, religious reformers saw their activities in economic or political terms, the fact was that, as earlier during the Reformation, the changing needs of an economy undergoing rapid expansion had called upon religion to advance its interests and, in so doing, created a new faith which at once facilitated and obscured the effects of industrialization and colonization. Underlying the new religious evangelism lay a doctrine designed to entrench the notion that the causes of social distress lay in the individual, not in the exploitive economic system. Thus, it was said, just as revelation was available to every person with sufficient faith and zeal, so by attention to strict personal discipline, chastity, sobriety and providence, every person could avoid poverty and even achieve wealth, if not in this world then at least in the next. It was a practical, social and utilitarian form of Christianity whose leading members—like prison reformer, John Howard and anti-slaver, William Wilberforce—were acquainted with and shared many of the ideals of philosophic radicals like Bentham and Mill. This convergence of interests was especially apparent in 1813 when the terms ending the East India Company's monopoly included a direction to the Company to alter its former respect for local religion and admit missionaries, a process which was seen as advancing both divine providence and economic growth.[36]

In the Australian colonies it was initially the Pacific Islanders rather than the Aborigines who claimed the lion's share of missionary attention. This reflected the involvement of early and influential missionaries in the maritime trading networks which they saw as a 'civilizing', quasi-religious force. This pattern was clearly established by 1798 when eleven out of the thirty missionaries sent the previous year by the London Missionary Society to Tahiti, Tonga and the Marquesas were forced to retreat to Sydney. Most then turned their missionary attention to convicts; the others, like Rowland Hassall, combined clerical duties with farming and pastoral pursuits. Only William Shelley interested himself in the Aboriginal people and then not until after nearly fifteen years of successfully combining commercial and missionary endeavour in the Pacific. Returning to Tahiti in 1801 Shelley believed that the mission could fund itself through trade with New South Wales. In 1806 he successfully exported rum secretly made in the mission still. Cargoes of pork followed and by 1811 eight of the original missionaries agreed to return to Tahiti. Allying themselves to Pomare II, by 1820 they secured the nominal Christianization of all 'his' people, while in 1814 a voyage by Shelley to attempt to re-open the mission at Tonga arrived back in Sydney with as large a quantity of pearls as had ever been procured by a single vessel. For Marsden, too, evangelism was inextricably related to trade. In 1814 he personally reconnoitred with warlike Hongi Hika (who was then displaying that keen interest in firearms which would prove so fatal to the Maori people) in order to establish a mission at the Bay of Islands. Marsden rightly judged that timber, flax and possibly potato production would soon more than cover his costs.[37]

In contrast, particularly after his failure to 'civilize' the Aboriginal children, Marsden repeatedly declared that Aboriginal people were so low down on the human scale that they were incapable of learning the time-discipline, the individualistic competitiveness and respect for private property which was part of the missionary creed. Shelley, however, having settled at Parramatta in 1814, was inclined to the view that perhaps conversion could be achieved if the process began in childhood. He conceived the idea of a special school or 'native institution' where Aboriginal children who had survived the Hawkesbury wars would be separated from their families and subjected to a course of study similar to that used in the institutions for other destitute children. This idea eventually found a sponsor in Governor Macquarie who was drawn also to the idea of an annual distribution of blankets and other goods in an attempt to win over the adults. When the institution opened in January 1815 it had only five inmates, and by 1820, even counting children taken as prisoners during the frontier wars and sent to the school, there had been only thirty-seven admissions, ten of whom had either died, absconded or been removed by their parents. The school was moved in 1823 from Parramatta to Blacktown but closed in 1824, the boys being sent to Reverend Robert Cartwright at Liverpool and the girls to the Female Orphan School.[38]

The demise of the native institution did nothing to divert

missionary action away from the Pacific to the inland, especially since Samuel Marsden, agent for both the Church and London Missionary Societies, was one of the school's severest critics. Marsden's well-publicized views, and the resistance of Aboriginal people, meant that even with the growth of evangelism in the 1820s missionary influence on the Australian pastoral frontier was negligible. In 1824 former Pacific missionary L. E. Threlkeld, encouraged by visiting agents of the London Missionary Society Daniel Tyerman and George Bennet, who had been sent to survey the Pacific stations, opened a mission at Lake Macquarie. Located at the gateway to the Hunter Valley where atrocities had occurred, the mission soon found itself to be largely irrelevant, its inmates either dying of disease or leaving in search of family or employment closer to traditional land. Similarly, the mission established by Wesleyan John Harper at the former government farm in Wellington Valley in 1825 could not prove viable while official policy condoned extermination and Aboriginal survivors still had access to traditional and other food sources.[39]

In Australia, it was not until land annexation had largely been completed that missionary activity could be successfully used as a colonizing technique for, in contrast with the Islanders, Aboriginal survivors could shelter and eke out a living in pockets of unoccupied land or on thinly settled back-runs. Others survived as fringe-dwellers and casual labourers on the edge of stations and settlements where, though in extreme poverty, they were able to retain aspects of their culture and technology. It was therefore no coincidence that it was in Van Diemen's Land, at a time when three long years of martial law (November 1828 to January 1832) were breaking Aboriginal resistance and every inch of fertile land had been sought out by pastoralists and farmers, that the Aboriginal people were obliged to submit themselves to the missionary experience. Nor was it coincidence that a different approach to conversion was tried. Governor George Arthur, who was known for his missionary work in his previous post (the British Honduras), together with George Augustus Robinson, a secular missionary employed by the Governor in 1829 to run a ration station on Bruny Island, were by the 1830s both coming to the view that since the Aboriginal people were so resistant to assimilation and trade, for them christianization must precede integration into the world of labour and commerce. Just as Shelley and Macquarie had attempted with the

Sydney children, now for adults total removal and prolonged segregation from European society was seen as the ideal formula, indefinitely postponing assimilation into the white workforce. Having succeeded in enlisting the assistance of the Bruny Island people—Wooraddy, Truganini, Pevay and others—in February 1830 Robinson set off on the first of his journeys devoted to rounding up every Aboriginal person left in Van Diemen's Land and persuading them to follow his party back to a reserve which he would prepare for their reception and re-education.

In August 1830 Governor Arthur mustered 2000 soldiers and armed civilians in a second attempt to deal with Aboriginal resistance by removing every Aboriginal person remaining in the settled areas, not by persuasion but by force. Forming a human drag-line which stretched across the island from the east coast as far as the central plateau, the aim was to drive men, women and children relentlessly southwards onto the Tasman Peninsula, where the Governor had created an Aboriginal reserve. Arthur's 'Black Line' succeeded in catching only two people. Two more were shot, but everyone else managed to slip away undetected. In contrast, by December 1834 Robinson had rounded up virtually every Aboriginal person who had survived the years of martial law, even those on the sparsely settled west coast. A total of some 300 surrendered to Robinson. Two-thirds of these people subsequently died in the various transit camps set up to incarcerate them as they were captured. By 1835 the remainder were relocated on a tiny, wind-swept island in Bass Strait. Named after Flinders and unwanted by the Europeans, this island prison made escape impossible. An intensive programme of missionary re-education was now implemented, with some forty-six Europeans supervising 123 Aborigines. Only the community of Aboriginal women and sealers on the adjacent islands in Bass Strait had been able to evade this removal policy.[40]

Despite the number of his captives who had already died, Robinson was well rewarded for his efforts, receiving from the state and settlers perhaps £6000 in land and cash.[41] Clearly, saving Aboriginal lives and assimilating them into the white workforce was going to be an expensive investment, both in terms of time and funds. Consequently, it was not surprising that while alternative and cheaper forms of labour were available, efforts to transform Aboriginal people into wanted workers would remain of secondary importance and the old policy of extermination would continue. Throughout the period of most rapid pastoral expansion, it was primarily the convicts who would be used to supply labour and to bear the responsibility for the genocide still to come.

6

NOT SLAVES, NOT CITIZENS
The Formation of an Australian Proletariat
1819–1839

Who built Thebes of the Seven Gates?
In the books stand the names of Kings.
Did the kings haul up the lumps of rock?
And Babylon, many times demolished,
Who raised it up so many times? In what houses
Of gold-glittering Lima did the builders live?
Where, the evening that the Wall of China was finished
Did the masons go? Great Rome
Is full of triumphal arches. Who erected them?

Bertolt Brecht[1]

WHEN HE ARRIVED at Port Jackson in 1819 Commissioner Bigge found the convict men hard at work building the town of Sydney. Some toiled at the docks and in the lumber yard, others laboured in stone-cutting gangs and brickyards, producing the materials for the simple yet monumental public buildings which, designed by ex-convict Francis Greenaway, seemed to speak of a grand future for Sydney and its satellite towns on the Cumberland Plain. At the Brickfields 180 men were employed in caring for the numerous horses and bullocks needed to haul the twenty-nine carts engaged on these and other projects. At the 280-acre Grose Farm 160 men and boys were grubbing out stumps, erecting farm buildings, and cultivating vegetables. Further along the Parramatta Road 110 men were at work on the 700-acre government

150

farm known as Longbottom, cutting and sawing timber for consignment to Sydney by boat along the Parramatta River. At the foot of the Blue Mountains nearly 300 men were clearing timber from a third government farm which had just opened at Emu Plains and were preparing the ground for the production of maize and wheat. At Pennant Hills, seventy-five men were sawing timber and shingles which others conveyed by bullock-dray to the Parramatta River, while further out at Windsor and Liverpool, gangs of government men were labouring at similar tasks. Even the penal station which had been established at the mouth of the Hunter River was essentially a labour camp supplying fuel and building materials for the colony. An important source of coal and timber, this settlement had been used increasingly to isolate and discipline recalcitrant convict workers, especially following the evacuation of Norfolk Island in 1811–14. By 1821 new wooden barracks accommodated 246 men who worked at cutting timber up to 70 miles inland, floating the logs down the river on the tide. Others toiled in the coal-mine, raising up to 20 tons of coal each day in spite of bad air in the shaft and the difficulty of clearing it of water. Other men collected oyster shells and burned them for lime for transport to Sydney; the smoke was admitted to damage their eyes, 'but not in greater degree than in England'.[2]

However, the Commissioner was not impressed with what he saw, for by keeping so many men under sentence in the service of the government, the system was failing to allow pastoralists sufficient convict workers to meet their labour needs. After all, what was the use of altering land laws so as to facilitate pastoral expansion unless something was done to ensure a steady supply of labour out on the frontier where it was urgently needed? Admittedly in New South Wales there were 6000 male convicts assigned into private service, two-thirds of the total number of male convicts then in the colony, but half of these were in the service of ex-convict businessmen and traders at the very time when the manufacturers of England needed wool. Moreover, the women convicts, instead of being confined neatly in the old Factory at Parramatta as a potential reproduction reserve were, because of overcrowding, largely out in the community where they and their children were, according to the Commissioner, proving an economic liability and a distraction to the men.[3]

The problems confronting Bigge and the pastoralists were not unique to the Australian colonies. The period from 1820 was one of greatly intensified forced migration of labourers right around the globe, as other imperial powers introduced experiments to solve their labour problems. The number of labourers forcibly removed to Siberia in order to reinforce Russia's hold on the North Pacific trade reached new proportions from this time, while the French would consider establishing penal stations in the Malouines and the Marquesas. From 1815 the British began to remove workers from India to Mauritius, Malaysia and Singapore, while convicts from Britain were sent to Bermuda from 1824.[4] In the Australian colonies the labour shortage was especially acute because of the speed and the nature of the pastoral invasion. Rural employers required a huge range of skilled and unskilled workers, as Alexander Harris observed. An emigrant mechanic employed on the station of a Hawkesbury land-holder and magistrate in the 1820s, Harris noted that, like almost all of the old settlers, his employer had a great many farms as well as cattle and sheep stations, hundreds of miles apart from each other.

He also, as usual, had at the home farm his smithy, flour-mill, tailors', shoemakers', harness-makers' and carpenters' shops, tannery, cloth-factory, tobacco sheds; beside stables, dairy, barn, wool-sheds, brick-kilns, saw-pits, . . . and all the necessary tradesmen for these various occupations.

Harris estimated that on these establishments there were altogether some 200 men, some bond, some free.

On the unimproved, unfenced back-runs the pastoral industry was remarkably labour intensive. Numerous shepherds were required to guard the flocks all day and to guide them back to the fold at night. In order to prevent disease it was believed necessary for workers to construct portable folds which they then moved daily onto new ground. At night, fires had to be lit and dogs tethered around the fold and at least one man was made to sit in a specially constructed watch-house in order to protect the flock from attack by dingos and other predators. Extra labour was also required for washing sheep and shearing, hut-keeping, droving, and for defence against Aboriginal attack. Because of the monotony, isolation and danger of the work, hut-keeping and especially shepherding or 'crawling', as it soon became known, were despised tasks for which free labour was difficult to recruit.[5]

Commissioner Bigge and the pastoralists believed the easy answer to the labour problem was to enlarge the existing system of transportation and reallocate most of the convicts out of the service of emancipists and the state and into the hands of the 'pure merino' wool-growers. This solution was attractive because in Britain the period following the end of the Napoleonic wars was one of unprecedented hardship and of rising criminal convictions. Unemployment was increased by the demobilization of some 250 000 men; in 1816 a new Corn Law to keep bread prices high and protect the British capitalistic farmer caused widespread distress. Mechanization was proceeding apace and with it the exploitation of female and child labour. The poor in the countryside were reacting by burning ricks, and in the cities by rioting and sabotaging machines which they saw as instrumental to their misery. In the factories, workers forced into close association over long periods with fellow sufferers began to develop further the idea of collective action and to articulate a radical political ideology. The authorities passed new Combination Acts, restricting political meetings and associations and, where necessary, empowering the militia to put down demonstrations. For example, at St Peter's Fields, Manchester, in 1819 crowds gathering to hear speakers demand universal suffrage, vote by ballot, and the repeal of the Corn Laws, were seen as warranting the same military repression as convict and Aboriginal protestors in the colonies.[6]

As part of this repression, and happily for the colonial pastoralists, criminal convictions were rapidly multiplying. In 1814 a mere 558 death sentences had been passed in England and 756 people had been sentenced to transportation. In 1817 the number of death penalties had grown to 1302, and 1734 people were sentenced to be transported. In the eastern colonies, whereas a mere 4700 convicts had arrived during the periods from 1804 up to and including 1814, just over 14 000 would arrive from 1815 to the end of 1820.[7]

As the plans at Swan River showed, any consignment of convict labourers into the service of private masters overseas was now ideologically problematic. This was not only because it conjured up images of slavery in the minds of the Utilitarians and religious reformers, but also because both groups believed it was not sufficiently intimidating to deter worker resistance in Britain. Although transportation had been primarily a form of labour, it had been expected to constitute a form of punishment. Finding further common ground with Utilitarians on this issue of penal discipline, evangelical theorists were now arguing that forced labour abroad should be replaced by incarceration. Since both groups placed such emphasis on individual freedom, what better way of discipling the new 'free' labourer than to deprive him or her of liberty? Where by 1785 plans to build two modern prisons in London had lapsed, by 1812 numerous prisons had been rebuilt or enlarged. In 1816 the first new national penitentiary opened at Millbank.

Inside these new houses of correction, any whips, chains and other signs of 'slavery' and force were now theoretically outlawed. A whole range of new rituals said to be capable of making obedience automatic was being introduced. According to the reformers, these techniques were absolutely humane, being invented by experts to replace useless and degrading violence against the body with more effective, scientifically guaranteed transformation of the mind. Methods which combined the latest medical prescriptions for hygiene with the inculcation of shame were considered ideal. Solitary confinement in special cells was said to 'soften' the mind and render it receptive to moral and religious values. In reality, solitary confinement broke up dangerous political affiliations while the prisoners, isolated in their tiny cells, were encouraged to find fault within their individual souls rather than the economic system. Also recommended was a rigid daily routine and repetition, believed to teach 'self-control'. By 1811 at Gloucester penitentiary a new device known as a treadwheel offered an unprecedented combination of physical exertion and stupefying monotony. Though many of these new techniques reflected the time-discipline required by the factory, and even employed some of its technology, it was not the function of the new houses of correction to produce commodities as Bentham had originally envisaged. The modern penitentiary was to be an entirely state-controlled institution separating punishment from labour, introducing religious instruction and outlawing sexual liaisons between inmates.[8]

These developments were strongly supported by a new generation of prison reformers who emerged after 1815. Led by Elizabeth Fry and the Prison Discipline Society, these people began systematic visits to women on convict ships and contributed to the formation of new penal strategies by their focus on the juvenile offender. They drew attention to the numbers of children living in prison who had either been incarcerated with their mothers or convicted independently of an offence. Given the scale of the destruction of working-class family life which war, colonization and industrialization had caused, the number of such children was increasing. Between 1818 and 1820 some 728 boys aged 18 or under were transported to New South Wales and Van Diemen's Land. In Sydney in 1819, in deference to the ideas of the penal theorists, arrangements were made to accommodate some convict boys at the new Carters' Barracks, where to assist in their training a treadwheel was introduced in 1823.[9]

All of these views about the need to incarcerate recalcitrant workers instead of employing them as a captive labour force, were dramatically opposed to the material interests of the employer in the eastern colonies. Here, because native-born and free immigrants were still a tiny minority, employers were heavily dependent on convict and ex-convict workers. In 1820 these people comprised over 94 per cent of the 'potential' male workforce and 69 per cent of the female one. Essentially a primary producer, the colonial employer preferred a system of forced labour. Admittedly these workers had to be fed, clothed and housed, but they were on call night and day, defending his back-runs from Aborigines, and in his home performing the huge amount of domestic labour which his life-style demanded.[10]

It followed that the system of convict labour devised by Commissioner Bigge had to be a compromise between slavery and the reformers' ideal of a free labour force intimidated by fear of incarceration in a modern penitentiary. For women, his recommendations were largely confined to the need for new Factories which, despite their old-fashioned name, would confine and punish the female convict according to the latest disciplinary techniques. In contrast, for men, his recommendations centred around ways to increase the number of landless labourers available for pastoral work. Thus, in addition to foreshadowing the end of the 30-acre grant, Bigge advised major changes in the remuneration of convicts for their work, the qualifications of masters who were entitled to benefit from their services, and in the allocation of pardons and tickets-of-leave, all of which increased the labour pool available for pastoral expansion. In 1823, for instance, the arrangements whereby convict men had been paid for work done in their own time were cancelled. In private

: their labour was to be wholly at the command of their
r, night and day. No ex-convict was to be assigned a
ict servant, though this proved difficult to enforce. By 1835
new assignment regulations would specify that no holder of less
than 20 acres was entitled to a convict servant. Bigge also recommended convicts be made to surrender any money on arrival, the
money to be kept in a savings bank until the convict became free,
or acquired a ticket-of-leave. This made them conform more to
the status of a prisoner during their term of servitude and helped
ensure they would become wage-labourers at its conclusion. [11]

The Commissioner also provided detailed recommendations
for disciplining this new labour system geared to wool production.
In particular, there was to be an extended system of secondary
penal stations to punish reluctant workers and isolate politically
dangerous ones. Though these stations would still be essentially
forced-labour camps, labour now would be focused more on
punishment than production. Coal River, and even Port Macquarie which was founded in 1821, were said to be too close to
existing settlements to achieve the kind of isolation which penal
ideology required, as well as being too close to land wanted for
'colonization'. Convicts were to be sent to new, more remote
stations where they were to do the most menial of labour on a
rigidly set, monotonous and minimum diet. Their dress was to
consist of a striped uniform and their bedding was to be limited
to one rug and a mattress filled with firm straw. Commandants of
the new settlements were vigorously to exclude visits by trading
vessels and traffic in spirits. Aborigines were to continue to be
encouraged to apprehend fugitives by rewards of corn, fish-hooks
and blankets. New secondary penal stations based on these
recommendations opened at Macquarie Harbour (1822), Moreton
Bay (1824), Maria Island (1825), Norfolk Island (1825) and Port
Arthur (1830). [12]

Despite their aversion to slavery, British manufacturers
accepted this system of semi-slavery in the Australian colonies in
order to obtain the wool they needed. Moreover, Commissioner
Bigge and his advisers in the eastern colonies were able hastily to
clothe the new scheme in the language of penal discipline which
gave it a gloss of modernity. It was said that far from being a
system of slavery, the new assignment system was designed to
reform offenders by placing them under the eye of 'persons of
responsibility'. Even living among sheep on distant out-stations

had an uplifting effect on the criminal mind, breaking dangerous associations with fellow felons and the temptations and luxuries of the towns. Besides, as the pastoralists had informed Bigge, they were generously prepared to bear the costs of maintaining the convicts while also ensuring that their labour produced only raw materials needed by Britain.[13] The pastoralists also pointed out that, unlike slave-owners, masters of assigned servants could not punish personally but had to bring every case before a magistrate so convict servants were protected by the majestic proceedings of the British criminal law. In any case, it was argued, during the Macquarie era a limit had been placed upon the number of lashes which could be inflicted, and the horrific sentences of the early decades were now outlawed. The problem with this argument was that where Macquarie had tried to make the upper limit fifty lashes, in practice the new maximum set by the magistrates was twice this number. Further, by 1825 the powers of magistrates had been increased. A single magistrate could order transportation to a secondary penal station for three years, and an unspecified number of lashes, provided life or limb was not endangered. Though a further change of rules in 1823 attempted to set an upper limit of fifty lashes, in practice this was evaded by 'splitting' offences, so that a reluctant worker could be convicted of two misdemeanours and receive a double sentence. A pair of magistrates were empowered to order 100 lashes or three years' imprisonment with hard labour.

Magistrates' powers were gradually widened over the period to 1837. In New South Wales in 1826 stipendiary magistrates were authorized to sentence convicts to penal settlements, and to work in chains. In 1832 magistrates gained the power to order up to fourteen days in solitary confinement for offences like drunkenness and disobedience. Exposure in the pillory was another punishment popular with magistrates, especially after growing evangelical influence caused the public flogging of women to decline.[14] Though there were twenty-four paid police magistrates in New South Wales country districts by 1839 (and thirty-two paid scourgers), the discipline of convict labourers was largely left to unpaid magistrates who, as in England, were selected from among the most wealthy local land-owners. This system in effect gave the colonial élite wide powers to punish their servants. Whereas in 1818 there had been only twelve magistrates in the whole colony, and only seven of these were in non-urban areas, by 1822, there were thirty-two magistrates (mostly unpaid), twenty of whom were in country districts. This meant that although pastoralists could not personally pass judgement on their own servants, they could rely on their friends to do so.

Employers in towns enjoyed similar magisterial power over their convict workers and, with a magistrate close at hand, convict employees had fewer chances of escaping punishment. In 1836 Sydney merchant and pastoralist, A. B. Spark, was quick to have his servant 'Charlie the Carpenter' brought before a magistrate and receive a sentence of fifty lashes for having borrowed tools and used them to manufacture goods on his own account.[15]

Despite all the efforts to conceal the violence of Bigge's assignment system it was still open to accusations of slavery because most punishments were meted out for work-related offences. Forms of indiscipline in the work-place such as absence without leave, absconding, indolence, idleness, or losing and damaging property, were criminal offences. Returns of corporal punishment in New South Wales for the years 1833 to 1836 reveal that on average some 25 per cent of the male convicts (including those in the penal stations) were flogged in any one year, and that of these, most received close to fifty lashes. By the 1830s flogging was so vital to discipling the convict worker and so common that pastoralists and magistrates were debating the efficiency of the implements used. 'They are made exceedingly careless', Lachlan Macalister complained from Goulburn in 1833, dwelling with savage relish on the length and strength of cordage which he thought would inflict the maximum amount of damage. George K. Holden, Police Magistrate at Campbelltown, disagreed. The construction of the cat should be such as to inflict the greatest pain with the minimum damage to the worker's health.[16]

Between 1820 and 1839, the new formula for combining punishment with profit provided some 54 000 convict workers for New South Wales and over 30 000 for Van Diemen's Land. In both colonies this resulted in a population structure where a high percentage comprised convicts under sentence. In New South Wales in 1828 the proportion would reach 46 per cent, the highest since 1796; in Van Diemen's Land, the extraordinarily high percentage of nearly 73 per cent of convicts in 1820, would settle down to average 43 per cent between 1821 and 1839.

Commissioner Bigge's assignment system formed a new kind of bridge between slavery and free labour and was, from the pastoralists' point of view, remarkably efficient, especially during the 1820s and early 1830s. A high intake of single male convicts ensured that an unusually large proportion of the population comprised able-bodied male workers, averaging 65 per cent in this period. Aged mostly between sixteen and twenty-five and bringing with them a cross-section of useful skills, both the men and the women provided the human resources necessary for sustained pastoral expansion. Most were first offenders, usually convicted of petty theft.[17]

However, more than even before, the fortunes of the convict men under the new scheme depended upon previous training. Those with skills in demand in the colony, such as carpenters and ploughmen, remained an important economic resource, and were less likely to find themselves reconvicted and consigned to a secondary penal station or chain-gang. On the other hand, those with skills unwanted in the local economy, such as nail-makers, tin-smiths, weavers and craftsmen of goods imported from British manufacturers, were likely to find themselves dispatched, along with the unskilled urban workers, into heavy or monotonous manual labour 'up the country'. Here, the purpose of the assignment system became very much to destroy unwanted knowledge and turn the craftsman into a labourer. Convict men confronted with this kind of experience explored the full range of punishments which the system had to offer. Nineteen-year-old Frederick Thomas, transported for life in 1835 for swindling, resisted the assignment system. A painter and glazier by trade, he was sent into the Snowy Mountains district as a shepherd. In 1836 he received fifty lashes for being illegally at large; in 1837 he spent twelve months in irons; in 1839 he received another seventy-five lashes for absconding, and two years later, another twelve months in irons for larceny. In April 1842 he was sentenced in Sydney to a further fifteen years for stealing in a dwelling house. This sentence had to be served in a penal settlement, and in due course he was consigned to Port Arthur.[18]

There were no prescribed hours for labour in assignment, but a convention had developed where male convicts worked between sunrise and sunset. Sunday was prescribed as a day of rest, and male convicts considered they were entitled to Saturday afternoon off, as were convicts in government service. Masters were responsible for providing specified amounts of food, clothing, and bedding for their servants, and those wishing to encourage obedience and industry provided extra rations, usually in the form of tea, sugar and tobacco. In cases of recalcitrance, offenders could be punished by withdrawal of these indulgences. This saved taking the case before a magistrate, a procedure which could involve much inconvenience to the master and loss of time.

Theoretically, convicts who were unfairly treated by their masters could use the legal system to get redress, but it was risky to leave one's master without permission in order to lay a complaint at the nearest Bench. Some convict labourers won their cases. At Scone in 1833 the men assigned to Hugh Cameron were ordered to be supplied with wholesome food after the magistrate agreed that samples of their meat ration were not fit for use. In another case before the same Bench, the servant of John Robertson, an absentee farmer living in Sydney, managed to get himself transferred after proving that he had not been supplied with shoes or clothing for six months, nor with a bed and blanket for four years. Cases where convicts attempted to use the law to secure redress were much fewer than cases where they were prosecuted by masters and overseers, and convict-initiated cases were not always successful. In 1835 James Brown brought a complaint before the Yass Bench that his master, John Hume, had beaten him because, having a headache, he had left his work to lie down. Hume responded by alleging past idleness and indolence, which was sufficient for Magistrate Henry O'Brien to dismiss the case. Hume was merely requested not to beat his servant again.[19]

Not surprisingly, a more common form of protest was passive resistance on the job. Convicts with a skilled trade were in an especially favourable position to try this, as missionary L. E. Threlkeld discovered. At Lake Macquarie he employed four unskilled labourers and a carpenter, a blacksmith and a shoe-maker. In an attempt to discipline them Threlkeld reduced their rations, but found this increased their 'obstinacy'. The shoemaker now produced three pairs of shoes a week instead of four, while the smith burned and destroyed the iron. The carpenter, reproved for working on his own account on a Sunday, 'cooly informed me that he was determined never to do me any good, that he wished to be turned in to the government'.

Convicts assigned to extremely remote areas could do little to improve their working conditions. On his journey to the Southern Alps in 1834 John Lhotsky found that, because of the absence of trees, shepherds and stockmen on a recently occupied run at Rock

Flat had not been able to build a hut. They were living in a shelter under the rocks and were inadequately clothed. Most were suffering from rheumatic complaints, while constipation, sore eyes, and 'the syphilitic disease' were common in Maneroo.

Convicts working in the government service were sometimes in a better position than those in assignment to offer resistance. From December 1831 those working on the construction of a tunnel to augment Sydney's water supply were able, as Governor Bourke admitted, 'to evade in every possible way' the labour they were supposed to perform. A project under the supervision of John Busby, the mineral surveyor of Sydney, that of the 2-mile tunnel connecting Hyde Park to the Lachlan Swamps, had to be driven for most of its length through solid rock. The work involved blasting with gunpowder and the tunnel was often waist-high with water. Busby initially estimated that the project would be completed in three years, with men working day and night in 8-hour shifts, six days a week, but by 1833 little progess had been made. Gratuities of tea, sugar and tobacco were offered to the industrious, and a variety of punishments meted out to the idle, but still the work did not progress. One overseer complained that the sixty to ninety men normally involved played 'hide-and-seek' with him in the tunnel and its twenty-eight shafts.

Some assigned convicts never came to terms with the discipline and subordination expected by their masters, nor did they acquire skills by which they could find a way out. One such was George Pettit, a young man of nineteen, sentenced to be hanged in Hobart in 1840 and his body dissected, for shooting an overseer. Pettit had been assigned to Roderic O'Connor, a wealthy pastoralist and large-scale supervisor of convict labour, both on his own estates and as inspector of roads and bridges during the Arthur regime. A letter dictated by Pettit to his father in England told the rest of the story:

My Dear Father,
I regret to state my misfortunes since I came to this country, but my situation now I don't expect to remain in this world more than few weeks as I am fully committed to take my trial for wilful murder at the next criminal court in Hobart Town. I have been 'signed off' to Mr O'Connor at Peter's Pass, and the overseer and I had some words on the 27th of this month, In consequence of my not going to work soon enough in the morning, and threatening to bring me in to Oatlands before the Magistrate for which reason I loaded my piece and shot him

in the breast and also in the hand. . . . My kind love to my sisters and brothers hoping they won't fret as it will do no good now

The overseer had promised Pettit a flogging which would strip the flesh from his back.[20]

Despite the large percentage of convicts in the population during the 1820s and 1830s, the opportunities for armed resistance were slight. Convict society lacked the predominantly Irish component which had provided solidarity and revolutionary experience in 1804. Certainly the numerous convict ballads and songs which have survived from the 1820s and 1830s suggest a strongly articulated desire for armed rebellion:

And some dark night when everything is silent in the town
I'll kill the tyrants, one and all, and shoot th' floggers down:
I'll give th' Law a little shock: remember what I say,
They'll yet regret they sent Jim Jones in chains to Botany Bay!

Experienced leadership, however, was lacking, since political prisoners were now a tiny minority of total convict numbers and care was taken to disperse them. Thus the fifty Luddites who had been transported in 1812 had been quickly submerged in the overall prison population. Of the twenty-five Cato Street conspirators transported in 1819—20 for an ambitious plot to assassinate the British Cabinet as a signal for revolution, one became chief constable at Bathurst, a second was assigned to him until he received a pardon and became a tailor; and a third became Bathurst's leading baker. The 164 village labourers and craftsmen, transported for rick-burning and other forms of political protest in 1830—31, tended to have the skills wanted in the colonial economy, and thus avoided the kind of oppression and tyranny which drove other convicts towards desperate protest against the assignment system. In 1834 six of the farm labourers known as the Tolpuddle Martyrs arrived to serve a seven-year term for taking an oath to protect their wages. Though highly politicized, they were too few to influence convict protest in the colonies.

As well as lacking political leadership, convict society was too scattered by the 1820s and 1830s for the formation of any concerted plan of action. Also the state had at its command the services of the military and the mounted police, whom the convicts 'up the country' could observe in action against the Aborigines. Clearly any uprising would be dealt with in the same manner as that in the West Indies in August 1823, when hundreds of slaves were shot dead and executed. No doubt the convicts learned of these reprisals from the 140 slaves who were transported to the Australian colonies following a similar uprising in Jamaica in 1831–32.[21]

In New South Wales, any convict contemplating organized rebellion had an example nearer to home. In November 1833 John Poole, a carpenter assigned to Waterloo veteran 'Major' Mudie at 'Castle Forbes' in the Hunter Valley, organized a small revolt. Of the sixty men who had been assigned to this estate, more than half had suffered corporal punishment, many at the direction of John Larnach. A former overseer of John Bowman, in 1827 Larnach had married Mudie's daughter and now managed his father-in-law's estate. Like so many of the gentlemen of the colony, Larnach did not shrink from personally defending his newly acquired possessions. In August 1826 he had accompanied the party of mounted police when one Aborigine was summarily shot on suspicion of being involved in the spearing of two of Bowman's fencers. At Castle Forbes, he had maintained order and industry by such stratagems as bringing one convict before the Bench twice on the same day for the same offence, so as to obtain two sentences of fifty lashes each.

In November 1833 John Poole was one of the minority who had not been flogged, for his trade made him such a prized and favoured worker that he was able to threaten that if he ever was flogged he would abscond into the bush. Ignoring the threat, Larnach arranged for Poole to receive fifty lashes for insolence. The same evening, Poole kept his word. Accompanied by two others he absconded, met up with a fourth who had departed earlier, and freed two others who were being escorted to Maitland by a constable. These six then chose to return to the 'Castle' and collect food, arms and horses. Here they informed Emily Larnach that they planned to sever her husband's head and use it as a gargoyle to ornament the 'Castle's' chimney. They also mentioned that had her father been at home, his head would have graced the other. They then rushed down to a water-hole where Larnach was supervising nine men washing sheep, and attempted to shoot him, but missed. Larnach hastily departed for shelter at Henry Dangar's neighbouring manor, Neotsfield, while the enraged convicts moved on to an estate occupied by another harsh employer, Edward Sparke. Here they changed their tactics and instead of attempting execution, commuted the sentence, tying gentleman to a post and flogging him with a cat-of-nine-tails. Larnach had meanwhile engaged a punitive expedition of mounted police and civilians, including himself. The six were caught and tried in December 1833 in Sydney, where three were executed. Poole and Hitchcock were escorted back to Castle Forbes for hanging, heavily chained and conspicuously arranged on two coffins as a warning to all the other convicts at work on the road or on adjacent stations along the way. In due course it was their bodies and not the heads of Larnach and Mudie which came to grace the 'Castle's' park. The gallows were left undismantled for months, as a ghoulish reminder of this display of the law in action against worker insubordination. The youngest of the six offenders was sent to Norfolk Island for life.[22]

If armed resistance was not an option, escape remained a possibility, especially for male convicts working around harbours and ports. In mid-1825 a gang of convicts loading coal onto the schooner *Eclipse* at Newcastle took advantage of a moment when all the crew were below decks, to fasten down the hatches, heave up the anchor, and make for the sea. Neither convicts nor crew were ever heard of again, though they were thought to have reached a Pacific isle. In 1835, five of William Wentworth's servants robbed his home at Vaucluse and boarded his ketch to sail to freedom. Wentworth was an unpopular master who had had the leader of the rebels flogged for insolence and drunkenness six weeks earlier. In August 1829, the capture of the brig *Cyprus* in Recherche Bay by convicts *en route* to the penal station at Macquarie Harbour helped inspire escapes of this kind. The leader of this mutiny became romanticized in the popular ballad tradition as 'bold Captain Swallow' for, having cast off the officer-in-charge, his wife and the soldiers, Swallow successfully steered for Japan. Arriving at length in England, however, he and his companions were identified. Swallow was returned to Macquarie Harbour and died of tuberculosis at Port Arthur in 1834.[23]

For many male convicts, escape into the bush also continued to be a possibility, but this too rarely resulted either in retribution or freedom. Writing in 1827, Peter Cunningham believed that bushranging was now so romanticized in ballad and song that convict men actually chose it in order to find fame and immortality. Certainly some escapees achieved such a familiarity with the bush that convict ballads by the 1830s began to depict it not as a hostile, antipodean environment but as a source of liberty. As the chorus to 'Bold Jack Donohoe' declared,

> Then come my hearties, we'll roam the mountains high!
> Together we will plunder, together we will die!
> We'll wander over the mountains and we'll gallop over plains—
> For we scorn to live in slavery, bound down with iron chains.

But Jack Donohoe was shot by police near Campbelltown while even the well-publicized exploits of Matthew Brady culminated in a similar way. Convicted of stealing a basket of butter, bacon, sugar, and rice, Brady was twenty-two years old when sentenced in Manchester in 1820 to transportation for seven years. An unskilled labourer, he soon proved to be one of those convicts determined to resist the work-discipline demanded of him. In the first four years of his sentence he received a total of 350 lashes and was sent to Macquarie Harbour. In 1824 he was one of a group of convicts who escaped from the penal settlement and sailed a boat to the Derwent River. For the next two years Brady managed both to evade capture and to establish a romantic reputation for courting women, and for daring gun-battles with members of the establishment. Persons whose property was singled out for his attention included Thomas Massey, Abraham Walker, and Richard Dry, while Thomas Jeffries, a former executioner who had cruelly bungled the hanging of a popular highwayman in Edinburgh in 1818, was a marked man.

Brady's most famous feat was to liberate all the prisoners in the gaol at Sorell and replace them with eighteen citizens and a number of soldiers. He was also reputed to have responded to rewards offered for his capture by posting a notice on the door of an inn offering twenty gallons of rum for the capture of the Governor. However it was the Governor's system of rewards which won the day. In May 1826 Brady was hanged following his capture by an indefatigable, native-born land-taker, John Batman, in the Western Tiers. Batman had been aided in the task by prisoners sent by the Crown to infiltrate Brady's gang and ultimately betray it.

In Van Diemen's Land bushranging had long been a special problem, to the extent that in 1815 Governor Davey had declared martial law. By the mid-1820s, so many armed bandits were again at large that, combining this with the fear of Aboriginal attack, some settlers deserted their stations and retreated to the towns.

No informing ideology was articulated but bushranging was not apolitical. 'Captain' Michael Howe's gang, active in Van Diemen's Land from 1814 to 1818 and dressed in a uniform of kangaroo skin and moccasins, frequently adopted the ritual disguise of the blackened face which had been the hallmark of organized rural resistance to enclosure in England, inspiring the *Black Act* of 1723. Nor could bushrangers have survived for long as bandits without the assistance of sympathetic convicts, ex-convicts and Aboriginal people. However, although the convict labourers of this time could be said to form the nucleus of the first Australian working class, the divisiveness and isolation of the assignment system deprived them of the ideological tools necessary for collective political action. It was all too easy for their essentially individualistic resistance to degenerate into a desperate battle for survival by anarchistic capitalists on the wrong side of the law. Some stole from struggling ex-convict farmers as well as the rich, and saw ex-convict women as property to be plundered. In May 1815, six armed men, including Michael Howe, having earlier fired the harvest of mineralogist and magistrate A. W. H. Humphrey, rampaged through his house, threatening to make him stand by 'while they did as thought proper' with his ex-convict wife.

Few succeeded in capturing the horses, the muskets, and the ammunition needed for stylish attacks on the settlements. In 1833 when Van Diemen's Land absconders Browne and Jeffkins appeared suddenly at a lime-burner's hut at Port Sorell and demanded food, they had had nothing to eat for five days but a parrot and a cockatoo. They had been on the run for two years and had lost their few possessions when crossing a river on a catamaran. Pieces of leather and blanket tied to their feet had to serve as shoes, and they wore ragged clothes of their own improvization. Both were subsequently shot by police, and a wounded comrade left in the bush while they sought food from the lime-burner was never found.[24]

In the two colonies gentlemen took to the task of hunting and capturing bushrangers with a relish only equalled by their punitive expeditions against the Aborigines. In July 1825 Robert Scott, with some of his servants and some soldiers, pursued and captured the gang known as 'Jacob's Mob'. The 'Mob' included a shepherd from Vicar Jacob's station who had been sentenced to receive fifty lashes but escaped on the way to Newcastle, and five men who had absconded from adjacent farms to join him. Though heavily shackled, the bushrangers escaped again, and over the next three months survived by robbing the houses of eminent settlers in the area, including those of James Reid, Dr Radford, and Leslie Duguid. From Sydney, A. B. Spark offered a reward of sixty Spanish dollars for their capture. Robert Scott and party were again in pursuit, but in October it was James Reid J.P. with soldiers who shot one of the 'Mob' dead at Hexham and captured the remainder. At Collector in 1833, the moment he was made a magistrate T. A. Murray joined in a relentless campaign against the bushrangers operating south of Goulburn, where armed men were still at large in the late 1840s.[25]

Masters were asking for an increased number of soldiers and police to aid them in these tasks from 1819. By 1828 in New South Wales the ratio of police to population was 1:44 in Sydney and 1:96 in the colony overall, a very high rate compared to 1:1000 in English rural areas at this time. Mounted police numbers also grew across the period. By 1835 in New South Wales they comprised over a hundred troopers, the bulk of whom were located in Goulburn, Bathurst and the Hunter. Their commandant, Captain Williams, claimed that they had captured 220 runaways in the first five months of that year alone. Notices in the *New South Wales Government Gazette* in 1835 confirmed that the capture of some thirty-five or more absconders per week was not unusual. Not all evaded capture long enough to become bush-rangers, but a constant stream of men was absconding from private service, road-gangs, watch-houses, and in one case, even from the *Phoenix* hulk, in irons. In December 1825 one Hunter River settler, James Phillips of 'Bona Vista', found that of twenty servants originally assigned to him in 1822 he had only eight remaining. The others had taken to the bush at different times.[26]

In an attempt to overcome the problem of convict resistance some employers turned to Aboriginal labour. Men and women were used, mostly as shepherds, but also in cutting bark for building purposes, and for washing and shearing sheep. In agricultural areas they milked cows, gathered potatoes, reaped wheat and erected fences. In 1822 Alexander Berry, who had acquired a huge number of acres of agricultural land on the Shoalhaven River, tried to use Charles Throsby's guide, 'Broughton', to

t a large Aboriginal labour force by presenting him with a
neck-plate proclaiming him 'Native Constable of the Shoal
Haven'. Berry had just been denied a request for 100 convicts to
work in his sawmill, grow subsistence crops and cut cedar for
shipment to Sydney. Aboriginal workers were seldom paid,
except in rations and, like the convicts, resisted this kind of
exploitation. Despite the official strategy to create enmity between bushrangers and Aborigines, numerous absconders were
aided by Aborigines, some of them women. In Van Diemen's
Land the presence of Aboriginal women working with bushrangers had been commonly noted by 1819. The same pattern
occurred in New South Wales where, for instance, the William
Macdonald gang, operating in the area between Bathurst and the
Liverpool Plains in 1834, included three women. Occasionally,
non-Aboriginal women also joined male absconders in the bush
but, as in the early days of the settlement, in general bushranging
was not an option for convict women.[27]

In New South Wales in 1830 a Bushranging Act attempted to
control the number of absconders and to tighten discipline.
Magistrates were authorized to enter any house at their own
discretion and seize any person suspected of being an absconder,
the onus being on the suspects to prove that they were not, rather
than on the Crown to prove that they were. Employers were
warned that all convicts who did not carry a pass while travelling
would be arrested, irrespective of the inconvenience to their
masters. However, the problem of convicts absconding and
convict resistance did not decrease. By the 1830s pastoralists
were responding with calls for more and severer discipline. Sir
John Jamison wanted to see the introduction of itinerant mounted
police magistrates travelling from station to station, complete
with a scourger to inflict punishment on the spot. At Collector
T. A. Murray found it convenient to hold police courts at his
own residence instead of at the Bench of Magistrates at Goulburn,
of which he was a member. He had arranged for a constable and
a scourger to be permanently stationed at his head-station,
Winderradeen. Prisoners brought in from Limestone Plains,
Maneroo and the Molonglo were installed in a strong-room on
his own premises pending their hearing, which was held in one of
the rooms of the house. Cases were heard at the rate of seven or
eight per week—indeed, scarcely a day passed without one.[28]

By the 1830s growing use was being made of the chain-gang to punish recalcitrant workers. In New South Wales in the decade from 1826 some 5000 men or 18 per cent of the male convicts spent part of their sentence in one of these gangs, labouring daily in the construction of the main roads and being locked at night in tiny, portable huts, still in their irons. Similar gangs were organized in Van Diemen's Land, where they were set to construct wharves at Hobart and the causeway at Bridgewater. Like the penal stations, the chain-gangs took workers out of the service of the pastoralists, yet throughout this period up to one-quarter of all male convicts experienced the especially brutal punishment for which both these forms of incarceration were notorious.[29]

The increasingly visible use of force was testimony to the fact that the assignment system was no longer the easy answer to pastoralists' labour problems that it had been two decades before. Like all systems of slave labour, which it increasingly resembled, it began to break down under the pressure of resistance. Contributing to the demise of the system was the fact that the dependence of the pastoralists on forced, unskilled labour was changing. Under the pressure of overgrazing, pastoral productivity was declining and new outstations in well-watered areas were now becoming much harder to find. Ruinous diseases of sheep, such as scab and catarrh, had made their appearance and could only be dealt with by more skilled and controlled methods of production.[30]

As the assignment system began to break down, so criticism of it by liberals and humanitarians increased. This was partly a reflection of the fact that for English manufacturers profits depended on a ready supply of low-priced raw materials and, in the 1830s wool prices were rising, as was British dependence on wool. Bipartisan agitation for the reform of the nation's major institutions was growing, as the Whigs's first taste of power in almost seventy years (November 1830 to November 1834), and the passing of Lord Grey's Great Reform Act in 1832 clearly demonstrated. Enfranchising adult males who had been enriched by industrialization, this Act, though it did not break the monopoly of the old aristocratic families on membership of parliament, did ensure that more attention would now be paid by them to meeting the needs of the industrialists. Almost immediately, in 1833 this Act was followed by legislation abolishing slavery throughout the British empire. Where the reformers had hoped their 1807 Act against the slave trade would gradually convert all employers to free labour, now employers in all British colonies would be forced to consider the moral and, in the long term, economic advantages of transforming their slaves into free workers and consumers. This achieved, it was inevitable that the uneconomic assignment system would also come under attack and in the 1830s the anti-slavers mounted a sustained attack upon it, using all the ideological weapons they had at their disposal. Convict workers, they declared, were brutalized slaves and their employers were tyrannical slave-drivers, for absolute power corrupted those who wielded it, while the bloody sight of public punishments tainted master as well as man.[31]

In particular, critics of the assignment system focused on the fact that transportation had produced a society where the disproportion of the sexes was extremely high. In New South Wales throughout the 1820s and 1830s the proportion of females in the total white population remained around 25 per cent while the proportion of adult women in the adult population was even lower, at around 20 per cent. By 1841 the equalizing effect of the immigration policies and of the female native-born would only slightly alter this pattern. Females would comprise only 33 per cent of the total population of adult women, and 28 per cent of the adult population. On the frontier even larger distortions existed. Whereas in Sydney in 1841 adult females comprised 38 per cent of the total adult population, in Maneroo there were only some 220 European women, comprising 14.5 per cent of the adult white population there.[32]

This unusual preponderance of males in the eastern colonies was of increasing fascination to Utilitarians—who saw it as demographically inefficient—and to moralists who saw it as a source of vice and disease. To some observers it seemed that the shortage of women increased the incidence of male homosexuality, which was both wasteful and morally repugnant. To others, it was seen as contributing an irresistible temptation to the 'weaker' sex to prostitute themselves and corrupt innocent males, who then turned to crime to pay these sultry temptresses their wages of sin. Sexual relations were ideally now to be universally confined to marriage and were to take place discreetly inside a private home. Once the home had functioned as a work-place where foodstuffs, clothing and other goods had been produced, now it was to be organized around the newly defined needs of the numerous children which every marriage was expected to produce. Though very much a site where the material possessions of the newly enriched middle class were to be displayed, the home was being ideologically elevated into a spiritual haven, absolutely superior to and separate from the sordid world of industry which had replaced it as the prime producer of consumer goods.

Many reformers were genuinely concerned for the plight of exploited women, but this ideal of sexual and domestic relations also reflected their underlying need for increased reproduction which was vital to the profitability of the free labour system. Their ideal of establishing a genteel, nuclear family life was based on the knowledge that numerous, separately housed family units would increase demand for manufactured goods. Through their philanthropy they were aware of the growing cost to private charity of the thousands of women and children left without the support of a male breadwinner. Legal marriage and a godly home were seen as the solution to all these problems. Instead of making marriage and family life impossible for the labouring masses, as the old mercantilist ruling class had done, these people wanted to make it compulsory.[33] The assignment system, in particular, was seen as exacerbating these alleged evils since it enabled masters to resist employing men with families, and to argue that women with very young children were 'useless encumbrances'. Employers had little interest in new, long-term demographic strategies to improve reproduction, preferring any system which would supply them with a constant stream of disciplined and cheap male labourers. As P. P. King, speaking for the pastoralists, pointed out in 1835, 'importing married male emigrants might benefit the colony, but it would not benefit the master who had to feed the families'.[34]

Therefore, in addition to their rhetoric of slavery the reformers used a rhetoric of sexual and domestic morality to attack the assignment system. This attack was taken up not only in Britain but also in the colonies, where the number of churchmen, urban professionals of liberal views and philanthropic wives and daughters was increasing. Catholic Vicar-General, W. B. Ullathorne, who arrived in Sydney in 1833, was concerned about male homosexuality, believing this was prevalent both on the pastoral frontier and in the chain-gangs and secondary penal stations. His *Catholic Mission to Australasia* was published in 1837, followed by *The Horrors of Transportation Briefly Unfolded to the*

People in 1838. Presbyterian Reverend John Dunmore Lang considered the system a moral catastrophe polluting the whole of colonial society. Arriving in 1824, he produced his critique of the system, *Transportation and Colonization*, in 1837.

These damning indictments of transportation as producing a licentious and sexually perverse society were shared by many of the missionaries, who believed that convictism introduced the Aboriginal people to depraved habits and alcohol, and therefore interfered with attempts at conversion. Others pointed out that the assignment system was failing to provide sufficient religious instruction for convict men and, by placing them alone in remote areas, was encouraging the rape of Aboriginal women and girls and the spread of venereal disease. In 1837 Governor Bourke declared that the abduction of Aboriginal women by shepherds was the major cause of war on the frontier and went so far as to prohibit whites from detaining Aboriginal women by force. This failed to prevent liaisons between Aboriginal women and convict men, merely stigmatizing such relationships and rendering them less likely to be permanent. At the same time, this preoccupation obscured the economic causes of violence on the frontier, and was used as an additional weapon with which to attack the assignment system.[35]

In this attack, the old issue of the sexual morality and reproductive efficiency of the convict women became of special concern. With growing evangelical influence, governors had been instructed to pay more attention to improving the religion and the morals of the colonies and to encourage marriage. In 1810 Macquarie had issued a proclamation condemning de facto relationships and prohibiting any woman in such a relationship from inheriting her partner's property should he die intestate. This of course was of no help to the women, merely encouraging them to be seen primarily as sexual commodities dependent on the support of a man. The skills of the convict women as general servants, laundresses, kitchen-hands and needleworkers continued to be undervalued and under-employed.[36]

For many of the women, Commissioner Bigge's assignment system had come close to achieving the penal reformers' ideal of making punishment a form of incarceration rather than a form of work. Following Bigge's censure of the old, overcrowded Factory, new institutions for women had been opened at Parramatta and Hobart in 1821 and at Georgetown in 1824. Despite some attention to cloth production, these new Factories were intended to be modern punitive establishments, devoted as much to disciplining women who committed misdemeanours as to sheltering new arrivals prior to assignment. This was especially evident at Parramatta where the new Factory, specially designed by Francis Greenaway to accommodate 300 women, contained six solitary cells and was surrounded by a wall almost ten feet high. In Hobart, the Factory was moved into new, enlarged premises at the Cascades in June 1828, while the design for a new Factory, opened at Launceston in 1834, from the outset reflected its role as a House of Correction. Reinforcing their role in incarceration, the new Factories were also nurseries where women who were pregnant on arrival or who became so in assignment could be housed and their children cared for until consigned into one of the orphan schools at about the age of three. Thus at Parramatta by 1835, there were some 150 children in the Factory, comprising just over one-fifth of the total number of inmates.[37]

Far from pleasing the critics of the assignment system, the Factories attracted increasing censure partly because they were no sooner opened than they were crowded with inmates and were thus expensive to run. Women continued to face sexual exploitation on board the ships and while in assignment and so many were destined to spend time in the Factories, bearing and rearing infants. The overcrowding was also a measure of the fact that to commit an offence while in assignment in order to be sent back to the Factory was one of the few means available for women convicts wanting to escape from intolerable working conditions. As domestic workers they were likely to be housed under the same roof as their employers and were subjected to constant scrutiny, by night as well as by day. This rendered their work particularly onerous and meant that they were much more likely than men to have their employer find fault with them. Reported offences like placing a mistress's child in the hands of a common 'prostitute' to nurse, refusing to work, or using threatening and diabolical language, reflected the special combination of vulnerability and resistance which explained why women convicts were especially likely to find themselves confined in the 'criminal' section of the Factories. In addition, free women as well as convict ones were sentenced to these institutions. As attempts to bring the women under discipline tightened during the period, women could be apprehended by a constable merely for being on the streets at night, where they were seen as constituting what was called 'a common pest'.

Pregnancy for convict women while in assignment could also constitute an offence, and a dangerous one, as the death of Jane Smith in 1834 revealed. Though married to a ticket-of-leave holder, she was assigned to a settler at Richmond who, a few days after she had given birth to a child, brought her before the Bench at Windsor where she was sentenced to be returned to the Factory. Meanwhile she spent a week in the Windsor cells where she could not sleep for fear that the rats would eat her child. Ordered to walk to Parramatta, she died soon after arrival. She was twenty years old.[38]

Growing humanitarian concern had thus done little to redress the traditional callousness with which convict women were treated, nor could it do so while it was based on the treatment of women primarily as sexual and reproductive objects. By the 1830s some theorists and administrators were becoming concerned that while the new emphasis on incarceration might punish women, it also interfered with reproduction. Some drew attention to the high infant death rate in the nursery of the Hobart Factory; others argued that reproduction would be better served by returning to the old policy of providing neither shelter nor modern punishments for the women while introducing some new and certain method of consigning the women as quickly as possible into wedlock. John Henderson, a self-styled political economist from Bengal who visited the eastern colonies in 1829–31, argued that those troublesome, expensive women presently cluttering the Factories would have been better disciplined and more useful if delivered into the hands of a husband before being permitted to disembark. This was the ideal way to discipline them and render them useful. Collectively they could produce perhaps a thousand children a year. It was well known, declared this sage, that the climate of Australia increased the reproductive powers of all animals, and all women under forty-two could bear a child a year. 'Females of a higher class are less affected by the climate', he conceded, but the present system of the Factories reduced female reproductive power by one-half. Peter Cunningham went further and suggested that even convict women who were already married should be divorced on arrival, so as to facilitate and legalize their function as sexual partners of colonial men.[39]

'An Exploring Party in New South Wales' (1826). This and other illustrations in James Atkinson's Account of the State of Agriculture and Grazing in New South Wales, *reveals the extent to which many pastoralists, in their assault on the inland, utilized the skills of Aboriginal guides.*

Augustus Earle's 'A Government Gaol Gang, Sydney, N.S. Wales' (1830) illustrated the growing stereotype of the convict men as innately cunning and vicious. Behind them, Greenway's elegant Hyde Park Barracks remains as a graphic reminder of the more egalitarian and now anachronistic plans of the colony's founders.

Pointing to the continuing importance of the military presence in the convict colonies, James Maclehose's illustration of the Sydney Military Barracks in 1839 also includes in the foreground the silhouette of Bungaree. Perhaps because of his distinctive clothing (a cast-off military uniform), Bungaree featured as a stock figure in numerous paintings and sketches during the 1820s and 1830s where, like others of his people, he was used to draw attention to the 'improvements' and 'progress' wrought by the colonizers. The Military Barracks had been erected by Macquarie in 1815 and included a fountain supported by nine classical columns.

J. S. Prout's Residences of the Aborigines, Flinders Island, 1844, evokes the bleak isolation of the settlement and the despair of its captives. Two Aboriginal figures evade the gaze of the missionaries' houses and church, which seem to have been designed so as to be the centre of focus and authority and, as in the Panopticon, to keep the inmates under constant surveillance.

In J. S. Prout's Hobart Town from the New Wharf (1844) a woman waits patiently, guarding goods unloaded from a vessel. The relative absence of ships and cargoes reflects the demise of the colony's former importance as a maritime and agricultural base.

Fancy Dress Ball given by Lord Mayor Hosking, Sydney, August 1843.

John Rae, Hyde Park, Sydney, 1842.

The efficacy of such modern eugenic programmes as suggested by Drs Henderson and Cunningham was never put to the test, although one state experiment in pushing women out of the new Factory and into the arms of convict men had already been tried. In May 1822 when the new Female Factory at Parramatta was already overcrowded, twenty-five women were dispatched to the government farm at Emu Plains where between 300 and 400 men were then at work. Apparently it was assumed that twenty-five men would easily be found who would marry the women and take them 'off the store'.

This experiment ended happily for the theorists, who rejoiced that by 1825 nineteen of the women were married. In the interim, the overseers prostituted the women to the convict men and to casual visitors who swam across the river from Sir John Jamison's Regentville or who were passing on the Bathurst Road. 'The cruel work going on in the women's huts was too brutal to be believed', a convict tailor who lived with his wife at the settlement later reported. An older woman, sent to the Plains as a hut-keeper, came to his hut and 'Begged for God sake, that she might be allowed to come in, stating as a reason that there were no less than six pair of buttocks at work in the hut and that she was tired of looking at such sights.' These statements were part of a report successfully used by Brisbane's enemies to contrive the termination of his regime. No future governor felt inclined to repeat such an experiment in enforced marriage and reproduction.[40] Instead Governor Darling initiated a new marriage policy. Under new regulations issued in 1826, selected government convicts considered able to support a family were offered special privileges if they would marry. In addition to being allowed to sleep out of the Barracks, they would be permitted to work on their own account at weekends. In 1830 Darling informed his superiors that this policy had been a great success, stating that in the past six months 163 prisoners had been married to free men and men holding ticket-of-leave. By the later 1830s the Parramatta Factory became known in New South Wales society as a market where approved applicants, including well-conducted men still under sentence, could have a wife for the asking.[41]

Convict women who left the Factory to marry were not freed but were assigned to their husbands. This policy was less successful for it permitted colonial men, as of old, to subvert the plans of the authorities and deny responsibility for their dependants. A husband could return a woman to the Factory for a misdemeanour or simply because he had tired of her. This practice became so common that an Act was passed in 1830 'to compel married men to withdraw their Wives from the Female Factory at Parramatta, or to maintain them after the expiration of her Sentence'.[42]

Despite the fact that most convict women sooner or later entered into reasonably permanent relationships with single male breadwinners where they had similar chances of security and happiness as working-class women elsewhere, the special problems faced by women in the convict colonies provided further fuel for the critics of the assignment system. Far from being punished or reformed, it was said, the women in assignment, with scarcely an exception, became drunken and abandoned 'prostitutes'. It was said that in the new Factories discipline was insufficient and that the Factories were virtually expensive lying-in homes for illegitimate children conceived as a result of the inefficient system. With homosexuality, juvenile vice and venereal disease running rife, the colonies were little more than cesspools of sexual perversion and godless waste.[43]

By the end of the decade, though not all were convinced that it was possible to continue colonial expansion totally without convict labour, nor to house all their refractory workers in penitentiaries, in Britain Whigs and 'radicals' had a plethora of reasons why they should at least end the uneconomic assignment system. In particular, Lord John Russell, Home Secretary in the second Whig government (1835–41) and Viscount Howick, Under-Secretary of State for the colonies (1830–33), both of whom had been active in the anti-slavery campaign, were deeply influenced by Archbishop Whately's criticism of the system in his *Thoughts on Secondary Punishments* (1833). The most trenchant theorist of penal reform since Bentham, Whately argued that to be effective, punishment must be totally separated from colonization. In addition, there was the indictment of the system by Quaker missionaries Backhouse and Walker, after personally inspecting the convict colonies between 1832 and 1838. In April 1837 'radical' reformer William Molesworth successfully secured the establishment of a House of Commons enquiry into the whole system. Chaired by Molesworth and with members including Charles Buller, Sir George Grey, Russell and Howick, the Committee recommended sweeping changes. By 1839 the task of phasing out the Bigge-Macarthur experiment in semi-slavery had begun.[44] In New South Wales, ideally no more convicts were ever to be sent to stain white society, nor to corrupt the native people. Only Van Diemen's Land, which had now removed its native people to 'safety' on Flinders Island, was to go on receiving convicts and then not into private assignment. Rather like the Aboriginal people themselves, all convicts were to undergo a crash course in moral re-education and respect for private property, housed in remote penal institutions, either in England or on Norfolk Island. Only after having completed this course would they qualify for release, and then they would each serve probationary stages of hard labour, at first wholly in the service of the state.

The termination of this now anachronistic labour system was only one of a number of moves being made throughout the 1830s towards implementing a brand new blueprint for colonization. Based on lofty ideals, this blueprint was intended to realize every aspect of the concept of individualism and liberty which the Utilitarian and evangelical reformers held dear, embracing free trade, free labour, free marriage and godly family life, as well as freedom of religion and, in due course, self-government. Also on the agenda was the elevation of native people to British citizenship, having first been taught to appreciate the blessings of British religion and law, for as a House of Commons Committee wrote in 1837, who could believe that Britain had been given mastery over distant lands and restless seas for commercial prosperity alone? Rather, when based on correct moral principles, colonization served a higher purpose, carrying civilization, peace, good government and knowledge of God to the uttermost ends of the earth.[45]

Once again Australia and the Pacific were to be one of the major arenas where these experiments were tested and tried. Indeed, already a new thrust of imperial expansion was occurring there, shaping but also being conditioned by contemporary liberal social, economic and political theory.

'ALL THAT CAPITAL'
South Australia and Port Phillip   1835–1842

WRITING IN ENGLAND in 1833, political economist E. G. Wakefield ruminated sadly over the fate of the Swan River settlement. His reflections on this, the most recent colony 'founded by Englishmen', were likely to bring a lump to the throat of every investor and a chill to the heart of any gentleman who contemplated leaving his native land:

On the west coast of New Holland there is abundance of good land . . . The capital taken out, in seeds, implements, cattle, sheep, and horses, cannot have been less, in money value, than 200,000:1.; and the labourers must have amounted to a thousand at the lowest. What is become of all that capital and all those labourers? The greater part of the capital has perished; . . . [and] one of the founders of the colony, Mr. Peel, . . . has been represented as left without a servant to make his bed or fetch him water from the river.[1]

Wakefield was not wrong. The new colony at Swan River was in a lamentable state, not only because gentlemen were in mourning for their deceased capital and, even worse, had to fetch and carry for themselves. It was also because the colony's potential had been much over-rated in the initial assessment by Captain Stirling and the botanist, Charles Frazer. The mouth of the Swan River was treacherous to ships and, in contrast with Stirling's glowing reports, land capable of supporting livestock and agriculture proved scant. All fertile land was rapidly alienated to first-comers, Stirling, Thomas Peel and an absentee investor, Colonel Lautour, being comfortably in possession of 100 000 acres each. Free land grants ceased in 1831. Those who imported live-stock suffered heavy losses both during and after the passage. The main difficulties of the colony, however, were derived from its system of commercial exchange. The first colony being founded exclusively by private capitalists, many settlers arrived fully qualified for a grant of good land which could not be supplied and with little if any alternative outlet for capital. Nor could they add to their income from the sale of surplus production, for all settlers produced similar goods. Most therefore lacked the means to buy imported commodities other than by barter or from borrowing from the few lucky settlers with access to overseas credit or funds. Emigrants like William Tanner, who were in possession of such funds, did very well. Despite a late arrival, he rapidly became one of the colony's largest land-holders. By mid-1832 the colony was facing economic crisis. There were still less than 2000 settlers, immigration had ceased, goods and labour were highly priced, the first harvests had been inadequate and Aboriginal people were finding mutton and flour a reasonable substitute for depleted supplies of bush food. Governor Stirling was petitioned by the settlers to return to England and ask for additional aid from the Colonial Office to save the colony from disaster and for an enlarged military guard to hold off the Abor-iginal raids.

As reports of these problems reached England some settlers, like Charles Viveash, altered plans to settle at Swan River and went to Van Diemen's Land. Others, like James Henty, considered moving on to one of the eastern colonies almost immediately after arrival, although with other members of the family in England who could secure access to goods and capital, he was one of the few who did well in Swan River. By 1830 he had made at least £1000 from mercantile dealings, and was already the agent for a number of ships and for dealers located in Algoa Bay, India and the Cape. By February 1832 he had departed to establish himself as a merchant in Launceston, where the family was in possession of a lease of 2000 acres on the Tamar, thirty-two merinos, two blood mares, seven pheasants, two dogs, a brace of partridges and a hive of bees, all recently arrived from England.[2]

The failure of the Swan River experiment was a great blow to British reformers who needed to find expanding sources of raw materials and markets. There was, too, much unrest in Britain. The census of 1831 showed that the population of England and Wales had increased by over two million in the past decade and now stood at sixteen-and-a-half million, while the Irish now numbered seven-and-three-quarter million. At no other period since the seventeenth century had there been such potential for revolution. In the northern manufacturing districts around Manchester and in the coalfields of Wales, there were strikes and machine-breaking; in London, Birmingham and other cities there was violent agitation on the eve of the Reform Bill of 1832; in the wheat-growing regions of the south and east there were agrarian riots. With rates for poor relief rocketing, it had come to be expected that new colonies such as Swan River might absorb some of these numerous, discontented labourers. Few theorists now argued that emigration would exhaust national wealth. Most began to see advantages in sweeping the paupers out of the workhouses and asylums and shipping them, instead of convicts, to colonies overseas. H. Wilmot Horton, Under-Secretary for War and Colonies from 1822 and Chairman of Special Emigration Committees called in 1826 and 1827, was one influential advocate of this view. Others argued that 'a well-regulated system of colonization acts as a safety-valve to the political machine and allows the expanding vapour to escape, before it is heated to explosion'.[3]

Against this background the political economists and moral reformers in Britain and the colonies again found common ground. Already united in their zeal for penal reform and free labour, throughout the 1830s they found themselves agreed in advocating a modern, 'systematic' scheme of colonization, more efficient and more humane than anything previously attempted. Ideally this would avoid the disasters which had befallen the Swan River experiment while sustaining a new wave of equally ambitious territorial expansion. By 1840 two new British settlements were founded in the South-West Pacific dedicated to these ideals. Based in South Australia and New Zealand, these focused on two organizing principles: first, an expertly calculated ratio of land, labour and capital designed to maximize profits; and secondly, the metamorphosis of both British paupers and indigenous people into contented and compliant colonial labourers and consumers. Commissioner Bigge's combination of punishment and profit was to be replaced by a new doctrine of piety and

progress. Though it was not a stated intention, in this new ideology
the political and economic ruthlessness underlying the acceler-
ating thrust of overseas expansion would be particularly well
concealed.

These two godly settlements would stand in stark contrast to a
third. Founded at Port Phillip in 1835 purely on the initiative of
local pastoralists, this settlement would be seen by moralists and
political economists as embodying all the worst features of the
bad old convict colonies. Essentially an extension of the existing
squatting system and forming a huge outstation of the pastoral
industry in New South Wales and Van Diemen's Land, these
squattocrats would display remarkable indifference to British
pauper problems and absolute contempt for missionary ideals.
Yet this particularly blatant and largely unplanned grab for land
would effectively colonize the entire south-east corner of the
continent, confounding its critics by its immediate and self-
perpetuating rate of growth.

The coming clash between these two apparently different
methods of colonization was foreshadowed in 1831 when the
governors of the three existing Australian colonies were informed
that a new system of state-assisted immigration would begin.
This, it was thought, would at once relieve the political unrest at
home and begin to dilute the evils of convictism in the eastern
colonies. To the horror of the local pastoralists, this system of
free immigration was to be funded by an entirely new method of
land allocation. The old practice of grants to men of capital was
to be ended. Under this system, it was said, settlement had been
allowed to spread over too much territory without attention to
improvement and cultivation. From now on, all land was to be
sold at a minimum price of five shillings an acre. Between 1832
and 1851 this new method of land alienation would bring 100 000
'free' immigrants to New South Wales and Van Diemen's Land.[4] In
Britain, this changed system of colonization was followed in 1834
by the New Poor Law. A Benthamite inspiration, this was seen
by its advocates as a brilliant way of correcting the disasters
caused by the misguided Speenhamland system which had increased parish rates and interfered with a programme which was
pushing workers out of the countryside and into the urban and
colonial labour markets where they were required. Now, by the
simple expedient of denying outdoor relief to the able-bodied,
the British pauper would be made to decide between entering the

workhouse or emigration. Conditions in the workhouses were made increasingly punitive and various schemes for funding the passage out of the country for paupers were tried. As early as 1820 assisted emigration to the Cape had been attempted, and in 1823, 1825 and 1827 to Canada. By the beginning of the 1850s more than three million people would have left the British Isles, more than 222 000 of whom came to Australasia.[5]

Employers in the labour-hungry eastern colonies were not particularly opposed to employing immigrant labour provided there was enough of it to keep wages low. However, the ending of free grants did not please them, especially when they discovered that the first ship loads of assisted immigrants were composed entirely of women. These had been gathered largely from the pauper institutions and workhouses which, like the Female Factory in New South Wales, were eager to get rid of some of their female inmates. In 1832 the *Red Rover* sailed for New South Wales filled with destitute women from Dublin and Cork, while the *Princess Royal* bound for Van Diemen's Land carried women from London charitable institutions and parishes. In the period from 1833 to 1836 a total of fourteen ships bringing 2700 women and girls were sent to the colonies.

Determined that their funds should not be used to import labour for which they had no use, the pastoralists turned to the rhetoric which the moral reformers used when criticizing the convict women, condemning the female immigrants in almost exactly the same terms. They could do this without difficulty, for the women were exposed to the same sexual exploitation as their convict sisters. On the ships, the officers did little to control the crew who, as the superintendent on the *David Scott* admitted, 'had an unrestrained intercourse' with the women during the voyage. Disembarkation was also a problem. When the *Bussorah Merchant* arrived at Sydney in August 1833 with 215 women on board, they were harassed by men who gathered around the gates of the lumber-yard where temporary accommodation had been provided. In August 1834 when the *Strathfieldsay* arrived at Hobart, the women confronted a similar scene of wild offers and obscene remarks.[6]

Local philanthropic ladies attempted to provide some assistance for new arrivals but on the whole failed to alter the poor reputation of female immigrants. In Sydney in 1833 a committee consisting of Miss Bourke, Mrs Broughton, Mrs Jones and Mrs

McLeay personally attended at a temporary barracks made available to shelter the women. Here, as with the convict women, the immigrants were subjected to a classification process during which some were consigned into domestic service, and a few instantly married off to applicants who met the ladies' approval. Women who preferred to make their own arrangements were seen as troublesome and immoral, while male moralists like the Reverend Mr Lang and Governor Bourke added to the condemnation of the immigrants.

Given that the colonial liberals had such a poor opinion of the women, the powerful pastoral lobby in the eastern colonies had no trouble in persuading the authorities that the whole experiment had been an abject failure. Robert Scott pointed out that the disproportion of the sexes existed only in the 'convict class'. It was worse than a waste of money to import women fit only to consort with them and thus propagate a race which, later, it would be policy to get rid of. A new scheme was planned to replace this disastrous experiment in female immigration. This scheme emphasized the importation of ready-made families. In deference to the interests of pastoralists, preference was to be given to married mechanics with three children or less. Unmarried women were to comprise no more than one-quarter of future state-assisted immigrants, and their character was to be subjected to strict scrutiny prior to selection by the emigration agents in Britain.[7]

By 1836 the pastoralists, still dissatisfied, gained permission to implement a scheme of their own. Alleging that the state system was bringing in too many useless women and children, settlers of means offered to bring out emigrants selected by their own agents in London, though the costs of the passage was to be paid, as before, by the state. Known as the 'bounty system', this scheme operated in tandem with the existing system and became an important means by which the free-labour market could be disciplined and wages controlled.[8]

Meanwhile, the pro-natalist colonizers found a new ally in the female philanthropist, Caroline Chisholm. The wife of an officer in the East India Company's army who arrived as a settler in 1838, with the help of Lady Gipps and a committee of ladies, in October 1841 Chisholm estalished a Female Immigrants' Home in a portion of the old immigration barracks. Within a few weeks of its opening the committee had gathered in ninety-six new arrivals, some of whom had been sleeping in the parks of Sydney. Like the male authorities in charge of the Female Factory, Chisholm immediately became convinced of a pressing need to disperse the women out of this institution and into marriage. Having gained from Governor Gipps permission to send hundreds of letters and circulars to country districts free of charge, she obtained information about the demand for female labour beyond Sydney. Hiring a bullock dray, she then personally consigned an initial group of sixteen captive girls up the country and into domestic service or, where possible, wedlock. The establishment of branches at Parramatta and Liverpool followed, and in country centres as far south as Goulburn and as far north as Moreton Bay. Persons requiring servants could register at these depots and female immigrants were dispatched to them by dray or boat.

As a female, Chisholm was less inclined than the male reformers to devalue working-class women as promiscuous misfits who could be transformed by marriage into a demographic resource only with the greatest difficulty. Far from being fickle creatures of appetite, she argued, women of all classes were morally superior to all men and a strong and rational force who, through their role as wives and mothers, would bring discipline, order and satisfaction into the lives of the errant colonial male. This view was essentially an attempt by women of the new industrial middle class to revise the concept of their sex as a demographic resource so that it elevated rather than debased women. Now celebrated as the 'angel in the house', all women were to be idealized as bearers and rearers of children. Essentially a female political economist, Chisholm believed that in Britain worker 'combinations' and trade unions were a new and intolerable threat; in the colonies, the imbalance of the sexes was a moral disaster and an impediment to reproduction. The solution to both problems lay in streamlining the immigration system, pushing working-class women into marriage and convincing them that problems lay, not in the political and economic values of the reformers and philanthropists, but in the innate vileness of all men.[9]

While Chisholm and other philanthropic ladies were evolving their plans for reconstructing the working-class family as a modern, nuclear unit presided over by a godly yet fecund wife, in Britain the male reformers, not content with merely patching up the land and labour laws in existing colonies, were creating brand new societies which would be run along 'systematic' lines from the start. In doing so, they looked to that arch-critic of the melancholy Swan River colony, E. G. Wakefield.

Though coming from a philanthropic Quaker family, Wakefield's philosophy was closer to the amoral pleasure-pain principles of the Utilitarians than to the rigorous self-denial of the religious reformers. His first publication, *A Letter from Sydney* (1829), was written while he was vegetating in Newgate gaol, serving a three-year sentence for having abducted the daughter of a wealthy silk manufacturer from a Liverpool boarding-school. Wakefield went on to publish works on penal discipline and emigration, producing *England and America* in 1833 and the *Art of Colonization* in 1849. Wakefield agreed that all colonial land should be sold and the revenue used to export Britain's 'surplus' working-class to sites where it was urgently needed. In Swan River, Canada, New South Wales and Van Diemen's Land, too much land had been alienated too fast, without proper attention to the problem of finding people to work it without reverting to slavery. In some areas the squatters were using huge tracts without even legal title. Most important of all, Wakefield alleged, it was all too easy for servants to save sufficient funds to acquire stock and land of their own, while their former masters, like poor Mr Peel, languished for want of labour. To cure all these evils, Wakefield believed not only should all land be sold but its price should be fixed at a level which would automatically prevent workers from acquiring too much too soon. Rather like the convicts under the old system of the 30-acre grant, assisted immigrants were to perform a term of hard labour before being qualified to hold land, and even the tiniest portion was to be purchased not given away. Wakefield considered transportation could be continued but convicts were to be employed only in the service of the government and kept well out of sight of the settlers, preparing the land on the inland frontier for the use of the employer class. He also believed in engineering a perfect demographic structure in colonies. In the selection of immigrants, he pointed out, special care was to be taken about their age. Just as importers of sheep selected only those animals which would provide the greatest numbers in the shortest time, so the colonies must not be encumbered with the very old, the infirm and the very young. Female immigrants were needed to moralize the colonies, to improve reproduction and to boost production. As in the factory so in the home, Wakefield pointed out, the laws of the division of labour must be brought into play. Two men having to cook their own food, mend their own clothes and make their own beds would produce less than one man who had a wife to do all these things for him.

Though he was only one of numerous writers theorizing on colonization at this time, Wakefield was the most influential. A supreme propagandist, his ideas influenced administrators like Viscount Goderich, first Earl of Ripon in charge of the Colonial Office under Earl Grey's ministry, and Viscount Howick, Grey's son. In 1838, in company with Utilitarian theorist, Charles Buller, Wakefield was appointed to assist Lord Durham (Grey's son-in-law) investigate the political crisis in Canada and compile a report advocating systematic colonization and responsible government. Families like Durham's and Howick's, along with those of Lords Russell and Stanley, owed their wealth to the iron and coal-mines, mills and factories which had fuelled the Industrial Revolution and so, directly and indirectly, had a vested interest in efficient imperial expansion and the ideology of free trade.[10]

Wakefield claimed to have found a solution to the problem of founding profitable and godly societies without reverting to slavery. He also argued that the sheer amount of territory coming under annexation, together with the new system of land sales, required a more coherent policy to deal with the problem of indigenous people and their legal title to the land. This was another issue of great concern to the industrial middle class by the 1830s. Though many of these people were genuinely concerned about the physical suffering and, as they believed, the heathen habits of colonized people, they were aware that from now on, colonization must proceed at an accelerated rate and that this could best be achieved not by force but by winning the co-operation of native people. Just as they were convinced that an automatic will to work was more efficient than the use of whips and chains, so also the reformers believed that native people could be persuaded to hand over their land voluntarily to the colonizing powers. With their hard-headed business sense and their desire to re-sell the land at the 'sufficient' price, for this purpose, the reformers favoured the idea of first recognizing the native people's title to their territory and then negotiating to 'purchase' it. This method would avoid bloodshed, promote settlement, and legitimize the process by which settlers purchased the land as absolute property.

This aspect of colonization was thoroughly aired during the debates that accompanied the foundation of the new colony of South Australia, where Sturt had drawn attention to the excellent pastoral land. In 1833 the area around St Vincent's Gulf was selected by a mixed group of social reformers, colonizing theorists and investors in Britain as a suitable site to test both their ideals and their capital. Calling themselves the South Australian Association, members of the group included Robert Gouger, Charles Buller and William Molesworth. By August 1834 they had persuaded parliament to pass an Act providing for the establishment of a new colony in southern Australia between the meridians of 132 degrees and 141 degrees east.

Chairman of the Colonization Commission, with much of the responsibility for attracting capital and emigrants, was founder of the Political Economy Club and later expert on land title transfers, Robert Torrens. The colony's supporters also included Samuel Mills, a retired merchant and Congregationalist with much capital to invest, and Jacob Montefiore, a banker whose brother Joseph had made a fortune from unsystematic colonization in New South Wales where he had settled in 1829. There was also George Fife Angas, a member of a Baptist family with trading interests in Britain, South America and the West Indies, and a generous supporter of the numerous charities then attempting to order the lives of the British poor. He was a founder of Exeter Hall, and in touch with Governor Arthur in Van Diemen's Land, and with missionaries in New Zealand and the Pacific. Despite some differences over detail, such as defining the 'sufficient' price to make the whole system work smoothly, planning of the new colony reflected Wakefieldian principles. Responsibility for land allocation was placed in the hands of three or more Colonization Commissioners. They were to arrange for the sale of parcels of land to investors at a minimum price of twelve shillings per acre. Revenue from land sales was to go towards the selection and transportation of suitably impoverished emigrants who were to be the sole labour force. There was to be no established Church of England, nor state assistance to any denomination. A constitution was to be established when the European population reached 50 000. Founded on free emigration, freedom of religion, and free institutions, the new colony was to be a model for liberal humanitarian colonization in the southern seas.[11]

In contrast with the founders of the eastern colonies, these new godly colonizers knew from the outset that they were going to annex those huge areas of land now required for pastoral capitalism and that it was morally and economically desirable to do so with the consent of the local people. Consequently, considerably more thought was given to reconciling the Aboriginal people to these happy plans. Testifying to their increased awareness of these issues, as an official seal for the new colony the planners suggested a draped figure of Britannia accompanied by a sheep and an unclothed Aboriginal man receiving in exchange for the land the gift of British 'civilization'. Actual details of this tricky trans-action remained noticeably absent. Former Attorney-General of New South Wales, Saxe Bannister, now back in Britain, advised using some of the revenue from the sale of crown lands for missionary purposes. The reservation of land and the appointment of a state-paid 'Protector' were also proposed. Theoretically the Protector was to ensure that no land became available for sale to Europeans until the 'natives' had formally surrendered or sold it, while special 'Letters Patent', which were to be issued before the first ship sailed, declared that nothing was to interfere with Aboriginal rights to occupy the land. However, the Act of 1834 had neglected to mention Aboriginal people, and in order for the colony to commence operations the Commissioners had merely to pre-sell in England £35 000 of 'crown' land. The first adver-tisements appeared in July 1835 and the surveyors, led by Colonel Light, sailed the following March to choose a site and begin carving up the land. Arriving off Kangaroo Island in August 1836 Light rejected Encounter Bay and chose instead a position on the east coast of the St Vincent's Gulf at Holdfast Bay.

The Colonial Office had appointed as Governor John Hind-marsh, a naval officer made redundant by the peace and more than willing to accept a civil appointment at £800 a year. He sailed on the *Buffalo* in August 1836 with his family, and with five preliminary orders for land to be taken up on his own behalf. By the time the *Buffalo* left England eight other colonizing ships had left for South Australia, and the first had reached Kangaroo Island. They carried the capital investors and labourers of the South Australian Company, which in January 1836 had purchased over 13 000 acres from the Colonization Commissioners at 40 per cent discount.

The *Buffalo* and the *Africaine*, a sister ship bearing the remainder of the civil officials, arrived at Holdfast Bay on 28 December 1836. Reflecting the division of authority between the Colonial Office, as represented by Hindmarsh and the civil officials, and the Colonization Commission, as represented by Light, there was disagreement on the site of the new settlement. As a naval officer used to absolute command, Hindmarsh thought the colony's capital should be on the sea and had expected Light to place it at Encounter Bay. Light had selected a site further to the north, some 6 miles inland on the River Torrens under Mount Lofty. Hindmarsh had to be content with naming the settlement Adelaide.[12]

Although no method had been clarified of persuading Aboriginal people to surrender their land, events elsewhere in the empire continued to highlight the problem of native title. Attention became riveted to this issue following a particularly daring private 'purchase' of Aboriginal land at Port Phillip in 1835.

While the saintly settlers of South Australia were translating some of their theories into action, exponents of a less 'systematic' and less humanitarian branch of liberal ideology were making preparations of a very different kind. In Van Diemen's Land the conclusion of the 'Black War' in 1832 had been followed by rapid occupation of the last of the good pastoral land. By the time the Hentys arrived in 1833 it was necessary to look elsewhere. While New South Wales underwent bad seasons in the late 1820s, being forced to import grain from Van Diemen's Land, the southern colony had experienced a period of prosperity. The opening of agencies to advance credit, like the Derwent Bank in Hobart in 1828 and the Cornwall Bank in Launceston in 1830, further stimulated commercial activity. Van Diemen's Land investors were reaching the point where they needed a colony of their own to absorb surplus stock and capital.

As early as 1834 the Hentys had noticed in their trading ventures between Launceston and Swan River that though whalers and sealers were in possession at Portland Bay there was suitable pastoral land further inland. They petitioned the Colonial Office for the purchase of 20 000 acres, taking care not to disclose the exact location. In October 1834 without waiting for a reply they sent their own vessel, the 55-ton *Thistle*, loaded with provisions, tools, timber, nails, and six working bullocks, across Bass Strait to take possession at Portland Bay. As the Hentys feared, other invaders were quick to follow. By mid-1835 investors in Van Diemen's Land were looking across the strait towards the site of Collins's original settlement in search of out-stations for their expanding flocks and herds. In 1835 John Batman, Joseph Gellibrand and John Wedge joined with ten other colonists from Van Diemen's Land to form the Port Phillip Association. Proposing an unofficial expedition to the mainland, all three were pastoralists who possessed a unique combination of useful skills. Batman had been born in 1800 in New South Wales and, like Wentworth and Hume, had proved himself able to move about the bush without becoming lost. He had also successfuly exploited the knowledge of Sydney Aborigines in tracking Tasmanian bushrangers and Aborigines near his land grant at Ben Lomond. Wedge was a trained surveyor who had arrived from England in 1824, but like Batman had been rewarded with a land grant for his special tenacity in helping to capture Matthew Brady and his gang. Gellibrand's contribution was legal knowledge. He was former Attorney-General of the colony and holder of extensive sracts of land. Other members of the Association were, like the Hentys, merchants, financiers or pastoralists. They included Charles Swanston, a former officer in the East India Company's army who had arrived in Hobart in 1829 and had already acquired large grants of land and a successful import and export business.

Aware that the British authorities were presently concerned to preserve and convert native people throughout the empire, the Batman colonization scheme included plans to contract a land sale with the Aboriginal people at Port Phillip and then force the authorities to recognize it. If this was allowed as a legitimate purchase then the 1831 regulations requiring all land in the Australian colonies to be sold by the crown would effectively be circumvented.

At the end of May 1835 Batman chartered the schooner *Rebecca* and left Launceston with seven Sydney Aborigines to negotiate with the people at Port Phillip Bay. Arriving at the junction of Merri Creek and the Yarra River, Batman's Aborigines signalled to the local people there that 400-pounds weight of blankets, tomahawks, knives, looking-glasses, handkerchiefs, shirts and flour could be theirs if they would allow him to annex 600 000 acres of the land located on the Yarra and the western shores of Port Phillip Bay. On 6 June Batman decided that the deal had been successfully completed and sailed for Launceston, remarking in his diary that the site of the transaction would be a good place to build a future village. News of the 'treaty' created sensational interest in Van Diemen's Land. By August, Wedge and Batman's brother were back at Indented Head, the site of the land claimed on the western shore of Port Phillip Bay, and by November the *Norval* was chartered to begin the transfer of equipment and stock. On 16 August 1835 another party had landed from Launceston on the southern part of the Bay. This was part of an expedition planned by John Pascoe Fawkner, an ex-convict innkeeper and newspaper editor who, like Batman, had long been interested in the reports of sealers and whalers of good land across Bass Strait.[13]

So even as the political economists and capitalists were tidying up the chaotic and inhumane system of land alienation in the colonies, they were confronted with a disturbing variation of the existing 'slovenly' and overtly self-interested system known as 'squatting'. Whereas state purchases were assumed to protect native interests, private ones like Batman's clearly violated the new rules about land sales which had assumed that all land in the colonies was crown land and could be ceded by the state alone.

Private land purchases of this kind were also being made in New Zealand. Here, Marsden's dream of making his missionary settlements a new base for Pacific enterprise had been attracting investors in Britain and Australia since the late 1820s. In addition to bay whaling and timber, the flax trade was booming as strong warrior chiefs like Hongi Hika, emerging from internecine wars, put their 'slaves' to work producing goods for sale to European traders. In 1826 a private company, whose directors included Robert Torrens, planned to establish a British settlement at the Bay of Islands to exploit these developments. Though this plan lapsed, focus on the area round the Tasman Sea sharpened after 1830 when the French turned to consolidate their claims to empire in the Pacific and in particular, to 'France Australe'. By the late 1830s bay whaling stations, chiefly American and French, stretched down the coasts of both main inlands; Catholic missionaries from France had gained a foothold at Kororareka; the Americans had appointed a consul and French naval vessels were making regular visits. Some 2000 permanent European residents were joined by hundreds of temporary ones, many of them seamen carousing ashore. The land was coming under pressure as speculators from Sydney, with an eye to drought-free pastures, 'purchased' large acreages from local tribesmen. By 1840 William Wentworth and some five or six associates had acquired twenty million acres in the South Island (virtually the whole of it) while other 'purchasers' included Hannibal Macarthur and William à Beckett, a London barrister who had arrived in Sydney in 1837.

These events, together with the traffic in firearms, rum and the introduction of infectious disease, were viewed with dismay by liberal reformers. Just as in the eastern Australian colonies, allegations of sexual immorality, alcoholism, and vice were used to attack the assignment system, so liberal reformers in New Zealand used similar descriptions, many dwelling on the number of escaped convicts in the area, to argue that the Maori people would be morally and physically destroyed unless 'rescued' by systematic British colonization. As early as 1831 Governor Darling, concerned about Maori involvement in violent clashes between traders, advised sending a British Resident, a move which was supported by investors like Henry Dumaresq and Reverend Ralph Mansefield, editor of the *Sydney Gazette*, who believed that New Zealand should be 'civilized' as a branch of Australian imperialism in the Pacific. Soon, however, there were calls for greater control than either the Resident (sent and funded from New South Wales) or the missionaries could manage.[14]

Faced with the convergence of these three separate thrusts of colonial expansion, along with similar problems in other colonies from Newfoundland to South Africa, the British had to clarify their ideas for a new form of colonization without delay. From 1834 they organized a series of House of Commons enquiries into the disposal of 'wastelands' and the fate of indigenous people all around the empire. Submitted in June 1837 the main report on 'aboriginal' people was written by Thomas Buxton, a leading anti-slaver, and revised by George Grey, a military officer who had become interested in liberal colonization ideas while posted to Ireland in 1833. Evidence collected for this report vindicated the system whereby the government negotiated with the people for the 'purchase' of their land and then re-sold it (at a higher price) to settlers. This method, it was said, had been used with great effect in North America and could be applied elsewhere, always depending on the number of indigenous people and the nature of their law. Though it drew a graphic picture of the destructive effects of colonization, the Report suggested that extermination, exploitation and costly events like the recent Kaffir War (1834) arose entirely because settlement had been allowed to proceed without first obtaining the consent of the local people. Outraged by the 'theft' of their land such unconverted 'savages' became 'dangerous enemies', 'unprofitable customers' or 'degraded denizens' who were a burden on the state. Yet imperial expansion could no longer wait while the missionaries undertook the laborious process of conversion and 'civilization'. It was hoped that, as in America, any purchase system would be accompanied by voluntary removal of the people to reservations where they would be subjected to re-education procedures. Invoking the anti-slavers' concept of the legal equality of all people throughout the empire, the Report suggested that when all 'barbarous' customs had been removed and conversion effected, all native people should receive full civil rights.[15]

This new policy of colonization by consent and of changing native people into British citizens meant that the former mercantilist practice of making trade treaties was now outlawed. This kind of treaty, arranged with people who had a visible political hierarchy and who were willing to negotiate, had established British rights to trade while leaving native people largely to rule themselves under customary civil and religious law. Now that a large amount of territory was required, and with the growing complexity of colonial commerce and land deals, and the need to transform native people into 'profitable workmen and good customers', this method of colonization was no longer an option. What was needed, it was thought, was to bring all native people under the full force of British law, as in Tahiti, for instance, which now had a legal code based on the British model. Along with christianization, this code protected merchants and extended commerce. It followed that from this time on, any new treaties would be 'protective' in nature, seeking permission to suppress 'savage' customs while also securing for the crown the sole right to make cheap purchases of native land.

Applying these principles to the Australian colonies Buxton and Grey, in effect, ratified the method adopted in South Australia and recommended a similar system for Port Phillip. They reported that although Aboriginal people were to be prepared for citizenship, it was not necessary to persuade them to 'sell' their land to the state. After nearly fifty years of British occupation, administrators and missionaries were no closer to understanding the relationship these people held to their land, nor why they had remained so resistant to trade. Like the African Bushmen, the Aboriginal people continued to be classified as an inferior racial type who were not qualified to negotiate the new kind of land deal and for whom, their own civil and religious law being invisible to Europeans, the 'gift' of British religion and law was seen as compensation enough. Official 'Protectors' were to be appointed to watch over their interests. Modelled on G. A. Robinson's exploits, these were to be peripatetic missionaries, travelling with and conciliating the Aboriginal people, preferably ahead of white settlement, becoming expert in their language, gathering statistical information and encouraging them to settle down and learn habits of industry on large areas of land temporarily set aside for this purpose. In this way, Aboriginal culture and law was to be systematically smashed and the people expertly prepared for assimilation into the white work-force, at which point the reserves could easily be resumed for other uses.

In New Zealand, though the aims of the colonizers were the same, Maori numbers, the presence of the French, plus the influence of Wakefield himself, made for a different solution. Eager to capitalize on the concept of colonization by consent, in May 1837 Wakefield had joined forces with Durham, Molesworth and Hutt to form the New Zealand Association. They proposed that this organization be given sovereignty over a large section of the country by Act of Parliament and then should proceed to 'purchase' land from the Maori people. This land would be re-sold to approved settlers along systematic lines and the proceeds used to finance further 'purchases' and orderly British immigration. Buxton and Grey, James Stephen (Permanent Under-Secretary for Colonies from 1836 to 1847) and Lord Glenelg (appointed Secretary of State for Colonies under the liberal Lord Melbourne's regime) had misgivings about whether the Association's 'purchases' would sufficiently conciliate Maori interests. However in 1840, when the French seemed about to claim the 'Middle Island', the British authorities had no hesitation in adopting a 'treaty' not so very different from the principles of Batman and Wakefield. Signed by a British officer and Maori chiefs at Waitangi, this agreement encapsulated the new principle for treaties for land purchase, giving the British sole right to 'purchase' land as well as power to impose British law. This feat accomplished and the new colony made, for the moment, a dependency of New South Wales, the authorities settled down to investigate all private purchases prior to 1840 in what would prove a prolonged procedure, bitterly debated by both Maoris and Europeans.[16]

After the immediate problems associated with native land, it remained for the reformers to deal with squatting in eastern Australia, bringing it more into line with systematic and missionary principles. As with the early traders in New South Wales, the squatters' bending of the rules raised the old problem of the extent to which ruthless profiteering could be permitted to jeopardize planning—in this case a system aiming to legalize the alienation of native land as private property and bring every citizen under the rule of law. Already this anarchic, do-it-yourself form of colonization was out-pacing the sober, systematic colonies of New Zealand and South Australia. By June 1836 some 20 000 sheep had been landed at Port Phillip from Van Diemen's Land in some forty-eight crossings, and at Christmas there arrived the first party overlanding stock from New South Wales. They were Joseph Hawdon, John Hepburn and John Gardiner, who having formed a partnership, left Howe's station on the Murrumbidgee with cattle in October 1836. Arriving at Melbourne at the end of December, they found only several horses and fifteen head of cattle in the settlement and had no difficulty in disposing of their herd at £10 a beast. By June 1837 the price of stock in Port Phillip was rocketing, with sheep fetching sixty shillings a head. By the end of that year there were 1000 settlers in the area, increasing to 20 000 within four years.[17]

To the horror of Wakefieldians, squatting would ultimately colonize Port Phillip, much of South Australia plus most of the land in New South Wales beyond the 'limits of location'. By 1848 a mere 2000 squatters would occupy a huge tract of land stretching from the South Australian border to southern Queensland, and tramping across this area would be nearly 900 000 cattle and eight-and-a-half million sheep.[18]

Just as the British reformers had not allowed their concern for Maori welfare to halt colonization in New Zealand, so in Port Phillip they were quick to realize that pastoral settlement, whether it was on land taken, granted, ceded or sold, was essential to meet the needs of industrialists. There would be no Rum Rebellion at Port Phillip, for now the British authorities and the local profit-takers had a compatible interest in imperial expansion. Both subscribed to the same liberal ideology, believing in the rights of the male individual to pursue profit in a free market-place for a personal enrichment which somehow contributed to the wealth and progress of the whole community. The authorities aimed to control squattocrat colonization, not arrest it. In September 1835 Governor Bourke in Sydney issued a proclamation warning that the interlopers at Port Phillip were trespassing on crown land, but in a dispatch to Glenelg the following month he recommended allowing them to settle. The pastoral industry was contributing to the wealth of the colony and it required a push beyond the nineteen counties in order to find sufficient pasture to maintain the flocks and herds throughout the year. Besides, the government had no means of effectively removing the intruders from the 'waste lands', and in any case such a happy spontaneous form of colonization should not be impeded. Towns should be laid out, a police and magistrates sent, schools established, the land surveyed and put up for rent or lease. Lord Glenelg agreed. It would be abysmal and uneconomic to repress such 'spirit, adventure and speculation'. Besides, these speculators were the forerunners of what would become a new and flourishing settlement for British people such as had already over the past fifty years converted unproductive waste into two great provinces.[19]

On 9 September 1836 the settlement at Port Phillip was officially recognized. Captain William Lonsdale was appointed Police Magistrate, and in March 1837 Bourke arrived in person via the coastal route to name the town after Lord Melbourne and deposit surveyor Robert Hoddle and his assistant, Robert Russell, who were to begin apportioning the land for private possession. It remained only to find a method by which the invasion could be controlled and revenue derived from it.

The pastoralists agreed that some kind of new control over the occupation of crown land was needed to prevent native-born, immigrant and ex-convict labourers from squatting on it. Although these people lacked capital to purchase stock, it was widely believed that they circumvented this difficulty by plundering the flocks and herds of the élite. In 1835 T. A. Murray declared there were several parties of such squatters in his neighbourhood, and he had actually seen their men in the act of slaughtering one of his cattle. Sir John Jamison pointed out that such nefarious activities were cramping the enterprise of graziers like himself, while P. P. King alleged that many of these audacious squatters were mere holders of a ticket-of-leave, and as such, a menace to the frontier:

They harbour the settlers' runaway servants; they steal his cattle and sheep; they receive stolen goods; they sell spirits 'on the sly'; they entice shepherds from the care of their sheep; and they shelter and feed bushrangers, and afford them information.

It was in response to these fears that the system of granting licences to approved persons to graze herds in designated areas outside the nineteen counties was introduced in July 1836. An Act ostensibly to 'restrain the unauthorized occupation of crown lands' allowed an approved settler, usually a wealthy male, to take out a licence which, for the payment of £10 a year, authorized him to graze stock on as much land as he pleased. As Bourke told Glenelg in September 1836, the aim was to encourage occupation by the stock owned by respectable men, and as Colonial Secretary Alexander McLeay reassured members of the élite who had petitioned for such a system in 1836, licences would be allowed only to those persons 'upon whom reliance can be placed' and 'speedily removed those of an opposite character'.[20] Bourke recognized, legalized, and facilitated the pastoral invasion beyond the nineteen counties and at Port Phillip. He also funded the largest exploratory expedition to date. Organized in March 1836 and led by Surveyor-General Sir Thomas Mitchell, this was intended to check whether the upper and lower Darling Rivers discovered by Sturt were in fact one river, and at the same time, determine the general nature of all the land between the Australian Alps and the mouth of the Murray.

Mitchell crossed the lush pasture of the Western District of Victoria only a few months ahead of the squatters who were moving in from Portland and Melbourne, and his heavy boat-carriage, bullocks and pack-horses left a trampled path wherever they passed. From the beginning of 1837 pastoralists from New South Wales were able to send stock along this 'line' into the country he had named Australia Felix. By 1840 it was said that there were some 20 000 cattle on the road between Yass and Melbourne, causing some heart-stopping moments for pastoral speculators when herds and flocks were forced to converge and collect at important river fords while waiting for a favourable opportunity to cross. One immigrant investor, new to squatting, lost horses worth £300 when trying to cross the Tumut River late in 1839. He was Edward Bell who had only arrived in Sydney in September with no more knowledge of the colony than what he had gleaned from reading books like Mitchell's, and treatises on sheep and cattle in the 'Library of Useful Knowledge'. None of these works warned him that horses harnessed to carts and made to swim a river would drown if the cart overturned, and Bell disposed of no less than three before making this discovery.[21]

The speed of this invasion in the late 1830s was facilitated by the licensing system and was on an unprecedented scale. Nor was it confined to Port Phillip District. In New South Wales the 1831 land regulations had already precipitated a search for more out-stations, while the maturing of a second generation of local pastoralists also contributed to the rush. Two sons of the Hunter Valley pastoralist, John Dight, who were among the first to claim holdings on the Liverpool Plains, now participated in a second push further north across the Gwydir and on to the land known as Maranoa. Here they joined other sons of Hunter Valley and Liverpool Plains squatters, many inter-related in a chain of busi-ness, pastoral and marriage ties. Meanwhile, two other sons of John Dight joined the rush to take land in the Albury district. In addition, there were numerous new arrivals from Britain. Patrick Leslie, who arrived from Scotland in 1834, followed by two brothers, set out northwards from the Clarence in 1840 to claim a huge section of the Darling Downs. Arthur Hodgson and his partner snatched another portion which they named Eton Downs and stocked it with sheep and educated younger sons fresh from English public schools. By May 1842 there were forty-five stations on the Downs.

Even late arrivals like Benjamin Boyd did not necessarily fare badly. Son of a London merchant, Boyd raised capital of £1 million in England and arrived amongst considerable publicity on his private schooner *Wanderer* in 1842. Though Monaro was crowded with land-takers by the late 1830s, Boyd nevertheless managed to acquire some 250 000 acres there for which he paid licence fees totalling £40 per annum. He also acquired extensive runs in the Riverina. Here, the rush along the Lachlan did not begin until after better land elsewhere had been taken up, but it was then rapid, stretching up the Darling to reach Wilcannia by 1850. Boyd's Riverina and Monaro runs totalled two-and-a-half million acres. Like the Hentys, he also invested in shore-whaling, having some thirty boats operating from Twofold Bay by 1844.[22]

Owing to the frenzied pace of the squatting rush, it was predictable that the state could delegate much of the task of exploration to the pastoralists themselves. One of these privately sponsored expeditions, while searching for fresh pasture during the dry summer of 1840, scaled the Snowy Mountains from the west and claimed to be the first to climb the continent's highest peak. Members of this party included James Macarthur, a minor star in the galaxy of the famous fleecing family, and Charlie Tarra, an Aboriginal guide who would later save all of their lives for, having descended into the dense wet forests of Gippsland, it was he who knew the value of a diet of uncooked koalas. Also in the party was 'Count' Paul Strzelecki, a visitor from Europe of scientific pretensions who, appropriately enough in this liberal age, named the highest mountain Kosciusko after a Polish nationalist.[23]

The authorities now turned their attention to the twin problems of survey and of settling the numerous boundary disputes between rival claimants to leasehold. Since money could be made from a quick turnover in livestock, fencing of runs was not a priority, and large holders, competing ruthlessly with each other for land, sometimes had difficulty in marking out their territory. At Port Phillip there was supposed to be a gentleman's agreement that no one was to take land closer than 3 miles to another station, with the land between being equally divided between the new arrival and the existing neighbour. Reality was somewhat different. 'I have scarcely time to eat my food, but from flying from one part to another to keep off the enemy—civilized man', wrote Neil Black in his journal. The son of a Scottish farmer, Black arrived in 1839 as manager and partner for a Scottish syndicate. He was provided with capital of £10 000 and claimed 44 000 acres at Glenormiston near Terang. To warn off intruders, out-buildings were constructed at 3- or 4-mile intervals and especially on waterholes or creeks where competition between land-takers was keenest. 'The jealousy with which we heard of the arrival of any one in our neighbourhood, notwithstanding the vast tracts of land that we each laid claim to, was one of the remarkable features of our early settlement', commented Edward Bell. In some cases quarrels resulted in blows; more commonly, appeals were made to the new Commissioners of Crown Lands. Authorized in 1833 in all districts beyond the nineteen counties, these agents of authority were also magistrates and in some cases were assisted by mounted police.[24]

Brash, brawling and belligerent, squattocrat colonization appalled both moralists and Wakefieldians. Some believed that in the Australian bush British character was fast regressing towards barbarity, with land-takers falling back 'in morality and energy even lower than their men'. On their runs, they constructed no churches and schools; no vineyards, fruit or flowers graced their huts. Some 'went so far with their indolence as to drop shaving themselves', a custom which, E. M. Curr noted in 1839, they kept up when they came to town. Even so they were in no way to be mistaken for their labourers, for squatters wore smart blue serge suits with their cabbage-tree hats; boots, spurs, sometimes a pistol and always a good horse completed their costume, while in the case of Samuel Winter from Van Diemen's Land, an Aboriginal boy in livery was also an accompaniment. Swaggering into the Melbourne open-air stock sales to partake of champagne lunches, cold fowls, ham, brandy and beer, no stronger contrast could be pointed to than the South Australians who, notwithstanding their equal interest in the profits from colonization, still found time to attend zealously to spiritual matters. In the future 'city of churches', even before being provided with a minister, the Wesleyans had erected a chapel by March 1838. The Independents, too, had completed a chapel of clay and reeds on North Terrace, while the Anglicans laid the foundation of Trinity Church in January of the same year. Even the tiny Lutheran community who arrived in December 1838 had two places of worship by the end of 1844.[25]

In particular, squattocrat relations with the Aboriginal people incurred the criticism of the liberal humanitarians. Like the early pastoralists in the convict colonies, most squatters did not hesitate to organize their own 'dispersals'. 'No consideration on earth would induce me to ride into a camp and fire on them indiscriminately, as is the custom here whenever smoke is seen', Henry Meyrick, a Gippsland squatter wrote to his mother in 1846, but 'if I caught a black actually killing my sheep, I would shoot him with as little remorse as I would a wild dog'. In the western districts, the Wedge brothers at The Grange and the

Campbells at Flooding Creek, took the same view. They mounted swivel guns near their homesteads and used them against Aboriginal attacks. Happily for the squatters, Aboriginal people in the eastern part of the continent were decimated by a second epidemic of smallpox, which between 1829 and 1831 killed an unknown number of people from the Darling Downs to Port Fairy, ahead of the main invasion of settlers. As in the earlier colonies, starvation and massacres were the other main consequences of colonization with which the Aboriginal people had to contend. It has been estimated that in Port Phillip, of an original population of about 15 000, some 2000 were killed in punitive raids by settlers and the state.[26]

Squatters not only murdered Aboriginal men, women and children, they also resented the efforts of liberals and missionaries to protect Aboriginal people as a future labour force. As in the debate over the utility of female labour, so with the protection of the Aborigines; the squatters remained committed to short-term profits rather than the long-term survival of the capitalist system as represented by the liberal state. Some of them went so far as to argue that the four Port Phillip Protectors appointed in January 1838 were actually responsible for the violence on the frontier because they had taught the Aborigines how to resist the invasion. Others resented the fact that, in some cases, the missionaries had been granted good pastoral land. To establish Buntingdale, for instance, a Methodist mission created in 1839 on an unusually generous 64 000 acres on the Barwon River near Geelong, five squatters had been forced to remove their flocks. The first local Victorian government would remove Reverend Tuckfield and his mission in 1850, allowing two of the original squatters to reoccupy the land. Yet the Commissioners of Crown Lands condoned atrocities committed by squatters or their employees. The Irby brothers, for example, dutifully reported the punishments they handed out to Aboriginal families in the New England district in 1842 and that was the end of the matter. Other cases were simply not reported and no questions were asked.[27]

Unfortunately for the pastoralists, such killings raised the old problem that certain members of the community were being permitted to take the law into their own hands. Now that it was so vital to liberals and humanitarians to emphasize the ubiquity of British law, such cavalier attitudes could no longer be permitted. There were also other anomalies in need of correction if the legal system was going to appear as an impartial upholder of justice, regulating commercial and race relations. Aboriginal people were being made to face the courts whether or not they understood the procedures or even the language while Aboriginal witnesses were barred from giving evidence unless they had been thoroughly converted to Christianity and were said to know the meaning of the oath. It was hardly surprising that, by the 1830s, though there were not many Aboriginal people enjoying the protection of British law there were plenty suffering its penalties. In part, the solution to these problems was seen to lie in stepping up the christianization process and passing Evidence Acts that would allow Aboriginal testimony in the courts. However, this did not solve the problem of two laws and, with it, the possibility of Aboriginal title to the land. Nor did the quashing of the Batman treaty, or the Report by Buxton and Grey, deal permanently with this issue at law. Pointing to the seriousness of this problem, in Sydney in February 1836, Alfred Stephen, defending Jack Congo Murrall against a murder charge for taking the life of another Aboriginal person, argued that the accused was answerable only to customary, not British, law. The outcome of the Murrall case set a useful legal precedent. In passing judgement, W. W. Burton declared that the Aboriginal people had no law, only lewd practices and irrational superstitions. Even so, if Aborigines and their land came fully under British law, they were entitled to at least the appearance of protection from the killings by whites occurring on the frontier.[28]

Hitherto, as in the case of Lieutenant Lowe, most of the few trials of white men for murdering Aboriginal people had ended in acquittal. In June 1838, however, more than thirty people, mostly women and children, were cruelly massacred at Henry Dangar's Myall Creek station on the Gwydir River. Eleven of the twelve men responsible were, or had been, convicts; the twelfth, the native-born son of a pastoralist, escaped arrest. Sydney's Liberal Solicitor-General, J. H. Plunkett, launched prosecutions, which Hunter Valley pastoralists like Robert Scott made more dramatic by for once siding with their workers; but seven out of the eleven men were found guilty and duly hanged.

The Myall Creek hangings served the liberal humanitarians extremely well. They reinforced Burton's 1836 decision that the Aborigines were under British, not customary law. They also eclipsed an impending and very awkward enquiry into the savage killings recently authorized by Major James Nunn. A military officer who had been conducting barbaric reprisals in the Gwydir area from December 1837, Nunn was apparently a model for the men at Myall Creek. When the Executive Council at length passed judgement on Nunn in July 1839, there was no liberal outcry against the verdict of self-defence. It was said the widest distinction had to be made 'between the case of the murderers of men, women and children, without personal provocation and in cold blood, and that of officers and men in repelling an attack made upon them, while under orders in the execution of their duty'. Like Lieutenant Lowe before him, Nunn was acquitted.

The Myall Creek trials also served the liberals by placing the blame for frontier violence squarely on convict shoulders while glorifying the apparent compassion of liberalism and the justice of the law. While the philanthropists, liberals and missionaries in New South Wales congratulated themselves and attended meetings of the newly founded Australian Aborigines' Protection Society, out on the frontier, following the hangings, official and unofficial action against the Aborigines was renewed. Many pastoralists and labourers now turned to the distribution of poisoned flour, a deadly technique which was almost impossible to prove in court. In 1839 Gipps raised a more economical quasi-military force to deal with Aboriginal resistance, the border police. With over two-thirds of the stock of the colony of New South Wales now outside the limits of location and justice having been seen to be done at Myall Creek, the task of dealing with Aboriginal 'depredations' by official means could really begin.[29]

Squattocrats and liberal humanitarians also fell out over the issue of supplying Indian and Melanesian labour to the Australian colonies. This conflict developed rapidly in the late 1830s as the pastoralists foresaw that their supply of convict labour would be cut off by the anti-slave lobby. In 1837 John Mackay, formerly of Bengal, submitted a memorandum to the governor of New South Wales urging that 'Boonah' or 'Dhangars' be imported from India. Mackay pointed out that these people were ideal workers, for they were used to having only a little rice to eat, and that usually only once in twenty-four hours. They were also accustomed to simple, scanty clothing, and quite unacquainted with the luxury of a bed on a dry floor. Admittedly, for any labour requiring muscular strength they were not equal to stout Europeans, but from their patient disposition and tractable habits they would make excellent shepherds. Any dry place 20 feet square and 8 feet high would suffice for twenty of such men. Mackay's views were supported by J. R. Mayo, a merchant from Mauritius.

Such ideas were anathema to liberal reformers like Sir James Stephen, for whom the free workers occupying the 'waste land' of Australia were to be kept white at all costs. As with Burton's judgement on Aboriginal law, Stephen's thoughts on this issue revealed the racist ideology which the liberals and missionaries were constructing. According to Stephen 'Indian coolies would debase by their intermixture the noble European race. They would introduce caste with all its evils. They would bring with them the idolatory and debasing habits of their country'. In Britain an Act attempting to make deportation of Indian coolie labour illegal was passed in 1839.

The imperial government's prohibition prevented most of the pastoralists' plans for importing coolie labour to replace convicts from eventuating. Exceptions were John Mackay, who managed to recruit two shiploads of 300 Dhangars ahead of the ban, and Robert Towns, a New South Wales pastoralist, Pacific trader and magistrate who, in 1844, introduced for himself and his friends some 100 Indians as 'domestic servants'. The enterprising Ben Boyd imported 185 Melanesian people to work his pastoral leases in 1847, but public opinion condemned his use of 'unlettered cannibals' and the government cancelled their indentures.[30]

In addition, squattocrats and liberal humanitarians came to differ over methods of disciplining free workers. Long used in Britain to regulate wage labour, a Masters and Servants Act had been introduced as early as 1828 in New South Wales. A draconian measure, this provided up to six months' gaol for 'free' workers in breach of contract. This penalty could be imposed for prematurely leaving a job or losing or damaging the master's property. In the colonies free labourers were potentially highly mobile and very independent. Indentured workers, hired in Britain for a fixed term and a set wage, were likely to attempt to break their contract when they discovered that much better rates of pay could be had in alternative employment. Moreover, single male labourers arrived with the expectation of bettering themselves and the determination to keep moving until they did so. 'Thear is no fear of me doing well sum whear', young Benjamin Boyce wrote back to his family in Lincolnshire from South Australia in 1842, 'for if a cant do well in oun place then i go to a nother i am not like you a fraid to go from the smoke of my mothers chinney for i av a rovin commishon throo the world . . .'[31]

Free labourers, even recent immigrants, knew that there were many ways in which employers could cheat them of their wages if they were sent to work 'up the country'. Cases were known where station-owners sold out when one or two years' wages were owing to their servants and the newcomers discharged the men without paying them. Other labourers, on the expiry of their service, were sent to Melbourne or Sydney with an order or a cheque for their wages, only to find that there were no funds to honour it. Some masters charged high prices for rations and other necessities; others paid their men with beer or spirits instead of currency. Such malpractices constituted one reason why many preferred to compete for city jobs rather than seek work on the frontier.

Theoretically, servants could use the Masters and Servants Acts against a defaulting employer, but in practice legal penalties of the legislation fell mostly on the employee. Workers who brought a case before a country Bench were especially likely to fail for, as with the convicts, the magistrate would be one of the master's friends. In 1848 when young Stewart Mowle, brother-in-law of T. A. Murray, found that one of his workmen had gone to Queanbeyan to put in a complaint that he had not been issued with flour, Mowle retaliated by obtaining a warrant against the man and having him imprisoned. As he later admitted, 'Terence and his brother, Dr Murray, were also on the Bench. I think we were inclined to be tyrannical'. While such visible injustice did not embarrass pastoralists, it was too blatant for the liberal code. Liberalism preferred to teach workers that the law stood above the protection of power and property, therefore workers should respect it and learn to use it for their own purposes. Already, in 1840 a new Act in New South Wales actually reduced the maximum punishment from six to three months, without hard labour. Though the new Act aimed at catching the indentured labourer who broke his or her contract, it also contained clauses for use by servants against their masters.

As a means of defusing worker radicalism, the Act was an unqualified success. By 1843 in Melbourne there was a flood of complaints taken before magistrates by employees. Liberals could congratulate themselves that servants were now using the law, rather than political action or violence, to gain redress. As well as benefiting the colony's legal profession, the practice of using Masters and Servants Acts against employers helped to individualize worker grievances and prevent collective action.[32]

Despite conflicts with aspects of liberal humanitarian ideology, squattocrat colonization throve. The new settlements south of the Murray and sprawling from Gippsland to South Australia were seeking separation from New South Wales, which they achieved in 1850. Named Victoria after the young queen, the new colony epitomized the ideals of *laissez-faire* pastoralism, its main town, Melbourne, becoming a prime financial centre, organizing the funds and the controls needed for pastoral profits.

By this time, though the two most recent southern colonies would continue to see themselves as fundamentally different from each other and especially from the old convict settlements, all four were becoming increasingly alike. Even the systematic colony, South Australia, had by now discarded many of its founding economic and moral principles. For instance, by 1839 the first South Australian Aborigines were on trial for the murder of two shepherds on the frontier. They were found guilty and executed. Missions and schools had been opened but venereal and other diseases were raging and out on the frontier, the Aborigines had declared war on the 'overlanders' droving stock from Port Phillip. The new governor called upon to deal with these problems was none other than the liberal George Grey (1841–45). Grey believed it was much more novel and effective to imprison 'nomadic' people than to shoot them, but he nevertheless authorized official punitive expeditions to clear the routes for the overlanders. In August 1841, one of these expeditions resulted in the deaths of thirty Aborigines in a single encounter.

Quite apart from its dealings with the Aboriginal people, the systematic colony now resembled the eastern ones in other ways. Surveyor Light had found it impossible to keep the survey ahead of the demand for land and had resigned. Buyers wanted to abandon the principle of concentration and in Adelaide the constant arrival of new settlers with cash and negotiable assets caused reckless speculation in land. By the end of 1839 two-thirds of the land sold was in the hands of absentees. By 1840 the colony's finances were in a state of collapse, and by 1842 the Board of Commissioners had been abandoned. Tough measures by Governor Grey, a series of good harvests, the discovery of

Emigrant women, 1850. Growing scrutiny by the ships' surgeons had reduced sexual exploitation but cramped quarters were still the norm.

CROSSING THE CREEK AT BACCHUS' MARSH.

In Thomas Ham's illustration for his Gold-Digger's Portfolio (1854), the men rushing to the goldfields seem indifferent to the dead or dying horse and the struggles of the bullock sunk to its chest in mud.

As S. T. Gill's sketch of Bendigo about 1857 suggests, though the gold rushes brought more white women and children into the interior, the opportunities for speculation and adventure remained confined chiefly to European men.

Dispossessed but defiant, an Aboriginal group is photographed by W. S. Jevons on the goldfields at Jembaicumbene, N.S.W. in 1859.

copper and the opening of wheat markets abroad, gradually brought improvement.[33]

However, the systematic colonizers had not been unsuccessful. In contrast with Swan River, where a convict labour force would be reintroduced between 1850 and 1868, all of the eastern colonies would remain committed to the principles of 'free' labour and would move rapidly towards preparing their population for those other major principles of their colonial policy, self-government and the entrenchment of the nuclear family as a moral and reproductive force. This goal required special educative procedures, in many cases ahead of those being applied in Britain. To these procedures colonial liberals were already directing their attention.

8

EDUCATION FOR DEMOCRACY

'THERE ARE LARGE numbers of children growing up in ignorance,' Robert Lowe told a New South Wales government enquiry into education in 1844, 'and if we do not educate them, other people will. Large drafts of criminals are coming over here and they will educate the children . . . Nowhere in the world is education more required than here.'[1]

Lowe was an English barrister who arrived to seek his fortune in the colonies in 1842. In declaring that education was an antidote to 'crime' he was voicing an opinion which had long animated social reformers. During the eighteenth century numerous theorists had argued that in order to prevent individual and collective rebellion it was more effective to educate the masses than keep them in ignorance, preferably by starting when they were still young and 'malleable'. By 1815–17, Jeremy Bentham had published *Chrestomathia* (or 'useful learning'), a collection of papers on how classrooms and curricula could be organized for mass education, while from 1829 James Mill was arguing that education was an exact science which could train the human mind so that all its responses were as predictable and automatic as a machine. The ability to read, write and perform simple arithmetical operations was clearly essential in the new, more technologically complex environments which industrialization was creating, in order to effect conformity to law and enable greater efficiency in the work-place. Together with the clock, the book was to be the chief symbol of the drive of reorganize the workforce for industrial capitalism.[2]

These pragmatic and political purposes of universal education were not always consciously articulated. Ever since the Enlightenment, the idea of education for every child was part of the rhetoric of egalitarianism. An elementary education, it was said, was designed to liberate the people from irrationality and ignorance, not to replace traditional forms of socialization in family, church and community. Religious reformers, too, had seen education largely as a means of enabling every person to read the word of God. Nevertheless, although different advocates of education justified the measure in different ways, all ultimately stood to gain economic and political advantages from this 'reform'. These deeper purposes of universal education were not necessarily widely accepted, either by educational theorists or the labouring masses. Far from being brainwashed into compliance, it always remained possible that working people might turn education to their own political advantage by using it to develop a counter-ideology. Adult workers in Britain by the 1830s were well aware of the importance of literacy, newspapers, broadsides, tracts and posters being found wherever discontent spilled over into active protest. The educational reformers were going to find that the problem would be how to control the workers' thirst for 'useful knowledge', not how to initiate it.[3]

During the 1840s, concern to implement a systematic programme of national education in Britain increased when a major depression ushered in a further period of working-class discontent. This pushed the liberals towards realization that, in order to pre-empt worker demands, certain political concessions such as manhood suffrage would eventually have to be made. As Locke had made clear long ago, such democratic rights could not be permitted without a prior period of carefully monitored education.

The economic crisis during this decade was particularly severe. In contrast with the periodic shake-outs caused by over-production which had struck both Britain and the colonies in the course of economic expansion since 1815, this depression was a distinct downturn caused by the saturation of domestic markets. Investors, now realizing that the greatest profits were to be made during the period of industrial take-off, were being forced to seek out newly industrializing countries in which to invest. To maintain the level of profits to which they were accustomed they would now need to export capital as well as manufactured products. Yet despite massive emigration, much of it to the United States, there were still over one-and-a-half million people officially classified as paupers in Britain in 1845.

In the colonies, the downturn in the British economy was immediately felt. As early as 1840 British financiers were pressing their colonial customers for the repayment of loans, while sources of local credit began to shrink. Even worse, sales of crown land began to fall, and the price of livestock to plummet. To the horror of pastoralists, sheep which in Port Phillip had commanded sixty shillings or more a head, plunged to one shilling or even sixpence a head by 1843. In New South Wales the end of transportation, which reduced government spending, accelerated the depression, while in South Australia the economy was in crisis. In Van Diemen's Land, the combined effect of the depression and the new probation system made for mass unemployment: by 1845 there were more than 3000 'passholders' out of work. The Australian colonies could not depend on being better situated to produce cheaper raw materials than competitors around the globe. This was brought home to colonists in January 1845 when shiploads of wheat arriving in Sydney from South America easily undersold those from Van Diemen's Land. The old notion of the island colony being the granary for New South Wales was gone forever.[4]

Conditions in New South Wales were worsened by the onset of a severe drought, the effects of which were compounded by overstocking and the total disregard of stockowners to the damage which their flocks and herds had caused to pastures, rivers and lagoons. By 1839 the Murray was almost dry and the western rivers had ceased to flow. Down on Monaro the large spread of Lake George had vanished by 1837 and a decade later was still dry. The whole of north-western New South Wales was reduced, as squatters admitted, 'to one vast desert'. Sheep and cattle died in their thousands and many stations were deserted. Some sheepmen discovered that they could save themselves, though not their sheep, by boiling down their flocks to produce tallow which could then be sold in England for candle-making. This ugly demonstration of the lengths to which pastoralists would go to wring the last drop of profit from their sheep resulted in at least fifty-six macabre 'boiling-down establishments' in New South Wales by the end of 1842.[5]

In Britain and the colonies one of the immediate effects of the depression of the 1840s was to reveal the new, two-class society created by industrialization. With numerous smaller investors being shaken out of the system, capital was being concentrated into fewer hands. In the colonies a series of spectacular bankruptcies occurred. In Van Diemen's Land, for example, there was the collapse in 1849 of the Derwent Bank and with it, Charles Swanston. His debts were found to amount to over £104 000, of which almost half was owed to the bank itself. Sydney's equivalent to Swanston was A. B. Spark. The son of a Scottish watchmaker, Spark had arrived in the colonies at the beginning of the pastoral boom and had gone on to reap a fortune from shipping, trade and pastoral pursuits. Unable to collect his debts, by mid 1840 Spark was in trouble. He responded by mortgaging and selling his assets, and eventually, discounting his own bills at the Bank of Australia, of which he was a director. When declared insolvent, Spark's largest creditor was found to be the bank, to which he owed nearly £44 000.

Others, more cunning and less dependent on borrowed capital, emerged from the depression even wealthier than before. They included pastoralists like George Wyndham who simply placed themselves out of reach of their creditors. In 1845, with his wife and ten children, servants and stock, Wyndham departed from 'Dalwood' in the Hunter Valley and disappeared over the lip of the New England plateau for two years. Descending on the Richmond River near present-day Kyogle, the sons were soon cheerfully engaged in dispossessing the Widjabal people from their land. A descendant, Judith Wright, writes that sixteen-year-old Alward enjoyed pursuing Aborigines, using his English rifle and the mountains echoed to this 'classical colonial scene'. Those who emerged unscathed from the depression also included merchants and pastoralists with wealthy friends to assist them. Of these, John Piper was a notorious example. Originally enriched through the trading activities of the New South Wales Corps, Piper had already been rescued once. This was during the previous shake-out of the late 1820s, when he had been dismissed by Darling for incompetence from the position of Naval Officer. As manager of the Bank of New South Wales, Piper had been held responsible for its shaky position in general and especially for the fact that some £57 000 had been lent to just four men. In April 1827, deciding to draw the attention of his friends to his plight,

Piper had made an excuse to leave guests invited to dinner at his harbour-side home and, ordering a large barge manned by members of his band, had himself rowed up the harbour and out to sea. Here, while the band played he leapt overboard, causing great inconvenience to the musicians who with difficulty retrieved him from the water and returned him to his dining-room where his half-drowned and dishevelled appearance created a sensation. The ruse was effective. Piper's humiliation in seeing his mansion sold to emancipist trader, Daniel Cooper, was cushioned by the support of his friends and his own removal to Alloway Bank, a land grant he was able to retain near Bathurst. In trouble again during the drought of 1838, Piper was again rescued by friends, most notably W. C. Wentworth, who purchased a 500-acre property for him on the Macquarie River.[6]

New political alignments were becoming apparent, reflecting the polarization of society into two classes during the 1840s. In New South Wales, by the end of the decade the old emancipist exclusive split had melted away and former dyed-in-the-wool conservatives were seriously considering the liberal formula of allowing major political concessions while introducing modern hegemonic strategies to educate the workers and control their demands. As early as 1828, a new Act had contributed toward meeting emancipist demands for more representative institutions and so to fusing old divisions. This Act allowed trial by jury in some civil cases before the Supreme Court (though only at the discretion of the presiding judge and when one party requested it). The Act also enlarged the Legislative Council to some ten to thirteen members nominated by the crown.

In New South Wales, for a while the exclusive faction continued to oppose the pressure of Wentworth and the wealthy emancipists for further involvement in government. In May 1835 these colonial liberals formed a permanent organization, the Australian Patriotic Association, to raise funds and retain an agent in the House of Commons. The conservative faction responded with a petition in mid-1836 declaring that the level of 'crime' in the colony rendered it as yet unfit for democratic institutions. Nevertheless, in 1833 Governor Bourke's Jury Act, which allowed an accused person to demand trial by a twelve-man civil jury, was accepted by the exclusive faction and removed one of the bones of contention. Then, in 1834 the British Government announced that the full cost of police and gaols, previously paid by Britain, had to be met by colonial revenue, a decision which was seen by the colonists as a threat to funds needed for immigration and as a form of taxation without representation. The raising of the reserve price of land from five to twelve shillings per acre in 1839 further enraged the land-takers, who considered any fixed price too high. By 1840 even James Macarthur had been converted, and his speeches in the Council on 7 January and 4 February 1841 attacked Wakefieldianism and urged colonists to stand together against the British authorities. Faced with the end of the cheap convict labour, emancipists and exclusives made common cause against the Colonial Office.[7]

The following year they were successful. The British Tories presented them with an Act providing for a new Legislative Council, comprising twelve nominees and twenty-four members elected from male property-holders. To qualify, members had to hold freehold land to the value of £2000 or have an annual income of £100, or hold £200 freehold or occupy a house with an annual rental of £20. Similarly, a £20 franchise successfully restricted the vote to men of substance, while actually leaving some squatters disenfranchised. Port Phillip was distinguished from New South Wales, and six of the elected men were to represent that colony. Though control over the disposal of land and land revenue remained with the imperial authorities, the Act provided the newly allied wealthy land-owners with an unprecedented degree of formal control over colonial affairs. The common economic basis which had always underlain the apparent exclusive-emancipist division was now clearly revealed.

Admittedly, by the mid-1840s new but equally nebulous political divisions developed. Newcomers to squatting, moving in over the ruins of bankrupt predecessors like A. B. Spark and Charles Swanston, found themselves temporarily at odds with some old hands who held both freehold and squatting leases and who were occasionally inclined to join Governor Gipps and urban liberals in opposing the attempts of the new chums to gain security of tenure over huge areas of rented land for a mere £10 a year. However, both groups used a liberal rhetoric, especially following the attempts of Gipps in 1844 to alter the squatting regulations and to collect quit rents in order to raise revenue for immigration. In a furious and united voice, again the pastoralists refused to pay 'taxation without representation' and in an ensuing deadlock with the crown which resembled that of seventeenth-century

England, demanded responsible government. In 1847 the squatters were able to modify their 'liberalism' when they gained what they wanted, namely the right to hold the land on long, fourteen-year leases, with provision for pre-emptive purchase on easy terms.

During the decade the liberal cause was also prominent among the growing numbers of urban professionals and merchants who opposed the claims of the squatters and flirted with 'radical' ideas. Like the landed élite, their chief concern was to ensure that the process of gaining greater independence from British control would culminate in liberal parliamentarianism rather than in other forms of social organization.[8] If the capitalist classes were obtaining a clearer grasp of the new industrial society, so were the workers. In contrast with the essentially anarchistic protest of the British Luddites or the colonial bushrangers, by the 1840s factory workers were beginning to develop a critique of liberal theories of society in which a clear counter-ideology was articulated for the first time. The Chartist movement in Britain, organized from 1838, limited its demands to manhood suffrage and other constitutional reforms. Even so, it supported its essentially liberal ideas with the radical threat of a mass general strike, and was in touch with the much more revolutionary political theories being evolved by socialists in Germany and France. From 1840 on, these radical theories were publicized by the Chartist press and in February 1848 the *Communist Manifesto* was published in London; by March worker-inspired uprisings had occurred in France and Germany; in April the Chartists were planning a huge demonstration in London to force parliament to enact its political programme.[9]

In the colonies, newly arrived convicts and emigrants kept workers in touch with the new political theories and uprisings and with their repression. By the 1840s in Sydney, a factory system had developed where numbers of labourers were now congregated under one roof and ideas for political organization could be exchanged. Some factories, like the Australian Gas Light Company, Tooth's Kent Brewery and Fowler's Potteries, were large organizations, while there were also numerous flour mills, many of them using steam-powered machines built in local engineering shops. The severity of the depression ensured that labourers were receptive to radical ideas. Unemployment soared and hundreds of workers who could afford to do so left Sydney for Valparaiso; starvation was not unknown to those who remained. In Sydney, by 1844 there were at least 1000 mechanics and labourers out of work with 2500 dependants. Families were going for periods of up to forty-eight hours without food, and children were seen eating vegetable scraps found on the streets.[10]

In 1848 the Duke of Wellington packed London with troops as a preparation for the planned Chartist meeting in a show of military strength which succeeded in persuading the leaders to call off the rally. Chartism was eventually broken and the progress of radicalism arrested, less by the use of force than by the implementation of educative techniques and ameliorative reforms. Principal among these was the repeal of the Corn Laws. Authorizing tariffs on imported wheat, these laws were a remnant of mercantilism designed by the landed interests to protect their grain from foreign competition. They formed an ideal scapegoat to explain the workers' misery while at the same time they came under attack as a traditional source of Tory wealth. Responsibility for the depression was blamed on the aristocrats who, it was said, were keeping up the price of bread to enrich themselves while the people starved. The repeal of the Corn Laws, effected in 1846, reduced the cost of bread and allowed the subsistence wage paid to labourers to be lowered so that profits increased and a period of capital expansion could ensue.

Equally successful as a liberal strategy was the encouragement of small industrial craft unions. These were an excellent vehicle for defusing worker political action, for they were élitist in ideology with membership confined to skilled urban workers like tailors, coachmakers, saddlers and painters, along with some white-collar workers such as clerks. These groups wanted to improve wages and working conditions, but they were more interested in the protection of their skills than in political action or large-scale worker co-operation. Their emphasis on thrift and on schemes to provide mutual benefit in times of sickness revealed their allegiance to the ideal of individual self-help. The craft unions were politically educative in function, their meetings being based on parliamentary procedure and their overall philosophy centred on respect for property and an improved form of political representation within the existing system. Though the old Combination Laws had been abolished in 1824 any workers who formed a more threatening form of union could be charged under the Conspiracy Laws.

In the colonies similar tactics defused resistance and collective organization among 'free' labourers. By the 1830s industrial trade societies, similar to those in Britain, were emerging in the towns. Though these groups were sometimes prepared to co-operate with each other in strikes and petitions, they were not unified organizations of workingmen against employers. Even organizations of a general kind, like the Society of Emigrant Mechanics, by 1833 were ideologically linked with liberal political economy and the urban democratic movement, accepting rather than challenging the leadership of liberal businessmen and professionals like W. A. Duncan and J. D. Lang. An admirer of American democracy, Lang's brand of liberalism focused chiefly on making a complete break with Britain and introducing ameliorative measures which he defined as social justice. In April 1850, assisted by emigrant ivory-turner Henry Parkes, and J. R. Wilshire, native-born son of a Sydney manufacturer, Lang formed the Australian League, a political organization based on achieving these limited ideals. Policies advocated in W. A. Duncan's *Australasian Chronicle* (1839–48) were not dissimilar, urging a stronger role for the paternalistic state including protection for the corn-grower and a state bank to lend money to the poor. E. J. Hawkesley, a Catholic and former schoolteacher and member of the Constitutional Association (1848), also adopted a moderate approach. This organization was branded by the *Herald* as a secret society, propagating 'Communist and Socialist Principles', but its aims were essentially democratic: to extend the franchise, re-distribute electorates on a popular basis, and encourage small agricultural holdings. Hawkesley's newspaper, *The People's Advocate*, adopted a motto from French liberal Lamartine, looking to political economy to bring about a less unjust distribution of wealth, and continuing to see the people's enemy as the aristocrat rather than the middle-class employer.

The reliance of workers on essentially middle-class leadership and ideology was revealed in 1843–44 in the fortunes of the Mutual Protection Society. This Sydney-based political organization, with a membership of 500, grew out of an alliance between workmen, intellectuals and political opportunists. It ran an employment agency in Sydney, petitioned the Legislative Council against competition from cheap coolie or British immigrant labour, and aired its views in a newspaper, *The Guardian*. However, with the improvement in economic conditions, the association virtually collapsed. By the late 1840s radical ideas survived only in a few transient journals such as *The Star and Working Man's Guardian* which still urged workers to combine against the 'vampire capitalists'.

Radicalism during the depression was also diffused in Sydney when the new Legislative Council took some action to alleviate worker distress. Select Committees were appointed in 1843 and 1844 to investigate the extent of poverty in the city. Twelve men working in pairs were appointed to go to 'every house that had the appearance of being the abode of a poor working-man' and enquire about the employment of the breadwinner and the size of the family. Members of the Council proved ready to conclude that the unemployed were not suffering want through their own folly, intemperance and error. They also accepted that it was the state's duty to alleviate distress and prop up the economic system. As in Britain, having virtually gained control of the state, liberals had no hesitation in extending its role to implement the kind of educative and remedial procedures which democracy was going to require. Accordingly, public works were begun in Sydney, jobs were created by the Colonial Architect and the City of Sydney Corporation, and immigration was temporarily suspended.[11]

In their efforts to provide palliatives to defuse radicalism the reformers turned especially to the principle of education. Ideally this was to be an extremely broad process, reaching into every aspect of working-class life so that eventually all but the most 'idle' and 'dissipated' would share liberal aspirations and conform to their cultural and economic expectations. In Britain, this process was apparent in a programme of adult re-education introduced in the 1820s. Directed specifically at skilled male workers and mechanics and organized by private charity, 'Mechanics' Institutes' offered evening lectures on a range of scientific and social topics. Their quasi-benevolent founders desired these lectures to function as a kind of 'university' for artisans, giving them access to knowledge which might produce practical results useful to commence. The alternative name for these institutions, 'Schools of Arts', reflected this belief that education would foster improvements in design, perhaps in architecture, civil engineering or of machines. In practice, however, the function of these organizations was very different, for the topics chosen were such as to inculcate desired moral and political values in the workers who attended. At the same time the leisure of the worker was commandeered and he was put in a position of dependence on and deference to his social superiors. Artisans, in particular, were made the main objects of this new form of instruction because they were potentially the most dangerous and troublesome and because it was still the case that the workers closest to the process of production made the technological discoveries so essential to profit. In 1844 John Ridley, a farmer near Hindmarsh in South Australia, was awarded a special prize by the Agricultural and Horticultural Society for a mechanical reaper which he had constructed from an illustration in J. C. Loudon's *Encyclopaedia of Agriculture* (1835). James Harrison, who designed and built the plant for the first manufacture of ice in Australia, was a compositor who had emigrated to the colonies in 1837. A self-educated son of a Scottish fisherman, Harrison went on to create a pioneer mechanical refrigerator, and by the 1870s to invent a system by which meat exports could be kept frozen during shipment to England.

Mechanics' Institutes quickly emerged in the colonies to educate the skilled workers politically and keep them in their place. Founded by Alfred Stephen, Hobart's Institute dated from 1827, and in 1833 Governor Bourke invited immigrant education theorist, Henry Carmichael, to begin a similar organization in Sydney. By 1835 the Sydney Institute had 153 financial members, and 263 by 1843; by 1850 similar institutions had been formed in all capital cities and many country centres.

Whether or not workers were fully aware of the political function of the Institutes, they certainly avoided attending them. The clientele of the Schools of Arts came largely from the middle classes, who were revealed to have a great zeal for self-improvement. In Sydney, first President was Sir Thomas Mitchell, and officials included other pillars of élite society like Reverend Henry Cartwright and Dr Bland. Lectures ranged from Mr David Taylor on the Natural History of Man to Mr Pattison on the Steam Engine and Thomas Shepherd on Horticulture. In June 1841 the Sydney Institute learned from Mr Rennie that knowledge was 'infinitely diffusable' and that even infants had basic knowledge of grammar, metaphysics, and science. All that was required was subsequent study and perseverance to improve these basic skills. It cost twelve shillings and sixpence per annum to join the Sydney Institute in 1841, and this gave access to the library as well as to lectures by the likes of Mr Rennie, who was known to speak for up to two hours. There was a table covered with 'beautiful models' of undefined objects presented by Sir Thomas Mitchell; 'fine apparatus' presented by R. Tertius Campbell; a 'moonlight landscape and lithographed scenery' by J. S. Prout; numerous specimens of American schoolwork lent by the Reverend T. Adam; and an Australian bird's nest from Goulburn, built chiefly of wool and showing, as Mr Rennie pointed out, 'that even wild animals adopt Colonial improvements'. Mr Rae, lecturing to Sydney Mechanics on Taste in 1841, admitted that rhetoric and grammar might not teach the mechanic much about pulley, wheel, axle, lever, or screw, but he declared they would help to exercise the reason; and should a mechanic one day have occasion to address a body of electors or even a Legislative Assembly, he would at least be able to speak the Queen's English with propriety. By 1855 it was admitted that Sydney mechanics formed a very small portion of the members, perhaps only 10 per cent of a total membership of 1000. Accordingly, the organization took a new name, 'The Sydney Literary and Scientific Institute'. It had fallen into the hands of a different class than had been intended, but middle-class membership, it was said, could only raise the character of the Institute.[12]

Workers may have resisted recruitment into the Mechanics' Institutes but the temperance movement successfully introduced many of them to similar values. Originating in the early nineteenth century in the United States, the first temperance society was founded in Hobart by the visiting Quaker missionaries Backhouse and Walker in 1832. In the same year Reverend Charles Price established a society in Launceston, and Reverend W. P. Crook established one in Sydney. In mid-1837 the *Australian Temperance Magazine* was launched, and by 1838 the first total abstinence societies appeared. By 1845 in Sydney alone, some 3000 people put themselves through the ceremony of signing an abstinence pledge. The new notion of temperance as an educative strategy was in strong contrast to the earlier encouragement of drinking to serve the short-term interests of the spirit trade and to promote the quiescence of the working class. Sober workers were required to operate industrial technology, while passivity was encouraged through the extension of middle-class morality into abstemious and godly working-class homes. Indeed, temperance missions became a major vehicle for transmitting middle-class domestic ideology.

The temperance and total abstinence societies were said to be civilizing agencies like the Mechanics' Institutes, designed to ameliorate the condition of the labouring masses and to promote social harmony. Similar emphasis was placed on individualizing social problems and encouraging 'self-improvement'. Drunkenness was seized upon as a cause, not a result of poverty, and was a major reason for domestic violence, vice and crime. As the *Temperance Advocate* wrote in 1840, alcohol was the evil

which has destroyed the peace and the comfort of so many families— which has made so many wives, widows, and so many children orphans— which is the parent of every vice, and of every crime—which has spread through our land disease, insanity and death . . .

Introduced by gentlemen and attracting viceregal patronage, the temperance movement, unlike the Mechanics' Institutes, successfully appealed to and were eventually taken over by people lower down on the social scale. In particular, whereas women had been largely excluded from adult education, they were involved in temperance campaigns from the outset, for the evils of drunkenness were seen as of being special relevance to wives and mothers. The colonial women who emerged as leaders— such as Isabella Dalgarno, Mary Ann Thomas, Sarah Crouch, Esther Bonwick, Hannah Crook and Sarah Walker—were from predominantly Nonconformist families, often teachers or women in modest financial circumstances, sometimes conducting their own private-venture schools. Public addresses, pledge-signing, processions and display became a regular feature of the movement, and many of these temperance rituals adopted a military theme. In Launceston abstainers formed what was probably the first civilian brass band in Australia, while the Melbourne Society organized the first performance on the saxhorn in that city. In Sydney in 1841 the Teetotal Society arranged a huge procession for Boxing Day, with two bands to encourage marchers and spectators to join the cause.

Temperance societies, like the craft unions, attracted newly arrived immigrants who derived social contacts and material aid from the movement. In small towns from Longford in Van Diemen's Land to Koroit in the Port Phillip district, members formed debating societies and youth organizations, with tea-meetings to raise funds and Bands of Hope to educate the children. Mutual Benefit Societies provided insurance against bereavement or death of the breadwinner; the temperance press offered hints on etiquette and how to control and educate servants, useful lessons for the socially ambitious. As with upper-class women in philanthropy, the experience gained by the wives of mechanics and craftsmen in organizing temperance meetings, writing and distributing tracts, and developing a presence outside their own homes, produced a feminist ideology: 'women in general are not such fools as men are; and secondly, they are not such knaves', an article in *The Teetotaller* announced in 1843. Entitled 'Ladies Should Have the Vote', this declared that:

If all the detestable and disgraceful public acts which have darkened the last quarter of a century could have been submitted to a jury of women, three out of four would have been stopped by the superior sense of virtue of the referees. Women, in fact, are vastly further advanced in civilisation than men are; vastly more removed from the instincts and passions of savage life. [13]

While advancing the liberation of women from some of the injustices they suffered by being treated as the property of men, this concept of a feminist sisterhood obscured the economic inequalities which divided philanthropic and temperance ladies from working-class and Aboriginal women, and implied that all women should seek the causes of their problems not in the economic system, but in their relationship to men. In failing to address the exploitation of one class of women by another, this ideology also implied that economic inequalities were the product of patriarchy, not the reverse. It thus potentially constituted a wedge which, like the notion of a separate skilled and sober aristocracy of labour, cut through the developing ideal of worker solidarity, in this case to prevent combined male and female challenges to liberal rule. [14]

In this struggle to deter workers from using education to build an alternative, radical ideology, it was the notion of gaining access to the young which especially appealed to the liberal reformers. 'Society must now be led, not driven', the Sydney Mechanics' Institute reported in February 1849, and 'sound and cheap education' was seen as a key element for defusion of revolutionary ferment and the maintenance of concord between classes. A working class that had been educated while young and impressionable might produce the occasional leader. As Wentworth wrote, even the poorest man could and should aspire to the seat of government and the couch of wealth, always provided that he was first educated to the sense of responsibility which men of substance like himself possessed. Social classes would remain but movement between them could allegedly be achieved by intellectual and moral merit. This was an ideal which particularly inspired colonial liberals determined to build a new society free of the social and political restraints of old. As J. D. Lang declared, ideally colonial society was like a collection of chemical salts thrown into a common solvent. Here a new form of crystallization would occur in which Nature's aristocracy would automatically rise to the surface.[15]

The liberals' faith in universal education was also based on their own child-rearing practice. In the colonies, the concept of the child-centred family, organized around the physical and educational needs of the 'innocent' young, was now established among the well-to-do. From Malthus's assumption that the wealthy always limited the size of their families according to their means it followed that a large number of children was a visible indication of their wealth. The wives of the colony's merchants, bankers and pastoralists devoted their lives to bearing and rearing as many children as possible, the number being limited only by miscarriage, child mortality, and the spacing of infants according to the dictates of breast-feeding. Some affluent men welcomed their wives' numerous pregnancies, perhaps seeing every child as an extension of their property. Certainly every symptom of conception was noted with pleasure by A. B. Spark, whose wife had already borne eight children during her first marriage to a Hunter Valley surgeon, and who duly presented the merchant with another six between 1840 and 1850: 'My Maria expecting a slight enlargement . . .'; 'A hint from Maria . . .'; 'Maria complaining of sickness—a token . . .'; 'Spouse not at all well—perhaps in a hopeful way'. Similarly, every occasion was recorded when such hopes were dashed: 'Another disappointment—my beloved has been in bed all day, and symptoms of increase have entirely disappeared'; 'She complained of a pain in the side, extinguishing late hopes . . .'[16]

Should breast-feeding fail, finding a wet-nurse of satisfactory character was a problem which absorbed fathers as well as mothers. 'I beg that you will not hesitate to engage a wet nurse should you be able to meet with one or do anything that may afford relief to him or you', James Norton, a Sydney solicitor and pastoralist, wrote anxiously to his wife, Jane McKenzie, in January 1834. She had recently produced a son and was staying with friends out of town. Norton scoured Sydney for a suitable nurse but one week later reported that there was not one to be had who could be trusted: 'hardly anything could overcome the fear I entertain of such women as are to be met with', he complained. He had been advised on no account to employ 'a woman from the factory' and indeed he could hardly endure to think of such a thing. The result was that Jane continued to nurse the child herself, despite her own failing health. She bore eight sons and two daughters between her marriage in 1824 and her early death in March 1840.[17]

The women were to produce children as property and to prepare them for the formal education which turned the sons into knowledgeable men of property and the daughters into obedient and accomplished wives. It was asssumed that mothers should teach early reading, arithmetic, and prayers. 'I continue to teach *Essington & Robert* their lessons every day', wrote Harriet King in March 1827.

I also try to keep them in proper subjection, but it is no easy task to manage so many Boys, for *Charles & Frederick* now come in for their share of correction. They have each a fine share of spirit which drilled into a proper channel will I hope make them good and steady, and be a comfort to us in our old age.

(Charles and Frederick were aged three and two respectively; Essington was six and Robert four.)

Pride was taken in dressing up children and displaying them. Georgiana McCrae, wife of a Port Phillip lawyer and pastoralist, was gratified when a visitor in 1844 was 'very much taken with little Lucia's appearance; her "lint-white locks" set off by a striped tabbinet frock, once part of an old dress of mine'. Baptisms provided ideal occasions for showing off one's offspring, and birthdays were 'strictly observed'. Affectionate fathers like A. B. Spark indulged their children with gifts while mothers provided miniature parties at which their offspring were expected to imitate the hospitality so dear to the hearts of their parents. 'Farquhar's third birthday Jenny McCrae came to dine with him and Aunt Agnes gave him a beautiful copy of Paul and Virginia, in English, with illustrations', Georgiana McCrae recorded in October 1841. For the third birthday of A. B. Spark's 'little Edith', her older sister Fanny, aged six, presided over the tea party, 'on which occasion a pretty tea service for children, very complete, was for the first time displayed'.[18]

Colonial children of wealthy parents had an idle though not unstructured childhood, especially the boys. James Hassall, born in 1823, a son of the clergyman and 'squire' of Denbigh, recalled numerous holidays spent there and with his uncle, Charles Marsden, at Mamre, the Marsden's farm near Penrith. The days were spent gobbling peaches, apples, pears, oranges and apricots which grew in abundance, picnicking and riding to South Creek for a swim. Assigned servants were available to do the farm and stock-work, and sons were expected to devote themselves to supervised amusements which closely appoximated those of their fathers. At Mamre, there were twenty to thirty convicts employed, freeing young James Hassall to visit the Cox's sons at Mulgoa, or the Lethbridges' and the Kings' sons at Werrington. These children rapidly reproduced the values of their class. In June 1841 young Francis Cox wrote to James Hassall from Mulgoa dwelling at length on his uncle Edward's house up on the hill 'which was getting on pretty quickly'. He noted it included a place fenced in for some deer procured from Van Diemen's Land. 'I think they will add greatly to the appearance of the grounds', added this miniature squire.

At Woden in the early 1840s the diary of Anna Maria Bunn's son, William, testified to the idleness and dependence of the sons of the élite: '22 February [1846] got up early. Read Phrenology. Frightened the servant.' Other activities for the day included firing pistols, making bullets and sketching. In July his short essay entitled 'A Day at Woden' was equally revealing:

I get up sometime between 8 and 11, read or, if Nowlan is at home, go to the dairy; have breakfast, write shorthand, Mamma reads, say lessons; if I do not write shorthand in the morning, write now (4 p.m. or 6), walk about, play—have dinner at dark. If Nowlan is at home go to the dairy—if not write, or make something, but not read. 8 p.m. or near it—go to tea. If post night (Tuesday, Thursday, or Sunday, but no papers are read on Sunday) read the papers, write and go to bed before 10. If the day is Sunday, play—namely run—jump—throw stones and walk about.

William was sixteen years old.[19]

Younger children were provided with pets to amuse them, parrots, cockatoos, and rabbits were imprisoned for their perusal.

Reflecting their parents' absorbing interest in botany and horticulture, gardening was an approved activity. The King boys were encouraged to plant vegetables, while even the lethargic William Bunn occasionally was stirred to plant lettuces, cabbages, and carrots, grapes from the Campbells at Duntroon, and peaches from the Wrights at Lanyon. Since a large amount of their time was turned over to entertainment and pleasure, the numerous minor accidents suffered by these children were the result of play rather than pioneering. 'Sandy took a fall off the brown pony and hit his head against the projecting root of a gum-tree', Georgiana McCrae's journal recorded in September 1843; the following February Johnnie was in disgrace for having allowed Wattie to chop his finger with an axe; in March George, returning from town with the newspapers, was thrown by the brown pony; in September Alick hit Lucia in the mouth with a flourish of his spade and knocked in one of her teeth; in October Willie's spear glanced off a tree and hit George near the eye.

Daughters of the élite also had a great deal of supervised leisure. At Port Macquarie, the girls in the Innes family had ponies to ride along the beach and were permitted to swim in the surf, for even during straitened circumstances early in the depression this household contained two personal maids, two housemaids, and a laundress. In addition, there was a butler, two footmen, a piper who also waited at the table, and two Spaniards who were 'attached to the stables, but appeared in livery at all times'. The girls were expected to attend to light household duties such as picking and arranging the flowers and gathering and preparing fruit for preserves and jam-making. On one occasion in 1844 they were set by their aunt to clean the windows. Annabella, amazed, recorded that they actually cleaned no less than seven French windows without breaking a single pane, 'I have no idea why we were set to this work', she wrote, 'or who usually did it'.

Girls enjoyed a shorter childhood than boys. From the age of about ten, their leisure was likely to be interrupted at any time by the need to help mothers, older sister, or other relatives with infant care and child-rearing. The expertise they acquired in those matters was rightly seen as invaluable to their future role as mothers or aunts. Georgiana Molloy's daughter Sabina, aged eleven when her mother died in 1842, helped to raise her four younger sisters even after her marriage at seventeen to Reverend

Matthew Hale. While Molloy went 'home' on a visit to England, the four little sisters were taken into the Hale family which already consisted of Hale's two children by his first marriage. While colonial boys of her age were still exchanging letters about the height their ponies could jump, or how many kangaroos their dogs had killed, Sabina was beginning married life with a household of six little girls.[20]

Wealthy colonial parents planning to secure land grants or leases for their sons did not have to face getting them into the overcrowded professions, a problem which was presently troubling their counterparts in Britain. On the other hand, they did believe in providing their sons with a classical education, seen as a device for moral training, as well as equipping them for army, church, medicine or law. Overseas, as educational theorists and moralists prolonged the period over which the young were said to be in need of special training and care, they began to focus on the physical changes of puberty, said to be a specially difficult period in child-raising. From 1828 Thomas Arnold, headmaster of Rugby College, and his followers began to devise new techniques for disciplining and hardening the increasing numbers of élite sons being incarcerated in the British public schools. Focusing initially on piety as the foundation of morality, by the 1850s new techniques such as team sports, designed to create and display aggressive masculinity, foster the competitive spirit, and teach absolute obedience to rules, began to replace classical influences on education with athletic and military ones.

From the late 1820s there were a number of private-venture institutions in the colonies offering at least the kind of discipline and training in the classics which middle-class parents wanted for their sons. In addition to Mr Lang's Caledonian Academy, and Captain Beveridge's Naval Seminary, there was Dr Laurence Halloran's 'establishment for a liberal education', also known as the Sydney Grammar School. Run by a litigious doctor of divinity who had been transported for forgery, this institution had opened in January 1820 and was patronized mainly by wealthy emancipist families. At the half-yearly examinations conducted in July 1823 the sons of Simeon Lord, James Meehan, and Samuel Terry underwent minute and public examinations in subjects like 'the Greek Testament', Horace, the commentaries of Caesar, and Ovid's *Metamorphosis*. According to the *Sydney Gazette* 'occasional exhibitions' of this kind were an invaluable pedagogical tool, 'in exciting and cherishing a spirit of laudable emulation and honourable competition among the students'. Rote learning of Greek and Latin grammar and the catechism was approved as developing desirable moral and mental 'faculties' in the mind of the young. At Bathurst, Mr Holloway's 'Classical and Mercantile School' offered young gentlemen a rather more utilitarian curriculum. This comprised Latin and Greek as well as 'Merchant's Accounts', bookkeeping, geography, geometry and trigonometry for a mere thirty guineas per annum.[21]

By the 1830s a growing colonial middle class produced a spate of secondary schools for boys modelled more closely on the latest British educative techniques. Archdeacon William Broughton's plan of 1830 for the foundation of 'King's Schools' was welcomed by the wealthy classes rushing to groom their sons for government. Established in Parramatta and Sydney, their aim was to provide 'a good classical, scientific and religious education' using schoolmasters especially imported for this purpose. In January 1832 the first of these schools opened in Parramatta, taking boarders and day-boys, and by June 1832 there were over a hundred pupils. Not to be outdone, that pillar of Presbyterian society, the Reverend John Dunmore Lang, was promoting a similar institution for non-Anglican youth. Believing that too many of the free immigrants arriving in New South Wales by the 1830s were Catholics, Lang was anxious to promote Protestant immigration and provide Protestant institutions to educate their young. Visiting England in 1830 he conceived a Wakefieldian plan for combining the promotion of emigration with the erection of a colonial college. He persuaded about 140 people, mainly Scottish tradesmen and their families, to emigrate to Sydney, and the Colonial Office to lend him £3500 to finance the venture. The emigrants were to be employed in building the school and to repay from their wages the cost of their passage. Named the Australian College, Lang's version of the English public school opened in Sydney in November 1831.[22] In Hobart, similar moves were being made to educate the sons of the élite for government. Pupils at William Gore Elliston's Longford Hall Academy included Thomas and James Reibey of Entally House, grandsons of Mary Reibey; and William Crowther, son of a quarrelsome emigrant doctor and, like Thomas Reibey, a future premier of the colony.

William Crowther junior and the Reibey sons were sent

overseas to complete their education in medicine and divinity respectively, but the arrival of Governor Franklin in February 1837 stimulated advanced education in the colony. Franklin was acquainted with Dr Arnold and consulted him when planning to revive a scheme for a college first mooted by Broughton and Arthur in 1833. Selecting an old Rugby boy, John Philip Gell, as headmaster, Franklin planned to call it Christ's College, and include Anglican instruction, but immediately ran into severe sectarian opposition. Presbyterian and Catholic critics damned it as élitist, while *Murray's Review*, inspired by the foundation of the secular University of London in 1828, demanded a University instead. The project lapsed, and the first of the colonies' major tertiary institutions was established in New South Wales. Sydney University which was founded in 1850, and Melbourne University which followed in 1853, were purely secular institutions, and though a system of denominational colleges developed, the universities remained autonomous.[23]

Having provided child-centred homes and local, structured schooling for their own children, it was small wonder that, when looking about for more subtle and effective means of controlling the population, the middle classes turned to universal education. They were extremely suspicious of the child-rearing provided by working-class parents or rather, it seemed, which they failed to provide in their homes. Far from being isolated in a special world of adult supervision and formal play, working-class children apparently were left unattended to run about the streets where, it was thought, they were in danger all sorts of moral contagion, especially the girls. These suspicions were further prompted by the growing visibility of the colonial child. Between 1832 and 1844, 57 000 immigrants arrived in New South Wales, many of them young married people with small children. This altered the age structure of the population. Children had comprised some 17 per cent of the population in New South Wales by 1804, by 1841 they comprised 25 per cent. This was still less than the 33 per cent then in England and Wales, but colonial children seemed more numerous because of their concentration in the cities and towns. In New South Wales, over two-thirds of the colony's children in 1841 were resident in the County of Cumberland. In Sydney the town crier could frequently be heard advertising lost children, and the streets seemed to be swarming with urchins, as A. B.

Spark noted with annoyance when he accidentally ran over one while driving into town in July 1838.[24]

The poverty, overcrowding and overwork in the working-class household made it impossible for many families to apply the developing, middle-class ideal of supervised play and prolonged formal training of their young. The long periods which many male breadwinners were required to spend away from home, often for an inadequate cash wage, continued to be inimical to stable, secure family life, and prompted many breadwinners to abandon their dependants altogether. In response to this problem Acts for the Maintenance of Deserted Wives and Children were passed in Van Diemen's Land in 1837 and New South Wales in 1840 but, though far in advance of similar legislation in Britain, these proved impossible to police. Working-class women especially, far from being able to provide a protected, pampered nest for their children, faced an on-going threat of institutionalization. As early as 1813 philanthropists established a Benevolent Society in New South Wales to provide first, outdoor relief to destitute families and, from 1820, an asylum to house, hospitalize and deliver the babies of the most outcast of colonial poor. By the 1830s similar societies had been formed in Launceston and Hobart and during the depression all were recording large increases in demand. Destitute women and children were always a conspicuous proportion of the people who came under their care. The 'Orphan' Schools, too, were crowded during the 1830s and 1840s. In 1819 Macquarie had opened a male equivalent of the original Female Orphan School, while Catholics had established an institution for boys and girls in 1837. Similar institutions had opened in Hobart in 1828.[25]

Nor were newly arrived emigrants necessarily in a position to provide for their young. Many families found the emigrant ship became a kind of mobile asylum where, given that they were expected to supply their own bedding, drinking mugs, plates and cooking pots, the poor found themselves and their children disadvantaged in comfort and in health. Mortality rates, especially amongst children, were high despite a series of Passenger Acts attempting to control the numbers herded into the steerage quarters and prevent unscrupulous captains from further curtailing passenger space by carrying cargoes of speculative goods. It was not unusual for families to arrive without their mother or breadwinner and so they immediately joined the ranks of the destitute on the shore. Emigrant families who survived these hazards discovered that the voyage out was only the beginning of their problems. Sarah Davenport, who disembarked at Sydney with her husband, a cabinet-maker, and four young children in 1841, was lucky to spend only a few days in the government tents before meeting an old neighbour from home. The two families then shared a two-bedroom house at the exorbitant rate of fourteen shillings a week where they and their combined total of eight children could count the stars as they lay in bed at night and were extremely uncomfortable in wet weather. In a typical Sydney two-roomed terrace, the rooms were usually only ten or eleven feet square and, as a later government enquiry conceded, 'scarcely high enough for a man to stand erect; the floor is lower than the ground outside; the rain comes in through the roof, and filth of all kinds washes in at the door . . .' In most of the workers' houses water had to be obtained from the nearest pump or purchased from a water-cart, while only the best dwellings had ovens and stoves. Most families round Lower George Street and the Rocks took their meat to the baker's oven where they paid to have it cooked. In Adelaide during the depressed conditions from 1841 to 1843 accommodation and relief for the alarming numbers of destitute families pouring off incoming ships was initially organized by the Resident Emigration Agent. In 1849 a Destitute Board was created to deal with new arrivals and the permanently poor.[26]

Survival of numerous families depended on the mother's taking paid work inside or outside the home, while neighbours or older children minded the young. In Sydney in the 1840s the wives of poorly paid constables kept cows and sold the milk. Fanny Doran, an immigrant who arrived in 1841 and who left her husband after he attempted to commit a rape upon her eldest child, aged eight, provided for her children for twelve years by working as a laundress. A sprained wrist terminated her earning capacity, and in the end she had no choice but to seek admission to the Benevolent Asylum for herself and one of her youngest children.[27]

Reflecting these problems, in the period up to the 1850s the large family appears to have been a luxury largely confined to the rich, together with successfully established innkeepers or farmers. A sample of 162 families in New South Wales, studied from the Mutch Index between 1820 and 1839, showed that some 60 per cent of families had four or fewer live births, the average being 5.3 live births. The 1828 census of New South Wales showed that most families had only one or two children resident with them, families with only one child were the most numerous. The poorer the family, the more the children were expected to be responsible little adults, contributing to the survival of the group by paid or unpaid work, often in the households of other people. In New South Wales only 13 per cent of the colony's young lived in families of seven or more children, while a massive 16 per cent were placed out either in institutional care or in the custody of a person to whom they appeared to be unrelated.[28]

These economic realities of working-class family life created a tension for the liberal reformer. Clearly unless something radical was done to alter the material condition of the poor, it was going to be very difficult to institute a system of education which cut across the dependence of the family economy on child labour. Though opportunities for employers to exploit children in factories and mines were absent, as William Macarthur pointed out in 1838, every 'healthy child of 8 or 9 years' was employable on a farm and work could also be found for those two or even three years younger. Of those children in New South Wales in 1828 who were in institutional care, most were aged around seven, while those in private care tended to be around ten, the age when they became most useful around house and farm.[29] There were, however, time-honoured solutions to these difficulties, given the observation long ago made by Locke that for the poor, education should comprise the barest minimum of literate, numerate and vocational skills, combined with a maximum of moral training. In fact, this was the policy followed in the 'orphan' schools, where inmates were apprenticed out from as young as twelve. A few of these children found their way into a skilled trade, but this was unusual, especially for the girls. Once apprenticed from an institution it was extremely difficult for parents to get their children back. Even children privately apprenticed out by their parents found their whole time subject to a master or mistress, and savage punishments could be authorized for those who defaulted or absconded.[30]

The way in which these educative institutions accommodated the needs of employers was especially evident in Lady Darling's Female School of Industry. Founded in 1826 this institution aimed to 'rescue' girls of humble origin from what was seen as the pernicious influence of their homes and a likely career in prostitution, and train them for a life of useful obedience as servants and wives. Nearly forty girls from the age of seven were enrolled, and the school insisted that parents sign a bond for £100 that they would not interfere with the child, nor attempt to remove her before the age of eighteen. Girls were placed out as servants at fourteen, preference being given to subscribers, so this rule provided élite women with trained servants for at least four years. Any girl who completed four years of service with one family was rewarded with a gift of £3, and marriage was also an approved achievement. Any girl consigned to the care of a husband before reaching eighteen was rewarded with £5 and a cow. Inside the institution the girls were subjected to a rigid course of instruction, partly in reading, writing and religion but especially in domestic duties. No servants were employed by the institution so the girls performed all of the housework as well as constructing suitable items for sale to offset costs.[31]

Another traditional solution to the problem of providing education while not interfering with child labour was the Sunday School. Founded in England in 1780 by Evangelical enthusiasts, Robert Raikes, Hannah More and Sarah Trimmer, Sunday Schools were specifically designed to teach religion and reading to child factory workers in industrial areas. Some relied on unpaid working-class teachers, and consequently attracted mass support for a time. By the 1830s, however, Sunday Schools were no longer reaching the neediest and were becoming another means by which working-class children were separated from the values and culture of their parents. Similarly in New South Wales where Sunday Schools had expanded rapidly during the Macquarie regime, by the 1830s they were seen as coming within the sphere of the colony's ladies, who were by then sufficiently numerous to control these classes as part of their philanthropic duties. By now too the Sunday School movement hoped to moralize the children and their parents and for this purpose, like the Aboriginal children in the Native Institution, the pupils were periodically expected to display publicly their knowledge of catechism, hymns and prayer, their parents observing these competitive performances. Following the arrival of the temperance movement, marches, banners and junior pledge-taking underlined the fact that these institutions were firmly in the hands of the advocates of self-help and sobriety as the answer to worker problems.[32]

In contrast with the Sunday Schools, there was never any possibility that parents might control the infants' schools. Founded during the 1820s these aimed to catch very young children, too small to contribute to the family's survival and whose mothers, it was correctly assumed, would be willing to surrender them during the whole of the day owing to their own labour commitments. In Sydney in June 1824 Reverend Richard Hill, having read only the month before of Samuel Wilderspin's experiments with educating very young children, established a school at St James' Church. By December some twenty to thirty children aged from eighteen months to four years attended daily where they learned to sing Dr Watts's hymns and to quote an Anglican catechism specially written in verse for the young. Attempts were made to teach the alphabet but progress, Hill admitted, was slow, owing to difficulties in fixing the eye of such young children. Using the metaphor from horticulture which German theorist Friedrich Froebel was currently applying, Hill saw the infant school as 'pre-occupying the ground to prevent the growth of noxious weeds' in the mind of the child too young to attend an elementary school. So well regarded were infants' schools that special provision was made for them in the Church and School Corporation. By 1829 there were Anglican infants' schools at St Phillip's in Sydney and at Parramatta and Windsor. By 1838 Presbyterian schools in Sydney also included special infants' departments. These claimed to follow methods of intellectual and physical instruction developed by David Stow, who had founded an Infant Training School in Glasgow in 1829.[33]

The underlying commitment to child labour which shaped the development of the Sunday and infants' schools was in contrast to the charity schools. Directed at children at the employable age of six to twelve, and growing in number by the eighteenth century these schools were based on a different philosophy. Whereas employers of child labour were attacking them as a threat to immediate profit, to more far-sighted liberals charity schools were based on the principle that in the long-term it was more important and economical to indoctrinate children and teach them some basic skills than to employ them. Ultimately the labour of this age-group was going to have to be foregone in the interests of the economic system. Governors since Bligh had been instructed to promote education, and in the absence of philanthropists to finance charity schools Macquarie had taken the principle of providing a daily education for children of this age and class one step further and provided state-funded institutions. By the end of 1814 some fifteen government elementary schools had been established in New South Wales. Small chapel-schools had also been established by churchmen and missionaries at Kissing Point, Green Hills and Ebenezer. Even so, in 1821 perhaps less than 20 per cent of the 7568 children in New South Wales and the 1021 in Van Diemen's Land were receiving instruction at established schools.[34]

In Britain, by the 1830s the changing labour requirements of industrial technology plus the development of worker radicalism rapidly fostered the priority of child education over child labour. In 1833, in spite of the vested interest of the manufacturers in employing children, liberals successfully introduced state aid for charity schools, while also urging that every child should eventually be transferred out of the factory into the school. Women, too, should ideally be removed from the workplace and into the restructured, nuclear working-class family, where they could improve their reproductive capacity and begin to monitor the lives of their children in the approved middle-class way. From the early 1830s the liberals also passed a series of Factory Acts aiming to regulate child labour and the length of the working day. The ideology of 'sacred' motherhood and 'innocent' child was now to be extended to every family, not merely the most destitute and 'criminal' ones.

The concept of a state-controlled system of 'national' education developed rapidly from these ideals. In the colonies, during the 1830s a special combination of factors brought about the implementation of this concept, some three decades ahead of a similar system in England. There were fewer factories and therefore less dependence on child labour, there was also the phenomenon of an unusually even distribution of the four main religious denominations, all attempting to establish elementary schools. Though united in their aim of moralizing and pacifying the population, the denominations were savagely divided and competitive on points of doctrine and method. To liberals, the result was a wasteful multiplicity of churches and schools in well-populated areas, while in outer settlements there might be none. Much more effective would be a state system of non-denominational schools where controversial religious doctrine could be avoided.[35] To some liberal reformers, rampant sectarianism was to be deplored. Utilitarians, in particular, were inclined to view churches as an outmoded vehicle of social control which would become increasingly irrelevant with state elementary education. In the classrooms of the national school, God was still seen to be of some utility but as a reinforcement of that special combination of individualistic values which the changing economic system required. Denominational affiliations which, in the case of Catholics, were often linked to an unwanted loyalty to the Irish community, could best be dealt with by assimilating them into a new allegiance to a common, national form of Christian faith. In England, an Act to end discrimination against Catholics, passed in 1829, reflected this confidence that divisive denominational rivalries had no place in the new, unified, democratic and educated nation. In 1833 the ending of the monopoly of the Church and School Corporation over education in the Australian colonies was based on similar ideals.[36]

Although Nonconformists and Evangelicals subscribed to a similar economic and moral code, their clergymen could not share the liberal ideal of national, non-denominational schools. Many were well aware of the threat to the power and influence of the churches which liberal, secular and scientific ideals implied. A multiplicity of faiths was seen as no bad thing, for it reflected that emphasis on the right of the individual to religious liberty which was such an important element in the Puritan tradition. Others held that competition between sects brought a large number of churches and schools directly into the working-class community, and this was especially important in new and godless centres of population such as the English industrial towns and the 'barbaric' convict colonies.[37] There was also the tacit belief that sectarianism, like liberal feminism, while it might cause some disorder nevertheless functioned as a mechanism for dividing the working class against itself. Whereas for gentlemen it might well be advantageous to minimize differences of doctrine for labourers, it was important to encourage rivalries between the different faiths. Though it was not the intention of its advocates, a Church Act passed in New South Wales in 1836 and in Van Diemen's Land in 1837 that provided state aid for all four of the main denominations, had the effect of greatly increasing sectarian warfare in these colonies. Even influential clergymen like Lang, who otherwise supported liberal ideas, remained implacably opposed to national education, effectively preventing Bourke's attempt to introduce such a system into New South Wales in 1836. A similar attempt made in 1839 by Gipps also failed.

By the 1840s, however, some influential lay opponents of national education began to change their minds. In particular, there was James Macarthur. Although he deeply mistrusted the masses and liberal secularism, he had read Adam Smith, Rousseau, and other more recent prophets of the liberal code such as Sismondi and Alexis de Tocqueville, and was coming round to the view that the best way to deal with the heaving mass of common humanity was to catch it while young and impressionable and educate it, if necessary with the aid of the state. Wentworth, and especially Lowe, were whole-hearted supporters of this principle. In 1844 they secured a Select Committee in the new Legislative Council to enquire into education in New South Wales. At this enquiry Lowe manoeuvred the cautious acceptance of witnesses, like William and James Macarthur, into more explicit endorsement of a 'national' system which had been successfully introduced in Ireland by Lord Stanley in 1832. Broughton and the Catholic Bishop, John Bede Polding, remained adamant that they preferred to leave children uneducated rather than have them exposed to teaching over which their denomination had no direct control. The recommendations of the 1844 Committee on Education in New South Wales for 'a general system of education' funded by the state and for a 'normal, or model, school' to be established to train teachers were shelved after strong sectarian opposition until 1847. In Van Diemen's Land Franklin successfully introduced a plan for organizing education on the British and Foreign School Society model in 1839.

Many theorists still rejected compulsory education but even the most vehement supporters of denominational schooling had no quarrel with a comprehensive system of elementary education based on meritocracy. Catholic teachers, in particular, would become zealous cultivators of competitive individualism in the interests of proving that their charges had transcended their convict and Irish origins. Nor were Catholics opposed to cultivating a unifying national spirit, though they would long prefer to teach allegiance to Ireland or to the colonies, rather than to

Britain. Similarly, even many of the anarchic pastoral magnates, in spite of the violence of their personal dealings with the Aboriginal people and their convict servants, subscribed to the developing ideal of an orderly universe of harmonious relationships where self-aggrandizement and social progress would march in step.[38]

Thus, in spite of denominational differences, every school formed part of a total educative programme, defusing radicalism and preparing the masses for democracy. However, formal, visible educative rituals were only one aspect of this programme. Other methods offered a much more complex and subtle control over the making of working-class aesthetic and cultural values. So far had these new cultural controls moved from the use of direct force, and to such an extent did they normalize existing economic arrangements and political values, that working people looked likely to be robbed of the intellectual tools which they had been developing to construct a counter-ideology with which to challenge the unseen hand of liberal hegemony.

9

CULTURE

ON 26 JANUARY 1842, the fifty-fourth anniversary of the colony of New South Wales, Sydney-siders gathered in Hunter Street to witness the opening of a brand new source of public entertainment. With a suitably patriotic name, this 'Australian Olympic Theatre' offered patrons the thrills and spills of tightrope dancing, clowns and equestrian performances. The *Sydney Gazette* reported 'notwithstanding the various attractions of other places', the new theatre 'was occupied to the fullest extent of the tickets issued', and no less than 300 applications for admission had to be refused.

Opened in the middle of the depression, this little circus-theatre was housed in a large if elegantly decorated tent, and was destined to have a short season. However, other forms of theatrical entertainment were by now more long-lived and much more permanently accommodated. In Hobart in 1834 a group of gentlemen planning to build a theatre consulted the talented Colonial Architect, John Lee Archer, and in March 1837 were presented with an impressive Regency-style building on which they bestowed an equally impressive name—the Theatre Royal. Port Phillip District, too, despite its recent origins, was not without play-houses. In 1842 the Pavilion Theatre, strategically located next to the Eagle Tavern in Bourke Street, was also given the name of Theatre Royal, only to be superseded by the new Queen's Theatre in 1845. Ten years later an enormous new

Theatre Royal was opened in Melbourne, offering seating for no less than 3000 people.

Now that labour was measured in terms of time spent on the job and was too onerous and too meaningless to be in any way considered as leisure, it was becoming commercially feasible in urban areas to provide structured activities to entertain people during the hours when they were not at work. The provision of leisure activities was also politically expedient, for as labourers became more radicalized and demanded a shorter working day, the men especially had more time which, if not channelled into approved pursuits, might otherwise be spent in dissipation or even worse, in worker political action. Public entertainments were being invented, some of which, like theatre, were held in pseudo-palatial settings and functioned to relieve workers of a portion of their wages and to improve them morally. As *The Blossom*, a quarterly magazine which had a brief life in 1828, frankly avowed,

a theatre would effect in the Colony much moral advantage—the hours and nights that are spent by many in debauchery and revelling; or at that universal scourge of all society, the gaming table; would be exchanged to the theatre where they would become refined, . . . and the mind impressed by the presented scene.[1]

Culture generally, not just theatrical entertainments, could be made to serve a similar role, for all societies produce some form of cultural expression and whether this is seen as embracing the simplest aspects of everyday life and work or is confined to 'higher', abstract forms of artistic, musical or religious expression, culture encapsulates disparate pieces of important information into a coherent form which is then remembered and understood. What could be more important, especially in a free society, than to secure and maintain control of the definition of what constitutes cultural excellence and the production and where possible, the sale, of cultural commodities? In contrast with schools and schooling, this kind of hegemonic control of cultural pursuits was going to be particularly difficult for workers to identify and resist. By the early nineteenth century many traditional forms of popular culture had, like the communities which sustained them, long ceased to exist. The worker mobility and time-discipline required by expanding trade and industry had proved incompatible with popular, week-long group celebrations such as carnivals and festivals, along with their parodies of civil and ecclesiastical rituals, mocking of heroic deeds and familiar indecent language. The emerging middle classes had distanced themselves from festivals, taking with them some of the popular traditions which, stripped of their economic and political significance, were then domesticated and literally brought into the home. Feasts, masks and fancy dress were being made part of the private life of the middle-class family, and used to celebrate birthdays, weddings, anniversaries and other occasions of significance. In England remnants of an oral tradition based around wakes, rush-bearings or the seasonal rituals of agricultural life did survive, especially in rural areas, but their function as occasions where social and communal relationships were affirmed and information conveyed to the young was already under threat, as was their ability to unite people as a participating political group, conscious of their rights and their power. Festivals had been reduced to displays of anarchistic disorder or challenges to the hardening moral code of the industrial middle class, not to their political and economic domination.[2]

Similarly, in theatre people of humble origin could still supply the actors, singers, acrobats and occasionally the playwrights and the entrepreneurs, for stage life was considered by the élite to be commercially risky and not quite respectable, especially for women and girls. Certainly, many plays included comedy and melodrama which in the eyes of some reformers blurred the distinction between theatre and tavern and contained material likely to inflame those very passions which it was the business of culture and learning to subdue.[3] However, in no sense did the participation of some working people, or the inclusion of some sexually suspect plays, alter the fact that modern theatre was a commercial rather than a community venture and, like many other forms of entertainment available to the working class, was 'popularized' rather than 'popular'. The forerunner of the mass culture of modern industrialized societies, far from conveying a proletarian radicalism, theatre contained a secret education, informing the audience how to live and love, how to succeed, how to buy, how to conquer, how to forget the past and suppress the future. Genteel observers constantly remarked on the turbulent behaviour of working-class patrons and the presence of prostitutes, but any criticism on the part of the audience was directed at the players rather than the gentry, who were separated by the gallery and private boxes from the masses in the stalls below.[4]

Theatre itself was censored. In England, every new play had to have the approval of the Lord Chamberlain before being staged while in the colonies each theatre had to be licensed and each play pre-examined by the Colonial Secretary, unless it had already been performed in England. Joseph Simmons, as actor formerly associated with Barnett Levey at Sydney's Theatre Royal, when writing for permission to stage his play 'The Duellist' in 1844, felt obliged to assure the Colonial Secretary that it was perfectly free in dialogue and plot from anything which was local, political, sectarian and immoral. Less successful was a play like the anonymous 'Life in Sydney; or, the Ran Dan Club' which contained thinly veiled and critical references to esteemed local magistrates, Charles Windeyer and Captain Innes. Submitted to the Colonial Secretary in August 1843 this play was a parody on W. T. Moncrieff's 'Tom and Jerry; or, Life in London in 1820' which had been staged in London and Sydney. In the parodied version an unpleasant 'old Windemere' was ridiculed for having fined street boys 'for whacking the constable' and for having made them pay for broken lamps and transposed street-signs. After joining the 'Cabbage-tree mob' in a fight against police, the three heroes were taken away by the officious 'Captain Innison' to the watch-house. Permission for this play was refused.

It was always possible, of course, for playwrights and actors to add local or subversive material more or less spontaneously during the performance. Also, as theatre became increasingly respectable, some players chose to remove themselves to the more ribald music halls and circus amphitheatres. However, since all these forms of theatre were commercial ventures their repertoire came to focus on a bizarre, best-selling formula which, as a combination of savage caricature of Black American life and nostalgic conservative Romanticism, by the 1860s also appealed to a large cross-section of the population overseas. This sometimes titillating and essentially escapist formula was presented in repertoires ranging from racist blackface acts and minstrel shows to Shakespearean and operatic tragedies. Pathetic child victims in moralizing melodramas, with titles like 'The Gambler's Fate' and 'The Foundling in the Forest', were also certain crowd-pullers. In Sydney, Barnett Levey's choice for the opening of his first theatre in 1832 was Douglas Jerrold's *Black-Eyed Susan*, and the performance was preceded by a formal rendition of the national anthem.[5] Also on the programme by the 1830s was pantomime. Though Evangelicals and Nonconformists disapproved of fairy stories and make-believe, figures from traditional folklore like Columbine and Harlequin, fairy queens and giants, were being resurrected to provide safe, amusing material for the nineteenth-century stage. Their original political and cultural significance had been lost and they were now seen as suitable only for the world of children or of adults at play. Pantomimes like 'Harlequin in Australia Felix' showed that in transplanting traditional fairy figures to a specifically colonial context the local producers were well aware of the growing commercial viability of fantasy, as families became more child-centred and devoted themselves to creating the approved world of the child, removed as far as possible from political reality.

Central to the pantomime and the circus was the clown. No longer representing a public figure to be mocked nor a wise fool lampooning figures of authority, he was now a complete dolt whose function was to admire the muscular, individualistic and gymnastic feats achieved by equestrians and other star performers, among whom aggressive roles like 'The Roman Gladiator' and 'The Fox-Hunter' were popular. In Hobart in 1848 the price of admission to one of the new circuses ranged from three shillings in a box, to one shilling in the pit.[6]

Theatre did more than suppress radical class consciousness—it was also hoped that the mixing of the social classes at these events would promote the alternative ideal of class harmony and unifying national ideals. A growing patronage of exhibitions and shows was also part of this trend. The public was invited to admire orderly displays of selected animals, agricultural and, in due course, manufactured goods, all of cultural significance to their producers. 'Wild' animals, too, were coming to be seen as of cultural importance and in London a public zoo to replace the old travelling menageries was opened in 1828. In the colonies, most of these 'shows' were seasonal and were sponsored by private scientific and cultural societies to which the élite belonged. The Agricultural Society of New South Wales, formed in 1822 with Sir John Jamison as President and Governor Brisbane as Patron, held its first show at Parramatta in that year, while by the 1830s its exhibitions of livestock and farm produce were an annual event. Similar organizations were formed in Hobart in 1821 and Launceston in 1833.[7]

These demonstrations of scientific farming obscured the surprisingly slow progress made by colonial gentlemen in the improvement of their flocks and herds. In 1826 the average weight of an improved fleece was still only two-and-a-half pounds. (In comparison, today a merino fleece would weigh about fifteen pounds.) Up to the 1850s pastoralists also paid very little attention to the improvement of their cattle, allowing them to run, as Peter Cunningham wrote, promiscuously together, and producing, as James Atkinson admitted, 'a very mixed and mongrel' herd. Horses were bred without care, their higher prices encouraging owners to focus on breeding for quantity not quality. The Australian stock-horse, already becoming well-known for its endurance and skill with flocks and herds, was evolving as much by accident as by design.[8]

Colonial ladies and gentlemen were enormously interested in horticulture, another rational pursuit which working people were encouraged to admire and emulate. Among the élite a wide collection of overseas flowers and especially fruits was seen as indispensable for creating a landscaped garden and for providing a variety of freshly grown delicacies to grace their tables. By 1835 Sydney could support a commercial nurseryman, Thomas Shepherd, and a large range of plants, English songbirds, and game which was being 'acclimatized'. Little thought was given to the possibility that some of these imports might adapt too well to their new environment. The aggressive prickly pear made its appearance in Sydney gardens by 1840 where in many cases it was used as a hedge to help privatize the home and discourage trespassers. In Van Diemen's Land the Jellicoes introduced gorse from Cornwall at Camelford, purely for sentimental reasons; by the 1840s scotch thistles were overrunning the land around Port Sorell, and settlers like James Fenton were carefully tending cuttings of blackberry plants introduced from England. 'I watered them! I watched them! I weeded them!' Fenton confessed later in his reminiscences, 'They made wonderful headway . . .'[9] If extended to the labouring masses, it was thought horticulture might usefully teach the delights of home-making and how to grow foodstuffs to supplement a meagre wage. In Hobart a Horticultural Society was founded in 1839 under the presidency of

Charles Swanston with botanist and overseer of Hobart Penitentiary, Ronald Campbell Gunn, as secretary. At its second annual exhibition Lady Franklin offered a prize for the most neatly kept cottage and cottage-garden. Unlike the labouring population in London and the new English industrial towns, early colonial workers' houses tended to have a plot of ground at the front, often surrounded by a paling fence. Urban imitations of the English country cottage-garden could be actively encouraged. A regulation in New South Wales in 1829 stating that all houses in towns had to be constructed at least fourteen feet from the front alignment confirmed this potential, though the rule was frequently evaded. In Sydney, an Australian Floral and Horticultural Society conducted flower shows where plants could be exhibited and prizes won, for as with agriculture, a spirit of individualistic competition in the garden was considered commendable. Similar horticultural organizations followed in Port Phillip and South Australia in the 1840s. A new organization, the Australasian Botanical and Horticultural Society, was established in Sydney in July 1848.[10]

A similar determination to encourage the working class to engage in approved cultural pursuits informed Bourke's decision in 1835 to form a 'commodious public walk' in Hyde Park where Sydney's inhabitants might find air and exercise in an environment of comfort and elegance. In the same year William MacPherson, Collector of Internal Revenue, suggested that the improvement of Hyde Park could also be used to absorb newly arrived emigrant labour. Footpaths and tastefully placed clumps of trees would render this part of Sydney 'highly ornamental and usefully beneficial for the promotion of health and pedestrian exercise', without encroaching on the space needed for exercising the troops, cricket matches, and the like. By the 1830s and 1840s the Botanic Gardens also took on a public, educative function. As conceived by Joseph Banks, the purpose of these gardens, founded in Sydney in 1816 and Hobart two years later, had been to test and acclimatize exotic plants of potential commercial value. This scientific purpose was still primary when Swan River was founded and a former curator of the Botanic Gardens at Cork accompanied Stirling's party to establish a public garden immediately on arrival. In Sydney in 1835, when Richard Cunningham, brother of the explorer, became curator of the gardens, he introduced artistic touches, such as sun dials, statues and decorative bridges so the poor were encouraged to appreciate the aesthetic values of the rich and the harnessing of science for commercial 'progress'.[11]

At the same time, efforts were made to stamp out the more noisy and unseemly leisure pursuits of the adult poor. In 1841 an editorial in the Sydney *Herald* named dog-fighting and cock-fighting as especially undesirable activities. Bull-baiting was not mentioned though this practice had been introduced in Sydney by 1831. These were some of the popularized gaming activities which had been imported from Britain and which, though cultivating the required competitive and aggressive spirit in the male, offered few opportunities for exploitation by respectable entrepreneurs. Even worse, they were the means by which male workers gambled away their savings and left their wives and children dependent on philanthropy and the state. 'Man-fighting' which had become common among unskilled London workers during the eighteenth century and which, as a Port Phillip judge noted in 1848, was essentially an urban variant of these sports, was also discouraged. Though apolitical, it was associated with tavern life and encouraged the collection of an unruly gambling crowd which was feared likely to turn to riotous behaviour.

As the censorship of the 'Tom and Jerry' play in Sydney showed, the crack-down on street behaviour was also directed against the 'Cabbage-tree Larkers', young native-born men who gathered in public places frequented by the better-off and annoyed them 'by rubbing shoulders with them' and shouting out 'all around my hat'. James Bates and John Kenny, arrested for this offence in Pitt Street in 1841, were fined ten shillings each plus one shilling costs, and warned that a second offence would be tried at Quarter Sessions. Though severe, these measures did not suppress the 'Cabbage-tree mob' who, according to G. C. Mundy, were still to be found round the doors of the Sydney theatres in 1852, wearing hats made of 'cabbage-palm' and knocking the 'ordinary black head-piece' from the heads of the respectable as they entered the theatre.[12] To replace these disgraceful pursuits the élite favoured patriotic celebrations such as 'Waterloo Day'. On this day in Sydney in 1841 'The Cricketers' Arms' was brilliantly lit up with the words 'Wellington and Waterloo' and a band was in attendance. Queen Victoria's birthday was also an approved celebration, when government offices and even the banks closed, vice-regal levées were held for the élite, and the military paraded through the streets to impress the *hoi polloi*. In

Sydney in May 1842 the appearance of the 28th Regiment and the mounted police in the Domain was accompanied by a salute from the Battery at Dawes Point and wild applause from old soldiers in the crowd. Fireworks were also permitted, though in Sydney, a town where most of the houses were roofed with shingles, the Superintendent of Police advised citizens to go to the racecourse to let off their crackers and squibs. Aquatic activities had long been a favoured Sydney recreation, so it was predictable that Queen's Birthday celebrations would focus on the harbour. Special regattas were organized and, in addition to the competing crews, the crowd took to the water in 'everything that would float from a washing tub to a steam-boat'. Sometimes there were melancholy consequences, as when the schooner *Eliza Ann* struck a sudden squall off Pinchgut and sank without trace, drowning seven people.

Attempts were also made to develop a distinctively local patriotic pride. In Sydney regattas were organized to celebrate Anniversary Day on 26 January, while in Hobart the Franklins conceived the idea of holding an anniversary water carnival on 1 December, in honour of Tasman's discovery of the island, with wattle blossom as an emblem of the event. The first of these regattas was held in 1838 at Sullivan's Cove, where races were organized between whale-boats, sailing boats and dinghies. Sideshows and amusement booths were provided, along with a regimental band.[13]

Organized sport was another device for ordering the leisure of the masses and turning their minds and bodies to competitive and patriotic pursuits. In England, by the late eighteenth century, country gentlemen used the traditional, spontaneous games played by tenants and employees, such as cricket, as part of their new public profile; these became formalized occasions where class barriers were temporarily lowered and the ideal of harmony was promoted. In the colonies, some members of the pastoral élite imported the idea of the ploughing match for this purpose. From September 1828, James Atkinson held these events annually at Oldbury and in 1833 a silver medal donated by the governor was won by Gabriel Nicholls, overseer to Mr Bowman. At Braidwood, Dr Wilson was fond of staging this quaint event, and personally donated prizes to the winning horse and bullock teams. By the 1840s the kinds of team games provided by employers for their labourers where changing. Instead of activities related to the leisure and work experience of villagers, games for workers were coming to be modelled on the organized team sports being introduced into the boys' schools of Britain. These activities bore no direct relationship to production but were seen as appropriate for developing discipline, obedience, and allegiance to approved group ideals. Formal lessons on common Christianity in the classroom were all very well but information about competitive individualism and the need to sacrifice it when required for a higher, national purpose could be taught more effectively on the playing field. In Britain, the regulation of games like cricket by organized rules enabled the introduction of formal matches between widely separated regional British teams.

In some ways, bringing the new team sports to the adult working class was like the theatre, an approved cultural spectacle from which profits could be derived. In Australia, where organized cricket clubs dated from the mid-1820s, following the introduction of regular inter-colonial cricket matches during the 1850s, a Melbourne catering company, Spiers and Pond, reaped a rich profit in 1861 from organizing the first tour by an English cricket team. A second team followed in 1863–64. However, from the outset, the idea of teaching the working class to appreciate organized team games was much more closely linked than theatre to the need to inculcate a male national type, physically and mentally superior to anything produced by other races. In contrast with the rather suspect and possibly effeminate world of the stage, outdoor sports were seen as manly activities where the working masses would both watch and play the game.

This sporting ideal was adopted with a special relish in the Australian colonies where the climate favoured outdoor activities and there was ample space which could be made available for the new team games. The native-born proved highly susceptible to the suggestions of wealthy emancipists that this sunny land, free of hereditary class distinctions, constituted a unique environment which would produce a superior, tall and athletic male, irrespective of the convict 'taint', a notion already present in Wentworth's rhetoric and aired in the *Australian*. During the 1820s local 'Bill Kangaroos', cooeeing about the bush on horseback, were still mocked in the *Sydney Gazette* as ignorant rustics, while 'Betsey Bandicoot', able to ride without a saddle and swim faster than English girls, was nothing less than absurd. Yet by the 1840s anti-English immigrants like J. D. Lang and the Catholic intellectuals found many to support them when (despite the Moles-worth Commission's attack on convict society) they asserted that the local male population would prove physically and morally superior to anything which England could produce.

These anti-British preoccupations made for a special encour-agement of approved sporting activities. In 1858 native-born cricketer Tom Wills, who had learned to play football when sent 'home' to Rugby College, met with a group of fellow Melbourne businessmen to draw up the rules for a local football club, he looked for a code which would be aggressive yet distinctive, without being so rough as actually to risk serious injury and thus prevent attendance at work. The need to maximize reproduction meant that women, of course, could not aspire to the sporting life, and it was not till much later in the century that the notion would be developed that certain forms of athletic exercise might improve women's health and therefore their reproductive power.[14]

Most Australian towns by 1860 were provided with a large arena for sports, visiting circuses and 'shows', and an even larger area for a racetrack. According to J. D. Lang, horse-racing was the 'universal accompaniment to Australian civilization'. Cer-tainly it had long been practised by the Australian élite. The first formal meeting was organized by military officers in October 1810 and held at a one-and-a-quarter-mile track at Hyde Park. With Macquarie as patron and the enthusiastic support of the indomitable Captain Piper and his brown horse 'Hawkesbury', the races and accompanying dinners and balls became an annual event. With racing temporarily brought to a halt by Governor Brisbane, Sir John Jamison constructed his own racetrack at Regentville in 1824. Jamison was also a founder of the Sydney Turf Club, established in 1825, and in March he and Piper organized a race-meeting on a new course opposite Piper's estate at Bellevue Hill. The more 'exclusive' Australian Racing and Jockey Club, with members like Blaxland, Cox and McLeay, followed in 1828. By the 1840s the races at Homebush attracted great crowds, from the governor to the common herd. In Van Diemen's Land the first recorded horse-race was held at New Town in 1814, while the Tasmanian Turf Club was formed at Jericho in April 1826. At Port Phillip, by 1840 an annual race-meeting was held beside the Salt Water River on a site later known as Flemington. From 1861 the popularity around Australia of the 2-mile race for the Melbourne Cup would testify to the successful promotion of racing as a form of public entertainment which later came to be associated with a unique Australian identity.[15]

Not every sport played by the élite was considered to be suitable for the working class. Golf, a game which could not easily be confined to a sporting arena and which was of no interest when viewed from a distance, remained largely confined to the colonial élite who were playing it from the 1830s. Hunting, too, was an indicator of superior social rank. John Macarthur at Camden Park kept fox-hounds and used them to hunt dingoes, a popular sport in the colonies. Members of the Bathurst Hunt Club, founded in 1825, undertook to keep a certain number of dogs and to meet on fixed days for 'a general turn-out'. On these occasions each member wore a conspicuous green jacket tastefully ornamented with a dingo embroidered in gold on the collar. As Peter Cunningham pointed out in his book for immigrant gentlemen, published in 1827, kangaroos and emus could also joyfully be hunted down, and many other animals besides. Even those which could run up trees to apparent safety could then be used as targets for a shoot. 'In this way', he assured his readers, 'you may return home after a few hours' pastime loaded with a dozen opossums, squirrels, bandicoots, kangaroo-rats and native-cats, if the forest has not been previously much hunted in'. Rabbits, Cunningham regretted to inform his readers, were not as yet acclimatized in the wild, though they were being carefully bred about gentlemen's houses. In Van Diemen's Land, Dr William Crowther had attempted to introduce the grey rabbit in 1826. Similarly, deer had been introduced to both colonies from India. On the Cumberland Plain near Sydney, many had run wild, but alas, instead of being reserved for the exclusive target-practice of the élite, they were constantly hunted down by the riff-raff and shot.[16]

Duelling, too, remained a pastime for gentlemen only, and they indulged in it from the colony's foundation years. Early duellists had included the choleric John Macarthur, and the quarrelsome Major Ross who fought a duel with Captain Hill in December 1791. Later gentlemen who kept the tradition alive included Thomas Gregson, who in 1836 fought a pistol duel with Henry Jellicoe, a supporter of Governor Arthur, and also horse-whipped the Governor's nephew, Henry Arthur, Collector of Customs. Jellicoe, who had arrived in Van Diemen's Land in 1823 and was elegantly ensconced in a villa on his grant at Camelford, was severely wounded in the fight and returned to England, while Gregson, seen as a popular leader in the struggle against the 'tyranny' of governors and the Colonial Office, had a three months' gaol sentence commuted after some 1400 gentlemen petitioned the new Governor, Sir John Franklin, on his behalf. In Port Phillip, a duel of a less political nature was fought in August 1841 between Redmond Barry and pastoralist Peter Snodgrass, an overlander from New South Wales who had squatted on the Goulburn River in the late 1830s. After the duel, honour was restored, though Snodgrass fired prematurely and shot his own toe off. He had already damaged a toe in a duel fought the previous year in Melbourne with William Ryrie, also a squatter. Snodgrass's father, Kenneth Snodgrass, an invalided army officer who had arrived in Sydney in 1828, was also a duelling man. In July 1842 he was fined £100 for attempting to incite a neighbour to fight a duel over the payment for a boundary fence at his Hunter Valley estate.[17]

The re-education of the worker for democracy involved more than the control of recreation and games. With increasing literacy cultural traditions did not need to be confined to spectacle but could include newspapers, journals, indeed the whole field of creative literature. Approved poetry and novels in school and at home could influence the way in which the people interpreted what they saw around them, thus shaping their view of the world. This process presupposed that the labouring masses were excluded from setting the current standards by which artistic merit was evaluated: just as some sports were for gentlemen only, so were the 'higher' branches of the creative arts. Control over what constituted literary, musical and artistic excellence was also related to the need to monitor the supply and therefore the commercial value of cultural artifacts. It established selected members of the middle class as experts on cultural issues. Needless to say, in the 1830s and 1840s, the authorities on 'high' culture were European and the fear of being seen as living in a cultural backwater prompted colonial ladies and gentlemen into a slavish attempt to keep up with changing literary and artistic fashion 'at home'. They also needed to keep abreast of the virtual explosion of new information on the social and physical sciences. In Sydney in 1826 a group of merchants and pastoralists formed an Australian Subscription Library. Financial members could equip themselves with the latest works on history, theology, biography, science, and travel, together with selected British periodicals like the *Edinburgh Review*, in which the scientific and social theories of the day were aired.

The need to keep in touch with the latest theory and taste led many colonists to create private libraries of their own. A. B. Spark's bookshelves at Tempe contained about 500 volumes; J. D. Lang's more than 600; Catholic schoolteacher, W. A. Duncan, who was adept in five languages, had acquired a library of over 2000 works by the time of his death. In Adelaide even colonists who used the local Mechanics' Institute Library prided themselves on being up-to-date. 'I recollect a newcomer being astonished at my sister Mary having read Macaulay's History', Catherine Spence recalled, '"Why, it was only just out when I left England"', said he. "Well, it did not take longer to come out than you did", was her reply. We were all omnivorous readers'. Even the rural élite read avidly. In the library at Archibald Innes's house at Port Macquarie there were three large book-shelves reaching from the floor to the ceiling filled with books, some of them supplied in regular batches from the Sydney Library. In the Western District of Port Phillip, squatters like George Russell collected biographical, historical, and scientific works.[18]

The private library of the 1830s was likely to include the work of writers who articulated middle-class values and whose style and technique conformed to current notions of literary excellence. In addition to Pope, Cowper and Goldsmith, works like Thompson's 'Seasons', Young's 'Night Thoughts' and Blair's 'The Grave' were part of the British nation's literary treasure-chest, thought fit to grace gentlemen's libraries and school curricula. Johnson, Smollett, Fielding and especially that doyen of the Romantics, Walter Scott, were also popular. Dickens's *Pickwick Papers* was serialized in Van Diemen's Land in 1838.

Numerous locally produced newspapers and periodicals also testified to Presbyterian clergyman David Mackenzie's remark in 1845 that 'Everybody reads'. In Van Diemen's Land, periodicals like Henry Melville's *Hobart Town Magazine* (founded 1833) and Dr James Ross's *Van Diemen's Land Monthly Magazine* (founded 1835) were some of the 200 000 journals being sent through the post in that colony by 1841. Coupled with the proliferating newspaper trade, these magazines showed that members of the colonial middle class were not only reading but writing, and were contributing personally to the process whereby information was monitored and cultural values formed. In 1835 Henry Melville published a safe Whiggish *History of the Island of Van Diemen's Land* in which the 'tyranny' of the Arthur regime was soundly criticized and the tradition established whereby the sad demise of the Aboriginal people was attributed largely to the sexual passions and violence of convict men. In 1830–31 Melville also published *Quintus Servinton*, a semi-autobiographical novel by Henry Savery. A former sugar refiner from Bristol, Savery had been transported for forgery in 1824 and his account of these experiences in his novel was such as to leave readers in no doubt that crime did not pay.[19]

Most colonial gentlemen writers were concerned to promote immigration and to tap the market for works about the colonies among curious readers abroad. Those who, like James Macarthur, found they were bereft of literary talent, could always have their books ghosted by a professional English writer. Macarthur's *New South Wales: Its Present State and Future Prospects* was published in London in 1837. Women with access to leisure also contributed non-fictional works of this kind. They included Louisa Meredith, wife of a Van Diemen's Land pastoralist, whose *Notes and Sketches of New South Wales* appeared in 1844.

As in England, women with leisure also articulated formal rules of social behaviour, so vital in societies where people were 'continually rising in the world'. Through contributions to temperance journals, fiction and verse, they developed the new domestic ideology which, focused on the sacredness of mother and home, was becoming central to conservative Romantic thought. In 1838 Anna Marie Bunn, mother of the idle adolescent at Woden, published *The Guardian A Tale by an Australian*, a melodramatic story of unrequited love which aired the problem of the double standard of sexual morality and its effect on marriage and the home. In the same year Mrs Dunlop, wife of the police magistrate at Wollombi, published 'The Aboriginal Mother', a poem which, while protesting against the violence of the Myall Creek massacre, did so in terms of private, nuclear family life and its assumed universal applicability.[20]

Many of the ladies whose work was published had been left financially stranded by the death of a spouse. Charlotte Barton, a former governess to Hannibal Macarthur, turned to writing after

being left with four children to support when her first husb
James Atkinson, died in 1834, and a second spouse became a
furious maniac who had to be kept under restraint. In 1841 she
produced *A Mother's Offering to Her Children*, a book aimed at the
market for children's literature in the new, child-centred family.
Dedicated to little Reginald Gipps, the son of the Governor, the
book contained a variety of anecdotes of the kind considered
instructive for children of all classes. Though rather old-fashioned
in its neglect of fairies, it abounded with lessons on the basic
cultural values and assumptions of the middle class. In 'A Visit to
an Iron Mine' little readers were treated to a picture of half-
frozen, emaciated 'criminals' in Sweden rightly punished by
being put to work to produce thousands of tons of valuable ore
every year. There was the story of the wreck of the *Stirling Castle*
off the north-east coast in 1836, and the adventures of a survivor,
Mrs Fraser, but this was carefully pruned of references to sexual
humiliation that could be found in versions of the story available
for adult readers. Here and elsewhere in the book, Aboriginal
people were stereotyped as savages who could expect nothing
better than 'extermination'. A copy of this useful and interesting
book 'should be in the hands of every young person', commented
the *Sydney Gazette*.[21]

Much of the verse produced by colonial writers was written in
the mock-heroic Augustan mode, its savage, cynical wit justifying
the economic and social policies of colonial land-takers. W. C.
Wentworth's 'Australia', submitted in a competition for the
Chancellor's Medal at Cambridge in 1823, was a classic celebration
of imperialism and commerce as 'progress'. Like Erasmus Darwin's
poem published with the first edition of Phillip's *Journal* in 1789,
Wentworth dwelt on the notion of British industry subduing the
wilderness. Wentworth's symbols were lengthening streets and
widening squares, as in Darwin's verse, though he added 'the
solemn churches and the lofty windmills' which together with
the 'column'd front of stately mansions' and the 'busy market
throng' had driven out the dismal, idle Aborigine. The poem took
second prize. Similar congratulatory and patriotic themes had
marked the odes of Michael Massey Robinson, written annually
from 1810 to 1820 to celebrate the birthdays of George III and
Queen Charlotte. A lawyer transported for blackmail, Robinson
was appointed chief clerk in the secretary's office by Macquarie,
who bestowed on him the title of Poet Laureate. Robinson was

fond of pretentious phraseology which celebrated 'Britannia's Sons' who had braved perilous seas and frowning rocks to plant commerce and arts in the 'Social Soil', their bold barques and swelling sails replacing the crude canoes of the sooty-faced native race.[22] Judge Barron Field was another poetaster, producing *First Fruits of Australian Poetry* in 1819. It contained just two poems, both displaying European fascination with what they saw as the weird permutations and combinations of antipodean mammals. The kangaroo, he wittily suggested, was a squirrel joined to the 'bounding hart'. The result was a 'large animal of chase', made 'by some divine mistake' but not without its uses to the sporting gentleman. Native-born Charles Tompson's *Wild Notes, from the Lyre of a Native Minstrel* (1826) covered a wider range of subjects. Educated at Henry Fulton's parish school at Castlereagh, in addition to conventional public poems, Tompson wrote verse 'In Imitation of Cowper' and in the style of Pope. He was partial to the Pindaric ode and wrote poems in praise of 'Sylvia', though the real object of his fancy was a Miss Hannah Morris whom he married at Windsor in 1830. Like most native-born sons Tompson did not rise to the ranks of the rich and powerful. His reward for introducing a not inconsiderable modicum of official European culture was a mere 100 acres of land.[23]

On the whole, up to the 1840s gentlemen poets were more comfortable with formal Augustan cadences celebrating industry and commerce than with Romantic verse. It fell to native-born son of convict parents, Charles Harpur, to be one of the first of the male writers to explore the political and creative possibilities of this medium. Born at Windsor in 1813 Harpur was encouraged to read English literature by his father who was made school-master there, and he was fortunate to be given access to private libraries of gentlemen in the area. Deeply influenced by these experiences, Harpur early became convinced that he was a cut above the common herd and decided to dedicate himself to the muse though this was a less than lucrative calling. Harpur found himself required to perform various demeaning tasks throughout the 1830s, especially after his father lost his small 200-acre grant. In his verse he made more extensive use of local scenery and other subject matter than had any previous poet and thus won the approval of another native-born son of a convict, Horatio Wills, father of the football founder and publisher of the *Sydney Gazette* and the *Currency Lad*, a weekly journal dedicated to improving

Australia (1832–34). Harpur's *Tragedy of Donohoe* appeared in the *Monitor* in February 1835 and was the first play by a native-born writer to be published in Australia. *Thoughts: A Series of Sonnets* followed in 1845, as did increasing estrangement from his family. In his most political verse, Harpur expressed the views of the urban liberals, attacking squatting and calling for education to cultivate 'The Mind of Man'. In company with Horatio Wills, W. A. Duncan and J. D. Lang, he was especially concerned to bring a new distinctively Australian fervour to officially approved literature. Like nationalists elsewhere, he was drawn to the idea that the nation underwent stages of maturity marked by historical events, especially battles, and wrought by writers into tragic and heroic myths which could be measured against the achievements of rivals. 'If we mean rise in scale of nations, we must possess a literature and a science of our own', declared Henry Carmichael in 1833. Romantic writers in Europe had a wealth of folklore which could be filched from popular culture and refashioned into an artificial and supposedly distinctive national identity, but in the colonies there was a paucity of material to inspire the muse. 'I sing not of wars, for our fields are unstained,/With the blood of our patriot men', W. A. Duncan complained in 1842. 'Tis in peace, and by commerce our honours were gained/Which in peace, or by war, we'll maintain.' Clearly, for these writers, the blood of convicts, Aborigines and Islanders was not the stuff of which local, nationalistic myths could be made.[24]

Similar problems troubled the song-writers, for the colonial middle class did not neglect music. In their homes a piano was to become a fundamental piece of furniture, especially after the invention of the upright model during the late 1820s. William Lawson had a piano at his new brick house at Prospect by 1824. A. B. Spark was considering importing these important and saleable items in 1836, while William Vincent Wallace, a recently arrived emigrant from Ireland, had a range of imported varieties on display at his musical repository in Hunter Street. At Capertee, 60 miles from Bathurst, Archibald Innes's brother George had a piano by 1838, while down in the Western District by 1843 the tinny notes echoed across Lake Purrumbete from a piano dragged overland by bullock dray and installed for the use of squatter Thomas Manifold and his wife. A veritable miniature orchestra, the piano was to become indispensable for creating approved family entertainment in the home and for taking selected songs to the masses. One of these instruments would eventually grace every theatre and church hall and, along with the brass band, would be the accompaniment to which the new, stirring, national songs would be sung.

As in Europe, the middle class was embracing the formal concert as part of its culture. In Hobart, concerts were held in the new court-house in Macquarie Street from September 1826, while at Swan River, despite the fact that neither the population nor the economy was 'prospering' in the approved manner, musical entertainments were not neglected. In September 1831 G. F. Moore, who had arrived with servants and capital entitling him to a grant of 12 000 acres of land, wrote an optimistic song about colonization and reproduction. 'Western Australia for Me' was sung by Moore at the colony's first ball:

> From the Old Western World we have come to explore
> The wilds of the Western Australian shore
> In search of a country we ventured to roam
> And now that we've found it we'll make it our home.
> For what tho' the colony's new sirs
> And inhabitants still may be few Sir's
> They'll soon be increasing here too Sir's
> So it's Western Australia for me . . .

These songs, like the officially sanctioned, middle-class literature, bore little relationship to those which were still being written and sung by convict workers and which the approved music was intended to replace. Ballads like Frank the Poet's 'Convict's Tour of Hell', composed at the Australian Agricultural Company's station at Stroud in 1839, were too subversive. Addressed to 'You Prisoners of New South Wales', the poem told the story of a bushranger who, after death, visited Satan's fold, expecting to be sentenced there, but found to his surprise that the Devil had accommodation only for 'the grandees of the land':

> Well cried the Poet since 'tis so
> One thing of you I'd like to know
> As I'm at present in no hurry
> Have you one here called Captain Murray?
> Yes Murray is within this place
> Would you said Satan see his face?
> May God forbid that I should view him
> For on board the *Phoenix Hulk* I knew him
> Who is that Sir in yonder blaze

Who on fire and brimstone seems to graze?
'Tis Captain Logan of Moreton Bay
And Williams who was killed the other day
He was overseer at Grose Farm
And done poor convicts no little harm
Cook who discovered New South Wales
And he that first invented gaols
Are both tied to a fiery stake
Which stands in yonder boiling lake
Hark do you here this dreadful yelling
It issues from Doctor Wardell's dwelling
And all those fiery seats and chairs
Are fitted up for Dukes and Mayors
And nobles of Judicial orders
Barristers Lawyers and Recorders
Here I beheld legions of traitors
Hangmen gaolers and flagellators
Commandants, Constables and Spies
Informers and Overseers likewise
In flames of brimstone they were toiling
And lakes of sulphur round them boiling . . .

Other notables being treated to the Devil's hospitality included Major Morisset, Dr Bowman and Captain Rossi. There was also Governor Darling who, though he had just arrived, was being given a special reception. 'With fire and brimstone I've ordained him', says Satan, 'And Vulcan has already chained him'.[25]

It was not until the convict system was long terminated that local writers like Marcus Clarke would turn to the pastoral frontier and the convict system to construct an Australian mythology, exploiting the ballads about convict and bush experience and subtly altering them in the process so that solidarity and resistance would be turned into a local version of the liberal rhetoric of egalitarianism and fraternity. Only in 1853, and after numerous revisions, was Harpur's play, based on the life of bushranger, Jack Donohoe, seen as fitting into the required mould, its hero embodying the 'national' spirit for which the culture-makers were already searching.[26]

Given the development of such a strongly articulated, oral counter-culture it was little wonder that, as the grip of the economic depression tightened in 1841, the *Australian* was lamenting the absence of a music school 'to elevate the mind and refine the manners of the people'. Fortunately relief came in

Sydney in April 1841 with the arrival of professional musician and teacher, Isaac Nathan. Nathan became choirmaster at St Mary's Cathedral and organized the largest concert of church music heard so far in the colony. In 1842 he composed *Australia the Wide and Free*, a 'Solemn Ode' for the inaugural dinner of the Sydney Municipal Council. *Long Live Victoria* and *Hail, Star of the South* were 'choral odes' produced to mark public occasions. In 1847 his *Don John of Austria* was the first opera to be wholly composed and produced in Australia.[27]

Following English taste, a private art collection was thought to be the mark of a gentleman. At Tempe, A. B. Spark's walls were weighted with over one hundred pictures that included Flemish and Italian works. By 1845 Charles Nicholson had begun to amass a huge collection of rare books, pictures, manuscripts and antiquities, as sought by cultivated gentlemen whenever they could lay their hands upon them as they roamed around the Mediterranean, reconstructing imaginatively and classifying scientifically the defunct civilizations of Egypt, Greece and Rome. In Sydney, there was sufficient interest in these pursuits for the formation of a Society for the Promotion of Fine Arts in May 1847. Within a month, an exhibition at the Australian Subscription Library mounted a total of 380 paintings. In Hobart, the first major art exhibition was held on 6 January 1845. It owed much to the activities of a sketching group, founded by G. T. W. Boyes and J. E. Bicheno, that included John Skinner Prout, a professional artist who had emigrated to Sydney in 1840, settling in Van Diemen's Land four years later. Prout's arrival stimulated a passion for landscape sketching and he was much in demand by gentlemen to paint their country seats. In New South Wales, Conrad Martens, a professional artist who had been on the scientific voyage of the *Beagle* before arriving in Sydney in 1835, found a similar demand for his work.

Most paintings appreciated by the élite were visual representations of the way in which the middle class wanted themselves and their possessions to be seen. Their houses were depicted as bastions of civilization in an impressively threatening wilderness: selected aspects of its vegetation or suitably spectacular geological formations were rendered in the detail which the Romantic, picturesque tradition required. In portraits of themselves, they appeared passionless, serene and just, their bodies decorously draped with the richest textiles, their persons as impenetrable a façade as their mansions, their furnishings or their gardens, against which they were usually posed. Even their children were transformed into perfect little pieces of property, angelic, doll-like and surrounded by possessions of their own.

For the portrayal of a less ordered world, artists turned to outcast groups such as convicts and Aborigines. As the first rush of interest in them as 'noble savages' faded, Aborigines had appeared in European art chiefly as stock foreground figures in early landscape paintings, the pictorial equivalent to the poets' smug contrast between 'primitive' life and the busy progress of the towns. By the 1820s and 1830s artists like T. R. Browne, in pictures like *Hump-back'd Maria*, caricatured Aboriginal survivors on the fringes of white settlement as grotesque, comic figures. W. H. Fernyhough and John Carmichael developed this genre, dwelling especially on the effect of alcohol on the Aboriginal communities. In Van Diemen's Land, emigrant land-taker and artist, John Glover, treated the Aboriginal people near his grant at Ben Lomond similarly. His paintings of his own house and garden were classic celebrations of the elegant home carved out of the wilderness, ordered and complete, but his pictures of the Aborigines suggested primeval savagery. Surrounded by eucalypts with distorted, snake-like limbs, Glover's people capered and leapt like exotic wild animals.

Similarly, in Augustus Earle's *Chain-gang* convict labourers appeared as sinister and bestial, like dogs too dangerous ever to be let off the chain. Son of an American artist and portrait-painter, Earle arrived in Hobart in 1825 after two decades spent roaming about the world. Transferring to Sydney in October 1825, Earle's portraits of Governors Brisbane and Darling, Dr Robert Townson, Governor Brisbane's astronomer James Dunlop, and Mrs Blaxland, were in marked contrast to his ruthless caricatures of the convicts. Elegantly attired and exuding a confident knowledge of their power, the élite subjects of Earle's portraits also seemed to occupy another world from that of Bungaree, whom Earle painted in the pose of a military hero, his officer's coat and hat deliberately and perhaps mockingly contrasted with his tattered trousers and bare feet.

Of the colonial artists, only Thomas Bock and S. T. Gill resisted the demands of official culture. An artist who had arrived to serve a fourteen-year sentence in 1824, Bock was commissioned almost immediately by the Van Diemen's Land

Bank to engrave the plate for a four-dollar note. He went on to establish a gallery in the city in 1831 and give lessons in art. He also painted Wooreddy, Truganini, and Mathinna, a child who was 'adopted' by Lady Franklin at the age of five and lived with the Franklins from 1839 to 1843. Compared with the other painters of the Aboriginal people at this time, Bock's portraits were sympathetic and not inaccurate, avoiding both caricature and idealization. S. T. Gill, an emigrant to Adelaide in 1839, was able to paint an Aboriginal corroboree in which the participants appeared to be engaged, not in mysterious savage ritual, but in a joyful form of group theatre. In other work, Gill satirized the land-takers rather than their victims and, in choosing to paint scenes from the lives of ordinary people, was the only artist who suggested there was an alternative to official culture and its aesthetics. He died an alcoholic on the steps of the Melbourne Post Office in October 1880.[28]

Architecture was especially important in forming and entrenching middle-class aesthetic and political values. Public and private buildings, consciously situated to dominate the landscape, made an unmistakable statement of power. Captain Piper's house, begun in 1816 on a headland overlooking Sydney Harbour, was notable chiefly for its large domed ballroom which had been designed essentially as a statement of its owner's commitment to pleasure. From the following decade, most gentlemen's houses made a much stronger political point. In 1824 Sir John Jamison's 'Regentville' constructed on his 1000-acre grant at Emu Plains was, as its name suggested, an impressive Regency mansion which sought to impress not by size alone but by strict formality of line, sophistication of detail, and borrowings from the classical public architecture of imperial Greece and Rome. Invariably two-storeyed, Regency houses had a rigid symmetry which dictated the arrangement of windows and doors, and the front entrance was exaggerated in importance, acquiring an imposing portico usually supported by Doric or Ionic columns. Chaste, ascetic and solid, this style became extremely fashionable among the expanding numbers of the colony's élite. In 1829 a classic example of the genre was erected at Hobartville near Richmond for William Cox, and during the 1830s there were numerous mansions built to similar design by architect John Verge. The son of a successful London speculative builder, Verge had arrived with a shepherd and a flock of Hampshire sheep in Sydney in

1828. Assigning pastoral pursuits into the hands of his son, Verge concentrated on designing Regency mansions which soon included Spark's Tempe on the Cook's River, Hannibal Macarthur's The Vineyard at Rydalmere and Alexander Macleay's Elizabeth Bay House. During the 1830s other landowners became attracted to a newer but equally imposing architectural style that was becoming fashionable in Britain. This was known as the Gothic Revival and was the architectural counterpart to the Romantic movement in the arts. Houses which conjured up visions of a more chivalrous age, the childhood of English civilization, had a special appeal to taste-makers wishing to cultivate a chauvinistic, British nationalism.

The potential of the new Romantic images for expressing national allegiance and legitimizing middle-class culture had been recognized by the Macquaries. The castellated Fort Macquarie, begun in 1817, featured a two-storeyed tower and drawbridge, intended both to adorn and defend Sydney Cove. On the western arm of the cove, Dawes Point Battery was embellished by the addition of a castellated battery tower and guard-house, while Macquarie also contemplated a new Government House in the same style. Only the stables were completed when he departed in 1822, and it was not till 1834 that plans were resumed for the erection of a new Government House. Designed in England by Edmund Blore and built under the supervision of Colonial Architect, Mortimer Lewis, its massive sandstone walls rose above Bennelong Point, towering over its modest predecessor further down the hill towards Sydney Cove, eclipsing the horse stables with its feudal embellishments and effectively conveying the suggestion that somehow a link existed connecting colonial figures of authority with the supposed triumphs of Britain's medieval past. The building was completed in 1843.

Quick to take the point, in 1835 the Colonial Treasurer, Campbell Drummond Riddell, had James Hume design 'Lindesay' on Darling Point while, not to be outdone, in 1839 Sir Thomas Mitchell commissioned for himself 'Carthona'. A much more extravagant version of the feudal fantasy, this house sported Gothic arches, a castellated roof-line, and carved stone bosses ranging from medieval figures of authority to Queen Victoria and the Duke of Wellington.

Most of the pastoralists who constructed country seats for themselves during the 1830s and early 1840s preferred the old-fashioned, solid Regency style, for with the addition of a wall, such as at 'Somercotes' and 'Bona Vista' in the midlands of Van Diemen's Land, the Georgian house could be made just as impregnable against attack by Aborigines as the more warlike Gothic castle. Some country settlers went so far as to incorporate a coat of arms over the portico, thus following a trend set in England at this time that attempted to revive aristocratic titles and alter surnames as the *nouveau riche* sought to conform to the fashionable cult of the medieval and conceal the recent origins of their wealth.[29]

The new code for advancing the lower orders from what gentlemen like Robert Lowe called their 'swinish repose' included a vigorous programme of church-building. Some gentlemen erected private chapels on their estates in imitation of the British gentry tradition, while the Church Acts of 1836–37 ushered in an era of subsidized and therefore more extravagant church construction, with more elaborate styles. Gothic designs were popular, as were internal fittings of cedar. Colonial churches of this period were similar to those erected in Britain from the 1820s and remarkably similar to each other. In Sydney, Broughton's St Andrew's Cathedral (1837), with its medieval mood and extra pinnacles and mouldings added by Edmund Blackett in 1846, was not dissimilar from St Andrew's Presbyterian Church built for the Reverend John McGarvie in 1833–35. Even the more proletarian Father J. J. Therry, planning St Mary's Catholic Cathedral in 1833, was tempted towards the militaristic grandeur of the Gothic. One of the first two Catholic priests permitted in the colony, Therry had arrived from Ireland in 1820. Enthusiastic and close to his parishioners, Therry harked back to the days of the Irish rebellion of 1798, when priest and people were closely linked, and was somewhat of an embarrassment to Catholic intellectuals. In 1835 he would be banished to Campbelltown following the arrival, first of the new Benedictine William Ullathorne in 1833, and then of Bishop Polding in 1835. In Hobart, convict James Blackburn's Gothic imagination was much in demand by church-builders. A former civil engineer and speculator who had attempted to retrieve his fortunes by forging a cheque, Blackburn was one of those whose skills enabled them to avoid the rigours of transportation. Soon after his arrival in Hobart in 1833 to serve a life sentence he found employment in the Department of Roads and Bridges where, in addition to town water and irrigation schemes, he contributed numerous Tudor-style buildings to the midlands landscape. These ranged from tiny watch-houses and Congregational chapels at Bagdad (1842) and Cambridge (1842–43) to the massive Holy Trinity churches in Hobart (1840–47) and Launceston (1841–42).[30]

In their search for enduring emblems and traditions, the colonial middle class, like their counterparts in Britain, found that the cult of the medieval served them doubly well. It not only provided them with an imposing and ancient-looking architectural style but with a code of manners which could be linked to national ideals. As popularized in the Waverley novels of Walter Scott and the poetry of Alfred Tennyson, the modern gentleman was to be a hero, personally helping the forge his nation's history by attempting the impossible, fighting battles without question, preferably against overwhelming odds. Indeed, his whole life was to be conditioned by a code of 'chivalry'. Close to the Arnoldian ideal of 'playing the game', this concept served a similar function, that of suggesting that the competitive individualism required by the economic system must never be taken too far.

The idea of chivalrous self-sacrifice for an allegedly higher, group ideal found its most spectacular public expression in the colonies in the field of land exploration. This was a concept attractive to those seeking to generate a unifying allegiance to Britain and those interested in forging a distinctively Australian patriotism. In either case, the explorer could become a national hero whose exploits, romanticized in glowing newspaper reports and celebrated in official art, would embody a unifying tradition for what were still largely migrant communities. The land would replace the foreign foe for whom blood had to be spilt to forge a unifying identity. Of course, there was also the hope that fresh grasslands might be discovered.

In 1844–46 a successful expedition led by Ludwig Leichhardt foreshadowed the kind of heroic aura which exploratory ventures into the still mysterious heartland of the continent could inspire. Sponsored by prominent New South Wales pastoralists and businessmen, he embarked on a long overland trek from the Darling Downs to Port Essington in search of an overland route to the markets of Asia. Coming upon fine pasture suitable for cattle, Leichhardt was shipped back to Sydney as a hero who had 'beaten the bush'. Exploratory parties like this one were much too visibly tied to the commercial interests of the pastoralists to be turned into truly patriotic and public cultural events. There was also the problem that the leader, Leichhardt, was very obviously a foreigner and therefore, not quite a gentleman. He had only arrived in Sydney in February 1842. During the journey he had fallen into a less than heroic fight with his Aboriginal guide, Charley and, even worse, had failed to win it, Charley relieving the impulsive Prussian of two of his lower teeth.[31]

Even less suitable for national myth-making was a small, privately funded party led by another European, Dr John Lhotsky, to the south-east of the continent in 1834. Though possessing admirable educational qualifications (he was suggested as co-editor of the learned *New South Wales Magazine*) Lhotsky's journey was virtually ignored and he sailed from Van Diemen's Land in April 1837, deeply in debt. 'Dr Lhotsky has gone Home', Ronald Gunn wrote to Sir William Hooker (Director of the Royal Gardens at Kew) in February 1838, 'be cautious of him. He is I am sorry to say a Black Sheep. He has made no friends in V.D.L. and is a good riddance . . .'[32]

Clearly, the explorer as national hero could not be a foreigner, and it was left for the South Australians to launch Edward Eyre as the prototype of the heroic explorer. While hoping to find cheaper overland access to markets for the colony's stock at Swan River, this expedition was given the aura of a cultural mission from its inception. Governor Gawler and Charles Sturt were enthusiastic supporters, and preparations for the expedition were completed in a mere seventeen days, in order that the party could be launched on the twenty-fifth anniversary of Waterloo. On the morning of departure an elegant *déjeuner à la fourchette* was held for Eyre at Government House and he was presented with a British flag, worked in silk by the ladies of Adelaide. This emblem, Gawler announced, had once 'floated triumphant in victory over the field of Waterloo'. The dangers faced by this expedition were equal to those of battle, and its purpose just as glorious. Eyre was to plant the flag in the very centre of Australia and leave it there, Sturt added, 'as a sign to the savage that the footstep of civilized man has penetrated so far'. A mere four weeks out of Adelaide the party ran into the dry salt bed of Lake Torrens and the northward course had to be abandoned. Eyre concluded (wrongly) that a vast formation of salt lakes curved like a horseshoe round the Flinders Ranges and decided to demonstrate a British gentleman's quality by marching westwards along the coast to seek a more favourable place to attack the continent's centre. Thus began a pointless but suitably epic journey along the Great Australian Bight, during which the Aboriginal members of the expedition kept the party alive by digging up roots from which water could be drained and by spearing stingrays for food. Nevertheless, having staggered into Thistle Cove near Esperance in June 1841, Eyre duly won himself a place in the annals of the colonies' official culture. In 1846 he was appointed Lieutenant-Governor of New Zealand and in 1861, Acting Governor of Jamaica. Here, however, as even some English experts conceded, the hero turned out to be a bully and a cad, ordering the execution or flogging of over a thousand blacks to put down a rebellion.[33]

Dramatic though it was, Eyre's performance was upstaged during the 1840s by a heroic sequence of pointless and often singularly unsuccessful expeditions. In Van Diemen's Land, the Governor, Sir John Franklin, already a hero for having been forced to eat his boots during an attempt to explore the mysteries of the Arctic Circle in 1827, decided to turn the visit of fellow polar heroes James Ross and Francis Crozier into a public cultural event. Following the unsuccessful attempt of the *Erebus* and the *Terror* to reach the South Magnetic Pole, Franklin welcomed the ships back to Hobart in June 1841 amid scenes of celebration and festivity. Then in 1842 the Governor launched an overland party along the river now named after him, to Macquarie Harbour. In a misguided attempt to suggest that a woman, too, could represent British heroism and leadership, Lady Franklin participated in this little voyage, travelling in a chair gracefully suspended on poles carried by convicts. In 1846 Franklin, his term as governor over, would achieve the ultimate sacrifice which the cult of the explorer required. Joining Crozier in another attempt to find the still elusive North-West Passage, neither explorer ever came back.[34]

Not to be outdone, Charles Sturt, now Registrar-General and Colonial Treasurer of South Australia, also yearned to lead an attack into the still mysterious and virginal centre of the continent. In 1844 he staged a repeat performance of Eyre's departure from Adelaide, this time with himself in the leading role. Though, like Franklin, he was not a young man with vision so defective that he could only see a few paces in front of him, like Eyre, Sturt carried a hand-sewn flag to be impaled in the continent's geographic heart. Skirting the imaginary horseshoe formation which had deterred Eyre, Sturt planned to go up the Darling and then strike a north-west course for the centre. Still a believer in the existence of an inland sea, his equipment included a boat. His route took him into the continent's most inhospitable deserts, where he discovered nothing of note except the difficulty of surviving in temperatures of over 130° Fahrenheit in the shade, one life being sacrificed to this illuminating piece of field research. Even so, as a dramatic performance of desert heroics the impact of the expedition was sensational, especially since Sturt chose to write constant letters home from the front, instructing his wife how to proceed in the event of his demise and detailing the daily dangers being faced. These missives and those of other members of the party were dispatched back to Adelaide by means of obliging couriers, a tactic guaranteed to stimulate public interest in the fate of the expedition.

In New South Wales, in December 1845 'Major' Mitchell was also eager to play the role of public servant as national hero. At the age of fifty-seven he chose to undertake a final journey in search of the fame which had so far eluded him. Travelling to the north-west interior via the Maranoa and Warrego, in December 1846 he returned to Sydney triumphant, having found a river named the 'Victoria' which, he alleged, was nothing less than the long-sought water highway to the Gulf and thus to Asia. The fact that he was soon proved wrong about the river did little to alter public acceptance of his own heroic estimation of his achievements.[35]

Leichhardt, that not so chivalrous Prussian, was also plotting greater glories. In March 1848 he led an expedition from the Condamine planning to cross the continent from east to west. He disappeared without trace, fifty bullocks, thirteen mules, twelve horses and 270 goats following him into oblivion.

As a feat of showmanship this was no easy act to follow, but in 1848 the death of Edmund Kennedy in the steamy tropical jungles of Cape York almost eclipsed it. An ambitious young surveyor who had been Mitchell's second in command, Kennedy had leapt into the limelight by leading an expedition proving that Mitchell's 'Victoria' River did not flow towards the Gulf but south-west towards the centre, where it became Sturt's Cooper's Creek. Moreover, Kennedy's new instructions were the stuff from which stardom might be made. He was to travel northwards along the mountainous north-east coast to the tip of Cape York, returning along the western side of the range till he met the tracks of Mitchell and Leichhardt. This was an impossible task because of the impenetrable tropical vegetation and swamps, and the encumbrance of a botanist, horses, carts and a flock of sheep. Kennedy's desert experience had not equipped him to confront the much more numerous Aboriginal population of the tropical north. After his party found occasion to shoot four people in a single engagement, it was only a matter of time until Kennedy, too, took a final bow. The colonial people might have thought the Kennedy débâcle a badly staged theatrical farce, but to the middle classes it had all the ingredients demanded by the patriotic myth of the British explorer as hero. The leader was young, male and British and, even better, did not return, and so could be said to have sacrificed himself gallantly to national 'progress', as a plaque erected to his memory in St James' Church, Sydney, attested. The fact that Kennedy was dispatched by Aborigines was also culturally useful, helping to denigrate these people as 'savages'. Even the awkward point that he was helped by an Aboriginal guide could be turned to advantage, for like Eyre's chief help-mate, Wylie, the guide could receive a brief public tribute as one of those rare, loyal Aborigines who had been successfully educated to the point where he knew which was the right side to be on.[36]

The spectacle of their top public servants jousting with the continent's interior and its inhabitants had important consequences for colonial society. Like organized sporting competitions of today, the feats of the explorers were thought likely to persuade people that they were part of a classless nation which, if they all played by the rules, would march on towards greater glories, as the bastion of white 'civilization' in the Pacific. While cultural influences significantly shaped societal attitudes, the physical and social sciences were offering much more radical methods for programming human bodies and minds towards desirable ideals. In order for the nation to survive in an increasingly competitive industrial world, educative and cultural strategies were not enough. It was necessary to breed a new, healthier man who would automatically adopt the militaristic physical and mental discipline which industry and empire increasingly required. Whereas women could not be heroes, any more than they could be sportsmen, science was offering an alternative medicalized version of domestic ideology whereby women could aspire to a special, biological status as 'mothers of the race'. This meant producing sons who were perfect human specimens, the embodiment of the national type, and daughters who would be devoted to a new, medicalized ideal of motherhood.

This application of the methods and the ideology of science to social problems was the more important since many of the masses were unimpressed by the moral and patriotic values in the spectacle and the literature of official culture. There were some who remained unfit, unchauvinistic and uninterested in laying down their lives in the interest of commercial, industrial or pastoral expansion. For them, other more coercive and scientific means of social incorporation would need to be found.

10

THE MANUFACTURE OF MAN
Social Science and the National Type

To believe that man in a savage state is endowed with freedom either of thought or action is erroneous in the highest degree. He is in reality subjected to complex laws, which not only deprive him of all free agency of thought, but at the same time by allowing no scope whatever for the development of the intellect, benevolence, or any other great moral qualification, they necessarily bind him down in a hopeless state of barbarism, from which it is impossible for man to emerge, so long as he is enthralled by these customs; which, on the other hand, are so ingeniously devised, as to have a direct tendency to annihilate any effort that is made to overthrow them.

George Grey, 1841[1]

WHILE LIBERAL THEORISTS were developing their new, cultural strategies for educating the male worker for the vote and creating a virile national type to which he should aspire, they also sought more scientific knowledge of human behaviour. The late-eighteenth-century assumption that such understanding depended on the scrutiny of so-called 'savage' people was now an accepted part of scientific method, as George Grey's remarks revealed. His perception of the intellectual defects in the Aboriginal people and the relationship of these perceived defects to Aboriginal law were part of a concerted effort to formulate new and apparently expert theories of the behaviour of individuals and whole societies, and to establish how these theories might be applied in the colonies and at home.

By the 1840s developments in physical and social science had come a long way since the days of Flinders, Dégerando and the dynamometer. Further development of Romantic thought brought to the fore the role of the unconscious in determining human character and the influence of passions, instincts and mental ability. Measurement of the body was not abandoned; on the contrary, it had simply been assumed that study of anatomical and physiological differences between races would yield information about physical strength and reproductive power, and could somehow be correlated with more abstruse concepts such as intelligence, personality and social organization.

These assumptions were reinforced by important developments in biological theory. Charles Darwin's fully worked theory of evolution would not be published till 1859 and T. H. Huxley's application of it, *Evidence of Man's Place in Nature*, would not appear till 1863, but from Lamarck onwards theorists were debating how physical, mental and even moral characteristics were determined by biological factors receptive to environmental and hereditary conditions. As in the earlier four-stage theory of social development, in evolutionary theory it was now assumed that so-called 'primitive' minds exhibited mental processes in their lowest form of biological development, a stage where the mind's 'most elementary laws and tendencies' could most easily be discerned.[2]

Parallel changes were occurring within natural history. The Linnaean system of botanical classification, centred on easily observed reproductive characteristics and the fixity of species, had given way to the more probing and technical system of Jussieu, based on the anatomy and physiology of animals, plants and man. Interest was stimulated by fossilized evidence of weird creatures, long extinct, now being brought to light by railway and canal construction, and by geologists who were attempting to classify rocks and other formations on the surface of the earth. By the time Charles Lyell published his *Principles of Geology* (1830–33) and Roderick Murchison was dating rocks of the Silurian era in 1835, controversial new theories were being discussed of the immense age of the earth and the origins of life upon it. By the 1840s, though Anglican clergymen were still prominent among geologists and most saw themselves as merely uncovering further evidence of God's wondrous design for human progress, daunting evidence from the remains of fossil vertebrae, together with information gathered from flints, tools, pottery and human remains, languages, fairy stories and myths, was dealing a death blow to clerical explanations of human origins and human behaviour. In particular, the seventeenth-century theories of Archbishop Ussher, dating creation in 4004 B.C., were now untenable. There were now at least three different theories to explain the origins of humankind, all of which placed great emphasis on quantifiable physical differences between races. Some theorists believed that the various races were the result of separate acts of creation; others believed all were created 'savage' but some had 'progressed'; others believed all were created perfect but some had regressed.

A far more predatory and chaotic universe was emerging than the old established hierarchy of species controlled by God. There was now a new determination to apply scientific solutions to social and political problems and to conceal the ruthlessness of these policies behind a rhetoric of scientific inevitability, hygiene and sanitary law. Evolutionary theory especially lent itself to political and economic purposes. In 1850 Herbert Spencer coined the phrase 'survival of the fittest', and Charles Lyell was predicting the 'speedy extermination' of the North American Indians. In 1855 Alfred Wallace, based on an island off New Guinea and perusing Malthus, linked evolutionary theory to the formation of racial characteristics. This 'self-actuating process', he declared, 'would necessarily *improve the race* . . . the inferior would inevitably be killed off and the superior would remain, that is, *the fittest would survive* . . .'[3] As Mary Shelley's novel *Frankenstein* warned in 1818, with growing interest in electricity, galvanism and the chemical sources of energy it was as if science thought it could actually manufacture an ideal human type. Charles Babbage's *Treatise on the Economy of Machines and Manufacturers* (1832) suggested this ideal type was not so much a whole person as an automated hand, the rest of the body and mind bred to perform faithfully even the most monotonous and tiny section of the production process, the total meaning of which should be understood only by a single overseer or manager. Thus, scientific intervention and classification would ensure that no labourer was too clever for his or her appointed task and all were perfectly adapted and content to perform that particular task to which they were 'vocationally' suited and into which they were ideally to be slotted. The physically and mentally 'fit' would be those who fitted in.[4]

Though the process of constructing scientific theory was becoming confined to professionals with access to information from every corner of a shrinking globe, general interest in science had never been greater, both for the challenges it presented to religious explanations of human origins and behaviour and for its promise of ameliorating so many of the problems of the age. The findings of physical science were now being made part of official culture and, applied to human society, were overtly linked to the silencing of worker and feminist protest, to the pursuit of empire and to the glorification of nation and race.[5]

Interest in science was especially marked in the Australian colonies, where many of the élite were in touch with the British and European 'experts'. Some gentlemen were personally involved as 'collectors' of the botanical, geological and zoological evidence on which the theorists depended. Thomas Mitchell was a collector for Sir Richard Owen, the 'British Cuvier' and leading authority on zoology and palaeontology. So, too, was Dr George Bennett, a visiting physician who settled in Sydney in 1836 and who was later appointed to the position of Colonial Zoologist for which the ill-fated Lhotsky had applied. In Van Diemen's Land, Ronald Gunn was a collector for Professor William Hooker, while Governor Franklin was well known to Sir Roderick Murchison.

Some colonial collectors aspired to being theorists in their own right. They included Sir John Jamison who was said to be compiling a 'natural history' of the colony and who in 1830 became a corresponding member of the Société d'Histoire Naturelle of Mauritius in 1830. William Sharp Macleay, son of the former Colonial Secretary, arrived in Sydney in March 1839 and was a classic specimen of the gentleman-scientist. He had already impressed the British scientific community with his *Essays on the Annulose Animals* (1819–21) and his *Annulosa Javonica* (1825), a learned study on insects gathered and impaled by a collector in the Dutch East Indies. He had continued this scholarly zeal for maiming beetles, butterflies, moths, and flies in Cuba between 1825 and 1836. By 1839 he was a member of the British Association for the Advancement of Science, the Zoological Society, and the Linnaean Society of London.

So great was the demand for specimens that some colonial scientists turned their collections to financial advantage. One who did so was William Crowther: when he departed in February 1839 for medical study overseas, he took with him sufficient skins, skeletons and live specimens that, when sold to the Earl of Derby, the profits covered the costs of three years' medical training in London and Paris.[6]

Colonial ladies shared the prevailing enthusiasm for natural history, and botanical drawing was an accepted feminine accomplishment, not far removed from the fairy land of talking animals, insects and birds in books being written specially for children. Few, however, were permitted to become serious scientific collectors, though Georgiana Molloy sent specimens to Dr Lindley, Professor of Botany at University College, London, and Director of the London Zoological Gardens. Lady Franklin was also a collector.[7] Colonial ladies and gentlemen kept abreast of overseas theories and their application to human society because they played host to the numerous visiting scientific expeditions which continued to see the Pacific as a fertile field of research. When Fedor Ivanovich Stein, surgeon and naturalist with the Russian expedition of 1819–21, examined the sandstone formations south and west of Sydney, he was accompanied by Allan Cunningham; and Charles Darwin arrived on the *Beagle* in 1836. James Dana of the United States expedition (1838–42) under Wilkes was in touch with Charles Nicholson and Anglican clergyman, Reverend W. B. Clarke. Owen Stanley and Thomas Huxley, who arrived in 1847, spent three months in Sydney, though Huxley, then surgeon on the *Rattlesnake*, outlaid rather more time courting Miss Henrietta Heathorn of Newtown, his future wife, than in collecting less interesting specimens.[8] Even after the departure of these great men, discussion of the new scientific theories and especially of their applicability to human behaviour was kept alive by numerous scientific societies. The model for these pursuits had been set early by Governor Brisbane who had seen his appointment as offering an unparalleled opportunity to contribute to knowledge of the southern heavens, largely neglected since the departure of First Fleet astronomer, Lieutenant William Dawes. Brisbane also presided over the Philosophical Society of Australasia, founded in June 1821 to collect information on 'the natural state, capabilities and resources of the country', and establish collaboration with learned bodies overseas. A number of papers on astronomy, geology, and meteorology were read, some of which were published in Barron Field's *Geographical Memoirs of New South Wales . . .* (1825), but the society became a victim of fractious colonial politics and expired in August 1824. Nevertheless, journals like the *New South Wales Magazine* (1831—33), and the *Sydney Guardian A Journal of Religious, Literary, and Scientific Information* (1847—48), although short-lived, provided a forum for gentlemen wishing to contribute to the increasing range of scientific theories appearing overseas. C. P. M. Wilton's *Australian Quarterly Magazine of Theology, Literature and Science* (1828—31) served a similar purpose.

The Franklins founded the Tasmanian Natural History Society in Van Diemen's Land in 1837, aiming to air overseas opinion and promote investigation locally. The earlier Van Diemen's Land Scientific Society, founded by John Henderson in 1829, had expired within two years, but under the zealous eye of Ronald Gunn the Tasmanian Society for Natural History survived the departure of the Franklins in 1843. For a time it functioned in tandem with the new Royal Society of Van Diemen's Land for Horticulture, Botany, and the Advancement of Science. This was founded by the new Governor, Eardley-Wilmot, in 1844 and was the first Royal Society established outside England. The Franklins' Tasmanian Society was amalgamated with it in 1848[9]

Far from being a scientific backwater, the Australian colonies were abuzz with discussion of the latest theories informing physical and human science. Gentlemen-settlers of the 1820s, casting their eye over the landscape, were looking for geological evidence to support current debates, as well as for mineral deposits or pastoral land. H. C. Antill, while crossing the Blue Mountains in 1815, speculated on whether he had found evidence of violent volcanic action at King's Tableland, while in an address to the Philosophical Society Alexander Berry declared that Neptunian theorist James Hutton would have found much to interest him in a single day's walk along the shores of Lake Macquarie. Henry Dumaresq believed the fossils found in local caves rendered the hypothesis that the continent was post-diluvial 'as groundless as that of its absorbent interior marshes'; J. D. Lang's *Mosaic Account of the Creation Compared with the Deductions of Modern Geology* (1846) was a classic attempt to weld local geological evidence onto Scripture. Lang speculated on the catastrophic origin of the continent, attributing to Blumenbach the view that the continent arose by the impact of a comet with the earth.[10]

Considered as unique evidence for scientific theory, the Aboriginal people continued to attract attention. Debate raged around the Tasmanians and their reputedly different physical appearance from mainland people. Robert Dawson declared the Tasmanians had invaded the island direct from New Guinea; Captain Robert Fitzroy of the *Beagle* postulated they had been driven by a storm from Africa; J. B. Jukes fancied they had drifted in from New Caledonia; hero of the Nullarbor, Edward Eyre, favoured a three-pronged migration from an original landing-place in the north-west of the continent. The Aborigines' own perception, that they were part of the creation of the land during the Dreamtime, was neither understood nor seen of relevance in a society whose economy and religion assumed the validity of migration, conquest, and colonization.[11] This familiarity of the colonists with scientific theory had dire implications for the Aboriginal people. In addition to collecting evidence to supply the experts abroad, the local land-takers had no compunction in applying the theories as a justification for extermination. In 1822 Judge Barron Field informed the Philosophical Society that his study of the skulls, the genius, and the habit and the language of the Aborigines proved that they were of an inferior 'Ethiopian' racial type and incapable of being 'civilized'. In 1827 pedantic pastoralist, Peter Cunningham, informed potential immigrants that these people were at 'the very zero of civilization, con-stituting in a measure the connecting link between man and the monkey tribe'. In 1838 while violence flared on the Liverpool Plains, in Sydney Dr F. L. Wallace broadcast his belief that there was a striking resemblance between the skull of an Aborigine and the skull of a monkey. In 1844 William Charles Wentworth, speaking in the New South Wales Legislative Council against the admissibility of Aboriginal evidence in courts of law, informed his fellow gentlemen that 'it was by deceit and cunning' that the Aborigines obtained their living in the wild woods of the interior, and 'it would be quite as defencible to receive as evidence in a Court of Justice the chatterings of an ourang-outang as of this savage race'.[12]

As overseas, the application of Darwinist ideas to society was facilitated by new theories of craniometry. Experts were becom-ing increasingly convinced that the key to understanding mental phenomena lay in the brain not the soul, and that the shape of the skull was a vital indicator of what might be going on inside it. It was assumed that Europeans had bigger heads and therefore more efficient brains than races lower down on the imagined evolutionary scale. In 1819 English anatomists Charles White and William Laurence, after a major comparative study of human brains, bones and teeth, alleged that a great distinction existed between the mental ability of 'civilized' nations of Europe and what they called 'the naked, shivering and starved New Hollanders' and other 'barbarous' tribes. Phrenologists, too, were convinced that the cranium was the clue to mental ability and emotional drives. Believers argued that by examining bumps on the human skull a trained phrenologist could know the potentialities of the individual worker and advise certain forms of exercise by which wanted faculties could be made to develop and unwanted ones shrink towards insignificance, especially if the patient were a white male. Women's skulls, being smaller, were assumed to have lower reflective powers.

Phrenology enjoyed enormous vogue in the colonies from about 1830, at first in scientific circles and later as an educative strategy which, like temperance, was successfully introduced to the upper working class. 'I have no doubt but that, if children's heads were carefully examined, and their organs studied, their propensities might be very materially guided as the teacher pleased', wrote Van Diemen's Land philosopher, Henry Melville, in 1834. In 1836 Dr William Bland presented a collection of sixty 'phrenological busts' to the Sydney Mechanics School of Arts, and lectures followed on the subject by Dr F. L. Wallace, Dr A. à Beckett, and James Hamilton, a professional phrenologist from Glasgow. Like craniometry, phrenology was used on criminals and other persons said to be a lower human type. In Sydney in 1844, following the hanging of John Knatchbull, a convict who bludgeoned a women to death in a shop in order to steal money, a cast was made of the head allegedly for scientific purposes. This was later reproduced as a wood-cut and offered for sale, the marks of the rope clearly visible around the neck. Knatchbull's skull was especially exploitable since he was of upper-class origins yet had apparently regressed towards savage ways. The populace was invited to speculate whether their craniums indicated that they had criminal instincts and thus were destined to feel the full force of the law.[13]

Phrenological science created for colonial collectors an enlarged and long-lived market for Aboriginal skulls among the theorists overseas. As early as 1819 Reverend Robert Knopwood was collecting Van Diemen's Land skulls for Alexander Berry who, in turn, passed them on to Archdeacon Scott, a keen student of cranial 'bumps'. From a major Aboriginal burial-ground on Berry's 10 000-acre grant at Crookhaven, that gentleman dispatched numerous remains, mostly to Edinburgh's School of Anatomy and its Museum of Natural History. In 1824 the collection of forty-five heads for dispatch abroad after a massacre in the Bathurst district appalled missionary L. E. Threlkeld, as did the measurement of Aboriginal heads, living and dead, by the French scientific expeditions. Dumont d'Urville's *Atlas: Anthropologie* included six modelled busts, three crania, one brain-cast of Tasmanian Aborigines, and two crania of mainland people. Even so, most missionaries shared an interest in craniometry, especially after the invention of the cephalic index (an apparently objective method of quantifying intelligence based on cranial measurements) in 1840.

Where pastoralists used scientific 'evidence' to justify policies of extermination, colonists of liberal persuasion were drawn to applying science to their existing educative attempts to 'protect' Aboriginal people and bring them under discipline. Expert 'proof' of Aboriginal mental inferiority could be used to explain why the first round of missionary education had failed and suggest the need for new more scientific and coercive methods. In Britain, the Ethnological Society of London, formed in 1844 by breakaway members of the old Aborigines Protection Society and under the presidency of physician, Dr James Prichard, illustrated the growing notion that only new techniques, systematically based on 'the Science of Man', could alter such allegedly retarded bodies and minds and find a role for them in the new, fragmented labour process into which they could ultimately be fitted. Specifically secular influence in the study of human origins would increase during the 1850s with the gradual discrediting of phrenology and Prichardian ethnology, which had relied on the study of language and culture as well as retaining Biblical concepts, and their replacement with wholesale acceptance of Darwinian ideas and physical anthropology.[14]

Dr John Henderson, already notable for his scheme for maximizing the reproduction of convict women, was one of a number of gentlemen in the colonies quick to apply ideas of genetic engineering to the Aboriginal people. There was hope, he declared, of finding a niche in the labour process for the 'half-caste' child, if given an education similar to Europeans. Alexander

Berry concurred: 'The cross-breeds are distinctly an improved race', he arrogantly asserted in his *Recollections of the Aborigines* about 1827. Other gentlemen were drawn to the idea of a positive eugenic programme. They included 'A Phrenologist' who wrote to the *Colonist* in October 1838 suggesting that 600 white female convicts should be distributed among the tribes and an equal number of Aboriginal women be placed among the white stockmen and shepherds.

In 1841 visiting Polish explorer, 'Count' Strzelecki dwelt on the problem of depopulation. The Aborigines, he argued, should have been declared a conquered people, entirely without rights. They could then have been rounded up as the Tasmanian Aborigines had been, and subjected to a scientific education which took account of their system of law. This done, they would then have proved 'an easy field for the missionaries'. As it was, the best policy was to ration the survivors and leave them to die out which, he alleged, since the women became sterile after mating with any man not of the full blood, they would soon obligingly do.[15] The colonial missionaries were moving towards similar views. The Reverend James Gunther of Wellington Valley believed the Aborigines were regressing because they were unable to imitate stencilling which covered the walls of nearby caves, and which Gunther saw as evidence of a past superior civilization. This view was not dissimilar from that of Sydney Police Superintendent W. A. Miles, who studied carvings in the Sydney area with Threlkeld. Arriving in 1840 Miles was a corresponding member of the Ethnological Society of London, of the Statistical Society, and of the Museum of Natural History in Paris and had worked on two official British enquiries into the anthropological causes of urban crime. One of his papers that attempted to prove that Aborigines resembled gypsies and were addicted to the same allegedly idle and vagrant habits was published in the *Journal of the Ethnological Society of London* in 1854. L. E. Threlkeld, though he drew the line at collecting skulls for the anatomists and biologists, was another who in the 1840s exploited to the hilt growing ethnological interest in Aborigines and other allegedly primitive peoples. Already considered an authority on Aboriginal languages, religion, and technology, Threlkeld went on to be received as a member of the Ethnological Society of London in 1851. Similarly, George Augustus Robinson, despite the failure of the Port Phillip Protectorate, by 1849 had gathered sufficient ethnological information about Aboriginal people to win acceptance in artistic and learned societies. Elected to the Royal Society of Tasmania in 1851 he became a Fellow of the Ethnological Society of London in 1853, and with the aid of pensions from the governments of Van Diemen's Land and Victoria, was able to lead a leisured life in England and on the continent until his death in 1860 at Bath.[16]

The early missions were now attacked as a wasteful, inefficient failure, but one novel, local experiment in educating and 'civilizing' the Aboriginal mind seemed an unqualified success. This was the Port Phillip Native Police force, formed in 1842, which was the brainchild of an expert in the application of the findings of physical science to human societies, Alexander Maconochie. Son of the local agent who succeeded Adam Smith on the Board of Customs in Scotland, Maconochie was one of those products of the Scottish Enlightenment who rapidly developed an interest in natural and social science. Following a successful career in the navy, Maconochie launched himself into scientific circles in 1813 by publishing a statistical study of commerce and trade in the South Pacific. In 1830 he was one of the founders and first Secretary of the Royal Geographical Society, and capped this in 1833 by becoming first Professor of Geography at the University of London. He came to Van Diemen's Land as secretary to his old naval friend, Sir John Franklin, in 1836, and during the voyage Maconochie marshalled his fellow passengers and lectured them on the 'Natural History of Man', informing them 'that it was possible to find specimens of the human species with tails'. Listeners also learned that the white races owed their colour to their civilization, and that their 'antidiluvian ancestors were in all probability black'. Not content with these dazzling displays of his knowledge, Maconochie also spoke on metaphysics and phrenology. In applying these new sciences to the Aboriginal 'problem', Maconochie saw the native police as a new form of adult re-education which, he declared, would succeed where the missionaries had failed, in reforming the minds and morals of selected Aboriginal men who would be appointed to a special army corps. Maconochie shared the prevailing view that Aboriginal people were like children, vacillating, unsteady and perverse, requiring much 'parental and inventive zeal' to win them from their 'savage' ways. Mounted on dashing steeds, clad in a distinctive uniform, and given a course in military discipline by European officers, members of the corps could gradually be made to leap

whole centuries of evolution and be brought to a proper appreciation of white culture and eventual assimilation into the community. They would be very useful in quelling disturbances and
tracking escaped prisoners and criminals.

After an abortive beginning, a Native Police Corps was
formed under Western District squatter, Henry Dana. Presented
with a green jacket, featuring opossum-skin trimmings, green
and red caps, and carrying a sword, short carbine, and bayonet,
sufficient young males were found who could be tempted to join
up. Once they had done so, they found themselves part of a
formidable and deadly force whose main purpose was to annihilate
other Aboriginal people still resisting the invasion, for their bush
skills immediately demolished the main advantage held by Aboriginal guerillas. The drill and regimentation undermined their
Aboriginal identity and encouraged them to imitate European
male behaviour in war. Stories were told of the zeal with which
they killed, and abducted Aboriginal women. This stereotype of
the native police further degraded the image of Aboriginal
civilization in the eyes of Europeans. In one stride the Europeans
created an effective constabulary which would do their killing
for them and which could be used to explain violence on the
frontier in terms of Aboriginal 'savagery'. Once he had realized
the purpose of the force, Billibellary, an elder of the Yarra people
who had encouraged about thirty young men to join, tried to
persuade them to leave, but desertion was a punishable offence
and the men had nowhere else to go, nor any other way to
survive.[17]

The Australian colonists proved especially susceptible to new
scientific programmes for dealing with Aboriginal people and
modifying the criminal mind. The eastern colonies, in particular,
seen by reformers as 'tainted' by their reliance on convict labour,
remained laboratories for testing theories of criminal behaviour
and its reform. This was the more so during the 1830s as the
British and local liberals, having moved to end the assignment
system, found themselves faced with many more convicts than
could be incarcerated in penitentiaries, at least for any length of
time. The number of 'criminals' was also increased by a new
series of English statutes which had made policing more efficient.
These included the Vagrancy Act of 1824, the Malicious Trespassing Act of 1827 and the Metropolitan Police Act of 1829. It
was hoped that, in the long term, by making detection and

punishment more certain the number of offenders would be reduced, but the short-term effect of these statutes was to increase the number of people convicted. In addition, since 1826 there had been passed a series of statutes reducing the number of capital offences.

It followed that there was now a need for more scientific methods of identifying potential criminal offenders and treating convicted ones. Even before the end of the assignment system, liberal reformers had been receptive to new theories of how people with allegedly criminal instincts might undergo a process of mental modification prior to speedy release into those areas of the work-force where their presence as free labourers was urgently required. So far, however, their ideas had tended to focus on intensification of the existing penitentiary formula. A House of Commons Committee called in 1831–32 was informed that occasional solitary confinement was not in itself sufficient to correct the hardened offender—to it must be added the principle of absolute separation and total silence at all times. Already the United States had constructed two model prisons on these principles, known as Auburn and Sing Sing. In Britain, by 1834 Coldbaths Prison had been converted to the principle of silence, while in 1842 a brand new penitentiary cast its shadow across workers living in North London. Occupying a 6-acre site, Pentonville was a formidable version of the feudal castle, surrounded by twenty-foot-high walls of stone; inside, it could accommodate 450 persons in silent, solitary cells.

In New South Wales, Governor Bourke had been quick to begin construction of facilities for solitary, if not silent confinement. Berrima Gaol was completed in 1839 and Darlinghurst in 1841. Work began on similar institutions at Parramatta, Port Macquarie and Norfolk Island, while the Female Factory at Parramatta became the scene of a particularly novel experiment in the principle of silence. In September 1839 Gipps informed his superiors that a new block of separate cells had been completed in which 'order, cleanliness and *silence*' prevailed 'to a degree scarcely surpassed in any Prison in England'. Half the cells were only eight by five feet and had been made as dark as possible. Unfortunately, when this information reached London, Gipps was advised that his cells actually exceeded the proper measure of pain now recommended by the British experts. The latest opinion was that dark cells had inadequate ventilation and hardened the offender. Suitably chastened, Gipps had windows chiselled out in the dark cells at Parramatta and included in the plans for new gaols at Port Phillip, Bathurst, Goulburn and Maitland.[18]

Alexander Maconochie, as interested in the criminal mind as the Aboriginal one, was developing a theory which, he declared, was the key to rapid release of convicted offenders as useful and tractable members of the working class. According to him, the clue lay not in separation or silence but in the development of social skills. A witness before the Molesworth Commission, in March 1840 he arrived back in Van Diemen's Land with full permission to test his theories on Norfolk Island, and a generous salary of £800. Though considered very radical by contemporary standards, Maconochie's programme was but another version of the old, Benthamite faith in architectural and educative solutions to social problems. It was based on moral reform rather than mental modification, with much emphasis on reading, music, prayer, and theatrical entertainments, preceded by the national anthem. By 1844 it had been decided that these methods were patently inadequate for permanently altering the criminal mind, as indeed was Stanley's 'probation' scheme which followed in 1842.[19]

Given these failures, it was fortunate for the propertied classes that concepts from phrenology, ethnology and evolutionary science were now available to be systematically applied. A new science of criminology was being invented, aimed at replacing the metaphysical speculation and bricks-and-mortar experiments of the philosophers, humanitarians and Utilitarians, with a new scientific method capable of dramatically reducing the incidence of crime. Believers in this new science declared that 'crime' could be measured and calculated just like any other physical phenomenon, for it was caused by abnormal, physical, mental and social characteristics which could be identified by anatomical and statistical studies. 'Criminal statistics', announced Brougham in 1860, 'are for the legislator what the map, the compass and the sounding line are for the navigator', and as early as 1835 Belgian statistician Adolphe Quételet had declared in an essay on the 'social body' that just as periodic examination of mortality and reproduction rates measured the health of the population, so regular statistical enquiries into criminal returns would throw light on the relationship of crime to age, sex, education, climate and race. By the 1840s the new criminal anthropologists and sociologists had invented the term 'the dangerous classes' to describe people who, because of the shape of their heads or the length of their arms, their fancy for tattoos or use of a distinctive habit of speech, were supposed to be pathologically different from the industrious working class and predisposed to savagery and crime. In 1855 Herbert Spencer would publish *Principles of Psychology* in England in which he would weld onto the old Benthamite concept of the association of ideas new biological arguments, while later Italian physician Césare Lombroso would add that all criminality was a form of mental regression to a more primitive stage in the evolution of the human species. This, he claimed, was a condition which the criminals shared with the 'primitive' races, who had exactly the same aversion to work and the same cranial characteristics.[20]

In this search for a more scientific understanding of criminal behaviour, theorists hit upon the notion that studies should be made of the mass of juvenile 'savages' who were eking out an existence in the slums of the ports and cities, now becoming known as the 'rookeries of crime'. Surely here lay important information about the early development and treatment of criminal habits of mind. Many of the new criminal statutes of the 1820s had targeted urban children, turning aspects of juvenile street behaviour into a criminal offence. Pranks like acquiring fruit from a garden or stall, which once might have merely earned a reproof, were now specifically criminalized, making street children very vulnerable to arrest. In the convict colonies, whole shiploads of boys under the age of eighteen had begun to arrive, and in 1834 a special institution to house them was opened on the Tasman Peninsula. Known as Point Puer, this was continuously overcrowded, numbers reaching 712 by the end of 1842. By this time boys from a new English juvenile penitentiary, Parkhurst, were being shipped to Western Australia. One of them, fifteen-year-old John Gavan, became in 1844 the first inhabitant of that colony to be hanged.

Working-class children had long been the object of 'rescue', but this notion of labelling them as juvenile offenders and incarcerating them in state-run, prison schools was entirely new. To treat these 'juvenile delinquents' theory and practice reversed some of the latest strategems being applied to adults. At Point Puer corporal punishment, long suspect as a satisfactory means of disciplining adults and infants, now found great favour as a 'wholesome punishment' for boys, as in the English public schools. In 1843 when there were 706 boys in the establishment, 54 per cent received corporal punishment and 78 per cent were placed in solitary confinement, many for a 'moral' crime.

Where adult offenders were being seen as people whose mental development had been arrested or had regressed, juvenile offenders were believed to have had the slow, quasi-evolutionary development of their bodies and brains dangerously speeded up by premature exposure to the adult world. Consequently, it was said, they were 'precocious' little adults instead of innocent children and as such, probably the most mentally and physically defective of all the 'dangerous' classes. Urban-dwelling boys, in particular, were stunted, shrivelled and smart instead of tall, muscle-bound and slow, and therefore likely to develop into fully-fledged specimens of the criminal type.[21]

This tendency to conflate the urban landscape and its homeless children with the presence of criminal instincts and vicious habits of mind was related to the fact that the densely populated industrial and trading centres of Britain, together with their fledgling counterparts on the colonial coastlines, had been permitted to expand without attention to waste disposal and water supply and were now sources of periodic epidemics of contagious disease. The findings of phrenology—that individual behaviour was controlled by specific organs located in the brain and that mental processes had a somatic base—made it easy for theorists to assume that such unhealthy living conditions produced diseases of the body and also of the mind. This concept gained greater currency when it was taken up by members of the emerging medical profession whose interest in botany, anatomy and physiology made them ideally situated to assume expertise on the modification of the human body and brain. By the 1840s they were claiming superior knowledge on issues ranging from urban health and demography to the 'diseased' mind, whether juvenile, criminal or 'savage'. As a group, doctors had a vital need to establish their expertise in such matters of the mind, for as yet they had not achieved a monopoly on the art of healing the body. Women were still in control of all matters affecting reproduction and infant care, and the numerous cures offered by the medical chest. There was also competition from the busy drug-vendors, bleeders, cuppers, and tooth-extractors, whose low-priced and not necessarily less-skilled services were often preferred to those offered by the 'qualified' practitioner. At the New South Wales Select Committee on the Medical Practices Bill in 1838, Drs Bute Stuart, Patrick Hill and Thomas Black declared that the health of the colony's women would never be improved until action was taken to do away with the services of the female accoucheur. Others combined this strategy with mystifying medical techniques. Dr James Russell alleged angrily there was not a druggist in Sydney who could name the artery from which he extracted the blood, neither was there one 'capable of distinguishing a molar tooth from an incisor or bicuspidatus, nor one who would properly explain the principles or degree of atmospheric pressure to keep up on the cupping glasses' and at the same time extract 'the requisite quantity of blood'.

Early in the nineteenth century doctors initiated a drive to tighten training procedures and expel 'unregistered' practitioners. This campaign for professionalization was to become integrally related to the process by which the findings of physical and biological science were both disseminated and applied to the solution of social and political problems. Already in England, apothecaries, formerly mere tradesmen and the servants of physicians, had dissociated themselves from the retailing of drugs and from 1815 set a minimum standard of education, and assumed the title of general practitioner. The surgeons had drawn a sharp distinction between themselves and barbers, who had once shared the same skills. Gaining a Royal Charter in 1800 they now specified that training had to be by apprenticeship, followed by attendance at a charitable hospital or service in the armed forces, as in both of these arenas they were assured of gaining plenty of practical experience. These developments were being watched with some misgiving by the physicians whose formal training already won them the prestige claimed by these newcomers.[22]

The doctors' need to control medical knowledge was especially acute in the Australian colonies which were more than generously supplied with trained practitioners, many of whom had come out as surgeons on convict or emigrant ships. In 1838 James C. Russell, who had arrived as a surgeon on the *Enchantress* in 1833, told the New South Wales Select Committee on the Medical Practices Bill, that there were no less than twenty-eight legally qualified practitioners then in business in Sydney. In the Hunter Valley, apothecary and druggist, William Lipscomb, believed there were at least one dozen surgeons practising within a radius of 10 miles of Maitland. Colonial doctors may also have been especially professionally ambitious since those who had been ships' surgeons had been accepted there as experts not only on health but on discipline. Having wielded an authority at sea second only to that of the captain himself, many expected to command a similar status when settled on the shore.

Some colonial practitioners, like Peter Cunningham and Charles Nicholson, solved the problem of an overly competitive market for medical services by turning their talents to pastoral pursuits. Others found employment in the government service where they were thoughtfully provided with corpses fresh from the scaffold, and had access to the steady supply of bodies, dead or alive, which cluttered the corridors of the colonial hospitals. Dr William Bland was able to capitalize on his position as medical officer to the Benevolent Society (1821–63) and staff member of the Sydney Dispensary (1826–45), to develop procedures which enhanced his reputation and that of the profession. In 1832 he was one of the first to perform an operation for the cure of an aneurysm of the subclavian artery, and published an account of the procedure in the *Lancet*. No part of the pauper body escaped this doctor's scrutiny. A veritable wizard with the scalpel, patients coming under his care rapidly found themselves relieved of physical impediments ranging from cataracts clouding the eye, to crystals clogging the bladder.[23]

In the absence of a high survival rate to advance their cause it was fortunate for the medical profession that the ensuing decade saw the discovery of anaesthetics. Almost overnight doctors gained access to the knowledge which would make possible unprecedented feats of heroic surgery, and while in some cases it could alleviate suffering, it would also facilitate further research into the modification of human beings. Following the invention of 'laughing gas' by Sir Humphry Davy in 1799, ether was first used successfully as an anaesthetic for an operation in Massachusetts in October 1846. By January 1847 the success of the experiment was reported in the *Lancet*, and on 7 June 1847 the *Launceston Examiner* was able to report that Dr William Pugh, a local practitioner who had enjoyed a long association with St John's Hospital, had used the new discovery. In Sydney just one week later, dental practitioner John Belisario in conjunction with a physician, Dr Charles Nathan, reported a successful adaptation of the anaesthetic for the extraction of teeth. Members of an admiring audience, invited to watch the procedure, pinched and squeezed the patient who obligingly remained in a state of stupor during their experiments and while the triumphant surgeons punched out two of his teeth. By August 1847 ether had been used by Dr David Thomas at Port Phillip. At the Royal Melbourne Hospital in 1848 surgeons had the use of both ether and chloroform, demonstrated by James Simpson in Edinburgh earlier in 1847.

In their campaign to dominate and extend medical knowledge, the doctors formed professional associations. Organized in Britain by the 1830s, these were used as lobby groups and produced learned journals in which the latest medical discoveries could be communicated to the registered practitioner. In 1846 the Port Phillip Medical Association made its appearance, to be followed in 1852 by the Victorian Medical Association. The Sydney-based *Australian Medical Journal* began publication in 1847.[24] At the same time, the doctors' claim to expertise in human science generally was being advanced through their efforts to improve sanitation in the urban centres. This was in spite of their commitment to an inaccurate concept of the causes of epidemics. The theory of miasma, or impure air, which was believed to emanate from swamps, damp cellars, cesspools and the like, would persist even after James Lister in the early 1860s publicized and developed Pasteur's theories that disease was spread by organic particles later known as germs. Conveniently for the doctors, the notion of miasma, while no help in the operating theatre or sick room, did demand attention to issues like sewage disposal and water supply. Action taken on these problems undoubtedly improved people's chances of avoiding some common forms of contagious disease.

Colonial doctors lost no time in identifying areas like the Rocks in Sydney as classic sources of infectious disease, and, as in Britain, whereas their campaign clashed with the economic interests of the speculative building trade, it soon became clear that the liberties of the working-class household were also going to be curtailed in the higher cause of public health. Writing to the *Herald* in June 1841 a medical gentlemen declared that the cause of the recent scarlet fever epidemic was filth accumulated in poorly drained areas. The government should have the right to compel residents in these places to wash their houses inside and out with chloride of lime, which had the power to destroy the miasma arising from decomposing animal and vegetable matter. This correspondent also favoured the idea of a local Board of Health, comprising eminent gentlemen such as himself, to investigate every cause of epidemic disease and discuss methods of prevention and cure. The formation of city councils employing doctors as health officers followed by the end of the decade.

The doctors' intervention in the field of public health helped entrench the notion that 'deviant' moral and political attitudes had a physiological cause which, with proper town-planning and medical surveillance, could somehow be allayed. As influential British reformer Dr Edwin Chadwick argued, health and longevity had nothing to do with poverty or hunger, for disease arose from 'effluvial poisoning' to which people who had misused their bodies were especially prone. In addition to cleaning up water supplies and drainage (he had shares in several companies planning to make a profit from the sale of sewage), Chadwick wanted compulsory drill and callisthenics introduced into factory schools to correct enervating, immoral habits. The public health campaigns facilitated 'field research' by the inspectors and 'social scientists' now venturing personally into the urban ghettos to provide information about hygiene and collect the statistical and sociological information on which further streamlining and streaming of the workforce would depend. The message carried by the public health officers was by no means culturally neutral. Taking up Chadwick's emphasis on the moral rather than economic causes of disease, they saw themselves as disseminating a 'gospel of health' and used phrases like 'cleanliness is next to godliness'. Intervention on behalf of public health would become an important means by which the newly medicalized moral and political values of the dominant class would be imposed on the working-class home.[25] While partly philanthropic, the public health crusaders widened their professional sphere of influence and served the new liberal regime. After all, efforts to preserve and prolong working-class life made sound economic sense, since such efforts were just as important as reproduction for keeping up a surplus labour pool. As many doctors pointed out, the new principle of universal schooling was of little use if children were going to die before they entered the workforce.

Like modern Prometheuses the doctors were in effect beginning to claim they were technologically creative divinities, wielding authority over life and death, interpreting the unseen and the unknown and pronouncing judgement on a wide range of moral and political issues. Their efforts to probe the hidden sources of life and to shape human behaviour were also extremely masculinist, as the doctors' attempts to break into the field of obstetrics and infant health was soon to reveal. Medicalization of pregnancy, child-birth and infant care was of financial importance to doctors; it was also a key area where they rationalized their alleged expertise on domestic hygiene and 'juvenile' behaviour and widened their analysis to include the middle-class mother and child. Taking up the prevailing interest in child sexuality, according to the doctors bad moral habits like masturbation would cause effeminacy in boys and sterility in girls, both of which were pathological conditions predisposing the evolving brain towards deranged behaviour or even crime. So, just as the 'savage' was now a child, every child was a little savage and as such, potentially abnormal, requiring a medically monitored programme to bring it to civilized ways. Innocence was now a medical issue requiring, in some cases, surgical intervention.

Medical intervention in middle-class child-rearing coincided with celebration of women as mothers and glorification of the 'private sphere', and was very much an attack on the improved esteem which feminists hoped those twin ideologies would achieve for women. Mothers would prove increasingly vulnerable to this attack as, during the 1830s and 1840s, the infectious diseases of childhood became more virulent and defeated traditional family cures, eroding the confidence of women and prompting them to turn to doctors for advice. This process was especially marked in the colonies where immigrant mothers were cut off from the traditional expertise of female family and friends. Like public health, the medicalization of child-rearing looked to the miasma theory of contagion as its scientific base. This allowed the doctors to restructure the spatial organization and time-discipline of the home and demand that everything in it, including the child, be kept scrupulously clean. This formula would eventually help reduce mortality rates, a development for which the doctors would immediately claim responsibility, further advancing their cause.

Women were also coming under increasing scientific scrutiny as 'mothers of the race'. No longer was it sufficient for women merely to reproduce, their bodies and homes were now to become laboratories for the production of the new national type under the direction of the medical profession. Puberty, menstruation and menopause were being constructed as serious crises in the fragile life of every woman, and without their careful management sterility and other diseases would follow. Even prenatal care became an area of medical concern, with women being warned that moral habits and mental attitudes during this time could be transmitted to the unborn child. This medicalization of reproduction and child-rearing did not mean that woman's status was in any way improved; indeed, ideally she was now not even to be a manager who understood the total process of child-raising. Rather she was a mere minion who could barely be trusted to administer the complicated and cruel purgatives and emetics, blisters and embrocations which the doctor recommended.[26] Because the quality of motherhood, like the concept of 'primitive races', was seen as the key link in explaining human differences and therefore deviations from the norm, the doctors' alleged expertise in this area helped establish new medical strategies for dealing with 'abnormal' behaviour generally. Criminals, prostitutes, and so-called primitive people would all be diagnosed as medically problematic, and likely to be suffering from some form of mental deformity and disease. In particular, such perverse behaviour was increasingly seen as a form of insanity, which was another general area assumed to require medical and, in some cases, surgical expertise.

Early prison reformers such as John Howard had long been concerned that people thought to be lunatics were often incarcerated in the nearest prison instead of an asylum, while they also suspected that many of the people being convicted of criminal offences were mad rather than bad. As early as 1835 Dr James Prichard, in his *Treatise on Insanity and Other Diseases Affecting the Mind*, had coined the term 'moral imbecile' to describe otherwise rational people who, he alleged, were the prey of irresistible savage instincts which predisposed them towards vice and crime. By the late 1840s doctors in Britain were declaring that there were certain diseases such as epilepsy which caused an individual to turn to crime and for which the medical profession was developing cures. Alcoholism, too, was being redefined as a mental disease. The doctors' claims to expertise in dealing with such matters were now sufficiently established to challenge the role traditionally played by lawyers in assessing criminal behaviour and its reform.[27]

These developments in mental science were rapidly imported to Australia, where the convict colonies had a large number of potential 'patients'. In 1843 in New South Wales, a Dangerous Lunatics Act provided that persons coming before magistrates for disturbing the peace or vagrancy could be certified as insane on the advice of two medical practitioners. In 1846 the new asylum at Tarban Creek came under criticism for not being in the charge of a doctor. J. T. Digby, a non-medical appointee from England installed after the opening of the institution of 1838, was demoted to the position of steward and in January 1848 Dr Francis Campbell took over as superintendent. Similar asylums to treat cases of lunacy were founded in the other colonies. In Van Diemen's Land a special state institution for all convicts suffering from bodily or mental disease was completed in 1827 and soon became over-crowded. Extensions in the early 1840s enabled separation of those diagnosed as mentally ill from those seen as having purely physiological complaints and in 1845, Dr John Meyger, alleged to have 'expert knowledge of brain diseases', was appointed super-intendent. Purging, emetics, blisters and bleeding were the main treatments; 'electric therapy', introduced by 1850 as a shock treatment was an innovation which Mary Shelley's Dr Franken-stein would surely have approved.

In Adelaide, in 1841 a Dr James Litchfield offered to establish a 'mental hospital' as a business proposition, contracting to take government lunatics at a fixed rate per year and private ones for an individual fee. Unfortunately, the colony was too small to furnish sufficient patients. Undeterred, Litchfield went on to become first Professor of Forensic and State Medicine at Kingston, Canada, and later a lecturer in the lucrative field of obstetrics.[28] The ease with which this particular physician moved from insanity to childbirth reflected the fact that the doctors' solutions for most kinds of female 'deviance' involved greater attention by all women to medically monitored sexuality and reproduction. By the 1840s physicians were asserting that most diseases of the female mind could be traced to disorders in the reproductive system. In order to attain mental as well as physical health, strenuous mental education, all factory work and distracting interests outside the home were to be avoided.

Diagnosis and treatment of women at Tarban Creek during the 1840s reflected these ideas. Female insanity was often related explicitly to sexuality. For example, one woman was said to be 'in a state of lunacy induced by profligacy'. Another's mental disorder was diagnosed as 'induced by ignorance and injudicial management during and after confinement', which meant, presumably, that this event had not been managed by a medical man. 'Puerperal mania' was another cause of female insanity. It followed that the doctors were moving towards finding a solution to the old problem that institutionalizing women interfered with reproduction, for it could now be argued that only the most difficult and hardened of female 'cases' belonged in gaol. All others should be medically treated in a hospital for the insane or, better still, by male medical guidance in their own homes. In 1848 the old Female Factory at Parramatta, though recently turned into a penitentiary, abandoned its old role and was transformed into a new institution to house male and female paupers classified as insane. By 1850 its name was changed to the Parramatta Lunatic Asylum and in 1852 it came under control of a doctor, Patrick Hill.[29]

By the 1840s, as in the gaols, most of the inmates of the mental institutions were men, usually vagrants or itinerant workers. However, when allowance is made for the unequal sex ratios in the colonial population, the proportion of women to men was higher in the mental institutions than in the gaols. In response to the fact that women were especially vulnerable to being classified as 'moral idiots', the position was developing where, by the 1870s and parallel with Britain, most inmates in the mental asylums were women and most inmates in gaols were men.[30]

The growth of institutions like the lunatic asylum reflected the belief in new forms of therapy for reducing and dividing the population of those traditional institutions, the workhouse and the prison while increasing scrutiny of people considered potentially deviant or already outside the 'norm'. As a result costs would be cut and the most dangerous and vagrant members of the population identified and punished in modern, hygienic ways. In Ireland, another English colony where legislative provision for lunatic and other asylums was provided early, by the end of the nineteenth century the prison population would be reduced, but the number of people incarcerated in asylums would have multiplied.[31]

This ideal would not be achieved for some time in the Australian colonies where, despite the existing concern about the quality of the population, quantity remained of even greater importance. New measures were urgently required to create the

'surplus', free labour pool needed to speed up capitalist development and reduce worker radicalism. Also, as colonial liberals
rightly perceived, it was imperative to terminate transportation,
otherwise the colonies would continue to be seen as a gaol, free
emigrants would go elsewhere and the granting of self-government would be indefinitely delayed. Even worse, it was thought,
the presence of so many criminals was polluting the population,
counteracting attempts to create the ideal national type. Therefore, though the goals of the social scientists were being achieved
in the long term, other more immediate if haphazard incentives
were needed to recruit rapidly the labourers required to expand
the Australian population. The lure of gold was to replace the
threat of the penitentiary and the workhouse as the agent for
removing labourers to markets where they were urgently required.

11

ALL THAT GLITTERS . . .
Emigration and the Gold Rush

EARLY IN THE winter of 1851 three Aboriginal shepherds, Daniel, Thomas and Jeremy Irwin, employed by Dr W. J. Kerr near Wellington, New South Wales, noted a speck of glittering substance in the surface of a block of quartz. A portion of the rock was carefully chipped away to reveal three large nuggets of gold, the largest about a foot in diameter. Dropping a blanket over the rock to conceal it from the eyes of a neighbour's shepherd, the Aborigines reported their find to Kerr who, quick as horseflesh could carry him, rushed to the spot. The rock was later weighed at Bathurst and found to contain a hundredweight of gold valued at some £4000, which today would be worth over half a million dollars. As contemporaries noted however, it would have been worth perhaps ten times as much as an interesting geological specimen, but the frenzied doctor, in his anxiety to carry it away, smashed it into smaller portable fragments.[1]

The Aborigines' discovery of the 'Kerr nugget' came some two months after the beginning of gold rushes to New South Wales and Victoria. The first of their kind in any British colony, these were to prove a brilliant solution for colonial liberals—anxious to curb the power of the pastoralists and rekindle the economy without reverting to 'slave' labour—and for British investors, searching for fresh fields to absorb the vast accumulation of capital that had grown out of the first phase of industrialization and which had only been partly absorbed by the laying of local railway track (some 6000 miles of it since 1830). Moreover, by 1850 Britain was no longer able to feed itself from its own agricultural production. Thus, though at first antagonistic, both groups would prove ready for large-scale investment in mining, first for gold, later for other metals and minerals such as coal; here the advances in geology since 1830 would prove rewarding. At the same time the colonies would be supplied with an abundant new labour force for more intensive exploitation through mining, urbanization, agriculture and improved communications and transport; thus entrenching them as dependent yet democratic economies supplying primary products in exchange for British manufacturers, capital and military protection.[2]

A wave of propagandist literature had appeared in the late 1840s, aiming to persuade impoverished Britons that Australia was a land of opportunity, a paradise for the workingman. In 1848 *Sidney's Emigrant Journal* informed the prospective migrant that a mechanic or labourer would have no difficulty in obtaining employment even before he left the ship, for potential employers would come on board and bargain for his services. Females were advised that colonists made good husbands, kind, indulgent, and generous. 'They are rather rough in their language to each other' it was admitted, but 'no one ever heard of a Bushman beating his wife'. As for food, emigrants could expect to eat meat three times a day, and to sample the native fauna, said to be delicious and plentiful. Wild turkeys, parrots, and bronze-wing pigeons, it was said, were all good eating, while the wombat was equal to pork. Propagandists for emigration now also included novelists Charles Dickens (*David Copperfield* 1849), Bulwer Lytton (*The Caxtons* 1849), and Charles Kingsley (*Alton Locke* 1850). Unfortunately, this kind of propaganda did not reach the minds and hearts of the people whom the novelists and political economists believed ought to emigrate, most of whom remained strongly and stubbornly resistant to the idea of removal. Even in Ireland, the survivors of the famine still clung to their holdings and, as in England and Scotland, those who decided to emigrate tended to choose North America.[3]

The Australian colonies, not yet recovered from the economic reverses of 1841–43, were offering a limited field for British investment. The construction of the first railway-line began at Redfern, New South Wales, in March 1850, but the colony at Swan River was continuing to stagnate for want of capital and labour. As a means of recruiting ex-convict workers, the new 'exile system' was providing the wrong kind of workers in the wrong place at the wrong time. Exiles were convicts who, like probationers, had previously been admitted to one of the new British penitentiaries, and were then dispatched for labour in the colonies. Following the consignment of Parkhurst juveniles to Western Australia, adult exiles bearing conditional pardons were disembarked at Geelong and Portland in 1845. Shiploads continued to arrive at Port Phillip throughout 1847–48. They met rising opposition for their presence was thought to spoil the image of this colony as a free land of economic opportunity. Such workers were not welcome in Van Diemen's Land either, where the labour market had long since reached saturation point. Yet to the further detriment of its economy, some 8000 convict workers arrived between 1847 and 1850. Meanwhile, pastoralists in New South Wales were threatening to revert to 'slavery' by importing their own labour from India, China and the Pacific.[4]

Little previous thought had been given to a gold rush as a means of promoting either mineral exports or free emigration. In Britain, the extraction of gold by private individuals had been seen as a likely source of disorder, overturning power relationships between master and servant. When gold had been found in County Wicklow, Ireland, in 1796, soldiers had been sent to remove the panners from the field. In New South Wales in 1823, when assistant-surveyor James McBrien found particles of gold near the Fish River, no action was taken by the authorities to encourage a rush. No interest was taken in Lhotsky's demonstration in 1838 of auriferous sands brought back from his journey to the Southern Alps, while even the popular Strzelecki's collection of traces of gold and silver west of the Blue Mountains, was not welcomed. According to the 'Count', Governor Gipps told him to 'keep the matter secret for fear of the serious consequences which, considering the condition and the population of the colony, were to be apprehended'. Strzelecki's announcement in the *Herald* in August 1841 of his finds similarly fell on deaf ears. No more successful in attracting the attention of state or capitalist was Reverend W. B. Clarke. In 1841 his discovery of gold near Bathurst and Hartley, and in 1842 on the Wollondilly River, was greeted with official dismay: 'Put it away, Mr Clarke', Gipps is reported to have said, 'or we shall all have our throats cut'. From 1847 the attempts of Sydney mineralogist, William Tipple Smith, to create interest in the presence of gold west of the Blue Mountains, were equally unsuccessful. It was a similar story south of the Murray where as late as January 1849, when would-be diggers hurried to Amherst in the wake of shepherd Thomas Chapman's discovery of thirty-eight ounces of gold, they were dispersed by the use of the native police.

One of the first British pundits to perceive the use of gold as a boost to the Australian economy was Sir Roderick Murchison. Aware of the stimulus which the discovery of copper at Kapunda in 1842 and Burra in 1845 had given to South Australia, as early as 1846 he was urging that unemployed Cornish tin-miners should be encouraged to emigrate to New South Wales and search for gold using a simple tin-dish method. Then from 1848 a gold rush to California further demonstrated the potential of gold-seeking as a means of stimulating free emigration and the growth of colonial markets. This new American state, recently acquired from Mexico by force of arms, was being flooded by volunteer settlers, including some 2500 who departed from Sydney in the fifteen months from January 1849. These volunteer emigrants paid their own passage out, provided their own equipment, conducted their own feasibility studies, and proved that the arduous work of gold extraction could be performed by en-thusiastic amateur volunteers. Their willingness to do so was related to the fact that under American law the State had no prior claim to the gold. The United States, one of Britain's greatest commercial rivals, was apparently being enriched by new supplies of labour, new markets for consumer goods and the injection of gold into the economy. Further, it was apparent that the fever to find gold automatically imbued these self-funded labourers with the doctrine of capitalist property relations. They had no doubts about their right to displace traditional Indian owners from the land for the pursuit of material gain and, unlike a work-force pressed into labour, these self-seeking gold-winners showed no interest in collective political action. Any radical working-class ideology soon faded before the prospects of profit and property.[5]

By now, the exasperation of colonial employers, first with probation and then with the exile system, was compelling the British authorities to realize that other methods of emigration would need to be tried. As early as October 1845 in Van Diemen's Land, six members of the Legislative Council, incensed with the cost of the colony of the uneconomic probation system, marched out to the chamber and resigned their seats. Known as the 'patriotic six', this group, which comprised some of the colony's most influential employers (Swanston, Dry, Kermode, Gregson, Kerr and Fenton) ominously put their challenge to imperial control in terms of 'no taxation without representation' and went on to cultivate a local nationalistic and potentially republican sentiment. Destined to find wide public support, this campaign was aimed not merely at ending transportation but achieving self-government.

Even more threatening was the Australasian Anti-Transportation League. First mooted in Launceston in August 1850, this group co-ordinated the activities of existing anti-transportation committees in Hobart, Geelong and Sydney and founded another committee in Adelaide. Taking up the nationalist rhetoric of the Continental liberals, the League spoke of forming a 'great Australian confederacy' to unify the colonies. As further testimony to these aims, by the time of its official inauguration in Melbourne in February 1851 the League had designed a special Australian flag. This was described as 'a banner of deep blue, spangled with the Southern Cross'. In deference to the fact that the problem of the imperial connection was as yet unsolved, the Union Jack was still present but it was precariously poised in the top left-hand corner of the flag. Appearing on letterheads, pamphlets and colonial vessels, this flag was also used to inspire fervour at League meetings. A prize was offered for the composition of a local national anthem.

This challenge by the colonial liberal nationalists—who had never had much in common with the British liberals except a shared rhetoric—to an imperial system which was not meeting either their demands for political autonomy or their labour needs, was much more serious than the former republican-posturing of colonial traders and squatters. Robert Lowe told a crowd of 5000, gathered at Circular Quay to oppose the arrival of the *Hashemy* with a cargo of exiles in June 1849, 'the time was not far distant when they would assert their freedom, not by words alone. As in America, opposition was the parent of independence . . .' In Melbourne, there was talk of getting up an army, while according to Launceston Congregationalist leader, Reverend John West, even the larger flock-masters were producing manifestos demanding that all transportation cease.[6] Much use was made by the colonists of the language of social science to focus the campaign against the exiles. This usefully obscured the vested interest of the liberal nationalists in free labour and added new moral and medical justifications to their campaign. According to the Anti-Transportation League, exiles were a noxious source of British depravity, moral cripples who would only impede the progress of the new nation which their flag claimed to represent. 'Consider the helpless pauperism of improvidence', the delegates of the League declared, 'constitutions ruined by vice and profligacy; asylums and hospitals overflowing with degraded and wretched outcasts, descending to the grave without respect and without sympathy, quitting a world which they had only dishonoured and abused.' This concept of the exiles as medically and morally unfit was especially popular in Port Phillip where, although they had long been employing convict workers and absconders from the penal colonies, and had been receiving exiles since 1845, colonists became especially indignant at this threat to their alleged genetic superiority. At a public meeting in Melbourne it was declared that Port Phillip District would never be regarded as a penal settlement, and any ship attempting to land a cargo of criminal types would be capsized into the cleansing waters of the Bay.

The stereotyping of the convict workers as physical and mental defectives attracted some support from urban groups of skilled, free labourers, who feared cheap competition, and Henry Parkes spoke of the right of the free labourer to be protected from the degradation of working with convicts. Parkes was associated with republican campaigns such as J. D. Lang's Australian League, and Charles Harpur's and E. J. Hawkesley's *People's Advocate*. Although many convicts were Irish Catholics, the anti-transportation cause also found support among some Catholic intellectuals. Archdeacon McEncroe's *Freeman's Journal*, founded in 1850, combined a liberal republicanism with attacks on convicts as a source of dangerous and evil social and political ideas.[7]

Faced for the first time with a strong and unified liberal opposition in the colonies, the British authorities moved rapidly to make political concessions and defuse the republican threat. Firstly, they speeded up the process of self-government, while at the same time advocating an imperial patriotism. Any anti-British, republican nationalism would be diluted in a greater faith and pride in the Empire. As Earl Grey wrote, rule by force would be replaced by rule by love and the Empire would become like 'a large family of devoted children'. In 1846 he had sketched the outline that self-government might take when he permitted the Canadian colonies to set up ministries wholly responsible to their legislatures, and in August 1850 an Australian Colonies Government Act was passed. This provided that all the colonies, except Western Australia, might rewrite their constitutions. The existing franchise was widened so that squatters could now vote and thus be intimately involved in the process of drafting the new constitutions. Imperial control of lands and land revenue, however, was retained. Separation from New South Wales, for which the Port Phillip District settlers had clamoured for a decade, would create the new colony of Victoria.[8]

Secondly, the British authorities began to give more thought to the presence of minerals in the Australian colonies and the possibility of using this to boost exports and to attract free emigrants. In 1848 Murchison wrote to Earl Grey pointing out that geological experts should be appointed to conduct mineral surveys and advise the state where payable gold was to be found. He also pointed out that the British law would have to be changed so that ownership of precious metals no longer automatically lay with the crown. However, the extraction process was not to be entirely free: the field was to be laid open to settlers only after the payment of 'certain dues'. Grey was cautious. He feared that access to goldmining might tempt existing settlers from other 'branches of industry' where their labour was required. The Californian rush had demonstrated that it was not going to be easy to allow free access to the the gold while at the same time deriving revenue from it to finance policing and control. Accordingly, in April 1850 Samuel Stutchbury, Fellow of the Geological Society of London and Curator of the British Scientific Institution, was appointed Government Geologist for New South Wales, and in June 1851 the Governor of New South Wales, Sir Charles Fitzroy, corresponded with Murchison regarding the problems of controlling a rush in agricultural and pastoral regions.

While the officials and geologists were deliberating, Edward Hargraves, a fortune-hunter recently returned from California, took matters into his own hands and engineered precisely the kind of uncontrolled rush which the authorities were hesitating to unleash. The son of a Hampshire army officer, Hargraves was a classic hero from children's literature, setting off to seek his fortune in 1830 at the tender age of fourteen. Two years later he arrived in New South Wales where he worked at a station near Bathurst, gathered *bêche-de-mer* and tortoiseshell in Torres Strait, and in 1834 acquired 100 acres near Wollongong. In July 1849 he was one of those settlers who alarmed colonial demographers by joining the rush to California but by January 1851 he was back in Sydney. With him he brought knowledge of the Californian gold-panning technique and plans to claim a government reward by discovering a similar goldfield in New South Wales which would be amenable to this technique. By late March, tiring of the outdoor panning life, he decided to return to Sydney and begin publicizing his efforts while other in his party went on with the arduous work of the search. In April he persuaded a friend to write to the *Herald*, announcing that a large field had been found, while he himself wrote to the Colonial Secretary claiming a reward. Fortune smiles on the bold and in the interim, Hargraves' friends in the field found four ounces of gold at Yorkey's Corner, north of Bathurst. Ignoring their pleas for secrecy, Hargraves returned to the area, named it Ophir after the Old Testament place of gold, and gave a public lecture on gold-seeking at Bathurst, displaying specimens and telling an enthusiastic audience where to search. By 15 May he had escorted the Government Geologist to the spot where some 300 diggers were already at work. A Bathurst newspaper declared the area a 'second California' and the rush began.[9] Hargraves's plan was totally successful. The New South Wales government handed over £10 000 and later a pension of £3750. To this the new colony of Victoria added £2381, and together with an assortment of other gifts, such as gold cups, gold spurs and whips, and selected nuggets. Hargraves departed from the field with a fortune so great that even with lavish living he did not succeed in entirely squandering it for almost a decade.

In Victoria, as soon as the news of the Bathurst discovery was confirmed, a committee of wealthy citizens offered rewards for gold discoveries there. Faced with an exodus of labour to the Ophir, and suffering from a commercial depression, they now needed a rush of their own. Early in August 1851 traces of gold were found by T. Hiscock in the Buninyong Ranges and a rush to richer deposits at nearby Ballarat soon followed. Armed with the knowledge of the cradle-washing technique, diggers in the area abandoned attempts to pick out grains of gold from the surrounding rocks, and early arrivals began to win an average of more than an ounce of gold a day.

News of the gold discoveries was transforming the image of the eastern colonies from a hellish place of punishment and human degradation to the land of opportunity promised in the emigration literature. To the delight of local reformers, the last convict ship sailed for Van Diemen's Land in November 1852. Though no gold had yet been found there, already the island colony was seeking to shed its association with convictism by renaming itself Tasmania. The transportation of workers now continued only to Western Australia, where landholders and merchants agreed to receive convict labour as the only method of saving the economy from stagnation. The first shipload arrived there in June 1850, with Britain agreeing to pay much of the cost of local police. Reflecting the fact that fewer women were now classified as criminal, no female convicts were sent.

Appalled at the way in which Hargraves had seized the fame and fortune to be had from initiating the rushes, his former friends, John Lister and the Tom Brothers, began a long battle for state recognition of their contribution. Reverend W. B. Clarke also demanded a prize, while William Tipple Smith complained bitterly to Murchison that it was science which should have been rewarded, not mere knowledge of Californian washing technique.[10]

The state, however, had greater worries for, as it had feared, though the rush brought a surfeit of settlers, how was their behaviour to be disciplined and their digging controlled? By the end of May 1851 volunteer miners were trudging along the road to Bathurst in such numbers that Thomas Icely removed all his plate and valuables from his country seat, fearing uncontrolled pillaging. Retreating to Sydney he counted 138 men in one day headed westwards for the Ophir. The Governor lost his hall-porter in the early exodus and asked the Colonial Secretary 'Where will it all end?' 'Wages are rising and if the precious metal continues to be found in any quantity I am at a loss to know what the squatters are to do during the approaching shearing time', Western District pastoralist, Archibald Black, lamented early in May as labourers left on the long trek to New South Wales. Anxieties in Victoria were not necessarily alleviated in

August when news of the Ballarat discovery arrived. The whole town of Geelong was in 'hysterics', the *Argus* reported with some journalistic licence in September. Gentlemen were 'foaming at the mouth, ladies fainting, children throwing somersaults', as the town became the gateway to the Victorian rush.

The new colonial governments found themselves without legal precedents and guidelines to deal with the problems. Some settlers advised proclaiming martial law and barring the working-man from digging, but this was now impossible to effect. 'It would be madness to attempt to stop that which we have not the physical force to put down', Deas Thomson informed James Macarthur. In due course, Fitzroy decided to uphold the principle of the crown's right at common law to all deposits of gold in New South Wales, and on 23 May it was declared that no man could dig without permission. This entailed securing a licence, which had to be purchased in advance, and was only available to those able to prove they were not 'improperly absent from hired service'. The price of a licence was set at thirty shillings, beyond the savings of many labourers and similar in principle to the fixed price of land in the 1830s and 1840s. By this means, it was hoped, essential labour would be retained, revenue raised, and the pace and size of the rush controlled. Similar regulations were adopted in Victoria.[11] Even so, the immediate effects of the rush seemed alarming enough. 'There is no appearance of the demand for labour for our shearing and harvest being supplied . . .' the *Argus* reported in October 1851:

the police force are handing in their resignations daily . . . the custom house hands are off to the diggings; seamen are deserting their vessels. Contractors' men had bolted and left expensive jobs on their hands unfinished. What are the contractors to do? Why, follow their men; and off they go.

In New South Wales by July 1851, in addition to the diggers on the road, 1000 miners were moving from the Ophir along the creeks towards the Turon River, where Stutchbury's official report, received in May, had indicated payable gold. By December there were 5000 miners. The children of a tenant farmer near Bathurst remarked that they 'never thought there were so many people in the world before, and wondered what it all meant'. On the Turon, a new town, Sofala, was taking shape, as those with sufficient capital realized that gold was more easily won by supplying goods, equipment, and accommodation than by digging for it in the hard stony ground.

At the Victorian fields where the strikes were richer, the numbers were greater. By November 1851 there were 13 000 men digging there for gold, mostly at Mt Alexander. In this area, 70 miles north-west of Melbourne and later to be known as Castlemaine, a hut-keeper, C. T. Peters, had been prospecting since July. By September when the find was made public, his party had gathered fifty pounds of gold and a rush began which temporarily eclipsed that of Ballarat. The Mt Alexander find provoked mass emigration of men from Van Diemen's Land and South Australia, where gold had not been found. By the end of 1852, when 70 per cent of Victoria's 33 000 diggers were at Castlemaine, the adult male population of Van Diemen's Land had been halved, and whereas before the gold rushes there had been twice as many men as women, with the departure of more than 10 000 males, women were in the majority for the first time.

Similarly, in South Australia, by early 1852 half the men were leaving or had left for Mt Alexander. 'Supernumerary shopmen, failing tradesmen, parasol-menders, and piano-tuners, went first', Catherine Spence wrote at Christmas 1852,

but now everyone is going, without regard for circumstances or families . . . Our butcher's man has dwindled into a small boy, who tells us he's the only man in the shop. Our baker drives his own cart, and you see women driving about quite independently now . . .[12]

In August 1852 the first rush of emigrants from overseas was arriving in the golden colonies. The sailors of many nationalities who had left their ships to try their luck at the diggings were now joined by veteran prospectors from California and Chile, and European political refugees. It has been estimated that some 10 000 or 15 000 non-British Europeans, about half German, and about 10 000 North Americans visited the Victorian diggings in the five years from 1852. To the delight of the British advocates of emigration, by far the bulk of the emigrant gold-seekers came from the United Kingdom. Between 1852 and 1861 almost 300 000 persons departed from Britain for Victoria alone, 70 per cent of them paying their own passage.

With emigrant arrivals in the new colony leaping from around 11 000 in 1851 to over 90 000 per year in 1852 and 1853, it was Victoria which bore the brunt of this new experiment in using

gold as the catalyst for colonization. Cajoled from their com-
munties by the promise of instant wealth earned by the sweat of
their own brows, the democratic acquisitive spirit rapidly became
strong in the new arrivals. Most took to the doctrine of Samuel
Smiles' self-help and Carlyle's espousal of enterprise, becoming
as individualistic and rapacious as their pastoralist predecessors.
On arrival they were confronted with the example of former
workers making a killing from retailing essential goods and
services. For instance, after having been unceremoniously dumped
ashore at Sandridge in a heap of dust, boxes, picks and shovels,
new arrivals found the 3-mile ride by cart or dray into Melbourne
cost two shillings and sixpence for each passenger and one
shilling for every parcel. It cost more in 1852 to take goods from
the ship to the town than it did to bring them from England to
Australia.

In Melbourne, would-be diggers had ample opportunity to
witness and admire the success of men returned from the fields.
Newly enriched diggers, some with elaborately dressed female
companions, thronged the circuses and theatres which now
abounded. At the top of Bourke Street at the horse-market,
others gazed with a knowing air and a heavy horsewhip in their
hand at the four-footed goods there offered for sale. New chums
soon learnt to leap aside as many a successful digger, new to
equestrian arts, came rocketing out of the horse-yard and into the
street to gallop and rampage about in imitation of the fox-
hunting class.

In 1852 an indifferent riding hack sold for around £50 and a
strong cart-horse for twice that amount, so most new arrivals
joined the thousands tramping to the diggings on foot. During the
hot summer months they moved in a choking cloud of dust, and
were pestered by swarms of flies; in winter they struggled
through chilling rain and sank into mud tenacious enough to pull
the soles from their boots. Some of those coming from South
Australia travelled by sea to Geelong and there joined the
overseas emigrants on the road, but those without a fare travelled
in the tracks of the overlanders. C. F. Holland, a farmer turned
digger who was led on this long journey by 'a rough bushman',
recalled that his guide had little patience with men of more
fastidious taste. 'If his meat was fly-blown, [it] did not matter to
him, the maggot he declared tasted just as good as the meat and
was quite as nutricious.' Those who could afford conveyances

e not necessarily more comfortable. G. O. Preshaw, a medical ctitioner just arrived from Scotland and travelling from Melbourne to Ballarat in 1852, found himself and his medicine-chest tipped out of the horse-dray which sank into the very first rut it encountered in Elizabeth Street. Those travelling by coach and dray were also vulnerable to the sharp practices of entre-preneurs along the way. At the public houses which leapt up along the roads to tempt the tide of would-be capitalists washing past their doors, owners reaped an extra harvest by charging vehicles high prices to be heaved out of bog-holes or hauled across fords. In the frenzied rush to get to the diggings, sensibilities were further hardened by the sight of the struggling bullock-drays and carts, piled with shovels, sieves, cradles, iron buckets, picks, axes, pans, kettles, and iron pots, and forced forward only by the exertion and profanity of the drivers. It was not to be wondered at that 'every few hundred yards' the travellers came upon the carcasses of horses and bullocks, sacrificed to the entrepreneurial ideal.

Across this ancient land, from Ballarat and Beechworth to Braidwood and Kiandra, the diggers left a trail of destruction which exceeded that of the hard-hooved European animals who had preceded them. No patch of green offered comfort to the newcomer's eyes, surrounding stands of timber vanished early to provide bark-huts, shingles and firewood. New arrivals con-fronted a desert of pale clay and gravel heaps, littered with mud-bespattered tents, huts and awnings. Where once the gold-bearing rivers and creeks ran clear between banks protected by wattles, tea-trees and tussocks, now they were turned into rancid mud and stagnant puddles by the frenzied activities of the diggers. And everywhere the gold-seekers were removing the surface soil, sinking holes with pick, spade and crowbar; burrow-ing into the earth and dumping the heaps of mullock like excrement behind them; barrowing the wanted soil to be washed in what remained of the river, where every back was bent and every eye was fixed in a hard, single-minded scrutiny of cradle or dish.[13]

There were other lessons to be learned as well. New arrivals were taught to be secretive about any finds, for neighbours could not be trusted not to encroach; they learned to carry weapons to protect their persons and their property from assault; they learned of the need to 'shepherd' likely holes and how to 'jump' a fellow-worker's claim. They learned to mistrust storekeepers who, in purchasing gold either for cash or in exchange for goods, had developed numerous methods of cheating their customers, such as cultivating long fingernails to gather up extra portions of gold-dust from the unsuspecting new chums. Even children of the goldfields knew how to follow the wheelbarrow of a successful digger *en route* to the river, scraping up what was spilled and creating obstacles along the way to jolt the barrow and increase the spillage. Eventually the diggers learned to view everybody with distrust and watch even their friends closely. As Dr Preshaw noted, 'the mode and manner of all was "I care for nobody, no, not I, since nobody cares for me"'.

The acquisitiveness and suspicion of the Australian digger was increased by the smallness of the claims. The strip of ground to which an individual miner was allowed to lay claim was small by Californian standards. In New South Wales it was set at as little as fifteen feet of river frontage, or a twenty feet square on tablelands or river flats; in Victoria it could be as small as eight feet by eight, until in April 1853 the government introduced a uniform claim of twelve feet square. The result of this policy was to increase the size of the goldfields' population, and to encourage competition between miners forced to work cheek-by-jowl with neighbours who were just as likely to sink a shaft next door in anticipation of the direction of a lead. The smallness of the claims also encouraged rushes to new areas as soon as a field showed signs of being worked out. In April 1852 diggers dashing to the new find at Eaglehawk from Castlemaine, actually heaped themselves onto the favoured ground like ants on a mound in a frantic attempt to stake out a claim. 'Hundreds lay upon their backs, with outstretched arms, gripping perhaps a pistol in one hand, a sheath-knife in the other, and claiming to own at least all the ground they could encompass', an eye-witness reported.

By the time the newcomer had adopted the standard dress of the goldfields he had probably succumbed also to the frenzied cupidity and individualistic self-interest which this form of enterprise especially required. With cabbage-tree hat crushed down over a matt of hair, blue serge shirt belted over trousers stained with yellow mud, and pistols and knives thrust into the belt, the digger completed this aggressive appearance by having at his heels a ferocious dog.[14]

The diggers may have learned the economic and moral

principles of self-help, but they also learned to defy authority when it was seen as interfering with the white man's right to pursue his fortune in a free market-place. From the outset, the amount of money which the digger had to find in order to purchase his licence and begin his search for gold was seen as unduly high. This was so especially on the crowded Victorian goldfields where authoritarian police methods were adopted to enforce the licensing system and detect defaulters. The proposal to raise the monthly licence to £3 caused agitation on the Forest Creek field in December 1851. During 1852 there were complaints from Bendigo about the lack of police and the inefficiency of the Gold Commissioner who had been appointed to collect licence fees and to keep order and settle disputes on the fields. Then at the Ovens, where some 10 000 diggers were clustered in January 1853, the Assistant Commissioner's camp was stormed and smashed following an unpopular judgement over a disputed claim, during which one miner was shot by police. By 1853 miners at Bendigo were, as an American newspaper put it, in revolt against

the excessive gold licence tax, the insolence and cruelty of the Commissioner and the Police, and the insulting reception met with by a deputation sent to petition the Government for relief from a fellow named Latrobe, an ignorant, stupid, one-ideaed lump of arrogance, who exercises the function of Lieut. Governor of the Province.

Americans on the field and at home followed these developments with interest, some predicting that a republic was imminent, and then the United States would annex the country.

In reality the origins of the discontent of the diggers were more complex. The men were looking back to traditions of communal solidarity against oppression, but they had been so imbued with liberal political notions that they could believe that representation in the colonial legislature would be a solution to their problems. They had become workers without worker consciousness, and given that the Australian colonies were in the process of drafting new constitutions and lacked a hereditary ruling class, the diggers were the more easily seduced by the prospects of achieving apparently radical departures such as manhood suffrage and vote by ballot. They did not see that these concessions were the political equivalent of the decision to allow them to seek gold for themselves, a decision destined to steep them in individualistic acquisitiveness, and school them for democracy.

At Ballarat in December 1854 the ambiguity of the miners' demands became most apparent. The easily worked surface-gold was becoming exhausted, and the fear of wage labour for capital-intensive deep-mining companies haunted the miners' imagination. Already there were three steam-engines in use and a modified Chilean crushing machine under construction.

The diggers' first response to these problems was more characteristic of the colonial speculator than of a member of the working class. They became increasingly involved in displays of lawlessness and looting against each other. In October, following the release of three men brought before the Bench for the murder of a miner, an irate mob of diggers set fire to a hotel owned by J. F. Bentley, one of the three accused men. After systematically destroying it, the diggers dissolved into revelry and disorder, declaring that if Bentley could have been found they would have hanged him. Lynchings were rare but not unknown on the Victorian diggings, where in addition to one death by hanging and one man accidentally drowned while being ducked in a sack, public opinion favoured shooting thieves to kill. Other summary punishments included flogging, branding, and chaining of suspects to trees.[15]

The diggers' second response was to turn to liberal political ideals. On 11 November the inauguration of the Ballarat Reform League, demanding political representation, lent a more respectable political veneer to the diggers' fury at the arrest of three men for the burning of Bentley's hotel. After further harassment from the police, a group of some 500 diggers assembled in a stockade quickly erected at the top of Bakery Hill and swore allegiance to a flag similar to that designed by the middle-class Anti-Transportation League, though without the Union Jack. When put to the test, however, by a surprise raid of troopers called in for the occasion at dawn on Sunday 3 December, the digger army was routed in a skirmish which lasted only some fifteen or twenty minutes. Twenty-four diggers were killed and some 130 taken prisoner.[16]

In spite of this débâcle, the fracas at Eureka marked the end of political riots on the goldfields. This was partly because the alarmed Victorian Government hastened to redress the particular grievances of the diggers. A miner's right of £1 a year replaced the despised licences, and wardens replaced commissioners on the fields. The depoliticization of the diggers also came as their demands for political representation were overtaken by more general acceptance of democratic principles, for all the colonies chose to adjust their new constitutions to the same ideal. South Australia led the world in giving the vote to all white adult men in 1854; in New South Wales, the ageing Wentworth's plans for the crown to appoint selected land-holders to a title, and for these men and their male descendants to elect an Upper House, was effectively demolished by Daniel Deniehy. Would James Macarthur choose as his heraldic emblem a keg of rum? asked Deniehy. It was true that colonial specimens like Macarthur had, relatively speaking, 'antiquity of birth' but, said Deniehy, 'he would defy any naturalist properly to classify them'. Everyone knew that in this land of contrarities the common water-mole was transformed into the duck-billed platypus, but surely they were not going to be favoured by the same degenerate processes of evolution 'with a bunyip aristocracy'. In Victoria the goldfields were made part of electoral districts, and the possession of a miner's right automatically qualified a digger for voting in the new Legislative Assembly. Leader of the diggers at Eureka, Irish civil engineer Peter Lalor, further exemplified this process by which digger demands were satisfied by democratic concessions. After hiding for a season, Lalor reappeared in 1855 as first member of the Legislative Council for Ballarat and went on to become Speaker for the Victorian Legislative Assembly.[17]

Violence remained on the goldfields and was turned against outsider groups. In Victoria, reflecting that colony's concern with freedom from the alleged convict taint, it was not surprising that the first groups to be denied a share in the grab for gold were 'old hands' from across Bass Strait. 'It is confidently reckoned that above three thousand convicts have come over from Van Diemen's Land', grumbled 'An Australian Journalist' early in 1852, adding that this was 'to the great annoyance' of settlers in the new colony. At Ballarat in October 1854 James Bentley, the unlucky proprietor of the Eureka Hotel, and his wife were Van Diemen's Land ex-convicts, as was John Farrell, another of the trio accused of the murder which sparkled the trouble. Quarrels were numerous between the various national and regional groups

assembled on the goldfields. In one such battle at Ballarat, Ir___
diggers became involved in a fight against English, Scottish, and
American miners. However, one particular national group, the
Chinese, bore the brunt of the miners' bigotry both in New South
Wales and Victoria.[18]

Chinese labourers began to arrive in Australia in considerable
numbers from 1848, some 2500 being brought out as indentured
labourers in the period up to December 1851. Their mentors
were private British shopping agencies which, following the Treaty
of Nanking in 1842 and the forcible opening of Hong Kong and
five Chinese ports as new markets for British manufactured
goods, found a profit to be made in transporting Chinese workers
to labour-starved areas of the Empire. Chinese workers were
shipped to Mauritius from 1843, to Cuba from 1847, and to Peru
and Australia from 1848. After the discovery of gold, first in
California and then in the Australian colonies, broadsheets advertising the size and quality of the diggings were circulated by
shipping companies in Hong Kong and Canton. These proved
persuasive to a people whose economic and social life had been
irrevocably changed by the introduction of opium from India, the
importation of European commodities and the penetration of
Christian missionaries. Then, attempts to put down the peasant-
inspired Taiping Rebellion (1849—60) devastated the countryside
around Canton, causing widespread poverty and costing thousands
of lives. In the six months to June 1854, some 3000 Chinese
emigrants, mostly male, arrived in Melbourne. More than 25 000
had arrived by 1857.

Chinese entrepreneurs in Melbourne and China accelerated
the emigration process. Emigrants were offered passages out to
the diggings on credit, and agreed to work for the entrepreneurs
for one year to repay the debt, after that they would be free to
send their earnings to their families. Sponsors of the emigrants
usually chartered vessels from European shipping firms and
arranged the disembarkation and initial work of the bondees.
Met at the wharf by local representatives of the Chinese organization, the men were assigned straight to a predetermined
goldfield, though this did not necessarily protect them from the
attentions of local entrepreneurs—especially from 1855 when
Victoria imposed a poll-tax of £10 on each Chinese immigrant,
and forbade ships to carry more than one Chinese passenger for

every ten tons of the vessel's weight. The Chinese were thereafter landed at South Australian ports and left to travel overland to the Victorian fields.

Nor were the Chinese protected from the disputes which erupted constantly on the goldfields. Even before the most easily won deposits were exhausted, miners were encouraged to see the Chinese as, like exiles, cheap labour competition. In Bendigo in 1854 the press spoke of a 'worthless horde' of Asiatic 'intruders', alluding vaguely to 'disgusting practices, fearful immorality and unknown vices', warning that they were the forerunners of a countless population that would soon be arriving by the millions. Such statements invited the increasingly radicalized white labour-force to see its enemy as another worker, never the employer class. In March 1854 police had to be called in to protect Chinese landing at a Melbourne wharf. By 1857, with digger incomes declining and some of the Chinese beginning deep-mining, tradi-tionally reserved for Europeans, racial violence was endemic at Bendigo, Ballarat, on the Ovens fields, and especially at Ararat, a rich field discovered early in that year by a party of Chinese overlanding from South Australia. Here, in June a Chinese store was burnt down and Chinese miners stabbed, their tents pulled down and their mining implements destroyed. Even more violent was the treatment of the Chinese on the Buckland field in July 1857. Police Superintendent Robert O'Hara Burke (soon to perish in a mad attempt with William John Wills to be the first white man to cross the continent from south to north), merely petitioned for a check to be put on the number of Chinese already in the district, and for persons to be appointed 'to prevent them from annoying the diggers'.

Eviction of Chinese from the Victorian goldfields continued into the 1860s, by which time the Chinese were a depleted population, confined to working alluvial tracts already picked over by Europeans. In New South Wales, the most serious anti-Chinese rioting occurred in July 1861 at Lambing Flat, near Young, where 6000 armed diggers headed by a brass-band playing such lively airs as 'Cheer Boys, Cheer' and 'Rule Britannia', turned on the Chinese.[19]

Colonists who had made money during earlier phases of the exploitation of the continent's resources deplored the disorder and the threat of democracy brought by gold. Despite these fears, the existing pastoral ascendancy was further enriched by the rush. A rapidly rising local population increased the demand for mutton and beef, so that the boiling-down works of the depressed 'forties vanished from the land. 'Sheep have risen . . . from 7s. to 15s. and £1 per head,' visiting Quaker gentleman and penal theorist, William Howitt, reported in 1855, '. . . the squatting stations are now on an average, quadrupled in value'.

As a new means of colonization the gold rushes were acknowledged as an unprecedented success. That expert on imperialism, E. G. Wakefield, wrote in May 1852 that despite an initial tendency to *'Jacobinize'* the new society, gold would benefit it in the long run. For Britain the reality would be nothing short of superb, benefiting landlords and farmers and helping to promote economic expansion. British exports to the Australasian colonies quadrupled by 1857. Investment in mining companies to operate in the colonies was immediately stimulated, as were the shipping and ship-building industries. To the delight of the local advocates of immigration, the population of New South Wales grew from just under 200 000 in 1851 to over 350 000 a decade later. The population increase in Victoria during the decade was even more spectacular, rising from just under 100 000 to 540 000 in 1861.[20] These developments were seen by colonial liberals as both economically and morally beneficial. In 1852 Reverend John West's *History of Tasmania* dwelt at length on the horrors of the colony's past so as the better to contrast it with the future which he envisaged as prosperous, progressive and just. To West, all of the faults of the old Van Diemen's Land society had been caused by the convict system. Now, aided by education, the temperance movement and the Church, the old convict element would be re-educated or at least demographically submerged in a larger flood of industrious, ambitious, fortune-makers who would hopefully arrive to leave their mark on the land.

But it was not as simple as that. For one thing, the economic stimulus created by gold did not create permanent prosperity. Whereas in the United States most of the gold found was kept in that country, almost all the Australian gold was exported, mainly to Britain which, having experienced a shortage of coin, could now mint large quantities of it. The result was a boom in British commerce as capital became cheaper and the markets for manufactured goods expanded. Then, by 1855 Victoria and New South Wales were in the grip of a commercial crisis, as the initial stimulus given to the local housing and retail trade began to level out. In Victoria there had been fifty-two insolvencies in 1851–53, involving liabilities of some £2 116 000. There were more insolvencies in 1855 than in the period 1842–53.

Neither New South Wales nor Victoria could produce enough bread to feed its growing population and both colonies had to rely on large imports of grain. The immediate effects of the gold rush were disastrous for many local manufacturers who faced steep wage rises which made it impossible for them to compete with British imports. Indeed, by 1859, the only local industry which was flourishing was the building trade. In New South Wales, Byrnes's large cloth mill at Parramatta closed down for five years and the quantity of textiles produced in New South Wales fell dramatically.

These problems caused much hardship and poverty. Destitute diggers were in evidence as early as May 1851, and their population increased as the easily-won alluvial gold disappeared by the end of 1854. Though neither as dangerous nor unhealthy as conditions in the factories and mines of Britain, the goldfields exacted a toll in accidents and illnesses. Doctors on the diggings made fortunes as gold-seekers fell victim to dysentery and ophthalmia, gunshot wounds, stabs, and fractures. As one journalist wrote in 1852, the pestle and mortar was more reliable than the cradle as a gold-getting apparatus.[21] Health conditions in the government emigrant camps and in the expanding urban areas remained appalling. Melbourne's 'canvas town' was 'a hot-bed of disease and wretchedness', a doctor who arrived in 1853 reported. Passing the new cemetery at North Melbourne, he was told there had been thirty funerals that afternoon. 'One month ago I landed in this country with a wife and four healthy children', a mourner informed him. 'I go from this grave alone.' Similarly, at the gloomy Quarantine Station on North Head in Sydney, emigrants like Thomas Carr, arriving from Scotland in 1858, found that having survived the voyage they could still lose members of their family while confined in these comfortless wooden buildings, which had a hospital and adjacent burial ground conveniently provided.[22]

In the cities, poverty was compounded by the aftermath of the convict system. Only now, after some seventy years, were its harsh effects on labourers becoming fully visible: of over 150 000 convicts who had landed in the eastern colonies by 1852, many now lay, as John West remarked, in the unmarked graves to be found in every parochial cemetery. Others, along with old soldiers and marines, were conspicuous among the human ship-wrecks being steered in to the colonial Benevolent Asylums or left beached at the gates, often 'in a dying state'. Far from being a turning-point in Australian history it seemed that, with the gold rushes, history was repeating itself. The former attractions of wealth from maritime and pastoral capitalism had simply been eclipsed by the glittering prize of gold, the main difference being that this time the speculators were primarily labourers and artisans drawn from every corner of the globe, rather than British men of capital. Nor, despite the hopes of liberal idealists like West, were the Australian colonies to see the end of penal establishments. In Western Australia, convict labourers were arriving at a steady rate of shiploads a year and would continue to do so until the system became uneconomic—nearly 10 000 would have come by the time of the arrival of the last convict ship in 1868. Also during the 1850s, work was beginning on new gaols to house other labourers who failed to find wealth and satisfaction in the free society. In Fremantle, construction began in 1852 on a new penitentiary to re-educate and punish 882 men. In Victoria, extensions were in progress on Melbourne's Pentridge Gaol, and there were so many prisoners by the late 1850s that use had to be made of the old concept of accommodating men on hulks. These were moored off Williamstown and the prisoners sent to work on shore by day. It was here in March 1857 that convict justice finally caught up with John Price, hated Com-mandant of Norfolk Island from 1846–53. Now Inspector-General of Penal Establishments in Victoria, Price was battered to death by the men when he foolishly descended into their ranks to collect information for a parliamentary investigation into punish-ments and crime.[23]

In the new, free societies fashioned by gold there was no shortage of such enquiries. Throughout the 1850s a spate of local Select Committees appointed by the new legislatures looked into a huge range of social problems. In New South Wales in a mere two years, prominent parliamentarians and expert witnesses investigated juvenile vagrancy and delinquency, the adulteration of food, the problem of pawn-broking, intemperance, public health, city administration, immigration, Asian labour, education, the state of agriculture and, in 1859, the condition of the working class itself.

People who had ventured half-way round the world to make a better life for themselves and who had recently won political independence were particularly responsive to the latest scientific ideas about how to deal efficiently with human capital. Moreover, most of the colonies had begun as experiments in different forms of social engineering and the new, local ruling class was, therefore, not short of precedents for permitting a strong, interventionist role to be played by scientific and other theorists advising an ever-enlarging state. They had no qualms about instituting a scientific surveillance over the whole of the working class, seeking to detect and treat those who were suspected of being part of a defective, dangerous and expensive threat to the survival of the new nation and the British race. In New South Wales in 1854 a scheme for sweeping destitute boys off the Sydney wharves and onto a nautical school-ship seemed a natural and enlightened solution in a society which perceived itself as young and, therefore, as having a special right to shape its future citizens along lines which allegedly would eliminate the errors of the Old World. In a society where access to scientific circles was seen as a privilege and explorers had been turned into heroes, it was all too easy for reformers to speak of a need to 'explore the homes of the poor' in order to discover the underlying 'dense stratum' of moral and social problems of which, it was said, intoxication and police convictions were merely the 'outcropping'. An economy which continued to take men away from their homes and to stigmatize women who were without male pro-tectors guaranteed a continuing supply of raw material for such studies.[24]

Products of the industrial age, children of the Enlightenment, devoted to the ideal of progress, the colonial rulers considered that no experiment which benefited class, nation or race was too daring or too difficult to implement. While they congratulated themselves that the sight of men in clanking chains no longer disgraced their shores and blighted the minds of their children, they chose to ignore the less visible chains by which the new, free society was provided with an equally disciplined work-force. Everywhere there were new monuments to this ideal, many of them in the form of new, imposing Gothic and classical buildings constructed during this first golden decade: schools, Mechanics' Institutes, churches; theatres and sports grounds; universities, houses of parliament and banks; asylums, hospitals and gaols. The gibbet had been pushed out of sight and replaced with more subtle forms of punishment such as the strait-jacket and the solitary cell. Behind this hegemonic offensive, there was still the law and behind that, the use of terror, violence and force.

Nowhere did the savagery underlying the apparent beneficence of the bourgeois code more clearly show its hand than with respect to the Aboriginal people. In the north-east of the continent the new colony of Queensland, founded in 1859, was developing its own Native Police Corps to put down Aboriginal resistance across the vast areas now being annexed for pastoralism or gold. In the south, in 1858 a parliamentary committee in Victoria was moving towards passing the first of numerous 'protective' Acts. Copied by most colonies, these would apply a coercive science to G. A. Robinson's pioneering ideal of gathering up survivors of the violence and disease and concentrating them into camps, temporarily gazetted for the purpose. Here, parents and children, separated from each other, would be put through a compulsory course in conversion and the work ethic, until judged ready for assimilation into the labouring masses or, like the people on Flinders Island, they 'faded away'.[25]

Perhaps it was in the Pacific that change rather than continuity was most apparent. Norfolk Island, once a foothold of such crucial importance, had long since been denuded of its forests of gigantic trees, and was no longer of interest even as a laboratory for British penal science. In June 1856 its last convicts were evacuated to Hobart and, in a move underlining the island's association with the now anachronistic imperialism of the late eighteenth century, the island's buildings and farms, together with its goats, rats and birds, were handed over to the descendants of the Bounty mutineers, a little community of some 150 forgotten people who had outgrown the resources of Pitcairn Island where they had been living since 1790.

With the exception of New Zealand, the old maritime frontier now played only a tiny role compared with gold and wool. Nevertheless, missionary and merchant interest in the Pacific remained intense, for the focus of British imperialism was changing from the need to secure territory in the area to the need to maintain economic dominion in the face of increasing competition. The existing ideal of Free Trade would only be viable while there were still large amounts of territory to be divided between the western colonizing powers. As soon as they ran out of territory, they would revert to making wars for markets and the re-allocation of colonies. Stimulated by the gold discoveries in America and Australia and the restructuring of credit facilities and corporate organization, the expansion of capital around the globe would soon sweep the western economies into a new, monopólistic phase. The Pacific was destined to be one of the arenas where the competition for economic dominance would be most intense.[26]

Australian concern for military security and the control of markets was growing, especially following the outbreak of the Crimean War in 1854. Signalling the end of the long period of British withdrawal from European politics, the war brought local fears of Russian expansion southwards from their monasteries and commercial bases on the margins of the North Pacific or, even worse, an invasion of Australia's undefended coastline. Moreover, the French were again making their presence felt, beginning to extend their influence in North Africa and South-East Asia. In September 1842, to the alarm of prominent colonists like Windeyer and Lang, they annexed Tahiti. Some feared Tasmania would be next. In fact, however, it was in New Caledonia where the French at last achieved their ambition of copying the British blueprint for colonization in Oceania. In 1853 they landed a convict work-force, conveniently comprised of survivors of the workers' insurrection in Paris in 1848 and political opponents of Louis Napoleon's 1851 coup. They were far too late, for the new British method of free and 'systematic' emigration of labour and capital to self-governing democratic colonies was not only more economic but more politically stable. The Australian colonies would hold their position as the emporium for British commercial domination in the area until caught in the cross-fire of American and Japanese imperialism almost a century later. Some colonists used the French seizure of New Caledonia as an opportunity to call on Britain to annex Fiji, by way of compensation, pointing to its potential for large-scale cotton production and to the profits to be gained from initiating a new wave of Australian sub-imperialism in the Pacific.[27]

For the people upon whose land and labour these imperialistic and sub-imperialistic ambitions depended, it was not too late. As the Puritan theorists and later the *philosophes* had always known, no child was naturally a capitalist. Spiritual ties to community, to fellow human beings, to family and to the environment could be stronger than the pursuit of material gain and did not necessarily have to be channelled into destructive, nationalistic ideology, nor were softness, creativity and love necessarily gender-specific. The desire to accumulate material goods, to make war in the pursuit of fortune, to rape and to exploit, though potentially part of human nature were values which had to be instilled early and constantly reinforced. To change the future was going to require a courageous critique of the present and relentless reinterpretion of the past. And that, given the special grip of medical, social and political science at every level of cultural life, would be no easy task.

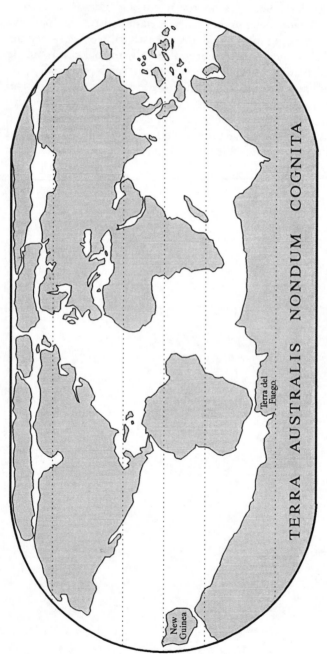

Abraham Ortelius, World Map, 1570 (NL)

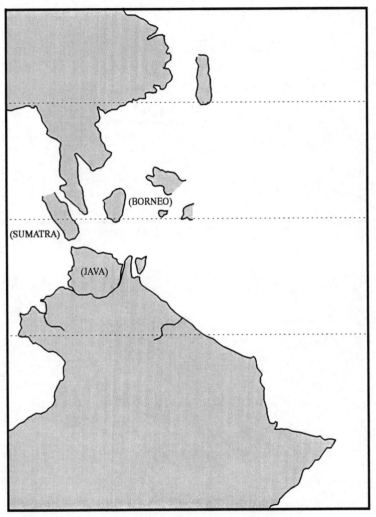

S. E. Asia and Java la Grande c.1555

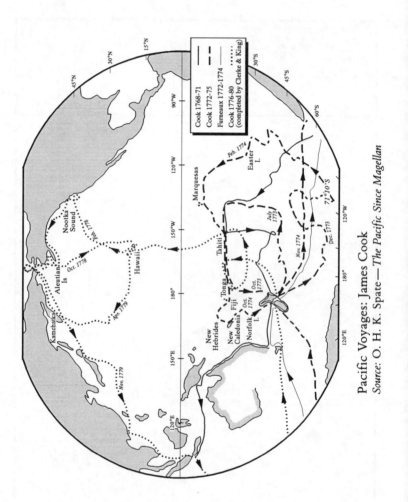

Pacific Voyages: James Cook
Source: O. H. K. Spate — *The Pacific Since Magellan*

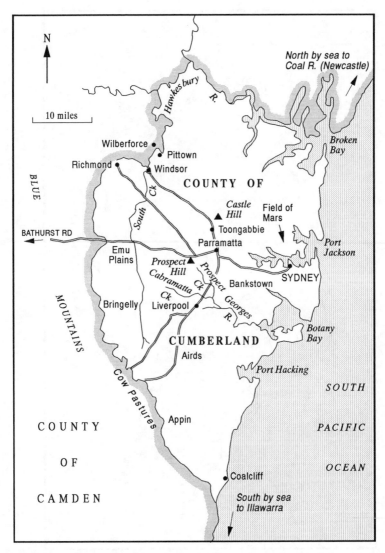

Location of British settlement in County of Cumberland up to 1821

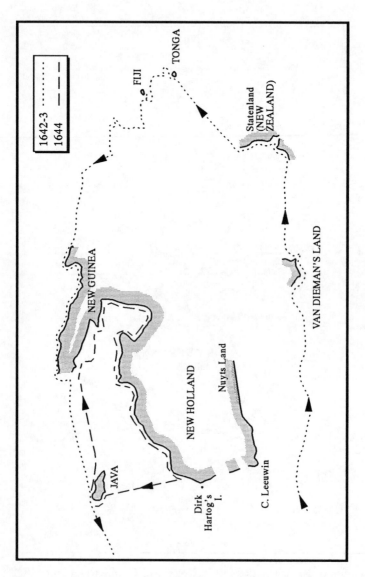

Tasman's Discoveries

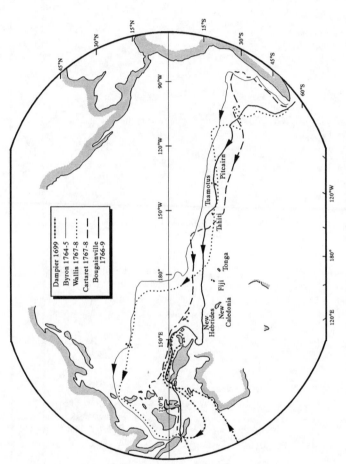

Pacific Voyages: Dampier to Bougainville
Source: O. H. K. Spate — *The Pacific Since Magellan*

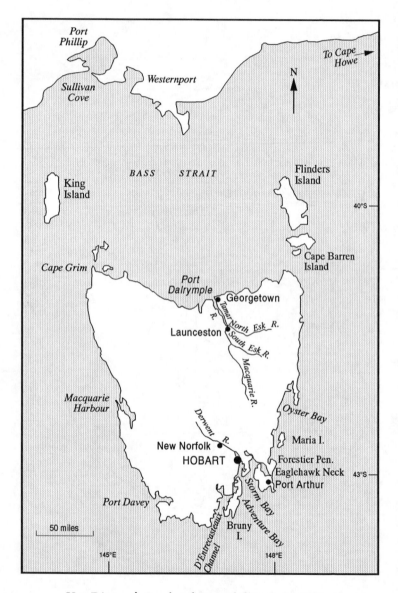

Van Diemen's Land and Port Phillip about 1821

NOTES

ABBREVIATIONS

ABC	Australian Broadcasting Corporation
AEHR	*Australian Economic History Review*
AGPS	Australian Government Publishing Service
AIAS	Australian Institute of Aboriginal Studies
AJPH	*Australian Journal of Politics and History*
ANU	Australian National University
ANUP	Australian National University Press
ANZJS	*Australian and New Zealand Journal of Sociology*
APSA	Australian Political Science Association
AQ	*Australian Quarterly*
CEDA	Committee for Economic Development of Australia
CLR	*Commonwealth Law Reports*
CPD	*Commonwealth Parliamentary Debates*
CPDHR	*Commonwealth Parliamentary Debates, House of Representatives*
CPDS	*Commonwealth Parliamentary Debates, Senate*
CSIRO	Commonwealth Scientific and Industrial Research Organization
CUP	Cambridge University Press
ER	*Economic Record*
FACP	Fremantle Arts Centre Press
HS	*Historical Studies* (earlier *Historical Studies, Australia and New Zealand*; from 1988 *Australian Historical Studies*)
JAS	*Journal of Australian Studies*
LH	*Labour History*
MUP	Melbourne University Press
NLA	National Library of Australia
NSWUP	New South Wales University Press
OUP	Oxford University Press
Proc. Royal Aust. Chem. Inst.	Proceedings of the Royal Australian Chemical Institute

SUP	Sydney University Press
UNSW	University of New South Wales
UQP	University of Queensland Press
UWAP	University of Western Australia Press
VHM	*Victorian Historical Magazine*

CHAPTER 1: BLUEPRINT FOR GROWTH

1   Cited in J. Mackinolty and H. Radi (eds), *In Pursuit of Justice: Australian Women and the Law 1788–1979*, Hale & Iremonger, Sydney, 1979, n.p. For convenience, the spelling here is modernized. All other quotations from Clark's journal retain original spelling and are taken from *The Journal and Letters of Lieut. Ralph Clark*, edited by P. G. Fidlon and R. J. Ryan, Australian Documents Library, Sydney, 1981.

2   *HRNSW*, I, ii, pp. 449–50.

3   *HRNSW*, I, ii, p. 429, II, p. 553.

4   Other opinions about the reasons for the settlement are discussed in Note 18 below.

5   *Journal of Arthur Bowes Smyth, Surgeon, Lady Penrhyn 1787–1789*, edited by P. G. Fidlon and R. J. Ryan, Australian Documents Library, Sydney 1979, p. 48.

6   Because most historians had uncritically accepted the officials' obsession with the convict women's sexuality, much early revisionist literature was particularly concerned to analyze this issue. (See Anne Summers, *Damned Whores and God's Police: The Colonization of Women in Australia*, Penguin, Ringwood, 1975; Miriam Dixson, *The Real Matilda: Women and Identity in Australia 1788–1975*, Penguin, Ringwood, 1976; Katrina Alford, *Production or Reproduction: An Economic History of Women in Australia 1788–1850*, OUP, Melbourne, 1984; Portia Robinson, *The Hatch and Brood of Time: A Study of the First Generation of Native-Born White Australians 1788–1828*, OUP, Melbourne, 1985. While providing a much needed critique, this approach caused them to share the view that the women's sexuality was the problem, not that of the male officials. They were also drawn into assuming that it is possible and necessary to categorize the women according to whether they were madonnas or magdalenes. M. Sturma, '"Eye of the Beholder": The Stereotype of the Women Convicts, 1788–1852' *Labour History*, No. 34 (May 1978) is a useful analysis of the class assumptions which informed male views of the convict women but tends to assume that the dislocation of working-class family life during industrialization was a 'cultural' experience, a 'revolution in eroticism', rather than the occasion of increased sexual vulnerability and exploitation of women. Though the need to work against the sexist assumptions in historiography has not abated (Kay Daniels, 'Feminism and Social History', *Australian Feminist Studies*, I, Summer 1985), the limitation of this debate to the morals of convict women has obscured the need for analysis of other issues, for instance, the variations between the experiences of women of different colour and class. See Note 24 below. For a recent overview of the literature on convict women, see Deborah Oxley, 'Female Convicts' in S. Nicholas (ed.), *Convict Workers*, CUP, Cambridge, 1988, pp. 85–97. For a mariner's view of the relationships formed between women convicts and the crew on the *Lady Juliana*, see *The Life and Adventures of John Nicol, Mariner*, Blackwood, Edinburgh, 1822, reprinted in R. J. Ryan (ed.), *The Second Fleet Convicts*, Australian Documents Library, Sydney, 1982, pp. 81–9.

7   A. T. Yarwood, *Samuel Marsden*, MUP, Melbourne, Carlton, 1977, p. 31.

8   For the fracturing of families, despite the appeals of women, see Portia Robinson, *The Women of Botany Bay*, Macquarie Library, Sydney, 1988, pp. 21–2. It became customary to remove all females sentenced to transportation aged under 45 years. See Report from the Select Committee on Transportation 1812 *BPP* (II, No. 341), (Irish Series—Crime and Punishment—Transportation, Vol. 1), p. 10.

9   For the practice of using soldiers as pioneer settlers in French and Spanish colonies as well as British ones, see B. H. Fletcher, *Landed Enterprise in Penal Society*, SUP, Sydney, 1976, p. 13. For the number of children on the First Fleet, see J. F. Cleverley, *The First Generation: School and Society in Early Australia*, SUP, Sydney, 1971, p. 7. Cf. Portia Robinson, *The Hatch and Brood of Time*, p. 23. As in most studies, child population figures should be taken as a guide only, owing to imprecise definition of the age of children in musters, victualling lists and other sources. In general I use 'child' to mean persons aged 14 or under. For the number of child convicts, see C. Bateson, *The Convict Ships*, Library of Australian History, Sydney, 1983, p. 79, which estimates over 1000 for the period 1812–17, but these figures include people aged 15 to 21 years.

10   Report from the Select Committee on Transportation 1812, p. 109; *Journal of Arthur Bowes Smyth*, p. 45.

11   M. Dobb, *Studies in the Development of Capitalism*, RKP, London, 1978, pp. 175–6; E. J. Hobsbawm, *Industry and Empire*, Penguin, Ringwood, 1981, pp. 26, 31–2; B. Fitzpatrick, *British Imperialism and Australia*, SUP, Sydney, 1971, pp. 30–1.

12   Alan Frost, *Arthur Phillip 1738–1814: His Voyaging*, OUP, Melbourne, 1987, pp. 37–42.

13   E. J. Hobsbawm, pp. 25, 27, 68–73; E. P. Thompson, *The Making of the English Working Class*, Penguin, Ringwood, 1981, pp. 237–43; M. Dobb, pp. 222–75; E. O'Brien, *The Foundation of Australia*, Angus & Robertson, Sydney, 1950, pp. 17–46; E. J. Evans, *The Forging of the Modern State: Early Industrial Britain*, Longman, New York, 1983, pp. 404–9.

14   M. Dobb, pp. 230–1, 281, 294; E. J. Hobsbawm, pp. 24, 28–9.

15   E. J. Hobsbawm, pp. 30–2, 62–3; M. Dobb, pp. 277–8.

16   D. Hay (ed.), *Albion's Fatal Tree: Crime and Society in Eighteenth-Century England*, Allen Lane, London, 1975, *passim*; E. P. Thompson, *Whigs and Hunters: The Origin of the Black Act*, Allen Lane, London, 1975, pp. 1–23.

17   A. G. L. Shaw, *Convicts and the Colonies*, Faber & Faber, London, 1966, pp. 23–4, 28–9, 31–3.

18   Some historians believe the hulks crisis was the sole reason, rather than the immediate catalyst, for the decision to found a penal settlement in New South Wales. Others argue that the need for a strategic base and/or access to supplies of timber and flax ('naval stores') was more important. The main arguments in this debate are reprinted in Ged Martin (ed.), *The Founding of Australia: The Argument About Australia's Origins*, Hale & Iremonger, Sydney, 1978. More recent contributions include M. Gillen, 'The Botany Bay Decision, 1786: Convicts, not Empire', *English Historical Review*, Vol. 97 (October 1982); A Frost, 'Botany Bay: An Imperial Venture of the 1780s', *English Historical Review*, Vol. 100 (April 1985), and *Convicts and Empire: A Naval Question*, OUP, Melbourne, 1980; M. Steven, *Trade, Tactics and Territory*, MUP, Melbourne, 1983; David Mackay, *A Place of Exile: The European Settlement of New South Wales*, OUP, Melbourne, 1985; G. J. Abbott, 'The Botany Bay Decision', *Journal of Australian Studies*, 16 (May 1985); R. J. King, 'Ports of Shelter and Refreshment . . .: Botany Bay and Norfolk Island in British Naval Strategy, 1786–1808', *HS*, Vol. 22, 87

(October 1986); O. H. K. Spate, *Paradise Found and Lost*, ANU Press, Canberra, 1988, pp. 300–6. While uncovering important information on late eighteenth-century British politics and society, this debate has become notable for a narrow empiricism and futile discussion of the respectability of minute scraps of evidence. Also, like the debate about the morals of the convicts, it obscures other issues. Arguably, analysis is better served by seeing the two apparently discrete issues of 'convicts' and 'empire' as fundamentally the same. That is, the problem of overcrowding in the gaols and hulks following the cessation of transportation to America was primarily an economic issue derived from consciously formulated policies towards the creation of a labour pool and the protection of private property. Thus the creation of criminality and its punishment was a product of the same processes of capital expansion which made strategic bases and naval stores of such crucial importance to British investors in the 1780s. See further Chapter 2, Note 7.

19   For the concept that private ownership of property was a 'law of nature' and 'liberty' was what the law allowed, see C. B. Macpherson, *The Political Theory of Possessive Individualism Hobbes to Locke*, Clarendon Press, Oxford, 1962. For John Locke, see Carole Pateman *The Sexual Contract*, Polity Press, Cambridge, 1988, pp. 50–3. For the Panopticon, R. V. Jackson, 'Luxury in Punishment: Jeremy Bentham on the Cost of the Convict Colony in New South Wales', *HS*, Vol. 23, 90 (April 1988); L. J. Hume, 'Bentham's Panopticon: An Administrative History', *HS*, Vol. 15, 61 (October 1973), Vol. 16, 62 (April 1974); D. Melossi and M. Pavarini, *The Prison and the Factory: The Origins of the Penitentiary System*, Barnes & Noble, London, 1981, pp. 31, 35, 40–1; J. Hirst, *Convict Society and its Origins*, Allen and Unwin, Sydney, 1983, pp. 9–15; M. Foucault, *Discipline and Punish: The Birth of the Prison*, Pantheon, New York, 1977, pp. 7–25, 200–21. For the traditional 'houses of correction', M. Ignatieff, *A Just Measure of Pain: The Penitentiary in the Industrial Revolution 1750–1850*, Macmillan, London, 1978, pp. 11–14.

20   For the politics of the arguments for birth control, D. E. C. Eversley, *Social Theories of Fertility and the Malthusian Debate*, OUP, Oxford, 1959, pp. 5, 29, 58–61, 125–7, 144, 209. For Bentham's views, Peter Fryer, *The Birth Controllers*, Secker & Warburg, London, 1965, pp. 31–6. For the child savers, William Langer, 'Infanticide; A Historical Survey', *Journal of Psychohistory*, Vol. I (1973–74). For the removal of parish children to the factories, E. O'Brien, pp. 27–8. For the participation of well-to-do women, F. K. Prochaska, *Women and Philanthropy in Nineteenth-Century England*, Clarendon Press, Oxford, 1980.

21   T. R. Malthus, *An Essay on the Principle of Population*, London, 1798, reprinted in E. A. Wrigley and David Souden (eds), *The Works of Thomas Robert Malthus*, London, 1986, Vol. I, p. 18.

22   For analysis of socio-economic differences between women in Britain, see Bridget Hill, *Eighteenth Century Women: An Anthology*, Allen & Unwin, London, 1984. The special problems of Aboriginal women are discussed below, esp. in Chapter 2, Note 32.

23   T. R. Malthus, pp. 20–1, 39–40; R. Porter, 'Mixed Feelings: The Enlightenment and Sexuality in Eighteenth-Century Britain' in P. Bouce (ed.), *Sexuality in Eighteenth-Century Britain*, Manchester University Press, Manchester, 1982, pp. 6, 18; Arthur N. Gilbert, 'Buggery and the British Navy, 1700–1861', *Journal of Social History*, Vol. 10, (1976); poem 'Botany Bay' reprinted in R. Ward and John Robertson (eds), *Such Was Life: Select Documents in Australian Social History*, Vol. I (1788–1850), Alternative Publishing Co., Sydney, 1978, pp. 13–4. Cf. M. Foucault, *The History of*

Sexuality, Vol. I, Vintage Books, New York, 1980, which describes but does not explain the growth of published opinion on these topics at this time. The attempts to define 'normal' sexuality remain part of a mysterious and allegedly liberating 'will to know'.

24 Bridget Hill, pp. 25–8; Portia Robinson, *The Women of Botany Bay*, pp. 51–60; Annette Salt, *These Outcast Women: The Parramatta Female Factory 1821–1848*, Hale & Iremonger, Sydney, 1984, pp. 17–31; Kay Daniels (ed.), *So Much Hard Work: Women and Prostitution in Australian History*, Fontana, Sydney, 1984, pp. 2–4, 22, 24–9. For eighteenth-century pornography, Ian Gibson, *The English Vice: Beating, Sex and Shame in Victorian England and After*, Duckworth, London, 1979, pp. 194–6; R. Porter, pp. 8–9. Cf. R. Hyam, 'Empire and Sexual Opportunity'. *Journal of Imperial and Commonwealth History*, Vol. 14, 2 (January 1986) which, though demonstrating the extent of sexual exploitation of subordinate women, both in Britain and overseas, assumes that white male promiscuity was so 'healthy' that it somehow benefitted those whom it abused. It was even 'good' for race relations (p. 75).

25 *HRNSW*, I, ii, pp. 14–20; B. H. Fletcher, p. 12.

26 *HRNSW*, I, ii, pp. 52–3.

27 *Journal of Arthur Bowes Smyth*, pp. 67, 70; W. Tench, *Sydney's First Four Years*, edited by L. F. Fitzhardinge, Angus & Robertson, Sydney, 1979, pp. xv, 39.

28 *Journal and Letters of Lieut. Ralph Clark*, pp. 96, 159.

29 D. Collins, *An Account of the English Colony in New South Wales*, edited by B. H. Fletcher, Reed, Sydney, 1975, I, pp. 66, 549; *Journal and Letters of Lieut. Ralph Clark*, p. 206.

30 D. Collins, I, pp. 346–7, 363.

31 This description of events in early NSW is drawn from *HRA*, I, i; D. Collins; W. Tench; John Cobley, *Sydney Cove 1788–1790*, Angus & Robertson, Sydney, 1963; *HRNSW*, II, pp. 561–3.

32 D. Collins, I, pp. 83–4, 94–5. For eye-witness accounts of the wreck of the *Sirius*, see *Journal and Letters of Lieut. Ralph Clark*, pp. 121–4; William Bradley, *A Voyage to New South Wales 1786–1792*, Ure Smith, Sydney, 1969, pp. 193–7; *HRNSW*, I, ii, pp. 381–2 (Lieut. Fowell). For the ensuing despair, *HRNSW*, I, ii, pp. 332–3 (Surgeon White).

33 'Marsden Family Letters to Mrs Stokes 1794–1824', ML MSS 719 (6 September 1799); *HRNSW*, I, ii, p. 184; see also, II, p. 747; D. Collins, pp. 69, 89, 96–7, 170, 552n.

34 W. Tench, p. 71; *Journal and Letters of Lieut. Ralph Clark*, pp. 137, 170; *HRNSW*, III, p. 749; C. M. H. Clark, *Select Documents in Australian History*, Angus & Robertson, Sydney, 1958, I, p. 406; D. Collins, I, p. 605n; R. J. Ryan, *Land Grants 1788–1809*, Australian Documents Library, Sydney, 1974, pp. 67, 81.

35 *HRA*, I, ii, pp. 454–64; M. Perrot, *A Tolerable Good Success: Economic Opportunities for Women in New South Wales 1788–1830*, Hale & Iremonger, Sydney, 1983, p. 26, 106; *Journal and Letters of Lieut. Ralph Clark*, p. 98; D. Collins, I, pp. 39, 70.

36 *The Voyage of Governor Phillip to Botany Bay*, edited by J. J. Auchmuty, Angus & Robertson, Sydney, 1970, p. 35; 'Journal and Letters of Daniel Southwell', *HRNSW*, II, p. 665; D. Collins, I, p. 14; C. H. Currey, 'The Law of Marriage and Divorce in New South Wales (1788–1888)', *JRAHS*, Vol. 41, Pt. 3 (1955).

37 D. Collins, I, pp. 244, 519n; M. Perrot, p. 42; Portia Robinson, *The Hatch and Brood of Time*, p. 69; *Journal and Letters of Lieut. Ralph Clark*, p. xvii.

38 D. Collins, I, pp. 244, 580n. Cf. Robert Hughes, *The Fatal Shore*, Collins,

London, 1987, p. 73; Report from Select Committee on Transportation 1812, *BPP*, p. 46.

39 *Journal of Arthur Bowes Smyth*, p. 72; D. Collins, I, pp. 607n, 332, 406; C. H. Currey, *The Transportation, Escape and Pardoning of Mary Bryant*, Angus & Robertson, Sydney, 1983; *HRNSW*, III, p. 392ff.

40 *HRNSW*, II, p. 747; III, p. 160; Report from the Select Committee on the State of the Gaols 1819, *BPP* (VII, No. 579), (Irish Series—Crime and Punishment—Prisons, Vol. I), pp. 29, 37; W. Tench, p. 251.

41 D. Collins, I, pp. 405, 607n; II, p. 87; Report from Select Committee on Transportation 1812, *BPP*, pp. 32–3, 35.

42 *HRNSW*, III, pp. 182, 508, 686; Report from Select Committee on Transportation 1812, *BPP*, p. 33; Alison Alexander, *Governors' Ladies: The Wives and Mistresses of Van Diemen's Land Governors*, Tasmanian Historical Research Association, Hobart, 1987, p. 19; *Journal and Letters of Lieut. Ralph Clark*, p. xvii, xviii.

43 These figures are based on *HRNSW*, III, p. 749; V, p. 679. See also, B. Gandevia, *Tears Often Shed: Child Health and Welfare in Australia From 1788*, Pergamon, Sydney, 1978, p. 32.

44 For instance, of the 221 women on board the *Friendship* in 1787, all were aged between 15 and 39 and more than half between 20 and 24 (*Journal and Letters of Lieut. Ralph Clark*, p. 35). Analysis of some 20000 convicts transported to NSW for the period 1817–40 shows 75 per cent of the women were aged between 16 and 35 (S. Nicholas *Convict Workers* (ed.), p. 205). See also, L. L. Robson, *The Convict Settlers of Australia*, MUP, Melbourne, 1965, p. 187.

45 B. Gandevia, pp. 34–7, 82–9; C. H. Currey, *Mary Bryant*, pp. 35–6.

46 *HRNSW*, III, p. 749; *HRA*, I, ii, p. 24; *HRNSW*, VI, p. 382; see also, Report from Select Committee on Transportation 1812, *BPP*, p. 40; *HRNSW*, VI, p. 151.

47 *HRA*, I, ii, p. 24.

48 The history of child-rearing practices now has a large literature. This summary is based on P. Aries, *Centuries of Childhood*, Penguin, Harmondsworth, 1973; L. Stone, *The Family, Sex and Marriage in England 1500–1800*, Weidenfield & Nicolson, London, 1977; L. De Mause, *The History of Childhood*, Psychohistory Press, New York, 1974; P. Laslett, *Household and Family in Past Time*, CUP, Cambridge, 1972 and *Family Life and Illicit Love in Earlier Generations*, CUP, Cambridge, 1977; G. Rattray Taylor, *The Angel Makers*, Heinemann, London, 1973. For the influence of non-conformist physicians in the construction of child sexuality, see Chapter 10 especially Note 26.

49 J. F. Cleverley, pp. 10–11, 88–92; *HRNSW*, III, p. 184; *HRNSW*, II, pp. 517–18; D. Collins, I, p. lxi, 45; *HRNSW*, III, p. 160. In addition to King's Orphan School on Norfolk Island, two day-schools were established there by 1796. In Sydney there were three day-schools in operation by the end of December 1797. (*HRNSW*, III, p. 1; D. Collins, II, p. 51.) See also, B. Gandevia, p. 52–7; J. Ramsland, *Children of the Backlanes: Destitute and Neglected Children in Colonial New South Wales*, NSWUP, Kensington, 1986, pp. 84–5.

50 *HRA*, I, iii, p. 123, 425; 'Marsden Family Letters to Mrs. Stokes', (22 August 1810); M. Bassett, *The Governor's Lady: Mrs. Philip Gidley King*, OUP, Melbourne, 1956, pp. 84–5.

51 Report from Select Committee on Transportation 1812, *BPP*, pp. 20, 25; *HRNSW*, I, ii, p. 437; T. A. Coghlan, *Labour and Industry in Australia*, OUP, Oxford, 1918, I, p. 129; M. Perrot, p. 33; *HRA*, I, iii, p. 433.

52 *HRA*, I, v, p. 12; *HRNSW*, VI, p. 151.

CHAPTER 2: THIRTY ACRES

1 W. Tench, *Sydney's First Four Years*, edited by L. F. Fitzhardinge, Angus & Robertson, Sydney, 1979, p. 256.
2 *HRA*, I, i, pp. 14–45.
3 Robin Hallett, *Africa to 1875*, University of Michigan Press, Ann Arbor, 1970, p. 183; J. D. Fage, *A History of Africa*, CUP, Cambridge, pp. 259, 263, 327.
4 For the revival of Christian evangelism in Britain and its link to industrialization and anti-slavery, see Eric Williams, *Capitalism and Slavery*, André Deutsch, London, 1964. For Governor Phillip's aversion to slavery in the 'free' colony of New South Wales, *HRNSW*, I, ii, p. 53. For Sierra Leone, K. E. Knorr, *British Colonial Theories 1570–1850*, Cassell, London, 1963, pp. 376–81.
5 For the need of manufacturers to curb the power of the East India Company see V. Harlow, *The Founding of the Second British Empire 1763–1793*, Longman, London, 1952, Vol. I, p. 67; M. Dobb, *Studies in the Development of Capitalism*, Routledge & Kegan Paul, London, 1978, pp. 166–7, 219–20; K. E. Knorr, pp. 246–50. For a contemporary view that this was part of the intention of the new Pacific settlement, G. Mackaness (ed.), *Alexander Dalrymple's 'A Serious Admonition to the Public on the Intended Thief Colony at Botany Bay'*, (1st edn 1786), Sydney, 1943, pp. 21–2. See also G. Martin (ed.), *The Founding of Australia*, Hale & Iremonger, Sydney, 1978, *passim*; M. Steven, *Trades, Tactics and Territory*, MUP, Carlton, 1983, pp. 82–3; A Frost, *Convicts and Empire: A Naval Question*, OUP, Melbourne, 1980, pp. 185–95. Despite the initial suspicion of the new penal colony by spokesmen for the manufacturers like Bentham, as early as 1789 others were celebrating the role which it might play in buying up 'northern treasures', planting civilization in the wilderness and turning convicts into useful citizens. See J. Auchmuty (ed.), *The Voyage of Governor Phillip to Botany Bay*, (1st edn 1798), Angus & Robertson, Sydney, 1970, especially pp. xxi, xxiii, 3, 347n.
6 K. E. Knorr, pp. 4–23, 81–94, 155–60; M. Dobb, p. 199. For the interrelationship between trade, empire and naval power in mercantilist theory and practice, see also Glyndwr Williams, *The Expansion of Europe in the Eighteenth Century*, Blandford Press, London, 1968, pp. 32–4. For shipbuilding materials, John D. Harbron, 'The Spanish Ship of the Line', *Scientific American* (December 1984), p. 127.
7 I draw here on information from the debate between historians on whether the reasons for the colony's foundation were 'penal' or 'commercial' and/or 'strategic'. As in Chapter 1, however, I argue that these factors were not mutually exclusive, but had a common economic basis in the policies being evolved in Britain to rationalize labour and protect investments at home and abroad during the take-off to industrialization. I also suggest that this present-day debate about the respectability of our 'criminal' versus 'commercial' origins has tended to obscure what was really at issue during the 1770s and '80s, namely the need to find new methods of and justifications for colonization, based around the changing needs of an expanding industrial middle class. For a summary of the main sources in the 'foundation debate', see Chapter 1 Note 18.
8 *ADB*, II, pp. 404–5 (Ruse).
9 D. Collins, *An Account of the English Colony in New South Wales*, edited by B. H. Fletcher, Reed, Sydney, 1975, I, p. 141; *HRA*, I, i, pp. 279–82; A. G. L. Shaw, *Convicts and the Colonies*, Faber & Faber, London, 1966, p. 69.
10 *HRA*, I, i, pp. 279–82; D. Collins, pp. 209, 585n.
11 *HRNSW*, I, ii, p. 7.

12 *HRNSW*, I, ii, pp. 355, 387. See also, C. Bateson, *The Convict Ships*, Library of Australian History, Sydney, 1983, pp. 128–31.

13 *HRNSW*, I, ii, p. 538; *HRA*, I, i, pp. 199–200, 203; I, ii, pp. 531, 554, 702–4; R. J. Ryan (ed.), *The Third Fleet Convicts*, Horwitz Grahame, Sydney, 1983, pp. xi–xiii. However, estimates of the number who died vary. See E. O'Brien, *The Foundation of Australia*, Angus & Robertson, 1950, pp. 284–6. See also C. Bateson, pp. 131–71; Robert Hughes, *The Fatal Shore*, Collins, London, 1987, pp. 144–51.

14 D. Collins, I, p. 331; II, p. 100; *Journal and Letters of Lieut. Ralph Clark*, pp. 131, 171, 199–200.

15 D. Collins, I, pp. 60, 280, 367; II, p. 280n; *HRA*, I, ii, pp. 75–6; J. Hirst, *Convict Society and its Enemies*, Allen and Unwin, Sydney, 1983, pp. 36–7; K. Buckley, 'Primary Accumulation: The Genesis of Australian Capitalism' in E. L. Wheelwright and K. Buckley (eds), *Essays in the Political Economy of Australian Capitalism*, ANZ Book Company, Sydney, 1975, p. 27.

16 D. Collins, I, pp. 205, 267, 327; A. G. L. Shaw, p. 75.

17 Report from the Select Committee on Transportation 1812, *BPP* (Irish series—Crime and Punishment—Transportation— Vol. I), p. 47; *HRNSW*, VI, p. 47; A. G. L. Shaw, 'Labour', in G. J. Abbott and N. B. Nairn (eds), *The Economic Growth of Australia 1788–1821*, MUP, Melbourne, 1978, p. 113.

18 *HRA*, I, i, pp. 212–13, 325–6; D. Collins, I, pp. 84–5, 551n, 115, 327, 375, 603n; *ADB*, I, p. 122.

19 D. Collins, I, pp. 274, 287, 399.

20 D. Collins, I, pp. 22, 68; *HRNSW*, I, ii, p. 645; *Journal and Letters of Lieut. Ralph Clark*, p. 68.

21 James Walvin, *Black and White: The Negro and English Society 1555–1945*, Penguin, Harmondsworth, 1973, Ch. 4; G. Williams ' "Savages Noble and Ignoble": European Attitudes Towards the Wider World Before 1800', *Journal of Imperial and Commonwealth History*, VI, iii (May 1978), pp. 309–11; Ian Duffield, 'From Slave Colonies to Penal Colonies: The West Indian Convict Transportees to Australia', *Slavery and Abolition*, Vol. 7, 1 (May 1986); 'Martin Beck and Afro-Blacks in Colonial Australia', *Journal of Australian Studies* (May 1985), p. 10; D. Collins, pp. 58, 76, 80. For the transportation of Africans from the Cape to the Australian colonies, 1828–38, see Leslie C. Duly, ' "Hottentots to Hobart and Sydney": The Cape Supreme Court's Use of Transportation, 1828–38', *AJPH*, Vol. 25, 1 (April 1979).

22 *HRNSW*, I, ii, pp. 487–8; III, p. 240ff; *Journal and Letters of Lieut. Ralph Clark*, pp. 169, 173–5, 211, 218; D. Collins, I, p. 354; *HRNSW*, II, p. 565.

23 Peter Lineburgh, 'The Tyburn Riot Against the Surgeons' in D. Hay (ed.) *Albion's Fatal Tree*, Allen Lane, London, 1975, p. 79ff; D. Collins, I, pp. 252, 329, 448.

24 A. G. L. Shaw, *Convicts and the Colonies*, pp. 141–2; D. Collins, I, pp. 112, 226, 356–7, 360, 384.

25 *HRNSW*, II, pp. 561–4; D. Collins, I, pp. 217, 573, 357–8; II, pp. 100, 146; *HRA*, I, ii, pp. 20, 354–5, 480–1.

26 B. H. Fletcher, *Landed Enterprise in Penal Society*, SUP, Sydney, 1971, pp. 11, 64; B. H. Fletcher, 'Agriculture', in G. J. Abbott and N. B. Nairn (eds), p. 199; *HRA*, I, i, pp. 35, 316, 365, 758–9; S. J. Butlin, *Foundations of the Australian Monetary System 1788–1851*, SUP, Sydney, 1968, pp. 4–5, 12–50; K. Buckley and T. Wheelwright, *No Paradise for Workers*, OUP, Melbourne, 1988, pp. 42–4.

27 *HRA*, I, ii, pp. 114, 136–40, 445–6; A. G. L. Shaw, *Convicts and the Colonies*, p. 66; M. J. E. Steven, 'Enterprise', in G. J. Abbott, and N. B. Nairn (eds),

pp. 121–2; G. J. Abbott, 'Economic Growth' in ibid., pp. 141–3, 160; B. Fitzpatrick, *British Imperialism and Australia 1783–1833*, SUP, Sydney, 1971, pp. 92–122; K. Buckley, 'Primary Accumulation', pp. 20–1.

28 *HRA*, I, ii, pp. 140–6; D. Collins, I, pp. 7, 219, 226–7, 274, 401, 606n; Report from Select Committee on Transportation 1812, *BPP* (II, No. 341), p. 43.

29 D. Collins, I, pp. 12, 13, 19, 539n, 28–9, 457; George B. Worgan, *Journal of a First Fleet Surgeon*, Library Council of New South Wales, Sydney, 1978, pp. 20–2; *Journal and Letters of Lieut. Ralph Clark*, pp. 98–9; *HRNSW*, II, p. 509. See also, Keith Willey, *When the Sky Fell Down: The Destruction of the Tribes of the Sydney Region*, Collins, Sydney, 1979.

30 D. Collins, I, pp. 18, 34–5, 47, 110–11; W. Tench, pp. 178–80; William Bradley, *A Voyage to New South Wales*, Ure Smith, Sydney, 1969, pp. 228–9. Cf. David Denholm's *The Colonial Australians*, Penguin, Ringwood, 1979, pp. 32–4 which, by over-emphasizing the ineffectiveness of European firearms, inadvertently implies that the Aborigines' failure to arrest the invasion was somehow their own fault.

31 N. G. Butlin, *Our Original Aggression*, Allen and Unwin, Sydney, 1983, pp. 12, 15, 22; 'Macassans and Aboriginal Small-Pox: The "1789" and "1829" Epidemics', *HS*, Vol. 21, 84 (April 1985), pp. 332–5; Patrick O'Brien, *Joseph Banks: A Life*, Collins, London, 1987, pp. 170, 181; William Bradley, p. 162. The question of how smallpox came to decimate Aboriginal society has long interested medical historians, who used to address the possibility that the 1789 epidemic, if not later ones, was introduced by the British, though possibly by accident rather than design (e.g. J. H. Cumpston, *The History of Small-Pox in Australia 1788–1908*, Government Printer, Melbourne, 1914, p. 2). More recently, with the exception of Butlin's work, the trend has been to excuse the destructive effects of European disease as an agent of colonization by suggesting that the Aboriginal people, through their traditional 'trading links' with Macassan fishermen, would have been exposed to smallpox anyway (see Judy Campbell, 'Smallpox in Aboriginal Australia 1829–31', *HS*, Vol. 20, 81 (October 1983) and 'Smallpox in Aboriginal Australia: The Early 1830s', *HS*, Vol. 21, 84 (April 1985). Alternatively, some historians now use doubtful judgements about pre-invasion culture to suggest that, though European diseases were a major factor in Aboriginal depopulation, alleged inter-tribal violence, 'sorcery', infanticide and mental predisposition towards alcoholism and despair were just as lethal (see B. Nance, 'The Level of Violence: Europeans and Aborigines in Port Phillip, 1835–1850', *HS*, Vol. 19, 77 (October 1981). In both cases, the effect is to obscure European responsibility for Aboriginal deaths.

32 W. Tench, pp. 223–37, 291; 'Journal of Lieut. King', *HRNSW*, II, p. 542; George Worgan, p. 47; D. Collins, I, pp. 464, 495–6. Cf. Ann McGrath, 'The White Man's Looking Glass; Aboriginal-Colonial Gender Relations at Port Jackson', *HS*, Vol. 24, 95 (October 1990). The officials' view that Aboriginal society was inherently violent and its women cruelly treated is shared by some historians who, believing that patriarchy is timeless and universal, point to reports of abduction, punishment and rape by Aboriginal men at other times and in other places in Australia to support this claim. However, these reports must be used with caution for, apart from their ideological function, none of them pre-dates the presence of Europeans. They therefore tell us less about pre-invasion life than about white values during the process of its destruction. See further Bobbie Sykes, 'Black Women in Australia — A History' in J. Mercer (ed.), *The Other Half Women*

in Australian Society, Penguin, Ringwood, 1983; Pat O'Shane, 'Is there any Relevance in the Woman's Movement for Aboriginal Women?', *Refractory Girl*, 12 (1976); Maureen Watson, 'First I am Black, Secondly a Woman', Socialist Feminist Conference. *Bulletin*, 1 (1987).

33　This account of the three Aboriginal captives is based on *HRNSW*, I, ii, p. 377; *ADB*, I, pp. 22, 84–5, 234; Keith Wiley; and the numerous references to them in Collins and Tench.

34　J. H. Cleverley, *The First Generation*, pp. 102–4; J. J. Fletcher, *Documents in the History of Aboriginal Education in New South Wales*, Sydney, 1989, pp. 19–26; and *Clean, Clad and Courteous: A History of Aboriginal Education in New South Wales*, Sydney, 1989, pp. 13–19; Rev. Samuel Marsden's Report to Archdeacon Scott on the Aborigines of NSW (1826) reprinted in N. Gunson (ed.), *Australian Reminiscences and Papers of L. E. Threlkeld*, Australian Institute of Aboriginal Studies, Canberra, 1974, pp. 347–8; A. T. Yarwood, *Samuel Marsden*, MUP, Carlton, 1977, pp. 112–13; George Caley, *Reflections on the Colony of New South Wales*, edited by J. E. B. Currey, Lansdowne, Melbourne, 1966, pp. 140–1, 171–2, 174, 177; *SG*, 28 September , 12 October, and 2 November 1816. The original information and depositions regarding prosecution of Moowattie for rape cannot be located (see Peter G. McGonigal, 'The Role of Law in the Foundation and Settlement of the Colony of N.S.W. Prior to 1828, in Relation to Aboriginal Inhabitants', LL.M. thesis, University of Sydney, 1975). Richard Partridge was convicted of theft and arrived on the *Scarborough* to serve a life sentence in 1788. In September 1794 he was one of eight convicts pardoned on condition of serving in the NSW Corps. In 1828 he was one of the few emancipists still farming (D. Collins, I, pp. 327, 591n).

35　W. Tench, pp. 209–15; J. F. Cleverley, p. 105.

36　D. Collins, I, pp. 326, 341, 346, 348. By March 1795, 77 per cent of Europeans at the Hawkesbury were convicts, emancipists or expirees (*HRA*, I, i, pp. 492–3).

37　*HRNSW*, II, p. 307; D. Collins, I, pp. 348–9; *HRA*, I, v, p. 503.

38　*HRNSW*, III, p. 207, 309; *HRA*, I, iii, p. 466; D. Collins, I, pp. 356–7; II, pp. 12–13.

39　Information on Wilson and Knight is drawn from *HRA*, I, ii, p. 79; *ADB*, II, pp. 610–11; and from D. Collins. For John Caesar, see Collins.

40　D. Collins, II, pp. 20, 24; *HRA*, I, iii, pp. 331, 466, 582–3, 800; Keith Willey, p. 164; *HRNSW*, IV, p. 784; see also Eric Willmot, *Pemulwuy The Rainbow Warrior*, Weldons, Sydney, 1987.

41　Keith Willey, pp. 168–70, 180. Willey believes that after his arrest Mosquito was transported to Norfolk Island and, following the closure of the penal settlement there, to Van Diemen's Land where he arrived about 1813 (ibid. p. 180–2). Here, aided by local Aboriginal people, he is thought to have resumed resistance activities until tracked down and hanged in Hobart on 24 February 1825. See also Christine Wise, 'Black Rebel', in E. Fry (ed.), *Rebels and Radicals*, Allen and Unwin, Sydney, 1983, pp. 1–7; G. Mackaness, *Lags and Legions*, Angus & Robertson, Sydney, 1944, pp. 113–15. Certainly the resistance led by a Sydney Aboriginal man of this name in Van Diemen's Land is well documented. See Mary Edwards (ed.), *The Diary of the Rev. Robert Knopwood 1803–1838*, Tasmanian Historical Research Association, Hobart, 1977, p. 429; H. Melville, *The History of Van Diemen's Land*, edited by G. Mackaness, D. S. Ford, Sydney, 1959, I, p. 26; C. Turnbull, *Black War*, Sun Books, Melbourne, 1974, p. 62; Lyndall Ryan, *The Aboriginal Tasmanians*, UQP, St Lucia, 1981, pp. 79, 87–8, 101. However, according to the *Sydney Gazette*, Mosquito was killed by the relatives of a man whom he had killed in a ritual battle outside the military barracks in January 1806, see *SG*, 12 January, 19 January, 2 February, and 23 March 1806. The belief that he was transported to Norfolk Island and Van Diemen's Land appears to be based on Samuel Marsden's testimony, see 'Reverend Samuel Marsden's Report to Archdeacon Scott . . .' (1826) in N. Gunson (ed.), p. 348.

42 George Rudé, *Protest and Punishment*, Clarendon Press, Oxford, 1978, pp. 9, 37, 91–3, 182–3; Thomas Pakenham, *The Year of Liberty: The Story of the Great Irish Rebellion of 1798*, Hodder & Stoughton, London, 1969; E. P. Thompson, *The Making of the English Working Class*, Penguin, Harmondsworth, 1968, pp. 183–8; J. Waldersee, 'Father James Dixon and the Wexford Rising', *Journal of Religious History*, Vol. 6, 1 (June 1970); D. Collins, II, p. 77. According to Collins, the authorities noted 'a new spirit of resistance' among the convicts recently arrived from England and Ireland as early as December 1791 (I, p. 160).

43 *HRA*, I, ii, pp. 575–83, 595–6, 636–9, 642–51; D. Collins, II, p. 216; A. T. Yarwood, p. 79.

44 *HRNSW*, IV, pp. 122–3, 266–7, 309, 325; H. McQueen, 'Convicts and Rebels', *Labour History*, 15 (November 1968), p. 14; *HRA*, I, iii, pp. 9, 15, 260, 586–7.

45 *HRNSW*, V, pp. 58, 74–5; R. Connell, 'The Convict Rebellion of 1804', *Melbourne Historical Journal*, Vol. 5 (1965), pp. 27–37; *HRA*, I, iv, pp. 564, 568, 619; A. T. Yarwood, p. 97; H. McQueen, p. 26.

CHAPTER 3: HUNTERS AND COLLECTORS

1 *HRNSW*, III, pp. 382–3; M. Flinders, *A Voyage to Terra Australis . . .*, G. & W. Nichol, London, 1814, reprinted Libraries Board of South Australia, Adelaide, 1966, I, p. lxvii, 8–9.

2 F. Horner, *The French Reconnaissance: Baudin in Australia 1801–1803*, MUP, Melbourne, 1987, Ch. 2–4; L. R. Marchant, *France Australe: A Study of French Explorations and Attempts to Found a Penal Colony and Strategic Base in South Western Australia 1503–1826*, Artlook, Perth, 1982, pp. 51–66, 101–83; M. Flinders, I, p. 6.

3 J. M. Ward, 'British Policy in the Exploration of the South Pacific, 1699–1793', *JRAHS*, Vol. 33 (1947), pp. 25–49; Paul Hazard, *European Thought in the Eighteenth Century*, Penguin, Harmondsworth, 1965, pp. 145–60; M. Foucault, *The Order of Things: An Archaeology of the Human Sciences*, Tavistock, London, 1970, p. 125. Cf. R. MacLeod, 'On Visiting the "Moving Metropolis": Reflections on the Architecture of Imperial Science', *Historical Records of Australian Science*, Vol. 5, 3 (1982), pp. 1–8; David Mackay, *In the Wake of Cook: Exploration, Science and Empire 1780–1801*, Victoria University Press, Croom Helm, Wellington, London, 1985.

4 T. M. Perry, *The Discovery of Australia*, Nelson, Sydney, 1982, pp. 78–85; M. Flinders, pp. lxix–lxx, xcvii–ciii, cviff; *HRNSW*, III, pp. 312ff, 363, 474; *ADB*, I, pp. 71–3 (Baudin), 177–8 (Flinders); John Bach, *A Maritime History of Australia*, Nelson, Melbourne, 1976, p. 40; M. Flinders, *Trim*, Collins, Sydney, 1977.

5 J. D. Bernal, *Science in History*, Watt, London, 1957, pp. 334–44; O. H. K. Spate, *The Pacific Since Magellan: III. Paradise Found and Lost*, ANUP, Canberra, 1988, pp. 55–64, 70–7; K. R. Howe, *Where the Waves Fall: A New South Sea Islands History*, Allen & Unwin, Sydney, 1984, pp. 69–70; G. Williams and A. Frost (eds), *Terra Australis to Australia*, OUP, Melbourne,

1988; K. G. McIntyre, *The Secret Discovery of Australia: Portuguese Ventures 200 Years before Captain Cook*, Souvenir Press, Adelaide, 1977.

6 K. R. Howe, pp. 71–8; O. H. K. Spate, *The Pacific Since Magellan: I. The Spanish Lake*, ANUP, Canberra, 1979; J. C. Beaglehole, *The Exploration of the Pacific*, Black, London, 1966.

7 G. M. Badger (ed.), *Captain Cook: Navigator and Scientist*, ANUP, Canberra, 1970, p. 52 (dead reckoning); C. M. H. Clark, *A History of Australia*, MUP, Carlton, 1962, I, Ch. 1–2; T. M. Perry, Ch. 1–3; G. Williams and A. Frost, Ch. 3; O. H. K. Spate, *The Pacific Since Magellan: II. Monopolists and Freebooters*, ANUP, Canberra, 1983, Ch. 1.

8 *The Voyage of Governor Phillip to Botany Bay*, edited by J. J. Auchmuty, Angus & Robertson, Sydney, 1970, pp. 288–93; Abel Janszoon Tasman, *Journal of Discovery of Van Diemen's Land and New Zealand in 1642*, reprinted in C. M. H. Clark, *Sources of Australian History*, OUP, London, 1957, pp. 5–24; O. H. K. Spate, *Monopolists and Freebooters*, pp. 43–51; G. Williams and A. Frost, p. 103. See also Günter Schilder, *Australia Unveiled: The Share of Dutch Navigators in the Discovery of Australia*, Theatrum Orbis Terrarum, Amsterdam, 1976; Günter Schilder (ed.), *Voyage to the Great South Land: Willem de Vlamingh 1696–1697*, Royal Australian Historical Society, Sydney, 1985.

9 For more information on the advent of British mercantilist imperialism, see O. H. K. Spate, *Monopolists and Freebooters*, especially pp. 30–6, 131–59, 253–68; Vincent Harlow, *The Founding of the Second British Empire 1763–1793*, I, Longman, London, 1952, pp. 12–22.

10 B. Smith, *European Vision in the South Pacific 1768–1850*, Clarendon Press, Oxford, 1960, pp. 8–9; W. Dampier, *A New Voyage Round the World*, 4th edn, Knapton, London, 1699, I, p. 462–7, reprinted in C. M. H. Clark, *Sources*, pp. 24–7; *A Voyage of Governor Phillip to Botany Bay*, pp. 294–301. See also R. White, *Inventing Australia: Images and Identity 1688–1980*, Allen & Unwin, Sydney, 1981, pp. 2–4; Leslie R. Marchant, *An Island Unto Itself: William Dampier and New Holland*, Hesperian, Carlisle, 1988.

11 G. M. Badger (ed.), pp. 7–8, 35, 53–60; O. H. K. Spate, *Paradise Found and Lost*, pp. 65–8; E. P. Thompson, 'Time, Work-Discipline and Industrial Capitalism', *Past and Present*, 38 (1967).

12 G. M. Badger, pp. 43–4; A. Frost, *Arthur Phillip 1738–1814: His Voyaging*, OUP, Melbourne, 1987, pp. 28–9; O. H. K. Spate, *Paradise Found and Lost*, pp. 191–4.

13 T. M. Perry, pp. 11–13, 58, 60–3; M. Stevens, *Trade, Tactics and Territory*, MUP, Melbourne, 1983, pp. 16–28; L. R. Marchant, *France Australe*, pp. 3–44; O. H. K. Spate, *Paradise Found and Lost*, pp. 55, 86–98. See also John Dunmore, *French Explorers in the Pacific*, Clarendon Press, Oxford, 1965.

14 O. H. K. Spate, *Paradise Found and Lost*, pp. 79, 81; G. Mackaness (ed.), *Alexander Dalrymple's 'A Serious Admonition to the Public on the Proposed Thief Colony at Botany Bay'*, G. Mackaness, Sydney, 1943, pp. 4–14; G. Williams and A. Frost, pp. 72–3; Alexander Dalrymple, *An Account of the Discoveries made in the South Pacifick Ocean, previous to 1764*, London, 1767, reprinted in C. M. H. Clark, *Sources*, pp. 28–34; G. M. Badger (ed.), pp. 8, 118–35; J. C. Beaglehole, *The Life of Captain James Cook*, Adam & Charles Black, London, 1974, Ch. 3–5.

15 A. Mozley Moyal (ed.), *Scientists in Nineteenth-Century Australia: A Documentary History*, Cassell, Melbourne, 1976, p. 37; G. M. Badger (ed.), pp. 38–41; J. C. Beaglehole (ed.), *The Journals of Captain James Cook on his Voyages of Discovery* (3 vols), Cambridge, 1955, 1961, 1967, I, pp. 84, 86, 97–8; J. C. Beaglehole (ed.), *The Endeavour Journal of Joseph Banks 1768–1771*

(2 vols), Angus & Robertson, Sydney, 1962, I, p. 258; II, pp. 330–4. For the use of firearms by Wallis and its effect on Tahitian attitudes to trade, see Colin Newbury, *Tahiti Nui: Change and Survival in French Polynesia 1767–1845*, University of Hawaii Press, Honolulu, 1980, pp. 5–6. Fort Venus was armed with two guns and six swivels (O. H. K. Spate, *Paradise Found and Lost*, p. 223).

16 *The Journals of Captain James Cook*, I, pp. 93–4, 98–9, 122–37; *HRNSW*, I, i, pp. 390–2; G. M. Badger (ed.), pp. 45–8.

17 *The Journals of Captain James Cook*, I, p. 387–90.

18 Captain Cook to Secretary Stephens, 22 March 1775, *HRNSW*, I, i, p. 378; *The Journals of Captain James Cook*, II, pp. 239, 567, 643.

19 The Spaniards, in fact, attempted to negotiate a treaty and establish a mission at Tahiti. See M. Steven, p. 20; O. H. K. Spate, *Paradise Found and Lost*, pp. 116–26; Vincent Harlow, pp. 48–55.

20 *The Journals of Captain James Cook*, III, pp. 101, 228–31, 529–39; *HRNSW*, I, i, pp. 415, 460–1, 468; G. M. Badger (ed.), pp. 22–3. For a critique of the literature on Cook as hero, O. H. K. Spate, *ibid.*, pp. 127–49.

21 Banks to Robert Brown, 8 April 1803, reprinted in A. Mozley Moyal (ed.), p. 25; *The Endeavour Journal of Sir Joseph Banks*, I, pp. 254, 351–2; II, pp. 52–60, 89, 91, 125; S. Parkinson, *Journal of a Voyage to the South Seas in H. M. S. Endeavour*, Caliban Books, London, 1984, pp. 15, 148–52.

22 *ADB*, I, pp. 52–5 (Banks); B. Smith, pp. 78–82.

23 *HRNSW*, I, ii, pp. 269–73, 695; T. M. Perry, pp. 76–7. See also William Bligh, *A Voyage to the South Sea*, London, 1792, reprinted by Libraries Board of South Australia, Adelaide, 1969; Gavin Kennedy, *Bligh*, Duckworth, London, 1978, and *Captain Bligh: The Man and His Mutinies*, Duckworth, London, 1988; G. Mackaness, *The Life of Vice-Admiral William Bligh*, Angus & Robertson, Sydney, 1951. For the longboat journey, see J. Bach (ed.), *The Bligh Notebook*, National Library of Australia, Canberra, 1986.

24 John Hunter cited in B. Smith, p. 125; George Caley, *Reflections on the Colony of New South Wales*, edited by J. E. B. Currey, Lansdowne, Melbourne, 1966, *passim*; A. Mozley Moyal, pp. 39–40; A. Moyal, *A Bright and Savage Land*, Collins, Sydney, 1986, pp. 22–4.

25 For Locke's theory that the American Indian people were the most 'primitive', and widespread use of ethnographic material relating to them, see Ronald Meek, *Social Science and the Ignoble Savage*, CUP, Cambridge, 1976, pp. 37–67, 119, 127–8; for early denigration of African people, M. F. Christie, *Aborigines in Colonial Victoria 1835–1886*, SUP, Sydney, 1979, pp. 31–4; for Dampier, *A New Voyage Round the World*, and *A Voyage to New Holland, etc. in the year 1699*, in *A Collection of Voyages in Four Volumes*, James Knapton, London, 1703, I, p. 468; III, pp. 100–1 (shooting).

26 For Linnaeus, see John S. Haller, 'Concepts of Race Inferiority in Nineteenth-Century Anthropoloy' *Journal of the History of Medicine*, (January 1970) pp. 41–1. Cf. A. O. Lovejoy's, *The Great Chain of Being: A Study of the History of an Idea*, Harvard University Press, Cambridge, Mass., 1957, pp. 231–7. Lovejoy provides much evidence of Great Chain imagery still used in some eighteenth-century scientific and creative writing. Arguably, however, this was less the 'fruition' of Great Chain theory than the revival of a now anachronistic concept by conservative writers, drawn to the reactionary implications of Romantic theory. For Adam Smith's frank avowal that the 'commercial' stage of development required an extremely unequal distribution of wealth and therefore new methods to protect property from the attacks of the dispossessed, see Ronald Meek, p. 123.

27 B. Smith, pp. 24–5; K. R. Howe, pp. 85–6; G. Williams '"Savages Noble

and Ignoble": European Attitudes to the Wider World Before 1800', *Journal of Imperial and Commonwealth History*, VI, iii (May 1978); E. J. Hobsbawm, *The Age of Revolution*, Weidenfield & Nicolson, London, 1962. Cf. O. H. K. Spate, *Paradise Found and Lost*, pp. 245–52; Alan Moorehead, *The Fatal Impact*, Penguin, Harmondsworth, 1985, Ch. 3.

28   B. Smith, pp. 65, 84–94, 107; *The Endeavour Journal of Sir Joseph Banks*, I, p. 227; II, p. 124. Curiously, having provided much evidence of how evolutionary science conflicted with the idea of the noble savage, Smith insists that, with the decline of Deism, changing Christian thought was primarily responsible for the new image of Pacific people as ignoble and depraved (p. 7). Arguably, when related to the socio-economic position of their makers, both scientific and missionary ideas can be traced to a common source in the increasing needs of industrialists for labour at home and territory overseas. That is, the tensions between scientific and missionary views of Pacific people were primarily about method, not aim, for they were conflicting ideologies of the same world view.

29   Lyndall Ryan, *The Aboriginal Tasmanians*, pp. 49–50; D. J. Mulvaney, 'The Australian Aborigines 1606–1929', *Historical Studies Selected Articles*, MUP, Melbourne, 1974, p. 13; J. M. R. Owens, 'New Zealand Before Annexation' in W. H. Oliver (ed.), *Oxford History of New Zealand*, OUP, Wellington, 1981, p. 30; L. R. Marchant, pp. 45–9.

30   B. Smith, pp. 100–3; W. Tench, *Sydney's First Four Years*, pp. 33–4; *ADB*, II, pp. 85–6 (La Pérouse). At Petropavlosk La Pérouse had received new instructions to check on reported British activities at Botany Bay and in France some rumours blamed the British for his disappearance (O. H. K. Spate, *Paradise Found and Lost*, p. 159). The mystery was unsolved until 1828 when trader Peter Dillon established that La Pérouse had been shipwrecked north of Vanuatu and some of the party put to death. See P. Dillon, *Narrative and Successful Result of A Voyage in the South Seas*, (2 vols.), Hurst, Chance & Co, London 1829.

31   B. Smith, pp. 70, 74, 110, 112; J. J. H. de Labillardière, *An Account of a Voyage in Search of La Pérouse*, Stockdale, London, 1800, pp. 302–13, 325. Cf. Lyndall Ryan, pp. 52–7. Arguably, however, the paintings of Piron, official artist for the voyage, avoided the caricature and grotesque exaggeration of facial features which were to characterize the work of artists on the Baudin voyage.

32   G. W. Stocking, 'French Anthropology in 1800', *Isis*, Vol. 55 (1964), pp. 134–43; F. Horner, especially pp. 205–6; G. W. Stocking, *Victorian Anthropology*, Macmillan, London, 1987, p. 26. For Pemulwuy, *HRNSW*, IV, p. 784. Cf. C. Wallace, *The Lost Australia of François Péron*, London, 1984; D. J. Mulvaney, pp. 13–14, who tend to assume that the Baudin party's artwork and 'experiments' were truly 'scientific' and therefore commendable. Paradoxically, others commend the French observers in general for being less 'scientific', more in touch with the ideology of the noble savage, and therefore especially 'humane' and 'imaginative' (Lyndall Ryan, pp. 49–65 and 'Reading Aboriginal Histories', *Meanjin* Vol. 45, 1 (1986), p. 53; G. Dutton, *White on Black: The Australian Aborigine Portrayed in Art*, Macmillan, Melbourne, 1974, pp. 22–4). Because the *Investigator* carried no ethnologist, Flinders's findings have attracted less attention but, foreshadowing the coming predominance of medical practitioners in physical anthropology, he arranged for the surgeon to conduct the required quantitative research. See, for example, M. Flinders, I, p. 68.

33   For earlier manifestations of the belief that a chauvinistic male virility and removal of women from production were central to a nation's achieving a

high rate of reproduction and therefore attaining the highest 'commercial'
stage of development, see Ronald Meek, p. 159 (Kames); p. 166 (Millar).
For Dumont D'Urville, see G. Dutton, p. 30.
34 *The Diary of Elihu Hubbard Smith (1771–1798)*, edited by James E. Cronin,
Amercian Philosophical Society, Philadelphia, 1973, p. 47 (October 1795).
I am indebted to Shane White for this reference.

CHAPTER 4: FREE TRADE

1   *HRNSW*, V, p. 313.
2   Report from the Select Committee on Transportation 1812, *BPP*, (Irish
Series—Crime and Punishment—Transportation), Vol. I, p. 65; M. Steven,
'Exports Other Than Wool' in G. J. Abbott and N. B. Nairn (eds), *The
Economic Growth of Australia*, MUP, Melbourne, pp. 287–91; M. Steven,
Trade, Tactics and Territory, MUP, Melbourne, pp. 85–6.
3   M. Steven, *Trade, Tactics and Territory*, pp. 64–81; C. Hartley Grattan, *The
United States and the Southwest Pacific*, Harvard University Press, Cambridge,
Mass., 1961, pp. 72–4, 78; O. H. K. Spate, *Paradise Found and Lost*, ANU
Press, Canberra, 1988, pp. 264–6, 294; *HRNSW*, V, pp. 379, 384, 387, 513;
HRA, III, i, p. 40. For the wreck of the *Sydney Cove*, see D. Collins, *An
Account of the English Colony in New South Wales*, edited by B. H. Fletcher,
Reed, Sydney, 1975, II, pp. 52, 56, 249n. For Bass Strait shipping, John
Bach, *A Maritime History of Australia*, pp. 125, 130.
4   *HRA*, I, iii, pp. 697, 737; M. Bassett, *The Governor's Lady: Mrs Philip Gidley
King*, OUP, Melbourne, 1956, p. 89.
5   *HRA*, III, i, pp. 1–8, 17, 783n. See also L. Robson, *A History of Tasmania*,
Vol. I, OUP, Melbourne, 1983, pp. 35–41, 537–44 (list of convicts in
Collins's party).
6   J. Earnshaw, 'Select Letters of James Grove, Convict . . .', *PTHRA*, Vol. 8
(1959), p. 33; *HRA*, III, i, p. 35; *ADB*, I, pp. 174–5 (Buckley).
7   *HRA*, III, i, pp. 196, 804n; L. Robson, pp. 33–5, 41–2.
8   *HRA*, I, iv, p. 304; *HRA*, III, i, p. 830n.
9   *HRA*, III, i, p. 761.
10 Report from Select Committee on Transportation 1812, *BPP*, pp. 78–9;
HRNSW, VII, pp. 359–61.
11 This description of the early settlement is based on *HRA*, III, i.
12 *HRA*, III, i, pp. 251, 286, 328; J. Earnshaw, p. 33.
13 D. Collins, II, pp. 121–2; *HRA*, III, i, pp. 242–3, 607, 649–50; C. Turnbull,
Black War, Cheshire-Lansdowne, Melbourne, 1965, pp. 31–2; Lyndall Ryan,
The Aboriginal Tasmanians, UQP, St Lucia, 1982, pp. 75–7.
14 *ADB*, II, pp. 379–81.
15 *HRA*, III, i, pp. 303, 308, 352–3, 403–4; *HRA*, I, vii, p. 129 (Bligh); W. G.
Rimmer, 'The Economic Growth of Van Diemen's Land 1803–1821' in
G. J. Abbott and N. B. Nairn (eds), pp. 331–48; S. J. Butlin, *Foundations of
the Australian Monetary System*, SUP, Sydney, 1968, pp. 33, 42–5, 52–3;
L. Robson, pp. 68, 71–5.
16 *HRA*, III, ii, p. 594; *ADB*, I, pp. 157–8 (Broughton).
17 M. Steven, 'Exports Other than Wool' in G. J. Abbott and N. B. Nairn
(eds), pp. 287–300; *HRA*, III, i, p. 329; N. J. B. Plomley, *Friendly Mission:
The Tasmanian Journals and Papers of George Augustus Robinson*, Tasmanian
Historical Research Association, Hobart, 1966, pp. 295–6; *HRNSW*, V, pp.
688–9; O. H. K. Spate, pp. 284–7. See also D. R. Hainsworth, *The Sydney
Traders*, Cassell, Melbourne, 1971, pp. 128–46; M. Steven, *Trade, Tactics and
Territory*, Ch. 5.

18 *HRA*, III, ii, pp. 575–6, 709; N. J. B. Plomley, pp. 297, 1017–21. Cf. Lyndall Ryan, p. 69. James Kelly, born at Parramatta in 1791 and engaged in sealing from 1812, left an especially rosy picture of the allegedly amicable relations between sealers and Aboriginal women on the north-east coast of Van Diemen's Land in January 1816. By then, Kelly was a master mariner investing in sealing on his own account and had no reason to be critical of the industry ('Boat Expeditions round Tasmania 1815–16 and 1824' in Tasmanian Legislative Council *Journal*, Vol. XXXI, 75, (1881) pp. 4–15. The comforting illusion that oppressed people were not 'victims' has proved extremely popular in academic accounts. It now animates but arguably distorts the experience of colonized people ranging from American slaves and Canadian Indians to Australian Aboriginal people including the native police. See, for example, E. Genovese, *Roll, Jordan, Roll: The World the Slaves Made*, Random House, New York, 1972; G. Friesen, *The Canadian Prairies: A History*, University of Toronto Press, Toronto, 1984; H. Reynolds, *The Other Side of the Frontier*, James Cook University, Townsville, 1981, M. Fels, *Good Men and True: The Aboriginal Police of the Port Phillip District 1837–1853*, MUP, Melbourne, 1988. For a critique of 'agency' in Aboriginal historiography, see Bain Attwood, 'Understandings of the Aboriginal Past: History or Myth', *AJPH*, Vol. 34, 2 (1988), especially pp. 266, 268. For the impact of the Canadian fur trade from the early 1600s, see Bruce G. Trigger, *Natives and Newcomers*, McGill-Queens University Press, Montreal, 1985, p. 203ff.

19 G. Blainey, *The Tyranny of Distance*, Sun Books, Melbourne, 1966, pp. 99–101, 105–9; M. Steven, 'Exports Other Than Wool', in G. J. Abbott and N. B. Nairn (eds), pp. 287–99; *HRNSW*, V, pp. 407–9, 554. For the impact of bay whaling stations on the Maori people, J. M. R. Owens, 'New Zealand Before Annexation', in W. H. Oliver (ed.), *Oxford History of New Zealand*, OUP, Wellington, 1981, p. 33; H. Morton, *The Whale's Wake*, University of Hawaii Press, Honolulu, 1982.

20 Colin Newbury, *Tahiti Nui*, University of Hawaii Press, Honolulu, 1980, pp. 7–14; M. Steven in 'Exports Other Than Wool', G. J. Abbott and N. B. Nairn (eds), pp. 295–8; D. R. Hainsworth, pp. 157–8; K. R. Howe, *Where the Waves Fall: A New South Sea Islands History from First Settlement to Colonial Rule*, Allen & Unwin, Sydney, 1984, pp. 91–2. The sandalwood trade remained important in developing Australian capitalism into the 1830s and did not become negligible until after 1865. See D. Shineberg, *They Came for Sandalwood A Study of the Sandalwood Trade in the South West Pacific 1830–1865*, MUP, Carlton, 1967. Applying the model of 'agency', both Shineberg and Howe insist that, far from being destructive or exploitive, the sandalwood trade was welcomed by Pacific people, giving them access to a superior technology and even allowing them the opportunity to exploit the Europeans. Invasion and socio-economic crisis are thus reduced to mere 'culture contact', with much unanalyzed ethnographic evidence being used to suggest that any trauma involved was caused by 'customary political ambitions and strategies', not the Europeans' presence. (K. R. Howe, pp. 259, 322–3; D. Shineberg, pp. 215–16). Even the introduction of firearms is said to have been of psychological importance only (K. R. Howe, pp. 219, 228; D. Shineberg, pp. 152–3).

21 The Rum Rebellion has a large literature. This summary relies mainly on *HRNSW*, VI; Gavin Kennedy, *Bligh*, Duckworth, London, 1978, pp. 333–74; B. H. Fletcher, 'The Hawkesbury Settlers and the Rum Rebellion', *JRAHS*, Vol. 54, 3, (September 1968); M. Steven, 'Exports Other than Wool', in G. J. Abbott and N. B. Nairn (eds), p. 297. M. H. Ellis, *John Macarthur*, Angus & Robertson, Sydney, 1955, was an early apologist for the rebels, writing aginst G. Mackaness's *Life of Vice-Admiral Bligh*, Angus & Robertson,

Sydney, 1931 and H. V. Evatt's *Rum Rebellion*, Angus & Robertson, Sydney, 1938. However, all saw the issue primarily in terms of personality, a clash between great and not-so-great men and, in so far as they provided any economic analysis, tended to see the issue in the rebels' own terms, that is, as a clash between the British state (committed to public and peasant farming) and nascent colonial private enterprise (committed to economic growth). W. G. McMinn's 'Explaining a Rebellion: An Historiographical Enquiry' in *Teaching History* (May 1970) provides a useful overview of these earlier debates without offering further analysis.

22 *HRA*, I, vii, p. 129; *ADB*, II, pp. 127–8 (Lord).
23 *ADB*, II, p. 3 (Ingle); *HRA*, III, i, p. 427; *ADB*, II, pp. 120–1 (Loane).
24 W. G. McMinn, *A Constitutional History of Australia*, OUP, Melbourne, 1979, pp. 1–3; *HRA*, III, pp. ix, xxvii–xxviii; J. M. Ward, *Colonial Self-Government*, Macmillan, London, 1976, pp. 8–20.
25 R. B. Joyce, 'Government Policy' in G. J. Abbott and N. B. Nairn (eds), pp. 68–70; Report from Select Committee on Transportation 1812, *BPP*, p. 9; *ADB*, I, pp. 288–9 (Davey), 119 (Bligh); II, p. 60 (King). Cf. E. Shann, *An Economic History of Australia*, CUP, Cambridge, 1930. Shann saw the British state as the opponent of local capitalism, a view which was disputed by S. J. Butlin. Brian Fitzpatrick's *British Imperialism and Australia*, Allen & Unwin, London, 1939, while arguing that the conflicts with the traders were not derived from any intention on the part of the British state to create a form of communism in the colonies, still insisted that the aim was to establish pre-industrial peasant proprietorship as a solution to the British problem of 'redundant' poor (pp. 13–16, 93). Related to the long debate about the reasons for the colonies' foundation, even recent analysis of this issue by Ken Buckley in 'Primary Accumulation: The Genesis of Australian Capitalism', E. L. Wheelwright and K. Buckley (eds), *Essays in the Political Economy of Australian Capitalism*, Vol. I, ANZ Book Company, Sydney, 1975 and David Clark, 'Australia: Victim or Partner of British Imperialism', ibid., and R. W. Connell and T. H. Irving, *Class Structure in Australian History*, Longman Cheshire, Melbourne, 1980, while recognizing that the activities of both governors and traders were part of developing British capitalism, nevertheless have not spelt out precisely how the clashes reflected the diverging economic needs of merchants and manufacturers in Britain during the shift from mercantilist to industrial production.
26 *ADB*, I, pp. 115 (Blaxcell), 115–18 (Blaxlands), 104–5 (Birch); John Bach, pp. 51, 72.
27 Elizabeth Brenchley, 'The Enlightenment in Australia: Attitudes of Alexander Berry Towards the Aborigines', BA Hons thesis, Macquarie University, 1982, pp. 26–30.
28 C. H. Currey, *The Brothers Bent*, SUP, Sydney, 1968, pp. 48–9; *ADB*, I, pp. 87–8.
29 S. J. Butlin, pp. 8, 26–113, 194–5.
30 D. R. Hainsworth, 'Trade Within the Colony' in G. J. Abbott and N. B. Nairn (eds), pp. 270–1, 274–5; *ADB*, II, pp. 128–31 (Lord); 31–2 (Kable). See also D. R. Hainsworth, *The Sydney Traders*, pp. 36–41.
31 M. Perrot, *A Tolerable Good Success: Economic Opportunities for Women in New South Wales*, Hale & Iremonger, Sydney, 1983, p. 14; *ADB*, II, pp. 373–4 (Reibey).
32 *ADB*, I, p. 306 (Dickson); Gwyneth Dow, *Samuel Terry*, Sydney, 1974, pp. 40–59; *ADB*, II, pp. 508–9 (Terry); J. T. Bigge, *Report of the Commissioner of Enquiry into the State of the Colony of New South Wales*, (*BPP*, XX, No. 448, 1822), p. 141.
33 *ADB*, II, pp. 579–82 (Wentworth); John Ritchie, *Lachlan Macquarie: A*

Biography, MUP, Melbourne, 1988, pp. 128, 133, 136–7; *ADB*, II, pp. 459–62 (Sorell); A. Alexander, *Governor's Ladies*, Tasmanian Historical Research Association, Hobart, 1987, 1987, pp. 70–80.

34 E. Halèvy, *The Growth of Philosophic Radicalism*, Faber & Faber, London, 1952, pp. 249–82; J. M. Ward, pp. 214–18; W. G. McMinn, pp. 6–9.

35 M. J. Steven, 'The Changing Pattern of Commerce' in G. J. Abbott and N. B. Nairn (eds), pp. 181–6; D. R. Hainsworth, 'Trade Within the Colony', ibid., pp. 277–80; W. G. Rimmer, 'The Economic Growth of Van Diemen's Land', ibid., pp. 340–3.

36 W. C. Wentworth, *A Statistical, Historical and Political Description of the Colony of New South Wales*, Whitaker, London, 1819, p. 126. H. Magdoff, *Imperialism: From the Colonial Age to the Present*, Monthly Review Press, New York, 1978, p. 105.

CHAPTER 5: INVASION OF A CONTINENT

1 M. Bassett, *The Hentys*, OUP, Oxford, 1954, pp. 40–3, 68.

2 *ADB*, II, pp. 320–2 (Peel).

3 *HRA*, I, xii, pp. 701, 774; *HRA*, III, v, pp. 737–9, 781–90; B. H. Fletcher, *Ralph Darling: A Governor Maligned*, OUP, Melbourne, 1984, pp. 131–4; L. R. Marchant, *France Australe*, Artlook, Perth, 1982, pp. 233–54. S. Murray Smith (ed.), *Dictionary of Australian Quotations*, Heinemann, Melbourne, 1984, p. 23 has information on Hyacinthe de Bougainville's secret report on the defences of the Australian settlements and the feasibility of arming the convicts to rebel against the British.

4 *HRA*, I, xii, pp. 777–80; *ADB*, II, pp. 484–5 (Stirling).

5 C. M. H. Clark, *A History of Australia*, III, MUP, Carlton, 1973, pp. 17–19; *ADB*, II, p. 321; M. Bassett, pp. 86–91, 99. See also J. S. Battye, *Western Australia: A History from its Discovery to the Inauguration of the Commonwealth*, Clarendon Press, Oxford, 1924, reprinted Perth, 1978, Ch. 4; F. K. Crowley, *Australia's Western Third*, Macmillan, London, 1960, pp. 4–13; C. T. Stannage (ed.), *A New History of Western Australia*, UWAP, Nedlands, 1981, pp. 181–7; 297–300; R. Appleyard and T. Manford, *The Beginning*, UWAP, Nedlands, 1979.

6 M. Bassett, pp. 318–19; B. Fitzpatrick, *British Imperialism and Australia*, SUP, Sydney, 1971, p. 177; K. E. Knorr, *British Colonial Theories*, Cassell, London, 1963, p. 269; R. B. Madgwick, *Immigration into Eastern Australia 1788–1851*, SUP, Sydney, 1969, p. 55; *ADB*, II, pp. 390–2 (Roe). For the ambitions of the new gentlemen emigrants, see also P. Statham (ed.), *The Tanner Letters*, UWAP, Nedlands, 1981, pp. xv–xvii.

7 M. Bassett, pp. 20–5; *HRNSW*, IV, pp. 648–9; M. H. Ellis, *John Macarthur*, Angus & Robertson, Sydney, 1955, pp. 221–5; B. H. Fletcher, *Landed Enterprise and Penal Society*, SUP, Sydney, 1976, pp. 73–6; G. J. Abbott, 'The Pastoral Industry' in G. J. Abbott and N. B. Nairn (eds), *Economic Growth of Australia*, MUP, Carlton, 1978, pp. 224–8. See also J. C. Garran and L. White, *Merinos, Myths and Macarthurs*, ANUP, Canberra, 1985; Hazel King, *Elizabeth Macarthur and her World*, SUP, Sydney, 1980.

8 B. H. Fletcher, *Landed Enterprise and Penal Society*, pp. 76, 229; A. T. Yarwood, *Samuel Marsden*, MUP, Carlton, 1977, pp. 104–5, 122, 132–6; *ADB*, I, p. 521 (Hassall); M. J. Steven, 'The Changing Pattern of Commerce' in G. J. Abbott and N. B. Nairn (eds), p. 185; G. J. Abbott, 'Economic Growth' ibid., p. 150; B. Fitzpatrick, *British Imperialism and Australia 1783–1833*, p. 201; W. G. Rimmer, 'The Economic Growth of Van Diemen's Land' in G. J. Abbott and N. B. Nairn (eds), pp. 336–7; J. C.

Garran and L. White, pp. 171–2; *HRA*, III, iii, pp. 584–5; L. Robson, *A History of Tasmania*, Vol. I, MUP, Melbourne, 1983, p. 115.

9   P. Cunningham, *Two Years in New South Wales* (2 vols), Colburn, London, 1827, I, p. 212; *HRA*, III, iii, pp. 250, 359; J. C. Garran and L. White, pp. 3, 168–9; J. Flood, *Archaeology of the Dreamtime*, Collins, Sydney, 1983, pp. 213–15; Sylvia Hallam, *Fire and Hearth: A Study of Aboriginal Usage and European Usurpation in South Western Australia*, Australian Institute of Aboriginal Studies, Canberra, 1979; E. Rolls, *They All Ran Wild*, Angus & Robertson, Sydney, 1969, p. 395, 'How We Savaged the Soil', *SMH*, 28 January 1988; G. Bolton, *Spoils and Spoilers*, Allen & Unwin, Sydney, 1981, pp. 83–4; D. N. Jeans, *An Historical Geography of New South Wales to 1901*, Reed, Sydney, 1972, p. 59; W. C. Wentworth, *A Statistical, Historical and Political Description of the Colony of New South Wales*, Whitaker, London, 1819, p. 97. See also T. M. Perry, *Australia's First Frontier: The Spread of Settlement in New South Wales 1788–1829*, MUP, Melbourne, 1963. The fact that the term 'squatter' was not applied to the 'respectable' man of capital until about 1840, by which time it meant a holder licensed under the system of leasehold introduced in 1836, has helped to obscure the fact that the large-scale pastoralist informally occupied land from the earliest years of the industry; see further Ch. 7. Cf. the misleading discussion of the term in S. H. Roberts, *The Squatting Age in Australia 1835–1847*, MUP, Melbourne, 1970, pp. 53–62.

10 I am indebted to Robin Williams for this information. See also Mary Coe, *Windradyne: A Wiradjuri Koori*, Aboriginal Studies Press, Canberra, 1989, pp. 14–17.

11 *ADB*, I, p. 116 (Blaxland); II, p. 96 (Lawson); II, p. 583 (Wentworth); G. Mackaness (ed.), *Fourteen Journeys Over the Blue Mountains*, Horwitz Publications & Grahame Book Co., Sydney, 1965, pp. 1–16; *HRA*, I, vii, p. 577; viii, pp. 122, 149. The journals of all three explorers are reprinted in Joanna Richards (ed.), *Blaxland–Lawson–Wentworth 1813*, Blubber Head Press, Hobart, 1979. See also H. K. Weatherburn, *George William Evans, Explorer*, Angus & Robertson, Sydney, 1966.

12 Mary Coe; *ADB*, I, pp. 258–9 (Cox); *HRA*, I, viii, pp. 557–8, 568–76; L. Macquarie, *Journals of his Tours in New South Wales and Van Diemen's Land 1810–1822*, Library of Australian History, Sydney, 1979, p. 98.

13 *HRA*, I, viii, p. 615; Bill Peach, *The Explorers*, ABC Enterprises, Sydney, 1984, p. 29.

14 J. Oxley, *Journals of Two Expeditions Into the Interior of New South Wales . . .* (1st edn 1820), Libraries Board of South Australia, Adelaide, 1964, p. xiv, 3; J. Oppenheimer, 'Survey and Settlement: New South Wales 1825–1836', *Push From the Bush*, 21 (October 1985), pp. 27–9.

15 J. Oxley, p. 274; *ADB*, II, pp. 306–7 (Oxley).

16 J. Oxley, p. 58; T. M. Perry, *The Discovery of Australia*, Nelson, Melbourne, 1982, p. 116, 119; *HRA*, I, xiii, p. 871n; P. Cunningham, I, pp. 29–31.

17 W. G. McMinn, 'Botany and Geography in Early Australia: A Case Study', *Historical Records of Australian Academy of Science*, Vol. 2, Pt 1 (1970), pp. 6–9; and *Allan Cunningham, Botanist and Explorer*, MUP, Melbourne, 1970, especially pp. 85–6.

18 Charles Sturt, *Two Expeditions Into the Interior of Southern Australia* (2 vols) (1st edn 1833), Doubleday, Sydney, 1982, I, pp. 86–7; II, pp. 158–60, 170. The Murray River had already been crossed by Hume and Hovell in 1824. See W. H. Hovell, 'Journal Kept on the Journey from Lake George to Port Phillip 1824–25', *JRAHS*, Vol. VII, Pt vi (1926), p. 332.

19 H. Reynolds, 'The Land, the Explorers and the Aborigines', *HS*, Vol. 19, 75

(October 1980); J. F. Campbell, 'John Howe's Exploratory Journey from Windsor to the Hunter River in 1819', *JRAHS*, Vol. XIV, Pt iv (1928); *ADB*, I, p. 564 (Hume); II, pp. 530–1 (Throsby), 597–8 (Wild); W. H. Hovell, pp. 357–8.

20   B. H. Fletcher, *Landed Enterprise and Penal Society*, p. 177; S. M. Onslow, *Some Early Records of the Macarthurs of Camden*, pp. 349–51, cited in M. H. Ellis, *Lachlan Macquarie*, Angus & Robertson, Sydney, p. 495. See also J. Ritchie, *Punishment and Profit*, Heinemann, Melbourne, 1970; *The Evidence of the Bigge Reports* (2 vols), MUP, Melbourne, 1971; *Lachlan Macquarie: A Biography*, MUP, Melbourne, 1988.

21   *HRA*, I, xi, pp. 434–44; xii, pp. 113–25. Cf. B. H. Fletcher, *Ralph Darling*, pp. 138–9. See also D. N. Jeans, pp. 106–15. Following the Blackburn been much debated by lawyers and, more recently, historians. Most assume that, had the British made treaties with Aboriginal people, some land for missions and reserves might have been set aside permanently or compensation paid. This ignores the experience of other colonized people with whom treaties were made. See V. Gollan, 'The Law of the Land', *Oceania*, Vol. 59, 3 (March 1989); M. Gumbert, *Neither Justice Nor Reason: A Legal and Anthropological Analysis of Aboriginal Land Rights*, UQP, St Lucia, 1984; P. Hanks and B. Keon-Cohen (eds), *Aborigines and the Law*, Allen & Unwin, Sydney, 1984. Cf. A. Frost, 'New South Wales as Terra Nullius: The British Denial of Aboriginal Land Rights', *HS*, Vol. 19, 77 (October 1981); Henry Reynolds, *The Law of the Land*, Penguin, Ringwood, 1987. The issue of Aboriginal status under British law is further discussed in Ch. 7.

22   For the allegation that emancipists made poor pastoralists and therefore should no longer be entitled to grants, see J. T. Bigge, *Report of the Commissioner of Enquiry into the State of the Colony of New South Wales*, London, 1822, reprinted by Libraries Board of South Australia, Adelaide, 1966, pp. 141–4; *HRA*, I, xi, p. 440. For the 1831 regulations, B. H. Fletcher, *Ralph Darling*, pp. 156–7 and see further chapter 7 below. For the proportion of emancipists holding land in 1828, R. Goddard, 'The Structure of New South Wales Society in 1828', MA thesis, University of Melbourne, 1967, p. 119, cited in J. Hirst, *Convict Society and Its Enemies*, Allen & Unwin, Sydney, 1983, p. 229n.

23   W. G. McMinn, *A Constitutional History of Australia*, OUP, Melbourne, 1979, pp. 19–24, 34; N. McLachlan, 'Edward Eager (1787–1866): A Colonial Spokesman in Sydney and London', *HS*, Vol. 10, 40 (May 1963); B. H. Fletcher, *Ralph Darling*, Chs 12 and 13.

24   Ibid., pp. 144–7, 154; P. Cunningham, II, pp. 157, 161.

25   D. N. Jeans, pp. 97, 100–5, 121–3; D. Denholm, 'Some Aspects of Squatting in New South Wales and Queensland 1847–1864', PhD thesis, ANU, 1972, pp. 50–1; Judith Wright, *The Cry for the Dead*, OUP, Melbourne, 1981, p. 41; *ADB*, I, p. 205 (Campbell); II, pp. 399–400 (Rossi); J. Lhotsky, *A Journey from Sydney to the Australian Alps*, edited by E. J. Andrews, Blubber Head Press, Hobart, 1979, pp. 49–50, 169; G. Wilson, *Murray of Yarralumla*, OUP, Melbourne, 1968; J. Jervis, 'The Great South Road', *JRAHS*, Vol. 25, Pt 5 (1939) pp. 413ff. See also W. K. Hancock, *Discovering Monaro*, CUP, Cambridge, 1972.

26   *ADB*, I, pp. 138 (Bowman); 299 (Dawson); J. Robertson, 'The Australian Agricultural Company and the Port Stephens Fiasco', *JRAHS*, Vol. 50, Pt 3 (1964); Judith Wright, p. 41.

27   L. Ryan, *The Aboriginal Tasmanians*, UQP, St Lucia, 1982, p. 83; R. M. Hartwell, *The Economic Development of Van Diemen's Land 1820–1850*, MUP, Carlton, 1954, pp. 31–9, 48; L. Robson, Ch. 10; *ADB*, I, pp. 269–70 (Curr):

II, p. 436 (Sharland); J. L. Davies, *Atlas of Tasmania*, Hobart, 1965, p. 39; see also Department of Main Roads, Tasmania, *Convicts and Carriageways: Tasmanian Road Development until 1880*, Government Printer, Hobart, 1988.

28 H. Reynolds, *The Other Side of the Frontier*, James Cook University, Townsville, 1981, pp. 37–41, 81–4, 131–4. Using valuable oral accounts which provide an Aboriginal point of view, Reynolds discredits the received interpretation that Aboriginal people just 'faded away' without opposing the invasion. Reynolds also goes further. Applying the model of 'agency' to resistance, he over-emphasizes the ferocity and cunning of the dispossessed. The Aboriginal people are turned into heroic Anzacs, employing aggressive battle tactics which other more imperialistic cultures admire. Like the historians who overplay the effectiveness of Aboriginal weaponry, this ultimately suggests that these people were beaten in a fair fight. See also Ann Curthoys, 'Rewriting Australian History: Including Aboriginal Resistance', *Arena*, 62 (1983).

29 *HRA*, I, ix, pp. 53–4, 139–40, 362–4; 854n; K. Willey, *When the Sky Fell Down*, Collins, Sydney, 1985, p. 196; ML MS A752 Throsby Papers, Charles Throsby to D. Wentworth (5 April 1816) pp. 183–6. See also Carol Liston, *Campbelltown: The Bicentennial History*, Allen & Unwin, Sydney, 1988, pp. 19–23.

30 *HRA*, I, xi, pp. 283, 431; Mary Coe, pp. 21–47.

31 *HRA*, I, xii, pp. 341, 610–12, 617, 621; J. O'Sullivan, *Mounted Police in New South Wales*, Rigby, Adelaide, 1979, p. 4; *ADB*, II, pp. 428–9 (Scott); N. Gunson, *Australian Reminiscences and Papers of L. E. Threlkeld* (2 vols), Australian Institute of Aboriginal Studies, Canberra, 1974, I. p. 95; *HRA*, I, xiii, pp. 177, 400–12. The best account of Wonnarua resistance is in James Miller, *Koori: A Will to Win*, Angus & Robertson, Sydney, 1985 Ch. 3. Cf. P. Cunningham, II, pp. 35–6; W. A. Wood, *Dawn in the Valley The Story of Settlement in the Hunter Valley to 1933*, Wentworth, Sydney, 1972.

32 *HRA*, I, xiii, pp. 858–9n; *SG*, 21 May 1827. Cf. R. H. W. Reece, *Aborigines and Colonists*, SUP, Sydney, 1974, pp. 110–5 which contains information on Lieut. Lowe and also on the Little Tommy case, as does B. H. Fletcher, *Ralph Darling*, pp. 183–90. Both however basically agree with Saxe Bannister that the problem was simply a legal one which could be solved by achieving a greater show of justice for Aborigines in the courts.

33 Alexandra Hasluck, 'The Battle of Pinjarra', *Australia's Heritage*, Vol. 2, Pt 29 (1970) p. 695. See also Neville Green, 'Aborigines and White Settlers in the Nineteenth Century' in C. T. Stannage (ed.), pp. 84–5.

34 For killings on behalf of George Cox of Clarendon, see *SG*, 30 September 1824; for Cox's advocacy of total extermination, N. Gunson, I, p. 49. For a similar policy adopted by the Lawson brothers, see Angus McSween, 'Some Lawson Letters 1819–1824', *JRAHS*, Vol. 50, Pt 3 (August 1964), p. 239, cited in James Miller, pp. 38, 266n.

35 J. D. Bollen, 'English Christianity and the Australian Colonies 1788–1860', *Journal of Ecclesiastical History*, Vol. 28, 4 (1977) pp. 361–85; A. T. Yarwood, *Samuel Marsden*, pp. 7–9, 11.

36 G. K. Cragg, *The Church in the Age of Reason 1648–1789*, Penguin, Harmondsworth, 1962, pp. 6–8; F. K. Brown, *Fathers of the Victorians*, CUP, Cambridge, 1961, pp. 3, 41, 437; G. Rattray Taylor, *The Angel Makers*, pp. 31–2, 39, 51–6; Lucien Goldmann, *The Hidden God*, Routledge & Kegan Paul, London, 1977, pp. 30–2; E. Halevy, *The Growth of Philosophical Radicalism*, Faber & Faber, London, 1952, pp. 81–2, 251; E. Stokes, *The English Utilitarians in India*, Clarendon Press, Oxford, 1959, pp. 34, 36–7. The parallels between the growth of Protestantism and the expansion of the

European economy have long been noted by historians, but the precise nature of the relationship between religious and economic issues continues to be debated. R. H. Tawney's influential *Religion and the Rise of Capitalism*, Murray, London, 1936, shares the tendence of the Weber thesis, from which it is derived, of assuming that the problem is to describe how certain mental and moral attitudes (such as 'cool intelligence', 'iron will', 'forethought' and 'thrift' (pp. 243, 248) were acquired by the Puritans from their religion and so contributed to their material success. Yet unless we believe that religious ideas have their own internal dynamic and somehow change by themselves, the question is rather why changes in the economic system required these ideas in the first place and how religious ideology was altered to suit the needs of that system. That is, the ideas to which individual theorists or artists are attracted are determined by the social group to which these people belong. Thus, the religion and culture of a society in which all members participate in production might stress unity and community in its ideology rather than individual competitiveness and self-aggrandizement (L. Goldmann, pp. 16–17).

37   K. R. Howe, *Where the Waves Fall*, pp. 113–21, 133–8, 212–22; C. Newbury, *Tahiti Nui*, pp. 34–48; *ADB*, II, pp. 438–9 (Shelley); A. T. Yarwood, pp. 105–9, 159–80. See also N. Gunson, *Messengers of Grace: Evangelical Missionaries in the South Seas 1797–1860*, OUP, Melbourne, 1978.

38   J. H. Cleverley, *The First Generation: School and Society in Early Australia*, SUP, Sydney, 1971, pp. 74–5, 105–14; B. Bridges, 'Aboriginal Education in Eastern Australia (N.S.W.) 1788–1855', *Australian Journal of Education*, Vol. 12, 3 (October 1968); R. H. W. Reece, 'Feasts and Blankets: The History of Some Early Attempts to Establish Relations with the Aborigines of N.S.W.', *Archaeology and Physical Anthropology in Oceania*, Vol. 2, 3 (October 1967); J. D. Bollen, 'English Missionary Societies and the Australian Aborigines', *Journal of Religious History*, Vol. 9, 3 (1977); J. J. Fletcher, *Clean, Clad and Courteous*, pp. 18–24.

39   N. Gunson (ed.), *Australian Reminiscences and Papers of L. E. Threlkeld, passim*; J. Woolmington, '"Humble Artisans" and "Untutored Savages"', *Journal of Australian Studies*, 16 (May 1985), and 'Wellington Valley in 1838; A House Divided Against Itself?', *Push From the Bush*, 16 (October 1983). See also R. H. W. Reece, pp. 64–5.

40   L. Ryan, pp. 88, 111–13, 183 and 'Aboriginal Policy in Australia–1838– A Watershed?', *Push From the Bush*, 8 (December 1980); N. J. B. Plomley, *Friendly Mission: The Tasmanian Journals and Papers of George Augustus Robinson*, Halstead, Sydney, 1966. For the notion that Aboriginal conversion required total isolation on reserves, see also *HRA*, I, x, pp. 263–72 (Cartwright to Macquarie 6 December 1819).

41   Vivienne Rae Ellis, *Black Robinson: Protector of Aborigines*, MUP, Melbourne, 1988, p. 102. For the cost of the early missions, see also B. Bridges, p. 239.

CHAPTER 6: NOT SLAVES, NOT CITIZENS

1   Bertolt Brecht, 'Questions From a Worker Who Reads' in *Poems*, edited by John Willett and Ralph Menheim, Methuen, London, 1976, pp. 252–3.

2   J. T. Bigge, *Report of the Commissioner of Inquiry into the State of the Colony of NSW (BPP*, XX, No. 448, 1822), (Irish Series—Australia—Vol. I), pp. 24–8, 115–116; J. M. Freeland, *Architecture in Australia: A History*, Penguin, Ringwood, 1982; W. Hardy Wilson, *Old Colonial Architecture in N.S.W. and Tasmania*, Ure Smith, Sydney, 1975, p. 8.

3   A. G. L. Shaw, *Convicts and the Colonies*, p. 96; J. Hirst, *Convict Society and its Enemies*, Allen & Unwin, Sydney, 1983, p. 96. In 1822 Edward Eagar believed emancipists employed some 4600 convicts (J. Ritchie, *The Evidence of the Bigge Reports*, Heinemann, Melbourne, 1971, II, p. 213 but in his desire to prove emancipist 'respectability' he may have exaggerated both emancipists' wealth and their role as employers. Certainly, those emancipists who could afford convict labour were mostly engaged in manufacture or trade. See B. H. Fletcher, *Landed Enterprise and Penal Society*, SUP, Sydney, 1976, pp. 216, 220–1. For Bigge's comments on the women, see his *Report*, pp. 68–70.

4   S. Nicholas and P. R. Shergold, 'Transportation as Global Migration', in S. Nicholas (ed.), *Convict Workers*, CUP, Cambridge, 1988, pp. 31–6; A. Grenfell Price, *The Western Invasion of the Pacific and its Continents*, Clarendon Press, Oxford, 1963, p. 89.

5   A. Harris, *Settlers and Convicts*, (1st edn, 1847) MUP, Melbourne, 1969, pp. 72, 182–8; J. Atkinson, *An Account of the State of Agriculture and Grazing in New South Wales*, (1st edn, Cross, London 1826) SUP, Sydney, 1975, pp. 74–8; M. Kiddle, *Men of Yesterday*, MUP, Melbourne, 1961, pp. 53–5, 59–61, 67–72. See also J. C. Garran and L. White, *Merinos, Myths and Macarthurs*, ANUP, Canberra, 1985, Ch. 19.

6   B. Fitzpatrick, *British Imperialism and Australia*, SUP, Sydney, 1971, pp. 174, 179; M. Dobb, *Studies in the Development of Capitalism*, RKP, London, 1978, pp. 273, 295; E. J. Hobsbawm, *Industry and Empire*, Penguin, Ringwood, 1981, pp. 65, 68.

7   H. G. Bennet, *Letter to Viscount Sidmouth*, Ridgway, London, 1819, p. 11; N. G. Butlin, 'Contours of the Australian Economy 1788–1860', *Australian Economic History Review*, Vol. 26, 2 (September 1986), p. 98.

8   M. Ignatieff, *A Just Measure of Pain*, Macmillan, London, 1978, pp. 96–100, 142–3, 170–1; *BPP*, Report from the Committee on the Laws Relating to Penitentiary Houses 1811 (III, No. 199), (Irish Series—Crime and Punishment—Transportation), Vol. I, pp. 17, 20, 35, 42, 66; *BPP*, Select Committee Appointed to Enquire into the Present State of the Penitentiary at Millbank . . . 1823, p. 30. For the increasing conservatism of Utilitarian thought by 1820, see Eric Stokes, *The English Utilitarians in India*, Clarendon Press, Oxford, 1954, pp. xiv, xvi; E. Halévy, *The Growth of Philosophical Radicalism*, Faber & Faber, London, 1952, p. 264.

9   Thomas Reid, *Two Voyages to New South Wales and Van Diemen's Land . . .*, Longman, London, 1822, pp. 16–17; BT, Box 16, Return of Prisoners ('Boys of the Age of 18 Years and under arrived in this colony from January 1818 to December 1820 inclusively'), (I am indebted to Jim McVie for this information); J. T. Bigge, p. 23; *SG*, 21 August 1823. See also B. Earnshaw, 'The Convict Apprentices 1820–1838', *Push From the Bush*, 5 (December 1979).

10 N. G. Butlin, 'White Human Capital in Australia 1788–1850', *Working Papers in Economic History*, ANU, 32 (April 1985), p. 19. 'Potential' work-force is defined as those aged 12.5 to 59 years. Though declining by 1840, convicts and ex-convicts then still comprised 71 per cent of the male potential workforce and 30 per cent of the female one (ibid., p. 21).

11 A. G. L. Shaw, pp. 191–2; J. Hirst, pp. 97–9, 123. See also B. Dyster, 'A Series of Reversals: Male Convicts in N.S.W. 1821–1831', *Push From the Bush*, 25 (October 1987).

12 J. T. Bigge, pp. 165, 183, 186.

13 J. T. Bigge, pp. 158–61.

14 J. Hirst, pp. 111, 112; A. G. L. Shaw, p. 200. For the use of the pillory and

frequency of floggings of 100 lashes or more in Sydney in 1811–17, see *BPP*, Report from the Select Committee on the State of the Gaols, 1819, (VII, No. 579), (Irish Series—Crime and Punishment—Prisons—Vol. I), Appendix p. 407ff. For the position in Van Diemen's Land by 1835, see A. G. L. Shaw, p. 199 and NSW LC *V&P*, 1835, Final Report of the Committee on Police and Gaols (Minutes of Evidence) p. 324. See also David Neal, 'Free Society, Penal Colony, Slave Society, Prison?' *HS*, Vol. 22, 89 (October 1987), p. 513. For Bourke's Summary Jurisdiction Act (1832) see Note 19 below. In Britain, flogging of women was outlawed in 1817, see J. Hirst, p. 17. Cruel treatment of women on the convict ships was, however, continuing at this time. See *BPP*, Report from the Select Committee on Gaols 1819, pp. 97–100 (voyage of the *Friendship*, 1817–18).

15   Estimates of the Expenditure of the Government of N.S.W. for the year 1840, No. VI, Police and Gaols, NSW LC *V&P*, 1839, Pt I; NSW LC *V&P*, 1835, Final Report of the Committee on Police and Gaols, p. 419; G. Abbott and G. Little (eds), *The Respectable Sydney Merchant: A. B. Spark of Tempe*, SUP, Sydney, 1976, p. 56.

16   The estimate of 25 per cent of male convicts flogged in 1833–36 is based on A. G. L. Shaw, p. 202. R. W. Connell and T. H. Irving, *Class Structure in Australian History*, Longman/Cheshire, Melbourne, 1980, p. 45 suggest the proportion may have been as high as 30 to 40 per cent, but do not specify time and place. See also A. G. L. Shaw, pp. 222–5; M. Sturma, *Vice in a Vicious Society*, UQP, St Lucia, 1983, pp. 16, 18, 126; L. L. Robson, *The Convict Settlers of Australia* MUP, Melbourne, 1976, pp. 101–2, 105; David Neal, p. 511; *BPP*, Report from the Select Committee on Transportation 1837 (Irish Series—Crime and Punishment—Transportation—Vol. II), Appendix No. 2, pp. 93–4 (Returns of Corporal Punishments, N.S.W. Magistrates Benches 1833). Though much of the oral evidence collected by this Committee reflected the vested interests and moral values of the anti-slave lobby and therefore must be treated with caution, the unsolicited, official information presented in the Appendixes speaks for itself. Cf. J. Hirst, pp. 57–69; S. Nicholas (ed.), pp. 11, 152–3, 180–3.

17   L. L. Robson, pp. 170–1; C. M. H. Clark, *Select Documents in Australian History 1788–1850* Angus & Robertson, Sydney, 1978, pp. 406, 408; S. Nicholas and P. Shergold, 'Unshackling the Past' in S. Nicholas (ed.), pp. 7–9.

18   B. Dyster, 'Convicts to Eastern Australia', paper presented to Royal Australian Historical Society, 24 June 1986; S. Nicholas, 'The Convict Labour Market' in S. Nicholas (ed.), pp. 105–7, 124–5; A. Conlon, '"Mine is a Sad but True Story": Convict Narratives 1818–1850', *JRAHS*, Vol. 55 (1969), pp. 70–1.

19   A. Atkinson, 'Four Patterns of Convict Protest', *Labour History*, 37 (November 1979), pp. 34, 36. Bourke's Summary Offences Act (1832) though at last limiting the number of lashes which magistrates could order made it easier for masters to punish workers for contriving ill-health. See W. Nichol, '"Malingering" and Convict Protest', *Labour History*, 47 (November 1984), pp. 18–27. The Act was an attempt to apply some of the latest principles of liberal penal theory; see *HRA*, I, xvii, pp. 313–30. For opposition to it, especially from Hunter Valley magistrates, H. King, *Richard Bourke*, OUP, Melbourne, 1971, pp. 162–5.

20   N. Gunson (ed.) *Australian Reminiscences and Papers of L. E. Threlkeld*, Australian Institute of Aboriginal Studies, Canberra, 1974, II, p. 269; J. Lhotsky, *A Journey from Sydney to the Australian Alps* edited by E. J. Andrews, Blubber Head Press, Hobart, 1979, pp. 171–3; *HRA*, I, xvii, p. 440; S. M. Ingham, 'A Footnote to Transportation to N.S.W.; James Ingham 1824–

1848', *HS*, Vol. 12, 48 (1967), pp. 527–9; NSW LC *V&P*, 1837, Report of the Committee on the Tunnel for Supplying the Town of Sydney with Water, pp. 678, 680; Richard P. Davis, *The Tasmanian Gallows*, Cat and Fiddle, Hobart, 1974, p. 44. In NSW during the 1830s, some fifty hangings took place per year, a much higher rate of executions in proportion to population than was then current in England (David Neal, p. 513).

21 'Jim Jones at Botany Bay' in Russel Ward (ed.), *The Penguin Book of Australian Ballads*, Penguin, Ringwood, 1978, p. 47; Russel Ward, *The Australian Legend*, Angus & Robertson, Sydney, 1958, (revised edition 1970), *passim*; R. W. Connell and T. H. Irving, pp. 47–8, 72n; H. McQueen, 'Convicts and Rebels', in *Labour History*, 15 (1968), pp. 19–20; I. Duffield, 'From Slave Colonies to Penal Colonies: The West Indian Convict Transportees to Australia', *Slavery and Abolition*, Vol. 17, 1 (May 1986).

22 C. M. H. Clark, *A History of Australia*, MUP, Melbourne, 1968, II, pp. 204–6.

23 N. Gunson (ed.), I, p. 45, 73n; P. Cunningham, *Two Years in New South Wales*, Colburn, London, 1827, II, p. 205; J. Hirst, p. 184; J. West, *The History of Tasmania*, (Launceston, 1852), II, p. 215; Frank McNamara, 'Seizure of the Cyprus Brig in Recherche Bay' reprinted in D. Stewart and N. Keesing (eds), *Old Bush Songs*, Angus & Robertson Sydney, 1976, pp. 30–2. L. Robson, *A History of Tasmania*, OUP, Melbourne, 1983, I, p. 150. A version of Swallow's story was used by Marcus Clarke in *For the Term of His Natural Life*, (1870–2).

24 P. Cunningham, II, p. 198; 'Bold Jack Donohoe', in Russel Ward, *Penguin Book of Australian Ballads*, p. 44; Charles White, *History of Australian Bushranging*, (2 vols) Lloyd O'Neil, Melbourne, 1970, I, pp. 98–109, L. Robson, *A History of Tasmania*, I, pp. 85–6, 142–5, 185; *HRA*, III, ii, pp. 120–2, 577; Richard P. Davis, p. 22. For the fear of collusion between Aborigines and bushrangers in the Hunter in 1826, N. Gunson (ed.), I, pp. 93, 120. See also E. J. Hobsbawm, *Primitive Rebels Studies in Archaic Forms of Social Movement in the Nineteenth and Twentieth Centuries*, University Press, Manchester, 1974, pp. 2–5, 13–28.

25 W. A. Wood, *Dawn in the Valley*, Wentworth Books, Sydney, 1972, pp. 83–4; G. Wilson, *Murray of Yarralumla*, OUP, Melbourne, 1968, pp. 68, 70.

26 W. C. Wentworth, *Statistical, Historical and Political Description of N.S.W.* Whitaker, London, 1819, pp. 32–5, 132ff; A. H. King, 'Police Organization and Administration in the Middle Districts of New South Wales 1825–1851', MA thesis, University of Sydney, 1956, pp. 76–9, Appendix L, cited in David Neal, p. 514; NSW LC *V&P*, 1835, Minutes of Evidence Taken before Committee on Police and Gaols, p. 347; NSW *GG*, 7 January 1835, p. 11; W. A. Wood, pp. 24, 84. See also B. H. Fletcher, *Ralph Darling*, OUP, Melbourne, 1984, pp. 180–2.

27 NSW LC *V&P*, 1841, Report from the Committee on Immigration with . . . Replies to Circular Letter on the Aborigines pp. 35–50; Brian J. Egloff, *Wreck Bay: An Aboriginal Community*, Australian Institute of Aboriginal Studies, Canberra, 1981, pp. 13–14; *HRA*, III, ii, pp. 94–6, 284, 603; L. Ryan, *The Aboriginal Tasmanians*, UQP, St Lucia, 1981, p. 77; *SG*, 22 November 1834. See also N. Gunson (ed.), I, p. 146. Some European women also joined the bushrangers; see *SG*, 4 January 1828 (Sarah Webb); *BPP*, Report from the Select Committee on Transportation 1838, p. 47 (Jemima Chapman); J. Oppenheimer, 'Colonel Dumaresq, Captain Thunderbolt and Mary Ann Brigg', *Push From the Bush*, 16 (October 1983).

28 J. Hirst, p. 125; M. Sturma, p. 102; A. Harris, pp. 75–84; NSW LC *V&P*, Minutes of Evidence Taken before Committee on Police and Gaols, pp. 332, 337–8.

29 A. G. L. Shaw, pp. 212–16; G. Karskens, 'The Convict Road Station Site at

Wiseman's Ferry: An Historical and Archaeological Investigation', *Australian Historical Archaeology*, Vol. 2 (October 1984), pp. 17–26; James Semple Kerr, *Design for Convicts*, Library of Australian History, Sydney, 1984, pp. 62–5.

30 NSW LC *V&P*, 1838, Pt I, Report from the Committee on the Catarrh in Sheep Bill, with the Minutes of Evidence; J. C. Garran and L. White, *Merinos, Myths and Macarthurs*, p. 155; M. Kiddle, pp. 63–4. The fact that flogging began to decrease in both colonies from 1836 did not mean that the assignment system was becoming more efficient, nor that resistance was declining. Rather it reflected the fact that magistrates now had recourse to alternative punishments, such as solitary cells (A. G. L. Shaw, p. 201).

31 Whereas in 1840 the Australian colonies supplied 20 per cent of British imports of raw wool, by 1850 they were the leading supplier, contributing 53 per cent of the British import of this material (N. G. Butlin, 'Contours of the Australian Economy', p. 122). In NSW (including Port Phillip District), the export of wool more than doubled between the phasing out of the assignment system in 1839 and 1844 (S. J. Butlin, *Foundations of the Australian Monetary System*, p. 316). Meanwhile, wool prices in NSW, after rising from 13 pence per pound in 1831 to 18 pence in 1837, fell steadily to around 13 pence for most of the 1840s (D. N. Jeans, *A Historical Geography of N.S.W. to 1901* pp. 99–100). For the attack on the assignment system as 'slavery', see *BPP*, Report from the Select Committee on Transportation together with the Minutes of Evidence (1838). See also J. Hirst, pp. 21–7; David Neal, pp. 497ff.; M. Dunn, 'Early Australia: Wage Labour or Slave Society?' in E. Wheelwright and K. Buckley (eds), *Essays in the Political Economy of Australian Capitalism*, I, ANZ Book Company, Sydney, 1975; S. Nicholas, 'The Convict Labour Market' in S. Nicholas (ed.), pp. 111–20.

32 M. Belcher, 'The Child in New South Wales Society 1820–1837', PhD thesis, University of New England, 1982, p. 119; *Census of New South Wales*, 1841. See also N. G. Butlin, 'White Human Capital', p. 16 (figures for NSW and Van Diemen's Land).

33 The construction of domestic ideology in early nineteenth-century Britain now has a large literature, but see especially E. Zaretsky, *Capitalism, the Family and Personal Life*, Pluto Press, London, 1976; S. Burman (ed.), *Fit Work for Women*, St Martin's Press, London, 1979; Leonore Davidoff and Catherine Hall, *Family Fortunes: Men and Women of the Middle Class 1780–1850*, Hutchinson Education, London, 1987. For colonial philanthropic ladies, E. Windschuttle, '"Feeding the Poor and Sapping Their Strength": The Public Role of Ruling Class Women in Eastern Australia 1788–1850', in E. Windschuttle (ed.), *Women, Class and History*, Fontana/Collins, Melbourne, 1980. For the intensified attempts to impose this ideology in the colonies by the 1830s, A. Summers, *Damned Whores and God's Police*, Penguin, Ringwood, 1975, and K. Alford *Production and Reproduction: An Economic History of Women in Australia 1788–1850*, OUP, Melbourne, 1984. For the relationship between the celebration of domesticity and the attempt to elevate the status of women as mothers, see Ch. 7 (Caroline Chisholm).

34 K. Alford, pp. 20–2; NSW LC *V&P*, 1835, Minutes of Evidence Taken Before the Committee on Immigration, p. 315.

35 W. Ullathorne, *The Catholic Mission in Australasia*, (1st edn, 1837), Library Board of South Australia, Adelaide, 1963, pp. 31, 47; J. Woolmington (ed.), *Aborigines in Colonial Society 1788–1850*, Cassell, Melbourne, 1973, pp. 65–6; NSW *GG*, 16 September 1837, cited in R. H. W. Reece, *Aborigines and Colonists*, Sydney, 1974, p. 53. See N. Gunson (ed.), pp. 282–3 for statistics showing the absence of Aboriginal women and girls from settled districts in NSW 1838–40.

36 J. Ritchie, '"Towards the Ending of an Unclean Thing": The Molesworth Committee and the Abolition of Transportation to N.S.W. 1837–1840', *HS*, Vol. 17, 67 (October 1976), pp. 130–1; Deborah Oxley, 'Female Convicts', in S. Nicholas (ed.), pp. 10, 91–3.

37 NSW *GG*, January–March 1835. See also H. Weatherburn, 'The Female Factory' in J. Mackinolty and H. Radi (eds), *In Pursuit of Justice*, Hale & Iremonger, Sydney, 1979; 'The Female Factory at Parramatta 1804–1848', BA Hons thesis, University of Sydney, 1978; L. Heath, 'The Female Convict Factories of New South Wales and Van Diemen's Land . . .', MA thesis, ANU, 1978; A. Salt, *These Outcast Women: The Parramatta Female Factory 1821–48*, Hale & Iremonger, Sydney, 1984.

38 L. L. Robson, *The Convict Settlers of Australia*, p. 136; A. Atkinson, pp. 32, 36; Paula-Jane Byrne, 'Women and the Criminal Law in New South Wales 1810–1821', Paper, Law and History in Australia Conference, LaTrobe University, April 1986, pp. 3, 12, 15; Kay Daniels, 'Feminism and Social History', *Australian Feminist Studies*, I (Summer 1985), p. 29. For Jane Smith, ML MS A269 Stiles Papers (S. Marsden to Reverend Henry Tarleton, 5 December 1834) cited in L. Heath, p. 268. For an earlier but not dissimilar case in Van Diemen's Land, see *HRA*, III, iii, pp. 408, 853ff (Alice Blackstone).

39 R. C. Hutchinson, 'Mrs. Hutchinson and the Female Factories of Early Australia', *PTHRA*, Vol. 11, 2 (December 1963), pp. 59–61; J. Henderson, *Observations on the Colonies of New South Wales and Van Diemen's Land*, Baptist Mission Press, Calcutta, 1832, pp. 21–2; P. Cunningham, II, pp. 287–92.

40 ML MS A1559-1 Brisbane Letter Book No. 1, pp. 85–97, 'Letters &c. respecting the Female Convicts at Emu Plains'; ML MS A2009 'Emu Plains Agricultural Establishment Inquiry 1826'; C. Liston, 'New South Wales under Governor Brisbane 1821–1825', PhD thesis, University of Sydney, 1980, pp. 387–90; *HRA*, I, xi, pp. 597–603, 620, 814–31.

41 *HRA*, I, xii, pp. 525, xv, 586. Pastoralist James Mudie provided an account of women being married from the Parramatta Factory in *The Felonry of New South Wales* (Whaley, London, 1837) and in his subsequent evidence to the House of Commons Committee on Transportation (1837–38). Though his statements were primarily intended to discredit his many personal enemies in NSW his evidence on this issue can be corroborated from other sources. See *BPP*, Report from the Select Committee on Transportation 1837, p. 197; 1838, p. ix, (James Macarthur); James O'Connell, *A Residence of Eleven Years in New Holland*, B. B. Mussey, Boston, 1836, pp. 69–71.

42 H. Weatherburn, thesis, p. 36; L. Heath, pp. 35, 171. The same arrangement did not hold for convict men assigned to free wives. See *SG*, 20 February 1834, for a case where, a husband having been successfully prosecuted by his wife and consigned into custody, was released following an order from the Governor himself.

43 Portia Robinson, 'The First Forty Years' in J. Mackinolty and H. Radi (eds), pp. 1–16; *The Hatch and Brood of Time*, OUP, Melbourne, 1985, pp. 7–8. For the belief that assignment caused special problems of sexual immorality, see *BPP*, Report of the Select Committee on Transportation 1838, especially pp. ix, xiii, 26–9 (Francis Forbes); 38–40 (James Mudie); 62–5 (E. A. Slade); 197 (James Macarthur).

44 J. Ritchie, pp. 145, 147; J. Hirst, pp. 21–2, 25.

45 A. G. L. Shaw, pp. 271–82; *BPP*, Report from Select Committee on Aborigines (British Settlements) 1837, (Vol. 7, 425) (Irish U. Series— Anthropology—Aborigines—Vol. II), p. 76; Minutes of Evidence, p. 204 (Reverend W. Yate).

CHAPTER 7: 'ALL THAT CAPITAL'

1   E. G. Wakefield, *England and America*, reprinted in *The Collected Works of Edward Gibbon Wakefield*, edited by M. F. Lloyd Prichard, Auckland, 1969, p. 484.

2   P. Statham (ed.), *The Tanner Letters*, UWA Press, Nedlands, 1981, pp. xvii–xxv; 'Swan River Colony 1829–1850' in C. T. Stannage (ed.), *A New History of Western Australia*, UWA Press, Nedlands, 1981, pp. 186–9, 197–203; N. Green, 'Aborigines and White Settlers in the Nineteenth Century', ibid., pp. 79–87; M. Bassett, *The Hentys*, OUP, Oxford, 1954, pp. 110–22, 174–9, 215.

3   B. Fitzpatrick, *British Imperialism and Australia 1783–1833*, SUP, Sydney, 1971, pp. 363; E. P. Thompson, *The Making of the English Working Class*, Penguin, Ringwood, 1981, pp. 284–5, 339; E. J. Hobsbawm, *Industry and Empire*, Penguin, Ringwood, 1981, p. 73; George Rudé, *Protest and Punishment*, OUP, Melbourne, 1978, pp. 22–3; R. M. Madgwick, *Immigration into Eastern Australia 1788–1851*, SUP, Sydney, 1969, pp. 31–2; J. M. Ward, *Colonial Self-Government: The British Experience 1759–1856*, Macmillan, London, 1976, pp. 214–25; K. E. Knorr, *British Colonial Theories 1570–1850*, Cassell, London, 1963, pp. 219, 270–9 (citing Torrens 'A Paper on the Means of Reducing the Poor Rates' 1817).

4   *HRA*, I, xvi, pp. 19–22; J. M. Ward, pp. 226–30; R. M. Madgwick, p. 223–5; R. J. Schultz, 'Immigration into Eastern Australia 1788–1851', *HS*, Vol. 14, 54 (April 1970), p. 273. See also R. C. Mills, *The Colonization of Australia 1829–1842: The Wakefield Experiment in Empire-Building* (1st edition), Sidgwick & Jackson, London, 1915, SUP, Sydney, 1974; P. Burroughs, *Britain and Australia 1831–35*, Clarendon Press, Oxford, 1967; J. Philipp, 'Wakefieldian Influence and New South Wales 1830–1832', *HS*, Vol. 9, 34 (May 1964), pp. 226–30.

5   R. B. Madgwick, p. 82; B. Fitzpatrick.

6   R. B. Madgwick, pp. 96–7; NSW LC *V&P*, 1835, Minutes of Evidence Taken Before the Committee on Immigration 1835, pp. 299–300; *SG*, 20 August 1833; *Colonial Times*, 19 August 1834, cited in A. Summers, *Damned Whores and God's Police*, Penguin, Ringwood, 1981, p. 277; A. J. Hammerton, '"Without Natural Protectors" Female Immigration to Australia 1832–1836', *HS*, Vol. 16, 65 (October 1975), pp. 543–4, 562–5.

7   *HRA*, I, xvii, p. 344; NSW LC *V&P*, 1835, Minutes of Evidence Taken Before the Committee on Immigration 1835, pp. 286, 295, 302, 307, 412–13. See also K. Alford, *Production or Reproduction*, OUP, Melbourne, 1984, Ch. 5. The prejudices of nineteenth-century male officials continue to be accepted by some historians, see A. J. Hammerton, pp. 546, 548–9. Further experiments in female immigration were tried in 1847–48, when some 4175 girls from Irish workhouses were shipped to New South Wales only to be castigated in the same manner (Gillian Wagner, *Children of the Empire*, Weidenfeld & Nicolson, London, 1982, pp. 23–6).

8   R. M. Madgwick, pp. 119–22; B. Fitzpatrick, *The British Empire in Australia*, MUP, Melbourne, 1949, pp. 66–9. R. J. Schulz compares ages, occupations, religion, literacy, though not gender, of bounty and state immigrants. For the demand for immigration to keep wages down, see NSW LC *V&P*, Evidence Before Committee on Immigration 1835, p. 306 (Sir John Jamison).

9   M. Kiddle, *Caroline Chisholm*, MUP, Melbourne, 1969, pp. 20–4, 29; A. Summers, pp. 300–1; K. Alford, pp. 45, 106–7. For the concurrent celebration of women and home in America, see Barbara Welter, 'The Cult of True Womanhood 1820–1860', in M. Gordon (ed.), *The American Family in Social-Historical Perspective*, New York, 1973.

10   E. G. Wakefield, *A Letter from Sydney* (1829), reprinted in M. F. Lloyd
      Prichard (ed.) *The Collected Works of Edward Gibbon Wakefield*, pp. 136–40;
      England and America, ibid. pp. 521–50, 561–9, 582–5; *ADB*, II, pp. 559–62
      (Wakefield); J. Philipp, p. 176; R. Lockwood, 'British Imperial Influences
      in the Foundation of the White Australia Policy', *Labour History*, 7 (November
      1964), p. 32.
11   C. M. H. Clark, *A History of Australia*, III, MUP, Carlton, 1973, Ch. 3; B.
      Fitzpatrick, *The British Empire in Australia*, pp. 23, 28–30; *ADB*, I, pp. 15–16
      (Angas); II, pp. 250–1 (Montefiore); D. Pike, *Paradise of Dissent: South
      Australia 1829–1857*, Longman, London, 1957, pp. 65–6, 83–144; E. Richards
      (ed.), *The Flinders History of South Australia* [Vol. 1] *Social History* Netley, SA.,
      1986 pp. 2–3.
12   C. M. H. Clark, *A History of Australia*, III, pp. 45–55; K. Hassell, *The
      Relations Between the Settlers and the Aborigines in South Australia 1836–1860*,
      Libraries Board of South Australia, Adelaide, 1966, pp. 4–7; D. Pike, pp.
      145ff; C. H. Spence, *An Autobiography*, Thomas, Adelaide, 1910, pp. 13–20;
      ADB, I, pp. 538–40 (Hindmarsh); C. Mattingley and K. Hampton, *Survival
      in our Own Land: 'Aboriginal' Experiences in 'South Australia' Since 1836 Told by
      Nungas and Others*, Wakefield, Adelaide, 1988. Cf. H. Reynolds, *The Law of
      the Land*, Penguin, Ringwood, 1987, which suggests that the intention of
      some reformers to 'treat' with the Aboriginal people or remove them to
      reservations was a beneficient solution to the problem of dispossession and
      one which constitutes a case for land rights today. See V. Gollan, 'The Law
      of the Land', *Oceania*, Vol. 59, 3 (March 1989).
13   B. Fitzpatrick, *The British Empire in Australia*, pp. 39–41; M. Bassett, pp.
      253–8, 283ff; *Historical Records of Victoria*, Government Printing Office,
      Melbourne, 1982, Vol. I, *Beginnings of Permanent Government*; C. P. Billot
      (ed.), *Melbourne's Missing Chronicle Being the Journal and Preparations for De-
      parture to and Proceedings at Port Phillip by John Pascoe Fawkner*, Quartet,
      Melbourne, 1982; A. J. Hopton, 'Rural Port Phillip 1834–1851', *JRAHS*,
      Vol. 36, Pt 5 (1950) and Vol. 36, Pt 6 (1950); C. M. H. Clark, *A History of
      Australia*, III, pp. 84–93; *ADB*, I, pp. 67–71 (Batman); 437–8 (Gellibrand);
      368–71 (Fawkner); II, pp. 500–1 (Swanston), 575–6 (Wedge); Lyndall
      Ryan, *The Aboriginal Tasmanians*, UQP, St. Lucia, 1982, pp. 95–7, 98, 102;
      M. F. Christie, *Aborigines in Colonial Victoria 1835–86*, SUP, Sydney, 1979,
      pp. 24–9.
14   J. M. R. Owens, 'New Zealand Before Annexation', in W. H. Oliver (ed.),
      Oxford History of New Zealand, OUP, Wellington, 1981, pp. 28, 34–43;
      Claudia Orange, *The Treaty of Waitangi*, Wellington, 1987, pp. 6–18, 95; R.
      C. Mills, pp. 284–9; Roger Thompson, *Australian Imperialism in the Pacific:
      The Expansionist Era 1820–1920*, MUP, Melbourne, 1980, pp. 10–11; W. H.
      Oliver, *The Story of New Zealand*, Faber & Faber, London, 1960, pp. 46–52;
      K. R. Howe, *Where the Waves Fall* Allen & Unwin, Sydney, 1984, pp.
      212–26; B. H. Fletcher, *Ralph Darling*, OUP, Melbourne, 1984, pp. 137–8;
      NSW LC *V&P*, 7 (23 June 1840), 8 (25 June 1840), 10 (30 June 1840),
      11 (1 July 1840).
15   *BPP*, Report from the Select Committee on the Disposal of Lands in the
      British Colonies 1836, Vol. 11, 512 (Irish U Series — Colonies — General —
      Vol. II), p. 108; *BPP*, Report from the Select Committee on Aborigines
      (British Settlements) 1837, (Vol. 7, 425) (Irish U Series — Anthropology —
      Aborigines — Vol. II), pp. 31, 43–6, 78–9, 81; Minutes of Evidence pp.
      11–21 (Saxe Bannister).
16   For this insight and information on treaties, I am indebted to V. Gollan. See
      further her 'Role of Law in the Colonization of Australia', PhD thesis,

University of Sydney (forthcoming). See also *BPP*, Report from the Select
Committee on Aborigines 1837, pp. 82–4; *BPP*, Report from the Select
Committee on Aborigines (British Settlements) 1836, (Vol. 7, 538) (Irish
Series—Anthropology—Aborigines—Vol. I) Minutes of Evidence espe-
cially pp. 14–24 (Broughton); 184–5 (Stockenstrom); 513, 542–3 (Coates,
Beecham, Ellis). Cf. H. Reynolds, pp. 84–102. For this Committee and its
recommendations, see also J. Woolmington (ed.), *Aborigines in Colonial
Society 1788–1850*, Cassell, Melbourne, 1973, pp. 65–6; M. F. Christie, pp.
85–8; A. T. Yarwood and M. J. Knowling, *Race Relations in Australia: A
History*, Methuen, Sydney, 1982, pp. 99, 109–11. G. A. Robinson was
appointed Protector for Port Phillip; see Vivienne Rae-Ellis, *Black Robinson:
Protector of Aborigines*, MUP, Melbourne, 1988, pp. 149–52. For New
Zealand, see further Claudia Orange, pp. 19–59, 92–100.

17   C. M. H. Clark, *A History of Australia*, III, p. 95; S. H. Roberts, *The Squatting
Age in Australia 1835 to 1847*, MUP, Melbourne, 1970, pp. 159–60; T. F.
Bride, *Letters from Victorian Pioneers*, Currey O'Neil, Melbourne, 1983,
pp. 63, 65–6; M. F. Kiddle, *Men of Yesterday*, MUP, Melbourne, 1961, p. 42;
M. F. Christie, p. 29.

18   D. N. Jeans, *An Historical Geography of New South Wales to 1901*, Reed,
Sydney, 1972, p. 135; S. H. Roberts, p. 362. See also G. J. Abbott, *The
Pastoral Age: A Re-examination*, Macmillan, Melbourne, 1971.

19   *HRA*, I, xviii, pp. 153–8, 389–81; H. King, *Richard Bourke*, OUP, Melbourne, 1971, pp. 184–90.

20   NSW LC *V&P*, 1835, Minutes of Evidence Taken Before Committee on
Police and Gaols 1835, pp. 332, 337, 338; S. H. Roberts, pp. 79, 81; NSW LC
V&P, 1836, p. 490, Reply to a Memorial presented to Governor (4 April
1836). For earlier attempts introduced from 1833 to confine squatting
outside the Limits of Location to 'reputable' pastoralists, see B. Fitzpatrick,
The British Empire in Australia, pp. 37–8; D. N. Jeans, pp. 152–4. In Port
Phillip District from 1840 to 1853, two women in partnership, Anne
Drysdale and Caroline Newcomb, secured a licensed run, but such cases
were unusual and confined to women of means. See K. Alford, pp. 141–4.

21   T. L. Mitchell, *Three Expeditions into the Interior of Eastern Australia . . .* (2 vols)
Boone, London, 1839; T. F. Bride, pp. 262, 281–5. On Mitchell's journeys,
cf. Paul Carter, *The Road to Botany Bay: An Essay in Spatial History*, Faber &
Faber, London, 1987. Arguably, Carter's view of Mitchell as a seeker after
knowledge, for whom the survey was 'a strategy for translating space into
a conceivable object . . . that the mind could possess long before the lowing
herds' (p. 113) is tenuous in the extreme. Such rejection of economic and
political context reduces explorers to mere agents or symbols of personified,
all-powerful ideas which are in turn produced by higher forms of language.
Eternal, self-generating and classless, this language constitutes a kind of
hidden code which exists beyond human experience yet somehow deter-
mines it.

22   R. McDonagh and F. Bridge, *Carroll Centenary 1847–1947*, Gunnedah, 1947,
n.p.; D. Denholm, 'Some Aspects of Squatting in New South Wales and
Queensland 1847–1864', PhD thesis, Australian National University, 1972,
pp. 53–60; Arthur Morgan, 'The Discovery and Early Development of the
Darling Downs', *Queensland Geographical Journal*, Vol. xvii (1902) pp. 98–100,
108; *HRA*, I, xxii, p. 35; W. K. Hancock, *Discovering Monaro*, CUP,
Cambridge, 1972, pp. 15, 46, 48; H. P. Wellings, *Benjamin Boyd in Australia
(1842–1849)*, Bega, n.d., pp. 3, 6; S. H. Roberts, p. 179. See also Judith
Wright, *The Cry for the Dead*, OUP, Melbourne, 1981, pp. 41–4.

23   Reverend George Cox, 'Notes on Gippsland History', (numbered news-

paper cuttings, June 1922, ML), pp. 80, 82; Charles Daley, 'Count Paul Strzelecki's Ascent of Mount Kosciusko and Journey Through Gippsland', *Victorian Historical Magazine*, Vol. 19, 2 (December 1941). James Macarthur (1813–62) was the son of Hannibal Hawkins Macarthur and held land at Yass and Port Phillip. The ascent of Kosciusko has been the subject of debate on two counts: whether Strzelecki gave the name to a lower peak and whether John Lhotsky had already climbed the mountain in 1834. Contributions to this debate include D. N. Jeans and W. R. Gilfillian, 'Light on the Summit: Mt William the Fourth or Kosciusko', *JRAHS*, Vol. 55, Pt 1 (1969); Alan E. J. Andrews, 'Strzelecki's Ascent of Mount Kosciusko: Another View', *JRAHS*, Vol. 74, Pt 2 (October 1988).

24 S. H. Roberts, p. 164; M. F. Christie, p. 30; M. Kiddle, *Men of Yesterday*, pp. 43, 49, 50, 57; T. F. Bride, pp. 95, 151, 170, 291.

25 T. F. Bride, p. 158 (John G. Robertson); E. M. Curr, *Recollections of Squatting in Victoria* (1st edn, 1883) MUP, Carlton, 1965, p. 5; M. Kiddle, *Men of Yesterday*, p. 78; D. Pike, pp. 258–67.

26 M. F. Christie, pp. 51, 68. For other frank admissions of private killings by squatters, see T. F. Bride, pp. 151, 164, 220–1; M. Kiddle, *Men of Yesterday*, p. 122; D. Watson, *Caledonia Australis Scottish Highlanders on the Frontier of Australia*, Collins, Sydney, 1984, Ch. 8; D. Watson, 'Exploring Australian Explorers; The Case of Angus McMillan', *Arena*, 52 (1979), pp. 59–60; P. Pepper and T. de Araugo, *The Kurnai of Gippsland*, Hyland House, Melbourne, 1985. The estimate of the number of Aborigines killed by punitive raids comes from M. F. Christie, pp. 78, 206. For discussion of this issue and of the second smallpox epidemic, see Ch. 2, fn. 31. For the politics of the white historiography of Aboriginal resistance, see Ch. 5, fn. 28.

27 For the Port Phillip Missions and the Protectorate, see M. F. Christie, Ch. 4 and 5; *Historical Records of Victoria*, Vols 2A and 2B, *The Aborigines of Port Phillip 1835–39*; H. N. Nelson, 'The Missionaries and the Aborigines in the Port Phillip District', *HS*, Vol. 12, 45 (October 1965). For the missionary movement of the late 1830s and 1840s in other areas, see John Ferry, 'The Failure of the New South Wales Missions to the Aborigines Before 1845', *Aboriginal History*, Vol. 3, 1–2 (1979); W. McNair and H. Rumley, *Pioneer Aboriginal Mission: The Work of Wesleyan Missionary John Smithies in the Swan River Colony 1840–55*, UWAP, Nedlands, 1981; N. J. B. Plomley, *Weep in Silence: A History of the Flinders Island Aboriginal Settlement*, Blubber Head Press, Hobart, 1987; Lyndall Ryan, *The Aboriginal Tasmanians*, Ch. 12 and 13. For the connivance of the Crown Land Commissioners, E. and L. Irby, *Memoirs of Edward and Lionel Irby*, Brooks, Sydney, 1908, pp. 58–81, 86–91. For an Aboriginal perspective, using the medium of fiction, Mudrooroo Narogin (Colin Johnson), *Doctor Wooreddy's Prescription for Enduring the End of the World*, Hyland House, Melbourne, 1983 and *Masters of the Ghost Dreaming*, Angus & Robertson, Sydney, 1991.

28 *SG*, 19 April 1936; V. Gollan, 'The Role of Law in the Colonization of Australia', PhD Thesis, Sydney University; A. C. Castles, *An Australian Legal History*, Law Book Co., Sydney, 1982, pp. 515, 519–32; Susanne Davies, 'Aborigines, murder and the Criminal Law in early Port Phillip, 1841–1851', *HS*, Vol. 22, 88 (April 1987), pp. 325–7. B. Bridges, 'The Extension of British Law to the Aborigines for Offences Committed *Inter Se*, 1829–1842', *JRAHS*, Vol. 59, Pt 4 (December 1973), pp. 264–6; 'The Aborigines and the Law: N.S.W. 1788–1855', *Teaching History* (December 1970), pp. 52, 59; N. Gunson (ed.), *Australian Reminiscences and Papers of L. E. Threlkeld*, Australian Institute of Aboriginal Studies, Canberra, 1974, I, pp. 26, 36n, 51, 97, 121–2, 133; *HRA*, IV, i, pp. 554–5.

29   The Myall Creek massacre has a large literature. For the liberal view, see J. Moloney, *An Architect of Freedom: John Plunkett in New South Wales 1832–1869*, ANUP, Canberra, 1973, pp. 140–7. R. H. W. Reece, *Aborigines and Colonists*, Sydney, 1974, rightly points out that the massacre was only one of many and that the trial culminated in greater violence, but even so insists that the incident was primarily a consequence of cruel instincts unique to the convict psyche (pp. 35–46, 58–61, 148–66). Others who take this view include A. T. Yarwood and M. J. Knowling, *Race Relations in Australia*, pp. 39, 76, 106–7 and David Denholm, *The Colonial Australians*, Penguin, Ringwood, 1980, pp. 36–7. M. Sturma, 'Myall Creek and the Psychology of Mass Murder', *Journal of Australian Studies*, 16 (May 1985), though pointing out that inhuman acts were and are not confined to convicts, also offers a psychological approach. Again this leads us to see the massacre in the same terms as the liberals, that is, as caused by personal human failings, not the pastoralists' search for profits. Convict moral degradation is simply exchanged for convict boredom, frustration and other neurotic disorders of the human mind. See also Richard Broome, *Aboriginal Australians*, Allen & Unwin, Sydney, 1982, pp. 37–8. For further details on Myall Creek, see *Push From the Bush*, 20 (April 1985) (Myall Creek number) and E. Webby, 'Reactions to the Myall Creek Massacre', ibid., 8 (December 1980). For Major Nunn, see *HRA*, I, xx, pp. 247–56, 280. For poisonings, see N. Gunson, pp. 165, 175; II, pp. 278, 279; R. Evans (*et al.*), *Exclusion, Exploitation, Extermination*, ANZ Book Company, Sydney, 1975, p. 49. For the Border Police, see M. F. Christie, pp. 70–1.

30   NSW LC *V&P*, 1837, Memoranda for John Mackay (October 1836, May 1837), pp. 582–4. See also NSW LC *V&P*, 1837, Minutes of Evidence Taken Before Committee on Immigration Indian and British into N.S.W., pp. 630–5; Paul Knaplund, 'Sir James Stephen on a White Australia', *Victorian Historical Magazine*, Vol. 12, 4 (1928) p. 242; R. Lockwood, p. 26; C. A. Price, *The Great White Walls Are Built*, ANUP, Canberra, 1974, pp. 39–45; M. Diamond, *The Seahorse and the Wanderer*, MUP, Melbourne, 1988, pp. 127–40.

31   T. A. Coghlan, *Labour and Industry in Australia 1788–1901*, (4 vols), OUP, Oxford, 1918, I, pp. 209–10; E. Richards, 'A Voice from Below; Benjamin Boyce in South Australia 1839–1846', *Labour History*, 27 (1974), p. 71.

32   NSW LC *V&P*, 1845, Report from the Select Committee on the Masters' and Servants' Act with Minutes of Evidence and Appendix, pp. 5–8, 15, 18, 40; G. Wilson, *Murray of Yarralumla*, OUP, Melbourne, 1968, pp. 202, 205; M. Sullivan, *Men and Women of Port Phillip*, Hale & Iremonger, Sydney, 1982, pp. 193–5. See also T. Rayner, 'Master and Servant in the New Norfolk Magistrate's Court 1838', *Push From the Bush*, 6 (1980), p. 34; J. Cashen, 'Masters and Servants in Early South Australia', ibid., pp. 23, 28–9; Cf. A. Merritt, 'Forgotten Militants: Use of the New South Wales Masters and Servants Acts By and Against Female Employees 1845–1930', (Paper, Law and History in Australia Conference, Latrobe University, May 1982) and D. Denholm, *Some Aspects of Squatting . . .*, pp. 134–41.

33   K. Hassell, pp. 36–7, 46–50, 62–70; M. F. Christie, p. 66; D. Pike, pp. 169–94; E. Richards (ed.), *Flinders' History of South Australia*, p. 12.

CHAPTER 8: EDUCATION FOR DEMOCRACY

1   Cited in R. Knight, *Illiberal Liberal: Robert Lowe in New South Wales 1842–50*, MUP, Melbourne, 1966, p. 84.

2   H. Braverman, *Labor and Monopoly Capital*, Monthly Review Press, New York, 1974, p. 436. See also R. L. Schnell, 'Childhood as Ideology; A

Reinterpretation of the Common School', *British Journal of Educational Studies*, Vol. 27, 1 (February 1979); David Vincent, 'Reading in the Working-Class Home', in John K. Walton and James Walvin (eds), *Leisure in Britain 1780–1939*, Manchester University Press, Manchester, 1983, pp. 208–41.

3   David Vincent, p. 216; E. P. Thompson, *The Making of the English Working Class*, Penguin, Ringwood, 1981, pp. 782, 788–90. Cf. G. Stedman Jones, 'Class Expression versus Social Control? A Critique of Recent Trends in the Social History of "Leisure"', *History Workshop*, 4 (Autumn 1977), who addresses the problem of assuming that nineteenth-century reformers were motivated by the political and economic need to 'control' the working class. He points to the origins of the 'social control' theory in conservative functionalist sociology, plus its emphasis on arbitrarily programmed human responses and its failure to throw light on the role of individual agency in history. Cf. also M. Ignatieff who, criticising his own work, adds that the model of 'social control' is too crudely reductionist and conspiratorial, inferring conscious manipulation where no evidence for this exists ('State, Civil Society and Total Institution; A Critique of Recent Social Histories of Punishment' in D. Sugarman (ed.), *Legality, Ideology and the State*, Academy Press, London, 1983, pp. 200–3, 206). For a refutation of these arguments, see A. J. Donajgrodski (ed.), 'Introduction', in *Social Control in Nineteenth-Century Britain*, Croom Helm, London, 1977. I rely here on Antonio Gramsci, *Selections from the Prison Notebooks*, edited by Q. Hoare and G. Norvall Smith, International Publishers, New York, 1971. Never in doubt that there is a ruling class which seeks to maintain order through a wide range of social and cultural institutions, Gramsci focuses on 'hegemony', that is, the common and appealing values implicit in ruling-class strategies and ideologies which make it difficult for working people to develop a counter-ideology for resistance and change.

4   E. J. Hobsbawm, *Industry and Empire*, Penguin, Ringwood, 1981, pp. 72–6; B. Fitzpatrick, *The British Empire in Australia*, MUP, Melbourne, 1949, pp. 71–9. Cf. S. J. Butlin, *Foundations of the Australian Monetary System*, SUP, Sydney, 1968, pp. 315, 318; and F. Crowley (ed.), *A New History of Australia*, Heinemann, Melbourne, 1976, pp. 107–8. These works see the depression as primarily caused by local conditions within the pastoral industry, which in turn affected British investment, not the other way round. For falling stock prices and their effects, see S. H. Roberts, *The Squatting Age in Australia 1835–1847*, MUP, Melbourne, 1970, p. 192; T. F. Bride (ed.), *Letters from Victorian Pioneers*, Currey O'Neil, Melbourne, 1983, pp. 65, 312; M. Kiddle, *Men of Yesterday*, MUP, Melbourne, 1961, pp. 133–6; R. Therry, *Reminiscences of Thirty Years Residence in N.S.W. and Victoria*, Low, London, 1863, p. 264. For South Australia, see D. Pike, *Paradise of Dissent*, Longman, London, 1957, pp. 194, 241–2; *ADB*, I, pp. 431–5 (Gawler). For V.D.L. wheat, M. Bassett, *The Hentys*, OUP, Oxford, 1954, p. 509; for convicts unemployed, A. G. L. Shaw, *Convicts and the Colonies*, Faber & Faber, London, 1966, pp. 300–1.

5   S. H. Roberts, pp. 204, 315; D. N. Jeans, *An Historical Geography of New South Wales*, pp. 48–9; G. Wilson, *Murray of Yarralumla*, pp. 79, 192; J. Henderson, *Excursions and Adventures in New South Wales* (2 vols), Shoberl, London, 1851, I, p. 187; II, p. 68; J. Wright, *The Cry for the Dead*, p. 63.

6   S. J. Butlin, pp. 345–66; *ADB*, II, 500–1 (Swanston); G. Abbott and G. Little (eds), *The Respectable Sydney Merchant: A. B. Spark of Tempe*, SUP, Sydney, 1976, p. 168; J. Wright, p. 67; M. Barnard Eldershaw, *The Life and Times of Captain John Piper*, Ure Smith, Sydney, 1973, pp. 139–40; *ADB*, II, pp. 334–5 (Piper).

7   W. G. McMinn, *A Constitutional History of Australia*, OUP, Melbourne, 1979,

pp. 25–30; J. M. Ward, *James Macarthur: Colonial Conservative*, SUP, Sydney, 1981, pp. 100–2; H. King, *Richard Bourke*, OUP, Melbourne, 1971, Ch. 11, 16, 17. Arguably, this period in New South Wales politics has attracted more attention than it deserves, especially given the difficulty of distinguishing between 'gentry' and 'squatters' in the period up to 1842, owing to their common interest in promoting personal wealth from pastoralism. This tendency to focus on the alleged differences between New South Wales politicians rather than their similarities extends also to attempts to classify individuals as 'conservative' or 'liberal', a framework which can lead only to the conclusion that the conservatives were really liberals at heart, or that the protagonists constantly changed sides. (See for instance, A. G. L. Shaw, *Heroes and Villains: Governors Darling and Bourke in N.S.W.*, SUP, Sydney, 1966. These confusions arise partly from the failure to address the fact that the main power to determine policy still lay with the changing ruling class in Britain; and partly from an absence of analysis of liberalism itself and the various strategies it evolved over this period to meet the threat of worker demands. See R. W. Connell and T. H. Irving, *Class Structure in Australian History*, Longman Cheshire, Melbourne, 1980, p. 53. Cf. M. Roe, *Quest for Authority in Eastern Australia 1835–1851*, MUP, Melbourne, 1965, Ch. 2, 3, 4.

8   It is thus only in the period from 1842–47 that the 'squatters' can be seen as a distinct political lobby, separate from the older pastoralists who owned freehold land as well as holding leases. For their political manoeuvres in gaining tenure, see K. Buckley, 'Gipps and the Graziers of New South Wales 1841–1846', *HS*, Vol. 16, 24 (May 1955) and Vol. 7, 26 (May 1956) reprinted in *Historical Studies: Selected Articles*, MUP, Melbourne, 1974; B. Dyster, 'The Fate of Colonial Conservatism on the Eve of the Gold Rushes', *JRAHS*, Vol. 54, 4 (1968); T. H. Irving, 'Some Aspects of the Study of Radical Politics in N.S.W. Before 1856', *Labour History*, 5 (November 1963); J. Molony, *An Architect of Freedom: John Herbert Plunkett in N.S.W.* ANUP, Canberra, 1973; M. Roe. *passim.*

9   E. J. Hobsbawm, pp. 77, 94; D. Fernbach (ed.), *The Revolutions of 1848*, Harmondsworth, Penguin, 1973, pp. 27-8, 35; G. Rudé, *Protest and Punishment*, Clarendon Press, Oxford, 1978, pp. 131–44, 213–18.

10 G. P. Walsh, 'Factories and Factory Workers in New South Wales 1788–1900', *Labour History*, 21 (November 1971); G. J. Abbott, 'The Emigration to Valparaiso in 1843', *Labour History*, 19 (November 1970); NSW LC *V&P*, 1843, Report from the Select Committee on the Petition from Distressed Mechanics and Labourers with the Minutes of Evidence, pp. 719, 725, 727; NSW LC *V&P*, 1844, Vol. 2, p. 603.

11 L. J. Hume, 'Working Class Movements in Sydney and Melbourne Before the Gold Rushes, HS, Vol. 19, 35 (November 1960); M. Sullivan, *Men and Women of Port Phillip*, Hale & Iremonger, Sydney, 1985, pp. 234–43, 45; T. A. Coghlan, *Labour and Industry in Australia 1788–1901*, (4 vols), OUP, Oxford, 1918, I, p. 427; R. W. Connell and T. H. Irving, pp. 57, 61; M. Roe, pp. 94, 97, 107; *ADB*, V, pp. 399–400 (Parkes); VI, pp. 411–12 (Wilshire); NSW LC *V&P*, 1844, Vol. 2, pp. 607–8.

12 H. Braverman, p. 157; Bernard Smith, *Place, Taste and Tradition*, Ure Smith, Sydney, 1945, p. 87; *ADB*, II, p. 379 (Ridley); I, pp. 520–1 (Harrison); L. Robson, *A History of Tasmania*, I, pp. 180–1; Peter Ling, *Education in Australia*, Phillip Institute of Technology, Melbourne, 1984, p. 127; *SG*, 22 June, 18, 20, 25 July 1833; 10 February 1834; B. Smith, *European Vision in the South Pacific*, Clarendon Press, Oxford, 1960, pp. 222–3; *SH*, 8 June, 30 July 1841; NSW LC *V&P*, 1855, Vol. I, Select Committee on Sydney Mechanics'

School of Arts Bill, p. 1036. Cf. D. I. McDonald, 'The Diffusion of Scientific and Other Useful Knowledge', *JRAHS*, Vol. 54, Pt 2 (June 1968); G. Nadel, *Australia's Colonial Culture*, Cheshire, Melbourne, 1957, pp. 83, 111–26.

13 M. Roe, pp. 165–6, 172; *Temperance Advocate*, 16 December 1840, cited in E. Windschuttle, 'Women, Class and Temperance: Moral Reform in Eastern Australia 1832–1857', *Push From the Bush*, 3 (May 1979), p. 13; ibid., pp. 9–11, 17–21; *SG*, 3 November 1841; H. A. McCorkell (ed.), *The Diaries of Sarah Midgley and Richard Skilbeck: A Story of Australian Settlers 1851–1864*, Cassell, Melbourne, 1967; *The Teetotaller*, 1 March 1843, cited in E. Windschuttle, pp. 19–20.

14 As Marilyn Lake has pointed out regarding the temperance movement in Australia during the 1880s and '90s, women in the movement rightly perceived that male drinking, smoking, gambling and sexual promiscuity were aspects of male privilege which were injurious to women and children (M. Lake, 'The Politics of Respectability: Identifying the Masculinist Context', *HS*, Vol. 22, 86 (April 1986). Arguably, however, the problem is that because of their economic and political position, the temperance women saw the source of this behaviour to lie in individual moral failings, principally in the working-class male, a view which conveniently did not explore the relationship between these attitudes towards women and the structure of the economic system.

15 *SMH*, 8 February 1849 (Sydney Mechanics' Institute) cited in M. Roe, p. 151; *ADB*, II, p. 588 (Wentworth): J. D. Lang, *Freedom and Independence for the Golden Lands of Australia*, Longman, London, 1852, p. 136.

16 G. Abbott and G. Little, pp. 122, 136, 137, 191, 206. For male rights to children as property in the early nineteenth century, see H. Radi, 'Whose Child? Custody of Children in N.S.W. 1853–1934', in J. Mackinolty and H. Radi (eds), *In Pursuit of Justice: Australian Women and the Law 1788–1979*, Hale & Iremonger, Sydney, 1979, pp. 119–21. For the demands of child-bearing in other élite families, see B. H. Fletcher, 'Elizabeth Darling; Colonial Benefactress and Governor's Lady', *JRAHS*, Vol. 67, 4 (1982) especially p. 306; D. Walsh (ed.), *The Admiral's Wife: Mrs. Phillip Parker King: A Selection of Letters 1817–1856*, Hawthorn Press, Melbourne, 1967.

17 ML MS 1389/2 Mackenzie and Norton Families Papers (11 January 1834); *ADB*, II, p. 289 (Norton). See also D. Walsh, p. 57; H. McCrae (ed.), *Georgiana's Journal: Melbourne 1841–1865*, William Books, Sydney, 1978, pp. 79–80, 123, 127.

18 D. Walsh, p. 62; H. McCrae, pp. 50, 70, 171, 177; James S. Hassall, *In Old Australia: Records and Reminiscences from 1794*, (1st edn Hews, Brisbane, 1902), Library of Australian History, Sydney, 1981, p. 25; G. Abbott and G. Little, pp. 70, 178, 190. See also P. Statham (ed.), *The Tanner Letters*, UWAP, Nedlands, 1981, p. 64.

19 James S. Hassall, pp. 25, 31–3; ML MS A1677 Hassall Family Correspondence (4 vols), Vol. I (14 January 1841); G. Wilson, *Murray of Yarralumla*, pp. 178, 180.

20 Hassall Family Correspondence; D. Walsh, pp. 18, 87; G. Wilson, p. 167; H. McCrae, pp. 137, 156, 159, 181, 186; M. Herman (ed.), *Annabella Boswell's Journal*, Angus & Robertson, Sydney, 1965, pp. 56, 102; M. Bassett, *The Hentys*, p. 278.

21 P. Aries, *Centuries of Childhood*, Jonathan Cape, London, 1973, pp. 83–7, 256–7; J. R. Gillis, *Youth and History*, Academic Press, New York, 1974, pp. 74–5, 82, 111; *ADB*, I, pp. 506–7 (Halloran); *SG*, 3 July 1823; P. Cunningham, *Two Years in New South Wales*, I, Colburn, London, 1827, pp. 169–70.

22   *SG*, 25 August 1831; James S. Hassall, pp. 14–15; *ADB*, I, p. 211 (Carmichael); II, p. 77 (Lang); *SG*, 31 December 1831 (Curriculum of Australian
College). See also C. Turney, *Pioneers of Australian Education*, SUP, Sydney,
1969, pp. 61–77; A. Barcan, *A History of Australian Education*, OUP,
Melbourne, 1980. The fears of Lang and later, Bishop Broughton, that the
colony would be swamped with Catholics were unfounded. It was true that
of petitioners applying for financial assistance for the passages of relatives
from 1824, well over half were Catholics. However, even after the formal
system of assisted immigration began in 1831, the number of Catholics
immigrating to New South Wales did not alter the overall proportion of
Catholics in the colony which remained at about 30 per cent (James
Waldersee, *Catholic Society in New South Wales*, SUP, Sydney, 1974, pp. 76,
81, 107–9). See also P. O'Farrrell, *The Irish in Australia*, UNSW Press,
Kensington, 1986.

23   *ADB*, I, pp. 455–6 (Gell), 436–7 (Elliston); K. Fitzpatrick, *Sir John Franklin
in Tasmania 1837–1843*, MUP, Carlton, 1949, pp. 181–92; J. M. Ward,
'Foundation of the University of Sydney', *JRAHS*, Vol. 37, 5 (1951);
C. Turney (ed.) pp. 81–99; G. Blainey, *The University of Melbourne*, MUP,
Melbourne, 1956. Plans for a local university dated from the early 1820s.
See F. L. Wood, 'Some Early Educational Problems and W. C. Wentworth's
Work for Higher Education', *JRAHS*, Vol. 17, 6 (1931), pp. 387–8.

24   R. Knight, p. 84; M. Belcher, 'The Child in New South Wales Society
1820–1837', PhD thesis, University of New England, 1982, pp. 130, 137;
Census of New South Wales, 1841; G. Abbott and G. Little, pp. 95–6.

25   Anne O'Brien, 'Left in the Lurch: Deserted Wives in New South Wales at
the Turn of the Century' in J. Mackinolty and H. Radi (eds), *In Pursuit of
Justice*, pp. 96–8; C. J. Cummins, 'The Development of the Benevolent
(Sydney) Asylum', N.S.W. Department of Health, Sydney, 1971, pp. 1–3;
Joan C. Brown, *'Poverty is Not a Crime': Social Services in Tasmania 1803–1900*,
Tasmanian Historical Research Association, Hobart, 1972, pp. 12–13, 21,
35–9, 58–9. See also D. Peyser, 'History of Welfare Work in Sydney
1788–1900', *JRAHS*, Vol. 25, 2 (1939); B. Dickey, *No Charity There: A Short
History of Social Welfare Work in Australia*, Nelson, Melbourne, 1984; John
Ramsland, *Children of the Backlanes: Destitute and Neglected Children in Colonial
New South Wales*, UNSW Press, Kensington, 1986.

26   NSW LC *V&P*, 1837, Minutes of Evidence Taken Before the Committee
on Immigration, Indian and British, pp. 652–5; NSW LC *V&P*, 1838, Pt 2,
Report From the Select Committee on Immigration with the Minutes of
Evidence, pp. 68ff, 87. See also pp. 7–8 (Evidence of James Lawrence) and
41 (James Stuart). For conditions on the emigrant ships, see also B. Gandevia,
Tears Often Shed, Pergamon Press, Sydney, 1978, pp. 49–51; P. O'Farrell,
Letters From Irish Australia 1825–1829, UNSWP, Kensington, 1984, pp. 20,
25. For Sarah Davenport, '"We Was Coming to Better Ourselves"
Memories of the 1840s' in Lucy Frost (ed.), *No Place for a Nervous Lady*,
Penguin, Ringwood, 1985, p. 243. For working-class housing, NSW LC
V&P, Vol. 4, 1859–60, Report From the Select Committee on the Condition
of the Working Classes of the Metropolis, p. 1268; Walter S. Campbell,
'Some Old Cries, Old Customs, and Old Practices in the Middle Ages of
Sydney, 1848–1861', *JRAHS*, Vol. 14, Pt 2 (1928). Brian Dickey, *Rations,
Residence, Resources: A History of Social Welfare in South Australia Since 1836*,
Wakefield, Netley, S.A., 1986, pp. 3–16.

27   Benevolent Society of N.S.W., 'Inmates Journal', ML MS A7227 (Fanny
Doran).

28   M. Belcher, pp. 162–4, 180. See also James Waldersee, p. 91. Average
completed family size was, however, almost certainly higher in other

colonies by mid-century. A study of a sample of women who married in Western Australia in the early 1850s and who registered the births of their children, found that these women each produced eight or more children by the close of their reproductive life. Similarly, a group of women who registered the birth of their first child in Castlemaine, Victoria, in 1861 and who were traced to the registration of their final child were found to have produced some nine children by the end of their period of family formation (M. Grellier, 'The Family: Some Aspects of its Demography and Ideology in Mid-Nineteenth-Century York', in C. T. Stannage (ed.), *A New History of Western Australia*, UWAP, Nedlands, 1981, pp. 489–90); P. Grimshaw and Charles Fahey, 'Family and Community in Nineteenth-Century Castlemaine', in P. Grimshaw, C. McConville and E. McEwen (eds), *Families in Colonial Australia*, Allen & Unwin, Sydney, 1985, pp. 96–7).

29   NSW LC *V&P*, 1838, Pt 2, Report from the Committee on Immigration with the Minutes of Evidence, p. 17. See also NSW LC *V&P*, 1835, Minutes of Evidence Taken before Select Committee on Immigration, p. 301 (Dr James Eckford); M. Belcher, pp. 180–3. For the dependance of Swan River settlers on the unpaid labour of children, including Aboriginal ones, aged from around nine years, see P. Statham (ed.), *The Tanner Letters*, pp. 30–2 (1831–32); A. Hasluck (ed.), *A Faithful Picture: The Letters of Eliza and Thomas Brown . . .*, Fremantle Arts Centre Press, Fremantle, 1977, p. 64 (1845). For the importation of boy labour to South Australia arranged by Lord Shaftesbury and the Ragged Schools Union in 1848–53, Gillian Wagner, *Children of the Empire*, Weidenfeld & Nicolson, London, 1982, pp. 26–33.

30   J. Locke, *Report to the Board of Trade on the Poor* (1697) cited in *Two Treatises of Government*, edited by P. Laslett, New American Library, New York, 1965, (Introduction) p. 56. M. Horsburgh's detailed analyses in 'The Apprenticing of Dependent Children in New South Wales between 1850 and 1885', *Journal of Australian Studies*, 7 (November 1980) refer to a later period, but this evidence on the 1830s and 1840s suggests his conclusions apply equally well to these decades. See also J. H. Cleverley, *The First Generation: School and Society in Early Australia*, SUP, Sydney, 1971, pp. 88–9, 94. Cf. P. Robinson, *The Hatch and Brood of Time*, OUP, Melbourne, 1985, pp. 121–44. Robinson's information on the punishment of apprentices (p. 136) would seem to undermine her argument that the system was about education rather than exploitation. For punishment, see also M. Horsburgh, p. 44 (treadmill and solitary confinement, 1842) and compare the notices issued for escaped apprentices and convict labourers, for example, *SH*, 29 June 1841. For a discussion of early plans to import child labour from Britain, see B. Fitzpatrick, *The British Empire in Australia*, pp. 64–5; G. Wagner.

31   Female School of Industry, *Annual Reports*, 1827, 1829; E. Windschuttle, '"Feeding the Poor and Sapping their Strength": The Public Role of Ruling-Class Women in Eastern Australia 1788–1850' in E. Windschuttle (ed.), *Women, Class and History*, Fontana/Collins, Melbourne, 1980, pp. 65–71.

32   Robert J. Hind, 'Working People and Sunday Schools: England, 1780–1850', *Journal of Religious History*, Vol. 15, 2 (1988); S. M. Johnstone, *The Founding of Sunday Schools in England and Australia*, Sydney, 1913; A. T. Yarwood, *Samuel Marsden*, MUP, Melbourne, 1977, pp. 208–9; *SG*, 27 June, 3 July 1823; *SMH*, 17 May 1842; John Barrett, *That Better Country: The Religious Aspect of Life in Eastern Australia 1835–1850*, MUP, Melbourne, 1966, pp. 147–52.

33   *SG*, 16 December 1824; *HRA*, I, xii, p. 315; M. Walker, 'The Development of Kindergartens in Australia', MEd thesis, University of Sydney, 1964, pp. 35–7, 46–7; *The Colonist*, 6 January 1838, 21 December 1839.

34   C. J. Cleverley, pp. 80–4; J. T. Bigge, *Report of the Commissioner of Inquiry on the State of Agriculture and Trade in New South Wales*, (*BPP*, X, No. 136, 1823), reprinted by Libraries Board of South Australia, Adelaide, 1966, pp. 74, 76. At first it was assumed that most children would leave the charity school by about the age of eight. See *HRA*, III, v, pp. 157–8 (Report on V.D.L. Schools, Scott to Arthur 13 February 1826). For discussion of the Lancaster-Bell methods in the charity school and their role in educating the 'faculties', see NSW LC *V&P*, 1844, Vol. 2, Report from the Select Committee on Education with Appendix and Minutes of Evidence, p. 475 (Reverend Ralph Mansefield), p. 477 ('Scriptural Enlightenment'—Extract from the Manual of the British and Foreign School Society). On the need for 'perpetual vigilance' in the elementary school, p. 505 (Polding). For Catholic schoolroom practice, see W. A. Greening, 'The Irish Christian Brothers' First Mission to Sydney 1843–1847', MEd thesis, University of Melbourne, 1981, pp. 78–101.

35   Bourke's Opening Address to Legislative Council, 2 June 1836 (NSW LC *V&P*, 1836, pp. 445–62); NSW LC *V&P*, 1844, Vol. 2, Report from the Select Committee on Education . . ., pp. 451–2. This committee estimated that, despite the efforts of the churches, less than half of the colony's children aged between four and fourteen were attending school and was also informed that attendance was very irregular (ibid., pp. 529, 569). Some secularists went so far as to argue that the Bible was unsuitable for children for it contained matter likely to excite 'lascivious sentiments' in the youthful mind. See ibid. p. 535 (John H. Baillie). For the attempts of Henry Carmichael to implement a curriculum based on Benthamite, secularist principles, see C. Turney (ed.), pp. 59–68.

36   J. S. Gregory, *Church and State*, Cassell, Melbourne, 1973, pp. 1–4, 11–13; John Barrett, pp. 31–2; A. R. Vidler, *The Church in the Age of Revolution*, Hodder & Stoughton, London, 1962, pp. 43–4; L. Goldmann, *The Hidden God*, Routledge & Kegan Paul, London, 1977, pp. 28–34.

37   John Barrett, pp. 20–3; Allan M. Grocott, *Convicts, Clergymen and Churches*, SUP, Sydney, 1980, pp. 91–6. For the Church Acts and their effect in increasing sectarianism, see John Barrett, pp. 29ff; Naomi Turner, *Sinews of Sectarian Warfare? State Aid in New South Wales 1836–1862*, ANUP, Canberra, 1972, especially p. 35.

38   J. S. Gregory, pp. 13–43; John Barrett, Ch. 6–8; J. F. Cleverley, 'Governor Bourke and the Introduction of the Irish National System' in C. Turney (ed.), pp. 27–58; H. King, pp. 226–31; J. Molony, pp. 203–8; J. M. Ward, pp. 3, 55–8; R. Knight, pp. 88, 90, 96; K. Fitzpatrick, pp. 174–80; *Hobart Courier*, 23 June 1837, cited in M. Roe, p. 151. See also G. Nadel, pp. 186–213.

CHAPTER 9: CULTURE

1   I. Brodsky, *Sydney Takes the Stage*, Old Sydney Free Press, Sydney, 1963, pp. 6, 9; M. St Leon, *Spangles and Sawdust: The Circus in Australia*, Greenhouse Publications, Melbourne, 1983, p. 13; J. Kardoss, *A Brief History of the Australian Theatre*, Sydney University Drama Society, Sydney, 1955, pp. 15–17, 20; M. Williams, *Australia on the Popular Stage 1829–1929*, OUP, Melbourne, pp. 35, 50. For Sydney's Theatre Royal, see E. Irwin, *Theatre Comes to Australia*, UQP, St Lucia, 1971. For the separation of leisure from work and for the economic and political need to provide official diversions for labourers, R. W. Malcolmson, *Popular Recreations in English Society*

1700–1850, CUP, Cambridge, 1973, pp. 71 (Adam Smith), 89–99. *The Blossom* cited in I. Brodsky, p. 6.

2　M. Bakhtin, *Rabelais and His World*, Indiana University Press, Bloomington, 1984, pp. 19–21, 31, 33; Peter Burke, *Popular Culture in Early Modern Europe*, T. Smith, London, 1978, pp. 204–81; R. W. Malcolmson, pp. 50, 53–4; E. P. Thompson, 'Patrician Society, Plebian Culture', *Journal of Social History*, Vol. 7 (1974), pp. 391–4, 396–401.

3　Formerly a medium of popular culture, theatre had been suppressed during the seventeenth century in England. See C. Hill, *Collected Essays*, Harvester Press, Brighton, 1985, Ch. 1 and 2. For suspicion of its revival in the convict colonies as an instrument of approved culture, see 'Cestria', *SG*, 9 December 1824. For its introduction to convicts at Emu Plains in 1825, E. Irvin, pp. 10–12.

4　M. Bakhtin, pp. 318–19; Ariel Dorfmann, *The Empire's Old Clothes*, Pantheon, New York, 1983, p. ix. In defining culture as information, potentially serving a political purpose, and distinguishing between 'popular' culture and 'popularized', I am working against the structuralist definition offered by anthropologist Clifford Geertz, which has proved so influential with historians. Though Geertz's concept of culture has altered during the 1960s and 1970s, for him culture, like utterance, is a system of encoded representations of a higher and hidden language by which all human beings order and make sense of space and time, thus constructing their own reality. In doing so, they are guided by permanent arbitrary structures of the human psyche. Therefore, more than merely patterned social behaviour, culture is a particular 'frame of mind'. As Kenneth Rice writes, for Geertz, a cultureless human being would not only lack vital sources of information but also certain mental attributes which are essential to the processes of human thought and without which individuals cannot make sense of their experience (Kenneth A. Rice, *Geertz and Culture*, Ann Arbor, 1980, pp. 219–21). The task of the anthropologist (or historian) thus becomes one of interpreting the meaning of cultural forms in terms of these hidden psychological universals and their complex layers of psychic and social messages, 'reading' ethnology as if it was a text. This anthropological approach has enabled historians to study numerous new areas of popularized culture, ritual and myth as legitimate areas for scholarly research. However, it is also theoretically problematic. For one thing, the definition of culture becomes so wide as to be almost meaningless, part of a system of significant 'symbols' ranging from language, stories, music, art and ritual events to mere acts of conventionalized behaviour and social institutions. A cultural symbol is 'anything, in fact, that is disengaged from its mere actuality and used to impose meaning upon experience' ('The Impact of the Concept of Culture on the Concept of Man' (1966) reprinted in C. Geertz, *The Interpretation of Cultures*, Basic Books, New York, 1973, p. 45). In this 'total' approach, the distinction between 'high' and 'low' or popularized culture disappears, along with analysis of how and why 'high' culture appropriated popular forms for its own purposes and how 'low' culture both exploited the people and served the status quo. See, for example, John Rickard, 'Cultural History: The "High" and the "Popular"' in S. L. Goldberg and F. B. Smith (eds), *Australian Cultural History*, CUP, Cambridge, 1988, pp. 18, 183 and *Australia: A Cultural History*, Longman/Cheshire, Melbourne, 1988, p. xi. A second problem with the Geertzian approach is that it rests on the a-historical notion that certain cultural universals exist beyond human action and to some extent determine it. Far from being created or invested with meaning by identifiable human beings with an identifiable purpose, cultural symbols are part of the timeless, pre-existing language which allegedly shapes human thought. The reason why cultural images and messages were formulated in the first place becomes of no interest, nor can it be explained whether or why these images change. For further discussion of cultural historiography in Australia, see Richard Waterhouse, 'Writing the History of Popular Culture', *AHA Bulletin*, 48 (September 1986); John Colmer, 'Australian Cultural Analysis: Some Principles and Problems', *Southerly* (September 1978); S. Alomes, 'Australian Popular Culture Revisited', *Overland*, 85 (October 1981).

5   M. Williams, pp. 29, 38; R. Waterhouse, *From Minstrel Show to Vaudeville: The Australian Popular Stage 1788–1914*, UNSW Press, Kensington, 1990, pp. 3–15, 22–30; H. Oppenheim, 'The Author of "The Hibernian Father": An Early Colonial Playright', *Australian Literary Studies*, Vol. 2, 4 (1966), pp. 279–80; J. Maclehose, *Picture of Sydney and Stranger's Guide to N.S.W. for 1839*, Sydney, 1839, p. 130; *SG*, 20 February, 9 August 1834; E. Irvin, Appendix, pp. 235–48. For the growing popularity of the dying child theme, P. Coveney, *The Image of Childhood*, Penguin, Harmondsworth, 1967, pp. 159–83.

6   M. Williams, p. 58; M. Bakhtin, p. 197; M. St. Leon, p. 19. For fancy dress balls, G. Abbott and G. Little (eds), *The Respectable Sydney Merchant: A. B. Spark of Tempe*, SUP, Sydney, 1976, p. 123 (12 August 1840); E. Irvin, Plate facing p. 132 (21 August 1844).

7   E. P. Thompson, pp. 387–90; J. J. Tobias, *Crime and Industrial Society in Nineteenth Century*, Penguin, Harmondsworth, 1976, p. 195; R. W. Malcolmson, pp. 20–5; B. H. Fletcher, 'The Agricultural Society of New South Wales and its Shows in Colonial Sydney', *Journal and Proceedings of the Royal Society of N.S.W.*, Vol. 118 (1985), p. 195; Report of the Agricultural and Horticultural Society of N.S.W. for 1828; L. Robson, *A History of Tasmania*, OUP, Melbourne, 1983, I, p. 182. See also H. M. Somer, 'Short History of the Royal Agricultural Society of New South Wales', *JRAHS*, Vol. 9, Pt 5 (1923); M. Roe, *Quest for Authority in Eastern Australia*, MUP, Melbourne, 1965, p. 38.

8   J. Atkinson, *An Account of the State of Agriculture and Grazing in New South Wales*, (1st edn, Cross, London, 1826), SUP, Sydney, 1975, pp. 31, 63, 80; J. C. Garran and L. White, *Merinos, Myths and Macarthurs*, ANUP, Canberra, 1985, pp. 57, 216, 235; P. Cunningham, *Two Years in New South Wales*, Colburn, London, 1827, I, p. 291; M. Kiddle, *Men of Yesterday*, MUP, Melbourne, 1961, p. 381.

9   L. Meredith, *Notes and Sketches of New South Wales* (1st edn, 1844), Ure Smith, Sydney, 1973, p. 41; L. Robson, p. 363; J. Fenton, *Bush Life in Tasmania Fifty Years Ago* (1st edn, 1891), Richmond and Sons, Devonport, 1964, pp. 108, 118–9. For the variety of plants available commercially by the 1840s, see *SMH*, 15 April 1848 (advertisement for John Baptist, Surry Hills). See also V. Crittenden, *The Front Garden: The Story of the Cottage Garden in Australia*, Mulini Press, Canberra, 1979; R. T. M. Pescott, *W. R. Guilfoyle 1840–1912*, OUP, Melbourne, 1974; B. Smith (ed.), *Documents on Art and Taste in Australia*, OUP, Melbourne, 1975, pp. 40–50 (Thomas Shepherd 'On Planning the Gardens of the Marine Villas of Port Jackson', 1836); B. Smith, *Place, Taste and Tradition*, Ure Smith, Sydney, 1945, p. 91. See also E. Rolls, *They All Ran Wild*, Allen & Unwin, Sydney, 1969, pp. 225–6; G. Bolton, *Spoils and Spoilers*, Angus & Robertson, Sydney, 1981, pp. 85–7.

10   K. Fitzpatrick, *Sir John Franklin in Tasmania*, MUP, Melbourne, 1949, p. 194;

J. M. Freeland, *Architecture in Australia: A History*, Penguin, Harmondsworth, 1982, p. 30; H. M. Somer, p. 321; G. Abbott and G. Little (eds), pp. 97, 138, 188; *SMH*, 10 July 1844 (summary of aims and members of Floral and Horticultural Society); B. Smith, *European Vision in the South Pacific*, Clarendon Press, Oxford, 1960, pp. 220–3.

11   N.S.W. LC *V&P*, 1835, Pt II, Minute of the Governor to the Legislative Council, Explanatory of Heads of Expenditure 1835, p. 211; Minutes of Evidence Taken Before the Committee on Immigration 1835, p. 294 (William Macpherson); A Mozley Moyal (ed.), *Scientists in Nineteenth-Century Australia*, Cassell, Melbourne, 1976, pp. 39–40; L. A. Gilbert, *Royal Botanic Gardens Sydney: A History 1816–1985*, OUP, Melbourne, 1986. For the Melbourne Gardens, see R. T. M. Pescott.

12   *SG*, 19 June 1841; 31 October 1831 (bull-baiting). For cock-fighting, see also *SG*, 29 December 1831. See also John O'Hara, *A Mug's Game: A History of Gaming and Betting in Australia*, UNSW Press, Kensington, 1988. In Britain, protest against working-class sports involving cruelty to animals grew rapidly from 1800. Legislation passed in 1822 against cruelty to cattle was extended to bears, badgers, dogs and cocks in 1835. In contrast, little action was taken against aristocratic blood-sports during the nineteenth century. See Brian Harrison, 'Animals and the State in Nineteenth-Century England', *English Historical Review*, Vol. 88 (1973); R. W. Malcolmson, pp. 119–38, 172–3. For 'man fighting', see R. W. Malcolmson, pp. 19, 42–3; Peter Corris, *Lords of the Ring*, Cassell, Sydney, 1980, pp. 4–7, 27. For 'Cabbage-tree larkers', *SH*, 10 June 1841; G. C. Mundy, *Our Antipodes* (1st edn, 1852), Bentley, London, 1857, p. 8.

13   *SH*, 19 June 1841; 24, 25 May 1842; Joseph P. Townsend, *Rambles and Observations in New South Wales . . .*, Chapman & Hall, London, 1849, pp. 258–60 (26 January 1846); M. Barnard Eldershaw, *The Life and Times of Captain John Piper*, Ure Smith, Sydney, 1973, p. 115; K. Fitzpatrick, pp. 168–70.

14   J. Atkinson, p. 18; *SG*, 30 July 1833; *SH*, 20 May 1842; W. Mandle, 'Games People Played: Cricket and Football in England and Victoria in the Late Nineteenth Century', *HS*, Vol. 15, 60 (April 1973); 'Cricket and Australian Nationalism in the Nineteenth Century', *JRAHS*, Vol. 59, Pt 4 (December 1973); Leonie Sandercock and Ian Turner, *Up Where, Cazaly?*, Granada, Sydney, 1981, pp. 9–10, 19–25. For the belief that the colonial environment was evolving a superior national type, see R. Ward and K. McNab, 'The Nature and Nurture of the First Generation of Native-Born Australians', *HS*, Vol. 10, 39 (November 1962). For 'Bill Kangaroo' and 'Betsey Bandicoot', *SG*, 30 October 1823, p. 4. Cf. C. M. H. Clark, *A History of Australia*, II, MUP, Melbourne, 1968, pp. 157–8. See also R. White, *Inventing Australia*, Allen & Unwin, Sydney, 1981, pp. 24–8.

15   M. Barnard Eldershaw, pp. 114, 135; R. Waterhouse, *The Principal Club; The AJC and the History of Australian Horse Racing*, Sydney, 1992, Ch. I; *ADB*, I, p. 475 (Gregson), II, pp. 10–12 (Jamison); B. H. Fletcher, 'Sir John Jamison in New South Wales 1814–1844', *JRAHS*, Vol. 65, Pt 1 (June 1979) p. 10; G. Abbott and G. Little (eds), pp. 133, 144; Leonie Sandercock and Ian Turner, p. 12; J. D. Lang, *Phillipsland*, Constable, Edinburgh, 1847, cited in M. Kiddle, p. 79. The popularity of racing in colonial Australia owed much to its promotion first by military officers with a professional interest in improving the breed and later by the rural elite. The Australian Jockey Club dates from 1842 (R. Waterhouse).

16   *ADB*, I, p. 475 (Gregson); P. Cunningham, I, pp. 112, 171, 304, 317. See also James S. Hassall, *In Old Australia*, (1st edn, Hews, Brisbane, 1902), Library

of Australian History, Sydney, 1981, pp. 31–2 (informal hunting of native animals at night). See also G. Bolton, pp. 89–90; E. Rolls, pp. 7–25, 210–12.

17 *ADB*, I, p. 475 (Gregson), II, p. 398 (Ross), p. 455 (Snodgrass), III, p. 109 (Barry), p. 501 (Crowther); L. Robson, p. 363; T. F. Bride (ed.), *Letters from Victorian Pioneers*, Currey O'Neil, Melbourne, 1983, p. 214. For other duellists, see *ADB*, I, p. 355 (John Montague and Henry Arthur), II, p. 572 (Robert Wardell and Saxe Bannister), II, p. 241 (Thomas Mitchell and Stuart Donaldson).

18 E. Webby, 'English Literature in Early Australia: 1820–29', *Southerly*, Vol. 27, 4 (1967), pp. 281–2; G. Abbott and G. Little, p. 3; G. Nadel, *Australia's Colonial Culture*, Harvard University Press, Mass., 1957, pp. 79–83; C. H. Spence, *An Autobiography*, Thomas, Adelaide, 1910, p. 20; M. Herman (ed.), *Annabella Boswell's Journal*, Angus & Robertson, Sydney, 1965, pp. 53, 56; M. Kiddle, p. 92.

19 E. Webby, p. 271. See also 'English Literature in Early Australia 1830–39', *Southerly*, Vol. 39, 1 (1976) pp. 73–87; '. . . 1840–49', ibid., Vol. 39, 2 (1976) pp. 200–13; G. Nadel, pp. 77–8, 96, 102; D. Mackenzie, *Ten Years in Australia*, Orr, London, 1851, p. 44 cited in M. Roe, p. 186; L. Robson, p. 183. See also R. B. Walker, *The Newspaper Press in New South Wales 1803–1920*, SUP, Sydney, 1976; H. Melville, *The History of the Island of Van Diemen's Land from the Year 1824 to 1835 Inclusive*, edited by G. Mackaness, D. S. Ford, Sydney, 1959, especially II, p. 25, III, pp. 46–54; H. Savery, *Quintus Servinton*, edited by C. Hadgraft, Jacaranda Press, Brisbane, 1962.

20 E. Windschuttle, 'The New Science of Etiquette', *Push From the Bush*, 7 (September 1980). See also Leonore Davidoff, *The Best Circles; Society, Etiquette and the Season*, Croom Helm, London, 1973. For Mrs Bunn, see G. Wilson, *Murray of Yarralumla*, pp. 89–90; for Mrs Dunlop E. Webby, 'Reactions to Myall Creek Massacre', *Push From the Bush*, 8 (December 1980), pp. 9–10.

21 M. Swann, 'Mrs. Meredith and Mrs. Atkinson', *JRAHS*, Vol. 15, Pt 1 (1929); M. Muir, *Charlotte Barton; Australia's First Children's Author*, Wentworth, Sydney, 1980; *A Mother's Offering to Her Children by A Lady Long Resident in New South Wales* (1st edn, *Gazette*, Sydney, 1841), Jacaranda Press, Brisbane, 1979; *SG*, 23 December 1841.

22 W. C. Wentworth, *Australasia: A Poem*, Whittaker, London, 1823 reprinted in J. Hennicker Heaton, *Australian Dictionary of Dates*, Robertson, Sydney, 1879; E. Darwin, 'Visit of Hope to Sydney Cove Near Botany Bay' in J. Auchmuty (ed.), *The Voyage of Governor Phillip to Botany Bay*, Angus & Robertson, 1970, p. xxiii; G. Mackaness (ed.), *Odes of Michael Massey Robinson*, Ford, Sydney, 1946; G. A. Wilkes, *Australian Literature: A Conspectus*, Angus & Robertson, Sydney, 1969, pp. 12–13.

23 B. Field, *First Fruits of Australian Poetry*, AGPS, Sydney, 1819, reprinted in *Geographical Memoirs of New South Wales*, Murray, London, 1825 (Appendix); C. Tompson, *Wild Notes From the Lyre of a Native Minstrel*, Robert Howe, Government Printer, Sydney, 1826; *ADB*, II, p. 533 (Tompson).

24 G. A. Wilkes, pp. 21–3; *ADB*, I, pp. 514–5 (Harpur); A. Mitchell (ed.), *Charles Harpur*, Sun Books, Melbourne, 1973; M. Roe, pp. 148–50; G. Nadel, pp. 60–73.

25 'Some Lawson Letters 1819–1824', *JRAHS*, Vol. 50, Pt 3 (August 1964); G. Abbott and G. Little (eds), p. 67; M. Herman, p. 16; M. Kiddle, pp. 95–6; G. F. Moore cited in P. Statham (ed.), p. 25; cf. H. McQueen, *A New Britannia: An Argument Concerning the Social Origins of Australian Radicalism and Nationalism*, Penguin, Ringwood, 1975, pp. 117–19 (pianos); 'A Convict's

Tour of Hell' reprinted in L. Murray (ed.), *The New Oxford Book of Australian Verse*, OUP, Melbourne, 1986, pp. 23–8.

26   M. Williams, pp. 14–16. Though R. Ward's *The Australian Legend*, OUP, Melbourne, 1958 cast new light upon the importance of the ballads as a historical source, he failed to distinguish the political purposes to which they were put by later, middle-class writers. H. McQueen rightly pointed to the conservativism and racism of these later writers, but because of the nihilism of his analysis, assumed that all culture, including the original ballads, must be equally bourgeois (*A New Britannia*, pp. 130–7, 101–16). D. Walker, (*Dream and Disillusion*, ANUP, Canberra, 1976), and R. White (*Inventing Australia*) pointed to the immediate vested interest which the professional writers and artists had in exploiting convict themes but did not explain the deeper purposes which national legends have served firstly in exploiting and depoliticizing worker communities and, by the 1890s, in preventing the growth of worker internationalism. For the romantification of the maritime frontier, see the novels of Louis Becke. See also Gavan Daws, *A Dream of Islands: Voyages of Self-Discovery in the South Seas*, Jacaranda Press, Brisbane, 1980 (Melville, Stevenson, Gauguin).

27   *Australian*, 7 September 1841 cited in M. Roe, p. 156; C. H. Bertie, *Isaac Nathan Australia's First Composer*, Angus & Robertson, Sydney, 1922; *ADB*, II, pp. 279–80. Nathan was also interested in Aboriginal music, as was Mrs Dunlop. See C. H. Bertie, pp. 19–20; *SG*, 19 October 1841, 16 April, 25 August 1842; *ADB*, I, p. 337 (Dunlop).

28   G. Abbott and G. Little (eds), pp. 3, 48–9, 185–6; *SMH*, 24 May 1847; J. Kerr (ed.), *A Dictionary of Australian Artists* (A–H), Power Institute, Sydney, 1984; B. Smith, *European Vision in the South Pacific*, pp. 165–6, 191–4, 201, 203; C. Turnbull, *Black War*, Sun Books, Melbourne, 1974, pp. 231–3; G. Dutton, *White on Black*, Macmillan, Melbourne, 1974, pp. 126–7; B. Smith, *Place, Taste and Tradition*, pp. 36–55, 67–9.

29   E. P. Thompson, p. 395; M. Barnard Eldershaw, pp. 123–6; B. H. Fletcher, 'Sir John Jamison in New South Wales', pp. 5–6; G. Mackaness (ed.), *Fourteen Journeys Over the Blue Mountains*, Sydney, 1965, pp. 94, 104; J. M. Freeland, pp. 75, 80; J. Broadbent, I. Evans and C. Lucas, *The Golden Decade of Australian Architecture: The Work of John Verge*, David Ell Press, Sydney, 1978; J. Kerr and J. Broadbent, *Gothick Taste in in the Colony of New South Wales*, David Ell Press, Sydney, 1980, especially pp. 91–7; M. Girouard, *The Return to Camelot: Chivalry and the English Gentleman*, Yale University Press, New Haven and London, 1981, pp. 21–4, 92–6. See also M. Dupain and J. M. Freeland, *Francis Greenaway*, Cassell, Sydney, 1980; E. G. Robertson, *Early Houses of Northern Tasmania* (2 vols), Georgian House, Melbourne, 1964; M. Cantlon, *Homesteads of Southern New South Wales 1830–1900*, Queensberry Hill Press, Melbourne, 1981; R. Irving (ed.), *The History and Design of the Australian House*, OUP, Melbourne, 1985.

30   R. Knight, *Illiberal Liberal: Robert Lowe in New South Wales 1842–50*, MUP, Melbourne, 1966, p. 93; J. Kerr and J. Broadbent, pp. 56, 66, 96; P. O'Farrell, *The Catholic Church in Australia 1788–1967*, Nelson, Melbourne, 1969, pp. 19–27; *ADB*, I, pp. 109–10 (Blackburn).

31   M. Girouard, pp. 130–42, 160–8; P. G. Spillett, *Forsaken Settlement*, Lansdowne Press, Melbourne, 1972, pp. 125–6; *HRA*, I, xxiii, p. 246, xxiv, pp. 50–5, 835; L. Leichhardt, *Journal of an Overland Expedition in Australia* (1st edn, Boone, London, 1847), Macarthur Press, Sydney, n.d., pp. 158, 538–44 (Appendix); *ADB*, II, pp. 102–4 (Leichhardt).

32   V. Kruta *et al.*, *Dr. John Lhotsky: The Turbulent Australian Writer, Naturalist and Explorer*, Australia Felix Literary Club, Melbourne, 1977, pp. 14–15, 45–6,

67; J. Lhotsky, *A Journey From Sydney to the Australian Alps* (1st edn, Sydney, 1835) edited by E. J. Andrews, Blubber Head Press, Hobart, 1979.

33   E. J. Eyre, *Journals of Expeditions of Discovery Into Central Australia . . .*, (1st edn, Boone Press, London, 1845), Libraries Board of South Australia, Adelaide, 1964. In fact, key British makers of the cult of chivalry were divided on the question of Eyre's actions in Jamaica. Carlyle, Kingsley and Tennyson defended him, but J. S. Mill, Spencer, Huxley and Thomas Hughes believed he had let the side down. See further G. Dutton, *The Hero as Murderer*, Collins, Melbourne, 1966.

34   K. Fitzpatrick, pp. 345–9, 287–300, 370–4.

35   C. Sturt, *Journal of the Central Australian Expedition 1844–45*, edited by J. Waterhouse, Caliban, London, 1984, pp. 2, 7–8; T. Mitchell, *Journal of an Expedition into Tropical Australia*, Longman, London, 1848, especially pp. 332–3.

36   W. Carron, *Narrative of an Expedition . . . for the Exploration of the Country Lying Between Rockingham Bay and Cape York*, (1st edn, Keep and Fairfax, Sydney, 1849), Libraries Board of South Australia, Adelaide, 1965, especially pp. 4, 26; M. Bassett, *Behind the Picture: H.M.S. Rattlesnake's Australia–New Guinea Cruise 1846 to 1850*, OUP, Melbourne, 1966, pp. 42–5; C. M. H. Clark, *A History of Australia*, III, MUP, Melbourne, 1973, p. 402; *ADB*, II, p. 7 ('Jackey Jackey'). Cf. E. Beale, *Kennedy of Cape York*, Rigby, Adelaide, 1970. For memories of Kennedy's militaristic and officious training of his men, see Dorothy Jones, *Cardwell Shire Story*, Jacaranda Press, Brisbane, 1961, p. 29 ('You had to wait for an order to put your foot in the stirrup and wait for another order to mount.').

CHAPTER 10: THE MANUFACTURE OF MAN

1   G. Grey, *Two Expeditions of Discovery in North-West and Western Australia . . .* (2 vols), (1st edn, Boone Press, London, 1841), Hesperian Press, Victoria Park, WA, 1984, II, pp. 217–18. For Grey's ethnology, see G. W. Stocking, *Victorian Anthropology*, Free Press, New York, 1987, pp. 81–7.

2   M. Foucault, *The Order of Things: An Archaeology of the Human Sciences*, Tavistock, London, 1970, pp. 145, 161; Reverend Thomas Dove, 'Moral and Social Characteristics of the Aborigines of Tasmania', *Tasmanian Journal of Natural Science, Agriculture and Statistics*, Vol. I, 1842, reprinted in R. S. Miller (ed.), *Thomas Dove and the Tasmanian Aborigines*, Spectrum Publications, Melbourne, 1985, p. 87.

3   E. Grainger, *The Remarkable Reverend Clarke*, OUP, Melbourne, 1982, pp. 15–21; J. A. Barnes, 'Anthropology in Britain Before and After Darwin', *Mankind*, Vol. 5, 9 (July 1960), pp. 367–77; A. Mozley, 'Evolution and the Climate of Opinion in Australia, 1840–76', *Victorian Studies*, Vol. 10, 4 (June 1967), pp. 411–19; M. Harris, *The Rise of Anthropological Theory*, Crowell, New York, 1972, especially pp. 93–8, 105–7; G. W. Stocking, pp. 64–5; R. Evans *et al.* (eds), *Exclusion, Exploitation and Extermination*, ANZ Book Company, Sydney, 1975, pp. 13–14.

4   Maurice Hindler, 'Introduction' in Mary Shelley, *Frankenstein or The Modern Prometheus*, Penguin, Harmondsworth, 1985, pp. 21–5; J. D. Bernal, *Science In History*, Watt, London, 1956, pp. 435–8; H. Braverman, *Labor and Monopoly Capital*, Monthly Review Press, New York, 1974, pp. 79–83, 316–18. For this insight on Babbage, and for general discussion of this chapter, I am indebted to Victoria Gollan.

5   Space does not permit discussion of the medium through which science as cultural ideology was perhaps most visibly promoted, namely public

museums and fairs. See Robert W. Rydell, *All the World's a Fair: Visions of Empire at American International Expositions 1876–1916*, University of Chicago Press, Chicago, 1984, pp. 2–4; G. Davison, 'Exhibitions', *Australian Cultural History*, 2 (1982), pp. 5–6; Susan Sheets-Pyenson, *Cathedrals of Science: The Development of Colonial Natural History Museums during the Late Nineteenth Century*, McGill/Queens University Press, Ontario, 1988, pp. 51–4, 72–9. For the Australian museums, Sally Gregory Kohlstedt, 'Australian Museums of Natural History: Public Priorities and Scientific Initiatives in the Nineteenth Century', *Historical Records of Australian Science*, Vol. 5, 4 (1983), pp. 1–4; Ronald Strahan (ed.), *Rare and Curious Specimens: An Illustrated History of the Australian Museum 1827–1979*, Australian Museum, Sydney, 1979.

6   A. Mozley Moyal (ed.), *Scientists in Nineteenth-Century Australia*, pp. 41–54, 73–4, 79–80, 204; K. Fitzpatrick, *Sir John Franklin in Tasmania*, MUP, Melbourne, 1949, p. 26; B. H. Fletcher, 'Sir John Jamison in N.S.W. 1814–1844', *JRAHS*, Vol. 65, Pt 1 (June 1979), p. 11; *ADB*, II, pp. 182–3 (Macleay); III, pp. 501–2 (Crowther).

7   Lyn Barber, *The Heyday of Natural History 1820*–1870, Doubleday, New York, 1980, pp. 56, 125–38; M. Bassett, *The Hentys*, OUP, London, 1954, pp. 269–74.

8   T. G. Vallance, 'Origins of Australian Geology', *Proceedings of the Linnaean Society of N.S.W.*, Vol. 100, 1 (1975) p. 24; E. Grainger, pp. 113–16; A. Mozley Moyal (ed.), pp. 87–91; A. J. Marshall, *Darwin and Huxley in Australia*, Hodder & Stoughton, Sydney, 1970; F. W. & J. M. Nicholas, *Charles Darwin in Australia*, CUP, Cambridge, 1989; M. Bassett, *Behind the Picture: H.M.S. Rattlesnake's Australia– New Guinea Cruise 1846–1850*, OUP, Melbourne, 1966. For the earlier Spanish expedition under Malaspina which visited Port Jackson in March 1793, see O. H. K. Spate *Paradise Found and Lost*, ANU Press, Canberra, 1988, pp. 177–80.

9   A. Mozley Moyal (ed.), *passim*; W. R. Browne and Ida A. Browne, 'The Royal Society of N.S.W.' in 'Scientific Societies in Australia', *Proceedings of Royal Australian Chemical Institute*, March 1961; D. F. Branagan, 'Words, Actions, People: 150 Years of Scientific Societies of Australia', *Journal and Proceedings of Royal Society of N.S.W.*, Vol. 104 (1972); M. E. Hoare, 'Doctor John Henderson and the Van Diemen's Land Scientific Society', *Records of the Australian Academy of Science*, Vol. 1, 3 (1968); '"All Things Queer and Opposite": Scientific Societies in Tasmania in the 1840s', *Isis*, Vol. 60 (1969); K. Fitzpatrick, pp. 193–9. See also D. J. and S. G. M. Carr (eds), *People and Plants in Australia*, Academic Press, Sydney, 1981.

10 T. G. Vallance, pp. 18, 24–5, 29; T. G. Vallance and D. F. Branagan, 'New South Wales Geology—Its Origins and Growth', *A Century of Scientific Growth*, Royal Society of New South Wales, Sydney, 1968, pp. 268–9.

11 D. J. Mulvaney, 'The Australian Aborigines 1606–1929: Opinion and Fieldwork', *HS*, Vol. 8, 30 (May 1958) and 31 (November 1958), reprinted in *Historical Studies: Selected Articles*, MUP, Melbourne, 1974; Patricia O'Shane, 'Some Perspectives on Australian History', *History Magazine of Royal Australian Historical Society*, 18 (August 1991), p. 6. This fascination with Aboriginal racial origins continues to colour modern studies. As in G. Blainey's influential *Triumph of the Nomads*, Macmillan, Melbourne, 1974, by seeing Aboriginal people as migrants, it is easier to suggest that they were the 'first Australians', driven by Western-style methods of production and resultant population pressure to search out new lands and then to colonize the entire continent, exploiting and depleting its resources by rapacious hunting and even mining activities. The implication is that they thus behaved in exactly the same manner as the 'second Australians', a

comparison which conveniently normalizes and validates the European invasion, while also suggesting that Aboriginal people today have no claim to special rights over other Australians. The fact that some Aboriginal communities make reference to migration in their Dreamtime myths does not alter the racist origins and political implications of European constructions of Aboriginal orgins. Cf. Josephine Flood, *Archaeology of the Dreamtime*, Collins, Sydney, 1983, pp. 29–30.

12   B. Field, 'Observations on the Aborigines of New Holland and Van Diemen's Land' (Address to Philosophical Society, 2 January 1822), reprinted in B. Field (ed.), *Geographical Memoirs of New South Wales*, John Murray, London, 1825, pp. 244–8; P. Cunningham, *Two Years in New South Wales*, Colburn, London, 1827, II, p. 46; *The Colonist*, 13 October 1838, cited in R. H. W. Reece, *Aborigines and Colonists*, SUP, Sydney, 1974, p. 91; *SMH*, 21 June 1844, pp. 2–3.

13   M. Harris, p. 99; N. Dain, *Concepts of Insanity in the United States 1789–1856*, Rutgers University Press, New Jersey, 1964, p. 61; H. Reynolds, 'Racial Thought in Early Colonial Australia', *AJPH*, Vol. 20, 1, 1974, pp. 49–50; R. I. Watson, *The Great Psychologists from Aristotle to Freud*, Lippincourt, Philadelphia, 1963, pp. 225–6; H. Melville, *Exposition of Various Admitted Theories*, Sydney, 1844, p. 80n, cited in M. Roe, *Quest for Authority in Eastern Australia*, MUP, Carlton, 1965, p. 162; R. H. W. Reece, p. 88; R. Knight, *Illiberal Liberal: Robert Lowe in New South Wales*, MUP, Melbourne, 1966, pp. 65–7.

14   E. Brenchley, 'The Enlightenment in Australia; Attitudes of Alexander Berry Towards Aborigines', BA Hons thesis, Macquarie University, 1982, pp. 18, 60, 94; N. Gunson (ed.), *Australian Reminiscences and Papers of L. E. Threlkeld*, Australian Institute of Aboriginal Studies, Canberra, 1974, pp. 49, 50, 66, 74, 78; H. Reynolds, p. 50; D. J. Mulvaney, p. 28; J. A. Barnes, pp. 373–4; G. W. Stocking, pp. 49–53, 74–7; Dr James Hunt, 'On the Study of Anthropology', *Anthropological Review*, Vol. I, 1 (1863) pp. 2, 8.

15   J. Henderson, *Observations on the Colonies of New South Wales and Van Diemen's Land*, Baptist Mission Press, Calcutta, 1832, pp. 152–3; E. Brenchley, p. 84; R. H. W. Reece, pp. 90–1; P. E. Strzelecki, *Physical Description of New South Wales and Van Diemen's Land*, Longman, London, 1845, pp. 349, 355. See also *SG*, 6 October 1832 ('Australian Sketches', 'I. Civilization of the Aborigines').

16   R. H. W. Reece, p. 75; *ADB*, II, p. 228 (Miles); W. A. Miles, 'How Did the Natives of Australia Become Acquainted with the Demigods and Daemonia? . . .', *Journal of the Ethnological Society of London*, Vol. 3 (1854); J. J. Tobias, *Crime and Industrial Society in the Nineteenth Century*, Batsford, London, 1976, p. 54; N. Gunson, pp. 29, 69, 77–8; N. J. B. Plomley, *Friendly Mission*, Halstead, Sydney, 1966, pp. 935–6.

17   *ADB*, II, pp. 184–6 (Maconochie); K. Fitzpatrick p. 47; M. F. Christie, *Aborigines in Colonial Victoria 1835–1886*, SUP, Sydney, 1979, pp. 71–8; *Historical Records of Victoria*, Vols 2A and 2B, Melbourne, 1982, pp. 237–68, 489–99. Cf. M. Fels, *Good Men and True: The Aboriginal Police of the Port Phillip District 1837–1853*, MUP, Melbourne, 1988.

18   M. Ignatieff, *A Just Measure of Pain*, Macmillan London, 1978, pp. 3–4, 179–87, 194–9; *BPP*, (VII, No. 276) Report from the Select Committee on Secondary Punishments, 1831, (Irish Series—Crime and Punishment—Transportation—Vol. I), p. 25; Second Report from the Select Committee on Secondary Punishments 1832, (VII, No. 547), pp. 7, 43–5; *HRA*, I, xxi, pp. 2, 538; J. S. Kerr, *Design for Convicts*, Library of Australian History, Sydney, 1984, pp. 90–100. See also L. Heath, 'The Female Convict

Factories of New South Wales and Van Diemen's Land: An Examination of their Role in the Control, Punishment and Reformation of Prisoners Between 1804 and 1854', MA thesis, Australian National University, 1978; H. Weatherburn, 'The Female Factory Parramatta 1804–1848', BA Hons thesis, University of Sydney, 1978; 'The Female Factory' in J. Mackinolty and H. Radi (eds), *In Pursuit of Justice*, Hale & Iremonger, Sydney, 1979.

19   J. V. Barry, *Alexander Maconochie of Norfolk Island*, OUP, Melbourne, 1958, J. West, *The History of Tasmania*, (2 vols) (1st edn, Henry Dowling, Launceston, 1852), Libraries Board of South Australia, Adelaide, 1966, I, p. 281, II, pp. 282–4; J. S. Kerr, pp. 122–9; M. Hoare, *Norfolk Island*, UQP, St Lucia, 1982, pp. 50–8.

20   Brougham cited in M. Parmelee, *The Principles of Anthropology and their Relations to Criminal Procedure*, New York, 1912, p. 65; R. I. Watson, p. 293; L. Radzinowicz, *Ideology and Crime: A Study of Crime in its Social and Historical Context*, Heinemann, London, 1966, p. 40. Cf. J. J. Tobias, especially pp. 62–5, 93–5, 101–8, 177.

21   For the precocious little adult, see, for example, E. G. Wakefield, 'Facts Relating to the Punishment of Death in the Metropolis' (1831), reprinted in *The Collected Works of E. G. Wakefield*, edited by M. F. Lloyd Prichard, (Auckland, 1969) p. 203; C. Dickens, *Oliver Twist* (1838). For the targeting of juvenile offenders, S. Margarey, 'The Invention of Juvenile Delinquency in Early Nineteenth-Century England', *Labour History*, 34 (May 1978). For Point Puer, F. C. Hooper, 'Some Observations on the Point Puer Experiment', *PTHRA*, Vol. 2, 2 (March 1953); *Prison Boys of Port Arthur*, Cheshire, Melbourne, 1967; A. G. L. Shaw, *Convicts and the Colonies*, Faber & Faber, London, 1966, pp. 243–4; D. Heard (ed.), *The Journal of Charles O'Hara Booth*, Tasmanian Historical Research Association, Hobart, 1981, pp. 32–4, 50, 60. For approval of corporal punishment, ostensibly as an alternative to imprisonment but actually accompanying it, *BPP* Report from the Select Committee on Secondary Punishments 1831, pp. 41, 52. For corporal punishment of juvenile convicts in Sydney in 1833, *BPP* Report from the Select Committee on Transportation 1837, (XIX, No. 518), (Irish Series — Crime and Punishment — Transportation — Vol. III), Appendix 2, especially pp. 92–3. From 1842 over 300 Parkhurst boys were transported to Western Australia and 1500 to New Zealand (Paul Buddee, *The Fate of the Artful Dodger*, St. George Books, Perth, 1984, p. 5). For the 'Exile' system of which this experiment in juvenile transportation was a part, see Chapter 11 below.

22   R. Cooter, 'Phrenology and the British Alienists' in A. Scull (ed.), *Madhouses, Mad-Doctors, and Madmen: The Social History of Psychiatry in the Victorian Era*, University of Pennsylvania Press, Philadelphia, 1981, pp. 76, 81; M. Foucault, pp. 137–8, *Birth of the Clinic: An Archaeology of Medical Perception*, Tavistock, London, 1973, pp. 9–12, 89, 127–46; NSW LC *V&P* 1838 Pt II, Report from the Committee on the Medical Practices Bill with the Minutes of Evidence, pp. 9, 13, 19–21; K. Inglis, *Hospital and Community*, MUP, Melbourne, 1958, pp. 26, 28–30. A. McGrath, 'The History of Medical Organization in Australia', PhD thesis, University of Sydney, 1975, pp. 3–4, 113–14, 188–9. In England, popular repugnance to the surgeon's trade was not allayed by the Benthamite Anatomy Act of 1832, which made the bodies of people who died in workhouses and other charitable institutions legally available for dissection. See Ruth Richardson, *Death, Dissection and the Destitute*, Routledge & Kegan Paul, London, 1987.

23   NSW LC *V&P*, 1838, Pt II, Report from the Committee on the Medical Practices Bill, pp. 21–2, 39; *ADB*, I, pp. 112–13 (Bland). Perhaps Dr

Bland's expertise on the bladder owed much to the practice he gained while operating on children incarcerated in the N.S.W. Benevolent Society's Sydney Asylum. Here in 1845, he and Dr a'Beckett performed seven operations for 'lithotomy' six of which were on children aged three to thirteen years (Benevolent Society of N.S.W., *Annual Report*, 1845, p. 23). Such a high incidence of bladder problems in children (fifty-six were admitted during that year) suggests some of this surgery might have been to 'cure' bed-wetting or masturbation. For surgical experiments on women and girls in charitable institutions in America from the 1840s, see M. Daly, *Gynaecology: The Metaphysics of Radical Feminism*, Women's Press, London, 1979, p. 224. For clitoridectomy as a cure for alleged 'moral' and 'mental' disease in private patients, see E. Showalter, 'Victorian Women and Insanity' in A. Scull (ed.), pp. 323–8. For the special authority of surgeons on the emigrant ships, see NSW LC *V&P*, 1838, Pt 2, Report from Select Committee on Immigration, pp. 75–6 (Surgeon Arthur Savage), 81 (Surgeon J. Sullivan); J. Hogg, *The Domestic Medical and Surgical Guide* . . ., Ingram, Cook, London, 1853, pp. 148, 150–2; P. O'Farrell, *Letters from Irish Australia 1825–1929*, UNSW Press, Kensington, 1984, p. 20.

24   *ADB*, I, p. 355 (Pugh); R. W. Halliday and A. O. Watson, *A History of Dentistry in N.S.W. 1799–1945*, Australian Dental Association, Sydney, 1977, pp. 33–6 (Belisario). For the medical societies, see T. S. Pensabene, *The Rise of the Medical Practitioner in Victoria*, A.N.U. Health Research Project, Monograph No. 2, Canberra, 1980, pp. 99–100; M. E. Hoare, 'Learned Societies in Australia: The Foundation Years in Victoria 1850–1860', *Historical Records of Australian Academy of Science*, Vol. I, 2 (1967).

25   K. Inglis, pp. 51–4; B. Barrett, *The Inner Suburbs*, MUP, Melbourne, 1971, p. 55; A. J. C. Mayne, *Fever, Squalor and Vice: Sanitation and Social Policy in Victorian Sydney*, UQP, St Lucia, 1982, pp. 23–8; *SMH*, 26, 28, 29 June 1841; 18, 27 May 1842; J. J. Tobias, pp. 127, 151, 181; F. B. Smith, *The People's Health 1830–1910*, Croom Helm, London, 1979, pp. 184, 218–19, 232, 420. For an example of the notion that political discontent among the masses could be cured by attention to insanitary living conditions, ibid., p. 218 (Lord Shaftesbury 1848).

26   The blurring of the physical with the moral in child-raising during this period, so that childhood became a problem requiring medical solutions, appears to have begun with Nonconformist physicians who medicalized the existing Puritan model of child-raising. (See, for example, M. Ignatieff, pp. 60–1.) This summary relies on Lloyd de Mause, *The History of Childhood*, Psychohistory Press, New York, 1974, pp. 48–9; J. H. Plumb, 'The New World of Children in Eighteenth-Century England', *Past and Present*, Vol. 67 (1975) pp. 92–3; N. Dain, p. 96; J. S. Haller and R. M. Haller, *The Physician and Sexuality in Victorian America*, University of Illinois Press, Urbana, 1974, pp. 196–7, 203–9. M. Belcher, 'The Child in New South Wales Society: 1820–1837', PhD thesis, University of New England, 1982, contains some evidence of similar developments in Australia but does not specifically address the issue of medicalization. For an example of the time-consuming and unpleasant medical treatments for infant disease in this period, see ML MSS 1389/2 Mackenzie and Norton Family Papers (Dr Black to Jane Norton, 10 March 1834). For medical 'cures' for women in Britain and America from the 1840s, see C. Smith Rosenberg, 'Puberty to Menopause: The Cycle of Feminity in Nineteenth-Century America' in M. Hartmann and L. Banner (eds), *Clio's Consciousness Raised*, Harper, New York, 1974, pp. 24–9 and E. Showalter.

27   M. Ignatieff, pp. 60–72; N. Dain, pp. 16–19, 56, 73–87, 100–11; E. Fee,

'Psychology, Sexuality and Social Control in Victorian England', *Social Science Quarterly*, Vol. 58, 4 (March 1978) p. 634; S. Garton, *Medicine and Madness: A Social History of Insanity in New South Wales 1880–1940*, UNSW Press, Kensington, 1988, pp. 13–16; C. J. Cummins, 'The Administration of Lunacy and Idiocy in New South Wales 1788–1855', NSW Department of Public Health, Sydney, 1967, p. 4. Some of the anomalies in interpreting the McNaghten rules are discussed by Roger Smith in A. Scull (ed.), pp. 363–73.

28 S. Garton, 'Policing the Dangerous Lunatic; Lunacy Incarceration in N.S.W. 1843–1914' in M. Finnane, *Policing in Australia: Historical Perspectives*, UNSW Press, Kensington, 1987, p. 76; C. J. Cummins, pp. 20, 22; J. Bostock, *The Dawn of Australian Psychiatry*, Australian Medical Publishing Co., Sydney, 1968, pp. 115, 138–40, 147, 200, 202; Joan Brown, *'Poverty is not a Crime': The Development of Social Services in Tasmania 1803–1900*, Tasmanian Historical Research Association, Hobart, 1972, pp. 98–105. See also D. I. McDonald, 'Gladesville Hospital: The Formative Years 1838–1850', *JRAHS*, Vol. 15, 4 (December 1965).

29 E. Fee, pp. 634–9; E. Showalter; J. Allen, 'Women, Crime and Policing in N.S.W. 1880–1939', PhD thesis, Macquarie University, 1983, pp. 45–6; cf. J. J. Tobias, p. 93; J. Bostock, pp. 182–5; C. J. Cummins, p. 22.

30 S. Garton, 'Policing the Dangerous Lunatic . . .', p. 81; E. Fee, p. 639. Cf. S. Garton, 'Bad or Mad? Developments in Incarceration in N.S.W. 1880–1970' in Sydney Labour History Group, *What Rough Beast? The State and Social Order in Australian History*, Allen & Unwin, Sydney, 1982, p. 93. When allowance is made for the fact that Garton's figures are for police admissions, and most women were not committed to lunatic asylums by police, the proportion of women in lunatic asylums would seem even higher. See also A. Summers, *Damned Whores and God's Police*, p. 285; A. Scull, 'Psychiatry in the Victorian Era', in A. Scull (ed.), p. 23.

31 M. Finnane, *Insanity and the Insane in Post-Famine Ireland*, Croom Helm, London, 1981, p. 13. Cf. M. Foucault, *Madness and Civilization: A History of Insanity*, Tavistock, London, 1967, which ultimately sees the growth of asylums as occurring independently of the changing needs of the economic system and the kind of worker it required. This approach normalizes asylums as educative in function rather than as providing the raw material for further punitive experiments in medical modification. See also E. Goffman, *Asylums*, Doubleday, New York, 1961, which similarly reduces events in the most 'total' of institutions to mere power relations which are seen as an inevitable part of the human psyche.

CHAPTER 11: ALL THAT GLITTERS . . .

1 N. Keesing (ed.), *History of the Australian Gold Rushes*, Sydney, 1981, pp. 42–4.

2 E. J. Hobsbawm, *Industry and Empire*, Penguin, Ringwood, 1981, pp. 109–14, 135; M. Dobb, *Studies in the Development of Capitalism*, Routledge & Kegan Paul, London, 1978, pp. 295–7; B. Fitzpatrick, *The British Empire in Australia*, MUP, Melbourne, 1949, pp. 100–1.

3 G. Serle, *The Golden Age: A History of the Colony of Victoria 1851–1861*, MUP, Melbourne, 1968, pp. 44–5; John and Samuel Sidney (eds), *Sidney's Emigrant Journal*, Orr, London, 1849, pp. 4, 10, 13, 15.

4 C. M. H Clark, *A History of Australia*, III, MUP, Melbourne, 1973, pp. 347, 454; A. G. L. Shaw, *Convicts and the Colonies*, Faber & Faber, London, 1966, p. 337.

5   L. Ramsay Silver, *A Fool's Gold: William Tipple Smith's Challenge to the Hargraves Myth*, Jacaranda, Brisbane, 1986, pp. 3–6, 14, 16; E. Grainger, *The Remarkable Reverend Clarke*, OUP, Melbourne, 1982, pp. 163–7; G. Serle, pp. 10–11; A. Markus, *Fear and Hatred Purifying Australia and California 1850–1901*, Hale & Iremonger, Sydney, 1979, p. 1; M. Roe, *Quest for Authority in Eastern Australia*, MUP, Melbourne, 1965, p. 98.

6   L. Robson, *A History of Tasmania*, I, OUP, Melbourne, 1983, pp. 420–4; F. Crowley (ed.), *A New History of Australia*, Longman, Melbourne, 1974, pp. 134–5; J. M. Ward, *Earl Grey and the Australian Colonies*, MUP, Melbourne, 1958, pp. 196–210; C. M. H. Clark, III, p. 418; J. West, *The History of Tasmania*, (2 vols) (1st edn, Henry Dowling, Launceston, 1852), Libraries Board of South Australia, 1966, I, pp. 290–1.

7   J. West, I, p. 306; C. M. H. Clark, III, pp. 416, 418, 443–4; *ADB*, V, pp. 399–406 (Parkes); II, pp. 165–6 (McEncroe); M. Roe, pp. 92–9, 108; R. Gollan, *Radical and Working-Class Politics: A Study of Eastern Australia 1850–1910*, pp. 4–17.

8   J. M. Ward, *Colonial Self-Government: The British Experience 1759–1856*, Macmillan, London, 1976, pp. 235–6, 295; *Earl Grey and the Australian Colonies*, pp. 19–20; W. G. McMinn, *A Constitutional History of Australia*, pp. 40–8. Formerly known as Viscount Howick (from 1807) Grey had succeeded to the earldom in July 1845.

9   L. Ramsay Silver, pp. 17–18, 34, 37–8; G. Blainey, 'The Gold Rushes: The Year of Decision', *HS*, Vol. 10, 38 (May 1962), pp. 132–3; *ADB*, IV, pp. 346–7 (Hargraves).

10 N. Keesing, p. 45; B. Fitzpatrick, p. 155; G. Serle, p. 11; L. Ramsay Silver, pp. 57, 88.

11 N. Keesing, p. 20; L. Ramsay Silver, pp. 66, 70; M. Kiddle, *Men of Yesterday*, MUP, Melbourne, 1961, p. 183; G. Blainey, pp. 134–6; B. Fitzpatrick, p. 155.

12 B. Fitzpatrick, p. 156; N. Keesing, p. 38; L. Ramsay Silver, pp. 79–80; G. Serle, pp. 23, 34, 388; C. Spence, *Clara Morison: A Tale of South Australia During the Gold Fever* (1st edn, Parker, London, 1854), Rigby, Adelaide, 1971, pp. 170, 172, Though a fictional account, Spence's careful dating of the exodus and documentary style make this a reliable source.

13 G. Serle, pp. 65, 383; M. Kiddle, pp. 187, 190, 191, 192; N. Keesing, pp. 56, 70, 81, 87, 97; Henry Handel Richardson, *The Fortunes of Richard Mahoney*, Vol. I, *Australia Felix* (1st edn, Heinemann, London, 1917), Penguin, Ringwood, 1971, pp. 5–7; [H. N. Baker] *Sketches of Australian Life and Scenery by one who has been a Resident for Thirty Years*, Sampson Low, London, 1876, pp. 86, 99–100.

14 G. Serle, pp. 24, 35 (citing W. E. Adcock, *The Gold Rush of the 'Fifties*, E. W. Cole, Melbourne, 1912, p. 80); N. Keesing, pp. 52, 62, 71, 154–6; G. Blainey, p. 133; M. Kiddle, p. 189; J. Sadleir, *Recollections of a Victorian Police Officer*, Robertson, Melbourne, 1913, pp. 60–1. See also *Thatcher's Colonial Songster*, Melbourne, 1857 and *Thatcher's Colonial Minstrel*, Charlwood & Son, Melbourne, 1864. Despite some patronizing exaggeration and self-conscious gestures towards egalatarianism, these ballads also reveal the individual rapacity which gold-seeking engendered in workers. Charles Thatcher was a well-educated English emigrant who arrived in Melbourne in 1852 and one of the first of many writers to exploit the market for popular songs and stories about Australian 'low life'.

15 B. Kent, 'Agitations on the Victorian Gold Fields, 1851–4: An Interpretation', *HS*, Vol. 6, 23 (November 1954) pp. 263–4, 266, 276; D. and A. Potts, 'American Republicanism and the Disturbances on the Victorian Goldfields', *HS*, Vol. 13, 50 (April 1968) pp. 149, 150; N. Keesing, pp. 170,

174–5; G. Serle, p. 83. For a police view of the 'digger hunts', J. Sadleir, p. 44.

16 B. Kent, p. 278; D. and A. Potts, p. 154; C. M. H. Clark, *A History of Australia*, MUP, Melbourne, 1978, IV, Ch. 5; G. Serle, pp. 161–9; R. Gollan, pp. 20–32. See also Raffaello Carboni, *The Eureka Stockade*, Atkinson, Melbourne, 1855. For the police view, 'A single volley from the ranks of the soldiers sent the silly sheep flying to the cover of their drill tent . . .' see J. Sadleir, p. 163. Like the Rum Rebellion, Eureka has a large literature. Again the conflict was primarily between the immediate interests of colonial wealth-seekers and the now essentially anachronistic policies of the imperial authorities—though oddly, where the liberal empiricist historians have tended to approve of the Sydney traders' fight for 'liberty', they have castigated the miners' very similar stand as somehow self-seeking and shabby. The Old Left historians have perhaps not helped by romanticizing the event instead of confronting its essentially liberal ideology.

17 Report of a speech by Mr Deniehy on the NSW Constitution Bill, 15 August 1853, in *SMH*, 16 August 1853, reprinted in C. M. H. Clark, *Select Documents in Australian History 1851–1900*, Angus & Robertson, Sydney, 1975, pp. 341–2; *ADB*, V, pp. 50–4 (Lalor); W. G. McMinn, pp. 62–3; R. Gollan, pp. 6, 17–21, 30–2. See also Ged Martin, *Bunyip Aristocracy*, Croom Helm, Surrey Hills, 1986.

18 N. Keesing, pp. 167, 173, 213; K. Cronin, *Colonial Casualties: Chinese in Early Victoria*, MUP, Melbourne, 1982, p. 106.

19 K. Cronin, *passim*; A. Markus, pp. 2–43; N. Keesing, pp. 120, 249–56; D. and A. Potts, p. 150; R. B. Walker, 'Another Look: the Lambing Flat Riots, 1860–1861', *JRAHS*, Vol. 56, 3 (September 1970). See also G. T. Blakers, *A Useless Young Man: An Autobiography of Life in Australia 1849–64*, Penguin, Ringwood, 1986, pp. 136–7; J. Sadleir, pp. 77–9, 84.

20 B. Fitzpatrick, pp. 166, 178; W. Howitt, *Land, Labour and Gold or, Two Years in Victoria with Visits to Sydney and Van Diemen's Land* (2 vols) (1st edn, Longman, Brown, Green & Longmans, London, 1855), SUP, Sydney, 1972, I, p. 141; E. G. Wakefield, *Spectator*, 15, 22 May 1852, cited in G. Serle, p. 40; C. M. H. Clark, *Select Documents in Australian History 1851–1900*, p. 664.

21 G. Serle, p. 42; B. Fitzpatrick, pp. 168, 180–1; G. P. Walsh, 'Factories and Factory Workers in New South Wales 1788–1900', *Labour History*, 21 (November 1961), pp. 6–7; N. Keesing, pp. 36, 104; see also p. 160.

22 *Sketches of Australian Life and Scenery*, pp. 66–7; K. Inglis, *Hospital and Community*, MUP, Melbourne, 1958, pp. 5–7, 22, 35; William Howitt, II, pp. 282–4; R. J. Pryor, 'Gold Rush and Health: Aspects of Victoria's Public Health in the 1850s', *Melbourne Historical Journal*, 2 (1962), p. 59; J. D. Foley, 'The Beginning of a Quarantine System at the Quarantine Station, North Head, Port Jackson', *JRAHS*, Vol. 71, 1 (June 1985); Carr Family Papers (private collection).

23 Benevolent Society of N.S.W. *Inmates Journal* 1852–3 (ML MS A7227); for overcrowding in the Sydney Asylum, Benevolent Society of N.S.W. *Annual Report* 1852, p. 8, 1853, p. 10. For similar problems in Van Diemen's Land, see H. Reynolds, '"That Hated Stain"; The Aftermath of Transportation in Tasmania', *HS*, Vol. 14, 53 (October 1969), p. 10. For convicts in Western Australia, see A. G. L. Shaw, pp. 356–7; A. Hasluck, *Unwilling Emigrants*, OUP, Melbourne, 1959. For penitentiaries, see J. Kerr, *Design for Convicts*, Library of Australian History, Sydney, 1984, pp. 166–7. For Price, J. V. Barry, *The Life and Death of John Price*, MUP, Melbourne, 1964.

24 A. W. Martin, 'Drink and Deviance in Sydney; Investigating Intemperance

1854–5', *HS*, Vol. 17, 68 (April 1977); NSW LA *V&P*, 1859–60, Vol. 4, Report from the Select Committee on the Condition of the Working Classes of the Metropolis; NSW LC *V&P*, 1854, Vol. 2, Report from the Select Committee on the Proposed Nautical School; Hobart Town Ragged Schools Association *First Annual Report*, Hobart, 1856, p. 18. For family desertion during the 1850s, A. O'Brien, 'Left in the Lurch; Deserted Wives in New South Wales at the Turn of the Century', in J. Mackinolty and H. Radi (eds), *In Pursuit of Justice*, Hale & Iremonger, Sydney, 1979, pp. 96–8; William Howitt, I, p. 50.

25   J. West, I, pp. 276, 283; Vic LC *V&P*, 1858–9, Replies to a Circular Letter and Evidence Given Before the Select Committee on the Aborigines; M. F. Christie, *Aborigines in Colonial Victoria 1835–1886*, SUP, Sydney, 1979, pp. 177–8. On Flinders Island there were only fifty Aboriginal people remaining when in 1847 the establishment was closed down and the survivors removed to an old penal station at Oyster Cove (C. Turnbull, *Black War*, Cheshire–Lansdowne, Melbourne, 1965, p. 230). Ignoring some 2000 people already forced into the white working class, in March 1869 devotee of social science, Dr William Crowther of the Royal Society, became locked in a ghoulish battle with surgeons at the Hobart Hospital for the remains of William Lanney, whom they saw as the last male Tasmanian. The surgeons captured his skull while the Royal Society had to be content with his hands and feet, see C. Turnbull, pp. 234–5; M. Mansell, 'Tasmania', in N. Peterson (ed.), *Aboriginal Landrights: A Handbook*, Australian Institute of Aboriginal Studies, Canberra, 1981, p. 129. For the Tasmanian Aboriginal community, see Ida West, *Pride Against Prejudice: Reminiscences of a Tasmanian Aborigine*, Australian Institute of Aboriginal Studies, Canberra, 1984. For the coercive legislation, see James Miller, *Koori A Will to Win*, Sydney, 1985; P. Pepper and T. D'Araugo, *You Are What You Make Yourself to Be: The Story of a Victorian Aboriginal Family 1842–1980*, Hyland House, Melbourne, 1980; Jimmie Barker, *The Two Worlds of Jimmie Barker*, Australian Institute of Aboriginal Studies, Canberra, 1977.

26   M. Hoare, *Norfolk Island*, UQP, St Lucia, 1982, pp. 34, 63, 69; Paul Sweezey, *The Theory of Capitalist Development*, New York, 1942, especially pp. 255–69, 299–300.

27   M. Lyons, *The Totem and the Tricolour: A Short History of New Caledonia Since 1774*, UNSW Press, Kensington, 1986, p. 42; R. C. Thompson, *Australian Imperialism in the Pacific: The Expansionist Era 1820–1920*, MUP, Melbourne, 1980, pp. 15–23; J. Connell, *New Caledonia or Kanacky?*, National Centre for Development Studies, Canberra, 1987, pp. 34–5.

SOURCES OF ILLUSTRATIONS

Every effort has been made to trace the original source of illustrations contained in this book. Where the attempt has been unsuccessful the author and publisher would be pleased to hear from the author/publisher concerned, to rectify any omission or error.

Cover Robert Dowling, *Masters William & George and Miss Harriet Ware with an Aboriginal Servant* Minyah Station near Warrnambool, Victoria 1856. Oil on canvas, private collection, Victoria.

1   [Port Jackson Painter] *An Attack by Aborigines c.*1788. British Museum of Natural History, London.
2   William Bradley, *Part of the Reef in Sydney Bay, Norfolk Island, on which the Sirius was wreck'd 19 March 1790*, William Bradley *A Voyage to New South Wales The Journal of William Bradley RN of HMS Sirius 1786–1792*. Public Library of NSW in association with Ure Smith, Sydney, 1969, p. 194.
3   Fernando Brambila, *View of the English Settlement at Sydney*, March/April 1793, *The Spanish at Port Jackson*, Australian Documentary Facsimile Society, Sydney, 1987.
4   Fernando Brambila, *Vista de la Colonia de Paramata*, 1793, *The Spanish at Port Jackson*, Australian Documentary Facsimile Society, Sydney, 1987.

5   *An Exploring Party in New South Wales*, James Atkinson *An Account of the State of Agriculture and Grazing in New South Wales*, Sydney University Press, Sydney, 1975 (facsimile of first edition, London, 1826), p. 9.

6   Augustus Earle, *A Government Gaol Gang, Sydney, N.S.Wales*, Augustus Earle *Views in New South Wales and Van Diemen's Land* (J. Cross, London, 1830).

7   *Barrack from George Street*, James Maclehose, *Picture of Sydney and Strangers' Guide in N.S.W. for 1839*, John Ferguson Pty. Ltd. Sydney, 1977 (facsimile of first edition, Sydney, 1839), p. 122.

8   *Residences of the Aborigines*, (Flinders Island), J. S. Prout *Tasmania Illustrated*, Hobart Town?, 1844.

9   *Hobart Town from the New Wharf*, J. S. Prout *Tasmania Illustrated* Hobart Town?, 1844.

10   Fancy Dress Ball given by Lord Mayor Hosking, Sydney, August 1843, Mitchell Library.

11   John Rae, *Hyde Park, Sydney, 1842*, Watercolour, Dixson Library.

12   *Between decks* (on a government emigrant ship), *Illustrated London News*, 17 August 1850.

13   Crossing the Creek at Bacchus Marsh, Thomas Ham, *The Gold-Diggers' Portfolio: Consisting of a Series of Sketches of the Victorian Goldfields taken by talented artists on the spot*, Melbourne, 1884.

14   *Bendigo c.1857*, S. T. Gill and N. Chevalier *Victoria Illustrated 1857 and 1862: Engravings from the Original Editions of S. T. Gill and N. Chevalier* (ed. W. H. Newnham), (first published in 2 vols, Sands and Kenny, Melbourne 1857, 1862), Lansdowne, Melbourne, 1971.

15   *Aborigines at Jembaicumbene, 1859*, photographed by W. S. Jevons, Historical Photograph Collection, Macleay Museum, University of Sydney.

BIBLIOGRAPHIC NOTE

AUSTRALIA'S COLONIAL HERITAGE continues to command attention, and for those interested in tracing the connections between past and present, the period to 1860 is very rich in terms of historical sources. A full coverage of all the available manuscript, statistical and archival material was beyond the scope of this project, and a bibliographical note can offer only selected suggestions for further reading. Both archival and published sources used in this volume are documented in the endnotes.

With respect to existing works by historians, the most recent are by no means always the most useful. Among earlier general histories of the period to 1860, C. M. H. Clark's monumental six-volume *A History of Australia* (Melbourne University Press, Carlton, 1962–88) remains unsurpassed. Clark's Volumes I–IV cover the period up to the 1880s, situating colonial life within the wider framework of European affairs. Brian Fitzpatrick's *British Imperialism and Australia 1783–1833* (George Allen and Unwin, London, 1939; reprinted by Sydney University Press, Sydney, 1971) and *The British Empire in Australia 1834–1949* (2nd edition, revised and enlarged, Melbourne University Press, Carlton, 1949; reprinted by Macmillan, Melbourne, 1969), also provide a broad political and economic context and thus remain of central importance. For the British social and economic background, Eris O'Brien's *The Foundation of Australia A Study of English Criminal Practice and Penal Colonization in the Eighteenth Century* (Shed and

Ward, London, 1937; reprinted by Angus and Robertson, Sydney, 1950) is still of major interest and offers a useful bibliographical guide to relevant *British Parliamentary Papers*. Earlier economic histories such as S. J. Butlin's *Foundations of the Australian Monetary System 1788–1851* (Melbourne University Press, Carlton, 1953; reprinted by Sydney University Press, Sydney, 1968) also merit re-reading. Older historians of imperialism in general and of the Pacific in particular continue to provide inspiration and widen the perspective to include the hemisphere of which Australia is a part; see for instance, Bernard Smith's *European Vision and the South Pacific* (Oxford University Press, Melbourne, 1960) and O. H. K. Spate's *The Pacific Since Magellan: Paradise Found and Lost* (Australian National University Press, Canberra, 1988).

Of the more recent general histories, the four-volume *People's History of Australia*, edited by Verity Burgmann and Jenny Lee (Penguin, Ringwood, 1988) brings together a diverse range of historians, including non-academic ones, in an attempt to provide a history of everyday life, presented in an affordable, accessible form. The more weighty eleven-volume *Australians: A Historical Library* (Fairfax, Syme and Weldon, Sydney, 1987–88) comprises a series of 'slices' or 'snapshots' of Australian society at fifty-year intervals. Inspired by the Bicentenary, the volumes of most relevance to the period to 1860 are *Australians to 1788*, edited by D. J. Mulvaney and J. Peter White, and *Australians to 1838*, edited by Alan Atkinson and Marian Aveling. *Australians: Historical Statistics*, edited by Wray Vamplew, and *Australians: A Guide to Sources*, edited by D. H. Borchardt and Victor Crittenden, also contain material pertinent to the colonial period. *The Push From the Bush: A Bulletin of Social History*, a periodical produced since 1978 by the editors of the 1838 'slice', is of particular value.

The *Australian Dictionary of Biography* Vols I and II, 1788–1850, edited by D. Pike (Melbourne University Press, Carlton, 1966–67), provides a more traditional approach to 'slicing' history. This biographical method, though necessarily concentrating on the lives of great and not so great men, often produces unexpectedly fruitful information about the private, day-to-day world from which these public figures emerged, raising questions outside the traditional range of historical enquiry. Larger biographies are similarly rich in detail, and many, like B. H. Fletcher's *Ralph Darling A Governor Maligned* (Oxford University Press, Melbourne, 1984) and J. Ritchie's *Lachlan Macquarie A Biography* (Melbourne

University Press, 1986), are impeccably researched. Biography has long attracted Australian female historians, many of whom provide special insight into domestic life and the experience of colonial mothers and wives. Marnie Bassett's *The Governor's Lady Mrs Philip Gidley King* (Oxford University Press, London, 1940; reprinted by Melbourne University Press, Carlton, 1956), M. Barnard Eldershaw's *The Life and Times of Captain John Piper* (Australian Limited Editions, Sydney, 1939; reprinted by Ure Smith, Sydney, 1973), and K. Fitzpatrick's *Sir John Franklin in Tasmania* (Melbourne Unversity Press, Carlton, 1949), are some of the older works of enduring value in this respect.

For readers interested in convict experience, Robert Hughes' *The Fatal Shore A History of Transportation of Convicts to Australia 1787–1868* (Collins Harvill, London, 1987) provides an excellent bibliography. Stephen Nicholas' (ed.) *Convict Workers Reinterpreting Australia's Past* (Cambridge University Press, 1988) also contains a useful guide to convict sources, as well as illustrating the variety of methodologies which computer analysis has brought to this subject. Babette Smith's *A Cargo of Women: Susanna Watson and the Convicts of the Princess Royal* (University of New South Wales Press, Kensington, 1988) illustrates the important contribution which private, genealogical research may make. Portia Robinson's *The Women of Botany Bay* (Macquarie Library Pty Ltd, Sydney, 1988) points to archival sources available in Britain through which historians may restore the humanity of convict women and explore the details of their individual experience.

The lives of free immigrants are of equal interest to many Australians. Eric Fry's *Flinders' History of South Australia [Vol. I] Social History* (Wakefield Press, Netley, South Australia, 1986) provides insight into the motives and fortunes of people who freely chose to transport themselves to that colony. Local histories, such as Carol Liston's *Campbelltown The Bicentennial History* (Allen and Unwin, Sydney, 1988), W. A. Wood's *Dawn in the Valley The Early History of the Hunter Valley Settlement* (Wentworth Books, Sydney 1972) and Margaret Kiddle's *Men of Yesterday A Social History of the Western District of Victoria 1834–1890* (Melbourne University Press, Carlton, 1961), should not be overlooked as detailed repositories of information about early pioneers.

Aboriginal experience, though long omitted from the works written by white academic historians, was extensively documented in both private accounts and the official correspondence of the day. For the latter, readers might begin by consulting *Historical Records of New South Wales* Vols 1–7 (first published in 1893, facsimile edition Lansdown Slattery, Sydney, 1978) and *Historical Records of Australia* Series I, Vols 1–26, Series III, Vols 1–6, Series IV, Vol. 1 (first published 1914–1922; reprinted by Federal Government, Canberra, 1971). Both these sources are well-indexed and reveal with sometimes surprising frankness the responses of government officials to Aboriginal issues. *Historical Records of Victoria* devotes two volumes (2A and 2B) to official and unofficial sources on Aboriginal experience. *Parliamentary Papers*, both for Britain and the colonies, are also important sources, as are published and unpublished descriptions of the colonies by traders, pastoralists and civil and military officials. Accounts by missionaries often prove enlightening; see for instance N. Gunson's edition of *The Australian Papers and Reminiscences of Rev. L. E. Threlkeld Missionary to the Aborigines 1824–1859* Vols I & II (Australian Institute of Aboriginal Studies, Canberra 1974). Most contemporary newspapers and periodicals were replete with information on Aboriginal people, together with discussion about official and unofficial policies being adopted. Of the more recent histories, the best are those written by Aboriginal people, such as James Miller's *Koori A Will to Win* (Angus and Robertson, Sydney 1985), Nigel Parbury *Survival A History of Aboriginal Life in New South Wales* (N.S.W. Ministry of Aboriginal Affairs, Sydney, 1986), Michael Martin *On Darug Land—An Aboriginal Perspective* (Greater Western Education Centre St Marys N.S.W., 1988). Aboriginal creative writers such as Colin Johnson (Mudrooroo Narogin), Jack Davis and Maureen Watson should also be consulted for their important and distinctive viewpoint of the colonial past.

INDEX